Driven from New Orleans

Driven from New Orleans

*How Nonprofits Betray Public Housing
and Promote Privatization*

John Arena

 University of Minnesota Press
Minneapolis
London

Original maps were created by Philip Schwartzberg, Meridian Mapping, Minneapolis.

Unless otherwise credited, photographs were taken by the author.

Published by the University of Minnesota Press
111 Third Avenue South, Suite 290
Minneapolis, MN 55401-2520
http://www.upress.umn.edu

Library of Congress Cataloging-in-Publication Data
Arena, John.
    Driven from New Orleans : how nonprofits betray public housing and promote privatization / John Arena.
    Includes bibliographical references and index.
    ISBN 978-0-8166-7746-7 (hc. : alk. paper)
    ISBN 978-0-8166-7747-4 (pbk. : alk. paper)
1. Public housing—Louisiana—New Orleans. 2. Nonprofit organizations—Louisiana—New Orleans. 3. Privatization—Louisiana—New Orleans. I. Title.
    HD7288.78.U52N745   2012
    363.5'850976335—dc23

                                                                    2012008139

Printed in the United States of America on acid-free paper

The University of Minnesota is an equal-opportunity educator and employer.

20 19 18 17 16 15   10 9 8 7 6 5 4 3 2

Contents

Abbreviations   vii

Preface   ix

Acknowledgments   xiii

Introduction: Nonprofits and the Revanchist Agenda   xvii

1. Confronting the New Boss: Struggles for Home
   and Community in the Postsegregation Era, 1965–1985   1

2. Undoing the Black Urban Regime: Resistance
   to Displacement and Elite Divisions, 1986–1988   29

3. Neoliberalism and Nonprofits: Selling Privatization
   at St. Thomas, 1989–1995   55

4. No Hope in HOPE VI: Dismantling Public Housing
   from the Nation to the Neighborhood   87

5. When Things Fall Apart: From the Dreams of St. Thomas
   to the Nightmare of River Gardens, 1996–2002   117

6. Whose City Is It? Hurricane Katrina and the Struggle
   for New Orleans's Public Housing, 2003–2008   145

7. Managing Contradictions: The Coalition to
   Stop the Demolitions   187

Conclusion: Lessons from New Orleans   215

Notes   227

Index   285

Abbreviations

ACLU	American Civil Liberties Union
ACORN	Association of Community Organizations for Reform Now
ACT	All Congregations Together
AEHR	Advocates for Environmental Human Rights
AFL-CIO	American Federation of Labor-Congress of Industrial Organizations
AFSCME	American Federation of State, County, and Municipal Employees
BNOB	Bring New Orleans Back
C3	Community, Concern, Compassion
CAN	Community Action Now
CAP	Community Action Program
CCH	Creative Choice Homes
CERD	Committee on the Elimination of Racial Discrimination
CETA	Comprehensive Employment and Training Act
CLU	Community Labor United
COPS	Community Oriented Policing Services
CRF	Community Revitalization Fund
CRP	Community Resource Partnership
CSA	Coliseum Square Association
CURE	Center for Urban Redevelopment Excellence (University of Pennsylvania)
DDD	Downtown Development District
FFLIC	Friends and Family of Louisiana's Incarcerated
FHA	Federal Housing Administration
GAO	General Accounting Office
GNOF	Greater New Orleans Foundation
HANO	Housing Authority of New Orleans
HIT	Housing Investment Trust (investment arm of AFL-CIO)
HOPE VI	Housing Opportunities for People Everywhere
HRI	Historic Restorations Incorporated
HUD	U.S. Department of Housing and Urban Development
ICERD	International Convention on the Elimination of All Forms of Racial Discrimination

IFCO	Interreligious Foundation for Community Organization
ILA	International Longshoremen's Association
ILWU	International Longshore and Warehouse Union
IMH	Institute of Mental Hygiene
LaRICE	Louisiana Research Institute for Community Empowerment
LIHTC	Low Income Housing Tax Credits
MLK	Martin Luther King Jr.
NAACP	National Association for the Advancement of Colored People
NGO	Nongovernmental Organization
NLIHC	National Low Income Housing Coalition
NOFA	Notice of Funding Availability
NO-HEAT	New Orleans Housing Eviction Action Team
NOLAC	New Orleans Legal Aid Corporation
NONC	New Orleans Neighborhood Collaborative
NOPD	New Orleans Police Department
NTO	National Tenant Organization
PBC	Police Brutality Committee
PHRF	Peoples Hurricane Relief Fund
PI	People's Institute for Survival and Beyond
PILOT	Payment in Lieu of Taxes
POC	People's Organizing Committee
PRC	Preservation Resource Center
PWA	Public Works Administration
QHWR	Quality Housing and Work Responsibility Act of 1998
RCP	Revolutionary Communist Party
RFQ	Request for Qualifications
RMCs	Resident Management Corporations
RTTC	Right to the City
SCLC	Southern Christian Leadership Conference
SDS	Students for a Democratic Society
STEDC	St. Thomas Economic Development Corporation
STICC	St. Thomas/Irish Channel Consortium
STRC	St. Thomas Resident Council
TCIA	Tremé Community Improvement Association
TIF	Tax Increment Financing
TINA	There Is No Alternative
TXI	Tulane–Xavier Initiatives
ULI	Urban Land Institute
UUSC	Unitarian Universalist Service Committee
WPA	Works Progress Administration

Preface

The origins of this book date back over twenty-five years, to when I first arrived in New Orleans to work as a community and labor organizer. My research began, unknowingly, in 1985 while working at a food, clothing, and rental assistance center in New Orleans's (upper) Ninth Ward that served the Florida and Desire public housing developments and their surrounding neighborhoods. Residents educated this young, white, aspiring activist about the daily struggles they faced paying rent, finding jobs, buying clothes for children, and putting food on the table, as well as the collective solutions they had forged, such as forming a Black Panther chapter at the Desire development. In 1986, I also collaborated with residents in writing a new chapter in this history of activism by helping organize a busload of residents to join a statewide rally at the state capitol to protest cuts in welfare. The following year, I gained a wider knowledge of New Orleans's public housing, including the workers, the housing authority bureaucracy, the importance of board meetings, and the location and characteristics of all ten developments, while organizing a union drive among housing authority employees. In the late 1980s, I met members of the St. Thomas public housing tenant council while employed as an organizer for an anti–death penalty group that had its office in a social service center next to the development. In the early 1990s, I worked as a case manager for low-income families with emotionally challenged children, which offered another opportunity to meet and learn from public housing residents. In addition, I was involved in many anti–police brutality and other community organizing efforts that brought me into contact with New Orleans's public housing communities.

Thus, when I repaired to the university in the late 1990s, it was with the goal of using my time to reflect and study the local movements I had been involved with over the previous dozen or so years. Indeed, this interest was a major factor in deciding to pursue my studies at Tulane University in New Orleans, rather than leave the city. In particular, I was interested in studying the city's public housing, which was, by the mid-1990s, facing a fight for its very survival as the neoliberal agenda of austerity, privatization, and demolition began to take hold. Yet this attack was coming

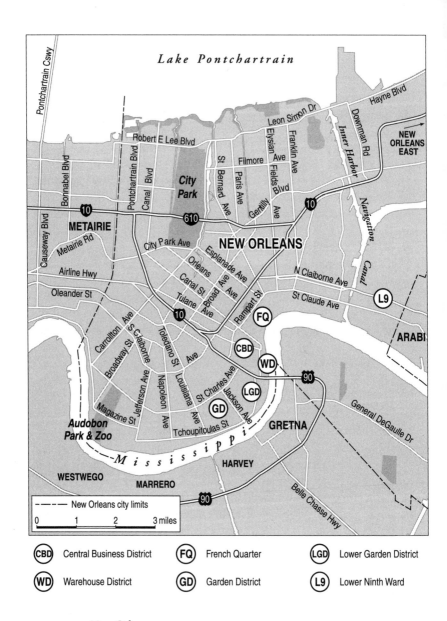

MAP P. 1. New Orleans

from some unanticipated sources. One was the university I was attending. Shortly before I arrived, Tulane signed an agreement with the Department of Housing and Urban Development (HUD) to assign the university's top lawyer and only African American vice president to oversee the operation of the local housing authority just as the agency began launching its demolition agenda. In addition, Tulane and the sociology department where I studied received a large grant from HUD to work with the C. J. Peete public housing development to, in effect, facilitate privatization and displacement. At the same time, many of the community activists and tenant leaders I had known were collaborating, to my surprise, in the privatization of St. Thomas during the mid- to late 1990s. People whom I thought would be allies in my study of public housing had moved in a different direction.

In the summer of 2001, I looked out at the recently bulldozed fifty acres that had been the St. Thomas public housing community. By June all the former residents had been evicted, with most having little or no chance of returning. Yet the heated controversy taking hold at the time, which added to New Orleans's brutally hot summer, was not the displacement of a vibrant yet economically deprived black community. Rather, the local media focused on the uproar by upscale homeowners over the placement of a Walmart on part of the former development. These "stakeholders" had cheered on the developer's effort to demolish St. Thomas but felt betrayed by his attempt to place a big box retail store in their historic neighborhood. "But what about the St. Thomas residents?" I asked myself. "Where did they go? Who would be able to return? What happened to the promises? How did this travesty happen? Why was there not more of a fight? How can this be prevented from happening again?"

Then, in the aftermath of St. Thomas's demolition, developers began turning their sights toward the Iberville development, located just outside the city's famed French Quarter. Drawing on lessons garnered from St. Thomas, I worked with residents and local activists to mount a successful campaign to defeat an attempt by the local housing authority to obtain a federal grant to demolish and privatize Iberville. After Hurricane Katrina struck New Orleans in August 2005, I immersed myself in organizing efforts to defeat attempts by federal and local government officials to demolish the city's remaining public housing communities.

These questions, concerns, motivations, and history are what drove and inspired the research that produced *Driven from New Orleans*. Clearly, my politics and values have shaped this study. But this feature is not unique to my study—politics is embedded throughout *all* research, from the questions asked to the theories and methods employed, the data drawn on, the funding received, and the ways research is used, or not. As political economists William Tabb and Larry Sawers underscore, "The research people choose to do and the selection of initial assumptions and methodology are in essence political decisions."[1] Or as Africanist scholar and activist John Saul put it, "Scholarly preoccupations—the questions asked—do not spring spontaneously from the data, but are themselves shaped by an ongoing process of 'ideological class struggle.'" Though all research is political, Saul suggests that "scholarship shaped by our activism" encourages an "impressive level of engagement" that leads researchers "to ask the hard and searching questions that a more conservative and passive scholarship would obscure."[2] At the same time, we cannot substitute political commitment for analytical rigor. Both are needed. The dictum enunciated by the late sociologist Oliver Cromwell Cox outlines the combination of scholarship and political commitment that informs this study. The "social scientist," Cox argues in his seminal study, *Caste, Class, and Race,* "should be accurate and objective, but not neutral." We "should be," he goes on, "passionately partisan in favor of the welfare of the people and against the interests of the few when they seem to submerge that welfare. In a word, the reason for the existence of the social scientist is that his [or her] scientific findings contribute to the betterment of the people's well-being."[3]

It is my hope and aim that this work will assist and strengthen the efforts of those fighting for societal betterment, for a world that places meeting human need as its organizing principle.

Acknowledgments

I owe a debt of gratitude to the many people who made this book possible. I am especially grateful for my friend and comrade Mike Howells. The innumerable conversations we have had on local, national, and international events and struggles during my more than two decades in New Orleans and his incisive intellect played a key role in developing the ideas that inform this study. I also want to acknowledge many other friends and comrades from New Orleans who have educated, inspired, supported, and sparred with me over the years, including Sharon Jasper, Sam Jackson, Kawana Jasper, Stephanie Mingo, Assata Olugbala, Andy Washington, Elizabeth Cook, Lance Hill, Art Carpenter, Llewelyn Soniat, Derrick Morrison, Brad Ott, Marty Rowland, Eloise Williams, Rev. Raymond Brown, Ben Gordon, Catherine Candy, Michelle Perez, Malcolm Willison, Angela Jaster, Les Evenchick, George Andrews, Dave Capasso, George Mahdi, and the late Gary Modenbach, Troy Avery, Patricia Thomas, and Gloria Irving.

The support and guidance I received from Kevin Fox Gotham during the initial stages of this work as a dissertation were invaluable. Special thanks go to Martha K. Huggins for the interest she took in this project from its earliest stages, including her patient listening to my first inchoate attempts to explain my central arguments and her insistence that the St. Thomas story reach a wider audience through a book. I also want to thank Joel Devine, Scott Frickel, and Mickey Lauria for reading the first versions of this work as a dissertation and providing helpful critiques.

The support I received from my colleagues at the College of Staten Island has been invaluable in completing this work. Special thanks go to Kate Crehan, who organized a departmental writing group that regularly met in the comfortable confines of a café in lower Manhattan. Over lunch careful readers provided encouragement and valuable feedback, including Kate Crehan, Ismael Garcia-Colon, Rafael de la Dehesa, Ananya Mukherjea, Leigh Binford, Nancy Churchill, Francesca Degiuli, Tom Volscho, Hosu Kim, Saadia Toor, Roz Bologh, and Cathy Lavender. I am appreciative of the support for this project that the City University of New York contributed since my arrival in 2008. A 2009–2010 faculty fellowship from the CUNY Graduate Center's Center for Place, Culture, and

Politics provided a collegial and intellectually stimulating environment to develop and rework various chapters of this book. I looked forward to every meeting of our weekly seminar and the friends I made, including facilitators Biswas Padmini, David Harvey, and Peter Hitchcock and the interesting mix of CUNY faculty, graduate students, visiting fellows, and guest speakers that made up the yearlong gathering, including Scott Larson, Tatiana Schor, Jeremy Rayner, Vinay Gidwani, Patricia Salazar, Fiona Jeffries, Andrew Greenberg, Mary Taylor, Mike Boyle, Joon Lee, Julie Skurski, Bertie Ferdman, Marjorie Rosen, Jenna Lloyd, Nikolina Nedeljkov, Ashley Dawson, Karen Strassler, Matilde Cordoba, and Simon Addison. A spring 2010 fellowship from CUNY's Faculty Fellowship Publishing Program provided further support to complete this project. I am thankful for the hard-nosed yet generous critiques I received from the group's mentor, Stephen Steinberg, and my fellow mentees, Libby Garland, Amy Wan, Tamara Brown, Deborah Gambs, and Katherine Chen. It was a special, and unexpected, privilege to have Stephen Steinberg lead the group. Reading his hard-hitting articles in the pages of *New Politics* and other venues during graduate school had convinced me that there was room in the discipline of sociology for politically relevant work. Finally, a PSC–CUNY research grant for summer research during 2009 and 2010 provided crucial financial assistance to complete this project.

I am indebted to the public housing residents, nonprofit representatives, government officials, developers, and others who agreed to be interviewed for this study. Furthermore, I want to recognize the staff of the New Orleans Public Library for outstanding service despite its shoestring budget. I express my gratitude to Hope House director Don Everard and researcher Brod Bagert for sharing their files on the St. Thomas redevelopment effort and to Michel Varisco, Roy Blumenthal, and Edward Lopez for allowing me to use their photographs. I am thankful for the guidance of Pieter Martin at the University of Minnesota Press and all the troubleshooting of editorial assistant Kristian Tvedten that helped move the project through its various stages. I thank Ed Goetz and Sanford Schram, who served as outside reviewers. The conversations I have held and the support I have received over the years from Eric Lerner, Jeannette Gabriel, Adolph Reed, Darwin Bond-Graham, Steve Rosenthal, Alan Spector, Cedric Johnson, Rodney Coates, and Levon Chorbajian further contributed to this study.

My family and the gifts I have received from them played an important part in planting the seeds of this project. The riveting family stories shared by those who have passed on—my grandmothers, Guiseppina Arena and Raffaela "Mary" Guidone; my father, Louis Arena; and my uncle Joseph Arena—as well as those still with me (my uncle Angelo Arena, my aunt Rae Albano Arena, and my mother, Jean Arena) helped me to develop and cultivate a sociological imagination. By sharing stories with their inquisitive son, grandson, and nephew, they helped me to recognize the relationships between biography and history, my own life and world-historical transformations. Finally, I thank Graciela and David for all their support and tolerance during our years at Rosen House. *¡Ojo Pelao! ¡Los quiero mucho!*

Nonprofits and the Revanchist Agenda

> Truth claims about cities must be conceived from the bottom
> upward, must be located and grounded in the street, in urban
> public space, in everyday life.
>
> —ANDY MERRIFIELD

Barbara Jackson and Fannie McKnight were fed up. On a steamy July New Orleans afternoon in 1982, these two leaders from the St. Thomas public housing development, along with scores of other public housing residents from around the city and their community activist allies, gathered outside the downtown headquarters of the Housing Authority of New Orleans (HANO). With pickets in hand and intent on having their grievances addressed, the group threw open the front doors, charged up five flights of stairs, and burst into the housing authority's boardroom, where board members were holding their monthly meeting. In the face of the Reagan administration's federal government cutbacks, public housing residents and their supporters demanded that the now black-led New Orleans city government and housing authority board immediately address their demands: to roll back recently imposed rent and utility rate increases, to improve maintenance, and to foster real, meaningful democratic input from residents on how their communities were run. When the board refused to change their agenda, residents pulled out their pillows and began what would become a two-day occupation of the housing authority's offices. A month after the conclusion of the sit-in, Barbara Jackson, Fannie McKnight, and other residents of the St. Thomas public housing development—a community situated amid the city's growing riverfront–tourist corridor—began an occupation of their own development offices and organized a yearlong rent strike to force authorities to meet their demands. These struggles forced HANO to withdraw its attempt to impose utility payments on all public housing residents and led to a multimillion-dollar refurbishing plan for St. Thomas. In 1986, these same activists organized a march on the Louisiana state capitol to oppose cuts in welfare. These actions were not anomalous events but representative of the aggressive organizing carried out by the St. Thomas and other public housing communities for housing, jobs, respect, and power.

Yet some ten years later, by the early 1990s, the St. Thomas tenant leadership and their erstwhile radical community activist allies had moved from protest against to cooperation with state and corporate officials. Spearheaded by Fannie McKnight, Barbara Jackson, and community activist Barbara Major, the St. Thomas community and their activist allies forged a partnership with Joe Canizaro, the city's most powerful real estate developer, to privatize the development and create a new "mixed-income" community that would drastically reduce the number of affordable apartments. From protesting federal and local government initiatives to scale back public housing, tenant leaders and advisers moved to embrace the Clinton administration's then new HOPE VI federal grant, designed to privatize and downsize public housing. In the end, the formally radical tenant leaders and advisers signed off on a redevelopment plan that reversed their stance: it both drastically reduced public housing at St. Thomas and fueled gentrification and tourist industry expansion in the surrounding neighborhood, ultimately reducing affordable housing opportunities.

How and why did this political transformation take place? Why did the tenant leaders and their community activist allies go from being combative opponents of developers and government officials to collaborators? How did they justify this defection to themselves and their erstwhile allies? Questions abound on the other side of this unlikely dyad. Why was their collaboration valuable to their previous adversaries? How exactly did developers win them over? What lessons can we learn from this case study? What does it portend for the neoliberal city if opponents can be co-opted into collaborators? Is there an alternative?

The answer to these questions lies in the transformation of grassroots activists into nonprofit officials. The process of radical public housing leaders and their activist allies entering into a government- and foundation-funded nonprofit complex is key to understanding their political transformation. No longer politically or financially accountable to their grassroots base, the new organizational framework led activists to abandon direct action as their key political weapon for coercing concessions and defending the interests of public housing residents. The political allegiances and financial benefits of the nonprofit model moved these activists into a strategy of insider negotiations that prioritized the profit-making agenda of real estate interests above the housing and other material needs of black public housing residents. The city's most powerful developer, local newspapers, and the city's black political elite embraced and cultivated this new found political "realism." Why their enthusiasm? White developers and black politicians now had willing partners that could provide crucially needed black working-class legitimation and cover for the regressive policies of the 1990s: the removal of poor people from now desirable urban real estate and the massive downsizing of public housing. More broadly, *Driven from New Orleans* argues that nonprofits play a central and crucial role on behalf of political and economic elites, facilitating the often politically difficult job of privatizing public housing and displacing communities and other regressive features of contemporary neoliberalizing cities.

To understand political transformation at St. Thomas and appreciate the role of nonprofits in that process, I employ a multilevel analysis. I identify the interconnections among global-, national-, city-, and community-level changes and dynamics to understand this unexpected political metamorphosis and its significance. This research strategy is what Michael Burawoy calls an "extended case study method," because it "encourages us," as urban sociologist Alex Vitale underscores, "to look at complex local events as being situated in a larger political and economic context, and not just a reflection of it."[1] That is, identifying the global, national, and citywide structures and actors that confronted the St. Thomas community is critical for appreciating the political choices available to residents and activists. This method helps highlight how, within those constraints, the conscious political decisions and actions of black public housing residents and their allies effected political and economic change.

Neoliberalism, Gentrification, and the Revanchist Agenda

Gentrification—defined as flows of capital into an urban core that create spaces for the affluent while displacing the existing low-income residents of the area—has taken hold in cities across the United States and globally over the last several decades. After decades of disinvestment and suburban growth, particularly in the United States, this transformation represents, argues geographer Neil Smith, "a dramatic yet unpredicted reversal of what most twentieth-century urban theories had been predicting as the fate of the central and inner-city."[2] The phenomenon of gentrifying inner cities is part of a larger transformation of U.S. capitalism and its relationship to the global economy.[3] Beginning in the 1970s and accelerating in the ensuing decades, the U.S. corporate and economic elite have overseen the dismantlement of the previous Fordist–Keynesian model of accumulation and the rise of a neoliberal–globalization one. In response to growing global competition and an increasingly combative working class, these elites have responded with a scorched-earth policy of dismantling factories and stripping assets while moving some manufacturing operations to capital security zones in the U.S. South and the global South, where "low wages and a union free business environment and close ties [of corporations] to state and local governments" predominate.[4] This capital offensive has produced draconian cuts in workers' wages and benefits and the devastation of countless cities, particularly in the Northeast and the Midwest. Instead of expanding the production of goods, the U.S. economy has increasingly veered toward an expanding service sector and, especially, financialization, with exploding debt at the state, corporate, and household levels helping to underwrite growth and consumption. The changing source of U.S. corporate profits underscores the dramatic restructuring of the U.S. economy. By 2006, the FIRE sector of the economy—composed of financial, insurance, and real estate firms— had generated an astounding 40 percent of all the profits for domestic industries, up from 15 percent in 1960.[5] This economic reconfiguration is reflected in the transformation of city waterfronts and former industrial districts into office buildings, upscale housing, and hotels replete with restaurants, malls, coffee shops, and other amenities, which serve the new affluent denizens of America's central cities.

Accompanying this spatial and economic restructuring has been a neoliberal political model to facilitate the emergence of a new model of accumulation.[6] The Keynesian welfare state, which provided varying levels of protection from the market, has now been identified by neoliberal elites as an impediment to capitalist restructuring. In its place governments have imposed a set of policies political scientist William Sites terms "primitive globalization" to advance a "damaging type of economic globalization."[7] The neoliberal national, regional, and local levels of the state promote the privatization and cutback of public services, tax reductions and subsidies for business, the lifting of regulatory controls, and of particular importance for this study, literally "clearing the ground" of poor people to make space for redevelopment.[8] Neoliberal states, as sociologist William Robinson evocatively describes them, incessantly push "for every layer of the social fabric ... [to be] opened up for accumulation." These states aim, he continues in wording that describes their actual impact on public housing, to "tear down all nonmarket structures that have in the past placed limits, or acted as a protective layer against the accumulation of capital."[9]

The policy agenda outlined above underscores that neoliberalism is, essentially, a "*political* project," as geographer David Harvey argues, designed "to re-establish the conditions for capital accumulation and to restore the power of economic elites."[10] This double mission—to increase both the power and the profits of the capitalist class—helps explain why privatization of public services is such a core element of neoliberalism. Privatization, understood through the lens of commodification as one instance of "the process through which things or services become market goods," has certainly helped to open up areas of social life previously closed off to profit making.[11] Privatizing—commodifying—formerly state-delivered goods and services, such as public education, public health care, and public housing, has created new "emerging markets" that allow private capitalists to generate profits from their provision. In addition, public housing privatization has also increased the *power* of, in particular, real estate and finance capitalists—the sections of the U.S. capitalist class most clearly in ascendency under neoliberalism—over poor and working-class urban communities. Commodification of public housing has helped break up the solidarities, "repertoires of contention," and everyday practices of poor, working-class communities that presented obstacles to the full spatial, cultural, political, and economic emergence and maintenance of the neoliberal city.[12]

The retaking of urban space from the poor, at the heart of what Neil Smith terms the "revanchist agenda," is not particular to the United States but represents a "global urban strategy" of development.[13] As geographers Brenner and Theodore underscore, national, regional, and local levels of the state across the world have adhered to "the basic neoliberal imperative of mobilizing economic space as a purified arena of capitalist growth, commodification, and market discipline."[14] Yet the actual creation of neoliberal spaces, such as those accomplished through public housing demolition, takes place in a particular locale, often at the municipal level. The city, as Brenner and Theodore underscore, is the "key arena in which the everyday violence of neoliberalism has been unleashed."[15] While a critical terrain of study, the extent to which market-friendly spaces are created at the municipal level is still a contingent process, one dependent on "the inherited institutional frameworks, policy regimes, regulatory practices and political struggles."[16] The local still matters. Broad global and national economic changes and political directives do not simply call forth the needed local regulatory and political changes to allow for the retaking of urban centers.

Neoliberalism, Public Housing, and New Orleans's Black Urban Regime

Central to the gentrification of U.S. cities has been the destruction of public housing. Between the mid-1990s and 2010 the federal government and local housing authorities demolished over 400 public housing projects, eliminating approximately 200,000 public housing apartments out of an original stock of 2.4 million.[17] The demolitions have, consistent with core neoliberal goals, removed physical impediments—what geographer Jason Hackworth terms "Keynesian artifacts"—that blocked profit-making opportunities not only on the former sites but in the surrounding area.[18] The implosion of high-rise developments has often been accompanied with extensive media coverage, with crowds gathering to watch local and often national officials give the signal to detonate what Vice President Gore labeled "monuments of hopelessness."[19] Developers and public officials choosing high-rises for special attention—which were only one, and not the modal, architectural form of public housing—underscores that public housing demolition was at the center of the racialized, revanchist agenda in the United States. In the public imaginary, high-rise projects signified black welfare dependency, crime, and much of what was perceived as wrong about urban America. Thus, the demolition of these "visual references to New Deal and welfare state policies" signaled, symbolically and physically, the "taking back" of the city from, in particular, poor African Americans, allowing for the "reimaging" of cities critical for increased flows of investment.[20]

The contemporary displacement generated by public housing demolition, with low-income African Americans being major victims, shares some similarities with the U.S. urban renewal of the 1950s and 1960s. This venture was dubbed ignominiously by many of its critics as "Negro removal" because of the way African Americans disproportionally bore the burden of removal to build highways, universities, office buildings, sports facilities, and upscale residential developments. White political leaders oversaw the displacement of this earlier era while real estate companies, construction firms, and residents garnered the benefits from the outlay of federal funds that subsidized this urban redevelopment. In contrast, under what sociologist Derek Hyra terms the "new urban renewal" of the 1990s and 2000s, upper-income African Americans, along with wealthy whites, have led and benefited from the gentrification and displacement of many low-income inner-city African American communities. Two of the best known examples of "black gentrification" are Harlem in New York and Bronzeville in Chicago.[21]

A central focus of works on black gentrification has been the role played by middle-class black homeowners and professionals, what sociologist Mary Pattillo refers to as the "middlemen," in displacing lower-income black residents from historically black neighborhoods.[22] For example, Michele Boyd's fascinating work *Jim Crow Nostalgia* analyzes how black middle-class gentrifiers in Chicago, drawing on an idealized version of the segregation era, constructed a particular, "authentic" black racial identity that, they lament, was lost through integration. This particular black identity is then harnessed to help legitimate a neoliberal urban redevelopment model of racial tourism districts, public housing demolition, and black gentrification designed "to recreate the (authentic) black communities that existed during the early twentieth century."[23]

Driven from New Orleans alters and extends the study of black gentrification in two ways. First, instead of focusing on the black middle class, my work centers on one of the principal targets of black gentrification—black public housing residents—and, in particular, how consent was won for displacement and the role that nonprofits played. Employing the vantage point of public housing residents also addresses what urban geographer Tom Slater critiques as the "eviction of critical perspectives from recent gentrification research." The trend has led to a glossing over of gentrification's negative impacts and, oftentimes, even celebrating the alleged benefits created by the colonization of inner cities by the new upscale entrants. In contrast, viewing the process from below draws us unavoidably to the underside of the process, to the "injustice of community upheaval . . . working class displacement . . . and the erosion of affordable housing."[24]

The second way this study extends our understanding of black gentrification is by moving beyond the iconic black neighborhoods of Chicago and New York to look at post–civil rights Negro removal within the context of what political scientist Adolph Reed calls a "black urban regime" form of government. This type of regime, which governed New Orleans from the late 1970s until the late 2000s, is one that emerged in many majority black cities in the post–civil rights era.[25] These political formations are characterized by a "governing coalition" composed of a primarily black public wing that holds a majority of the leading positions in local government and their allied, primarily black cadre of professionals, contractors, and ministers. Assembled on the other side of the power structure is a mainly white corporate private wing that controls the most important economic institutions. These elites are, for the most part, committed to a neoliberal, urban entrepreneurial development model, with their collaboration often taking the form of "public–private" partnerships. The governing elite favors constructing policy through these private and sometimes quasi-public entities, since they are buffered from extensive citizen participation and pressure, as compared with the traditional democratic organs of city government such as the mayor's office, city council, and elected boards. These corporate or entrepreneurial regimes facilitate and subsidize corporate-led economic development, while redistribution and welfare are jettisoned. Working-class communities are assumed to benefit from the trickle-down effect of government-subsidized economic development projects in which local governments, rather than entrepreneurs, assume most of the risk. The development agenda is characterized by what Gordon McLeod calls a "political economy of *place* rather than *territory,*" in which "the benefits of flagship projects like convention centers and festivals are often more readily experienced by those, like tourists and place-mobile capitalists, who live beyond the immediate locality."[26]

This procorporate development model promoted by the regime's governing elite comes into conflict with the interests of the largest and most loyal component of the black urban regime's electoral coalition—the black poor and working class. Thus, as Adolph Reed notes, the relationship between the regime's governing and electoral coalitions is a particularly "tenuous" one, with the regime's popular base expecting government policy to promote downward redistribution, "while those of its governing coalition . . . converge on the use of public policy as a mechanism for upward distribution."[27] Therefore, the challenge for the new post–civil rights black political leadership is "how to appear to be progressive," how to appear to address "the needs of the black community and yet meet the needs of the major business interests."[28] In his study Reed argues that the first generation of black urban regimes during the 1970s and 1980s were relatively effective in managing this contradiction. Key to this success was the ability of black mayors to shift black

> response to policy debate away from substantive concerns with potential outcomes and toward protection of racial image and status, as embodied in the idiosyncratic agenda of the black officials. *In this way it becomes possible for black officials to maintain support from both their black constituents and the development elites that systematically disadvantage them.*[29] (emphasis added)

Undergirding these powers of obfuscation was the legitimacy that came with being the first black mayor in their respective cities, an authority further bolstered by many having been leading participants in the civil rights movement. For example, New Orleans's first black mayor, Ernest "Dutch" Morial, was formerly head of the local NAACP and litigated various desegregation suits. Mayors Maynard Jackson in Atlanta, Coleman Young in Detroit, and Marion Barry in Washington, DC, enjoyed similar trajectories. Thus this first generation of leaders could portray their elevation to city hall as the culmination, indeed the institutionalization, of the civil rights movement. Further strengthening the ability of black mayors and city councilpersons to manage the black urban regime's class and racial contradictions was that in the 1980s, as Dennis Judd notes, many of the corporate, progrowth strategies were "not as divisive as the urban renewal clearance programs" of the 1950s and 1960s. Instead, they often dealt with issues of tax abatement and bond issuances that appeared more economic than political and were often dealt with by "quiet behind the scene transactions between a public authority and private institutions."[30]

Conditions changed in the 1990s and 2000s as the "new urban renewal," particularly in the form of demolishing black public housing communities, made a dramatic return to New Orleans and other cities across the United States. Complicating matters further was that this new round of "Negro removal" would have to be led by a second generation of black leaders that had no personal involvement in the civil rights movement and thus did not enjoy the same legitimacy as their predecessors. How might the post–civil rights urban black leadership in majority African American cities and their allied white developers successfully handle politically explosive endeavors such as public housing demolition? I argue that examining the politics and organizations at the neighborhood level can provide some answers. This context is crucial for solving a major conundrum of the postsegregation American politics addressed in this study: the consensual removal of poor, black communities.

Nonprofits and the Politics of Post–Civil Rights Negro Removal

The theory of hegemony developed by Antonio Gramsci offers a conceptual framework useful for understanding how the contradictions of black urban regimes and those of the broader globally and nationally driven neoliberal agenda can be addressed and managed at the neighborhood level. Gramsci holds that any political system is maintained by both coercive and consensual mechanisms. He identifies the formal institutions of the state, particularly the courts, prisons, police, military, and central bank, as maintaining control primarily through force and laws. This form of rule is accompanied by that of the "extended state"—that is, the private institutions in civil society, such as nonprofit organizations, that help generate consent to the ruling class's agenda without resorting to force. "These two levels correspond," Gramsci argues, "on the one hand to the function of 'hegemony' which the dominant group exercises throughout society and on the other hand to that of 'direct domination' or command exercised through the State and 'juridical' government."[31]

Key to the generation of consent is the dissemination of an ideology and corresponding political practice that appears merely as common sense. Hegemonic institutions contain dissent by portraying deviations from the ruling class's thinking and agenda as extremism and self-defeating, while at the same time they are dynamic enough to incorporate new ideas and practices generated by challengers. Therefore, Gramsci's theory of hegemony leads us to look at nongovernmental organizations and actors to address the paradoxes of the black urban regime. These organizations can provide insights into how the dominant group, in this case the black urban regime's governing elite, was able to consensually introduce public housing demolition and poor people removal.

What Are Nonprofits? Whose Interests Do They Serve?

The nonprofit or third sector refers to a wide range of organizations situated between the family at the microlevel and business and government on the other. Although technically independent of the government, in the United States many nonprofits, ranging from PTAs to unions to neighborhood associations, are registered with the federal government's Internal Revenue Service as tax-exempt organizations. The largest component of these state-recognized nonprofits, and one that plays a particularly important role at the neighborhood level, is the "religious, charitable, scientific and educational" subset of organizations covered by section 501(c)(3) of the federal tax code. Not only is this category of nonprofits exempt from federal income tax (as are the other nonprofits registered by the government), but contributions to these organizations are tax deductible for the donors. In addition, unlike most other nonprofits, they can receive foundation grants. In fact, for most 501(c)(3)s grants are their major source of funding. These privileges are accompanied with restrictions on lobbying, and they are barred from participating in partisan electoral campaigns.[32]

Foundations, which are also categorized as 501(c)(3)s, are divided by the IRS into three categories: operating foundations, public charities, and private foundations. The IRS defines private foundations as entities that are primarily grant-making institutions and whose income is primarily derived from investments. In contrast, organizations designated as public charities receive the bulk of their income from public donations, such as grants, membership fees, and individual contributions. Operating foundations have a similar funding source, but the bulk of their expenses are dedicated to its central purpose, such as operating a museum. For this study private foundations, which provide the bulk of revenues for 501(c)(3) nonprofits, have the greatest relevance. Because of their financial power, the private foundations act, in effect, as the "the planning and coordinating arm" of the 501(c)(3) sector.[33]

The nonprofit sector has grown dramatically over the last thirty years. Between 1998 and 2008, the number of nonprofits registered with the IRS increased by 30 percent, expanding from 1.16 to 1.51 million. Among the 501(c)(3)s—the largest component of IRS-designated nonprofits—the growth rate was even more robust during the same ten-year period, expanding from 597,236 to 958,398, an increase of over 60 percent. This rate even outstripped the impressive 50 percent growth in the government-registered, nonprofit sector over the last three decades.[34]

What explains the impressive growth and increasing importance of the nonprofit sector in the United States, as well as in other parts of the globe, both in the first and third world? Part of the explanation is in the neoliberal transformation of the state, particularly the privatization of public services. As the state—or at least its social service arm—has receded, nonprofits have emerged to fill the void. This expanded role has often taken the form of governments or foundations contracting with nonprofits to provide services previously delivered by the state.[35] A second important factor explaining their growth is the crucial *political* role they play, providing, to use Joan Roelofs provocative description, a "protective layer of capitalism."

This protective function provided by the nonprofits is centered on their capacity to undermine, contain, or prevent the emergence of social movements that challenge the power and prerogatives of the ruling class.[36] One key way nonprofits contain movements is through co-optation of leaders or, as Hester Eisenstein puts it, by "sopping up the energy of activists." Nonprofits help cultivate what Gramsci defines as the ruling class's "intellectuals," their "deputies"—operatives who exercise hegemonic power within the working class.[37] Central to the recruiting and co-optive powers of nonprofits and their foundation sponsors is the material rewards they can provide intellectuals—the "jobs and benefits for radicals willing to become pragmatic."[38] These perks, along with the legitimation that comes with being associated with "progressive," "humanitarian," and/or "social change" organizations, can be useful in both peeling away working-class, grassroots, organic intellectuals or preventing others from even dabbling in radical politics.

The power to channel activists, organizations, and movements into nonthreatening directions is a second crucial protective role performed by what the INCITE collective calls the "non-profit industrial complex."[39] The financial power of foundations, which helps discipline nonprofit officials who might have an inclination toward developing a radical, anticapitalist politics, is central to the channeling process. The hard reality faced by nonprofits, radical or otherwise, is that to obtain funding they have to fit their agenda into the issues and guidelines laid out by the funders. The liberal foundations—who are the major provider of funds for the 501(c)(3) sector, dwarfing monies provided by the conservative and left variants—encourage applicants to develop and forge campaigns with reasonable goals that do not represent a radical challenge to the status quo. The nonprofits are generally encouraged to approach social problems as technical in nature, requiring the application of expert knowledge, rather than to frame issues as deeply rooted, class-based conflicts. Any deviation can result in a cutoff of funds. Even if funding is not obtained, nonprofit "grassroots" organizations will often structure their initiatives and organizing to fit within a model acceptable to the foundation's funders. If a grant application is denied in one funding cycle, there is always hope for next year. There are undoubtedly radicals that enter into the nonprofit complex with the goal of gaming the funders and system to support a radical, anticapitalist agenda. Those attempting to subvert the system invariably confront an iron cage of constraints that encourages, indeed requires, accommodation.

Another important way foundations channel nonprofits and movements into nonthreatening directions is through the promotion of an identity politics form of organizing narrowly focused on a particular oppression. To garner funding, nonprofits are usually required to develop single-issue campaigns that address the needs of some oppressed group, based on age, race, sexuality, disability, or some other identity. The result of this type of organizing is a proliferation, as James Petras argues in his critique of the foundation-funded 2007 U.S. Social Forum, "of fragmented 'identity groups' each embedded in narrow sets of (Identity) interests totally incapable of building a national movement."[40] The promotion of identity politics–informed organizing focused on difference presents a major obstacle, or trench, to constructing a broad left that recognizes common class interests—a force that would have the social power to effectively combat racial, gender, sexual, and other forms of oppression through a mass challenge to the ruling class's neoliberal capitalist agenda.

New Orleans and Nonprofits

This book provides a critical look at nonprofits by analyzing their involvement in a core component of the neoliberal agenda in pre– and post– Hurricane Katrina New Orleans: the privatization of public housing and the displacement of poor, black communities. To explore the role of nonprofits in privatizing the St. Thomas development, I place primary attention on the St. Thomas/Irish Channel Consortium, better known by its acronym, STICC. Former radical community activists, St. Thomas tenant leaders, and various neighborhood social service providers formed the organization in 1990. STICC was the central organizational vehicle through which tenant leaders and community activists moved from protest to insider negotiations with developers, government officials, and foundations to work out a redevelopment plan for St. Thomas. I examine how in the post-Katrina period a host of foundations and nonprofits promoted, either directly or indirectly, the demolition of public housing and its replacement by smaller, privately run, so-called mixed-income developments. The role played by the post-Katrina nonprofit complex is contrasted with that of several non-501(c)(3) community groups dedicated to defending and expanding public housing.

Race, Class, and Public Housing: A Bottom-Up View

Public housing in this study is defined as federally financed low-rent housing directly owned and managed by local government, where eligibility and rent payments are based on need and income. "The central event leading to the adoption of the public housing program in the U.S.," urban planner Peter Marcuse underscores, "was certainly the Depression, and more specifically the forces of unrest and discontent it unleashed."[41] Clearly, public housing was one of the important social and economic concessions won by the radical social movements of the 1930s, along with union organizing rights, minimum wage and other government-enforced labor standards, a social security act that established old-age pensions, unemployment insurance and welfare, and a public works program. In fact, Catherine Bauer—a driving force behind its creation—argued that the Housing Act of 1937, which established the program, was "perhaps the most clear-cut and uncompromising [pro-working-class reform] adopted under the New Deal." The 1937 act was a radical initiative because of its frank recognition of the private market's inability to provide, as the act states, "decent, safe, and sanitary dwellings for lower income families" and of the need for state provision of this basic human need.[42]

Critics of public housing argue that although the federal government financed the construction of low-income public housing, it provided much more generous and expansive subsidies for private homeownership. Through the Federal Housing Administration (FHA), created in 1934, the government insured mortgages issued by private lenders, removing risk, and allowed borrowers to put up only a small portion of the principle, with low mortgage payments spread out over twenty and, later, thirty years. This program did dramatically expand homeownership and helped build wealth—for whites. African Americans were virtually barred from the program. The FHA and, later, the even more generous Veterans Administration housing program institutionalized the private housing industry's use of discriminatory racial covenants, legally enforceable restrictions that prevented sales and rentals to racial and ethnic minorities, especially African Americans.[43] Under FHA guidelines the covenants were given the imprimatur of official state policy and support, with government-backed mortgage insurance approved only if the home and the development in which it was situated was covered by a racial covenant. Even when the Supreme Court held racial covenants unenforceable in 1948, their effect continued as realtors—although sometimes challenged by block busters—abided by them and private appraisers continued to use racial criteria to determine home values.[44]

In the post–World War II era, as the radical social movements of the 1930s were tamed, U.S. housing policy became increasingly dominated by state subsidization for the racially discriminatory suburbanization model promoted by the FHA and supported by the real estate–banking–house building industry. In contrast to the first-tier FHA program, public housing became part of the bottom tier, disproportionally serving the inner-city black poor (although whites still outnumbered blacks in public housing). With passage of the 1949 and 1954 housing bills, public housing was progressively linked to rehousing inner-city poor communities displaced as part of federally financed inner-city urban renewal projects and highway construction.

This legacy has led many researchers and housing advocates, especially those concerned about racial and economic justice, to take a particularly negative view of U.S. public housing. For example, historian Arnold Hirsch, author of the influential *Making the Second Ghetto*, argues that public housing has essentially operated as a federally supported program to remove the poor, particularly African Americans, from land desired by developers and warehouse and segregate the displaced in isolated urban high-rise reservations.[45] Sociologists William Julius Wilson and Douglass Massey and Nancy Denton, historian Brad Hunt, and urban planner Lawrence Vale bewail the way public housing has led to a concentration of poverty among, in particular, inner-city African Americans.[46] The isolation and concentration of poor black families in public housing has helped foster, in Massey and Denton's words, a "pathological culture" among the black poor. It is a culture in which "traditional mores that assign value to steady work, family life, the church, and respect for others" is replaced by a "nihilistic and violent counterculture sharply at odds with the basic values and goals of a democratic society."[47] Influential urban scholars Thomas Sugrue and Nicholas Leeman add to the condemnation, pointing to the "failure" of public housing as the third key leg—along with white flight and transfer of capital to the suburbs—of what they characterize as the U.S. postwar "urban crisis."[48]

In contrast to these perspectives, *Driven from New Orleans* presents a more contradictory picture of public housing. It is one that, as Ian Gough argues in his study of the modern welfare state, exhibits both "positive and negative features . . . embod[ying] tendencies to enhance social welfare . . . and tendencies to repress and control people, to adapt them to the requirements of a capitalist society."[49] Underscoring these cross-cutting currents, historian Rhonda Williams, in her study of Baltimore's public housing, argues the program "offered African American women and their families a mixed bag of opportunity and discrimination, possibilities and restrictions, freedoms and surveillance."[50] This contradictory picture is critical to challenging the view—represented by many of the works cited above—that public housing was a total failure.

Clearly, an underfunded public housing program, compared with the much more generous federal subsidies provided for housing mortgages that have disproportionally benefited white and upper-income households, reinforced the racial, gender, and class hierarchies of American capitalism. Public housing and welfare were, unlike entitlement programs such as Social Security, means-and-morals-tested programs that separated the "deserving" and "undeserving" poor. The former were central components of the U.S. charitable state—an uneven, two-tiered, racialized and gendered welfare state that blamed the victims of poverty for their plight.[51] Although public housing was designed in many ways to control, stigmatize, and segregate poor black communities, it also resulted in politicizing and empowering residents. Not only did public housing fulfill a crucial human need for many low-income families, but through the provision of low-rent, subsidized, *public* housing, the government "implied a *right* to decent living conditions for U.S. citizens."[52] Through the provision of public housing, the state inadvertently helped facilitate what geographer Don Mitchell calls a "rights talk"—that is, by establishing the right to "safe, sanitary, and decent housing," the program "establish[ed] an important ideal against which the behavior of the state, capital and other powerful actors must be measured."[53] The creation of these rights or ideals and the official sanctioning of resident councils—originally designed to cultivate apolitical "community involvement"—worked to encourage political activism. It was the very idea of this right—and the recognition of government responsibility to provide such fundamental needs as housing that the market could not—that would face a withering ideological attack in the neoliberal era.

A further contradictory component of public housing was the power embedded in its geography. The close proximity of living arrangements in public housing promoted group identity and facilitated collective action. The Kerner Commission, established in 1967 by President Johnson, paid particular attention to this latter feature of public housing in its attempt to understand the root causes of and provide policy solutions to contain the black revolts sweeping U.S. urban centers in the mid- to late 1960s. The report repeatedly identified public housing projects as the epicenter of many uprisings and called for, as part of their recommendations for containing future "disturbances," the construction of smaller, scattered-site developments rather than the large developments associated with political disturbances.[54] Thus, the demolition of public housing communities at St. Thomas in New Orleans and across the country has destroyed not only badly needed affordable housing but political power, community identity, and neighborhood support systems, as well. This book highlights the role that nonprofits played in undermining and sapping the political power that St. Thomas and other public housing developments helped foster.

New Orleans's Public Housing: From Jim Crow to the Black Urban Regime

In New Orleans public housing has been a major housing source since the 1940s for the city's working class and for the black working class, in particular. At its peak in the 1970s, it provided a home for approximately 60,000 working-class people, almost all African American, about 20 percent of the city's total black population. At this time, HANO, established in 1937 and governed by a mayor-appointed board, operated ten large public housing developments and smaller collections of apartments, known as *scattered sites*. The large complexes ranged from the 1,800 apartments in the isolated Desire housing development, built in the mid-1950s, to the 858 apartments at the centrally located Iberville development, opened in 1941 and situated adjacent to both the historic Tremé neighborhood and the city's famed French Quarter. The St. Thomas development, the focus of this study, was one of the nation's first public housing developments approved for funding by the Roosevelt administration under the Housing Act of 1937. The 1,510-apartment complex, opened in 1941 as white only and expanded in the mid-1950s, was located in the "uptown" (west of Canal Street) Irish Channel neighborhood (see Table I.1).

Like almost all public housing projects in New Orleans, the St. Thomas was not a high-rise complex—the stereotypical image of public housing—but rather comprised two- and three-story walk-up apartments" (see Figure I.1). Initially, residents paid rent—which covered utilities, as well—based on the size of their apartment. This system was later changed to one based on a percentage of gross monthly income, which was set initially at 25 percent and then increased in the 1980s to 30 percent. With regard to race, federal regulators of public housing employed the neighborhood composition rule. Under this policy the occupants of completed projects were to reflect the racial makeup of the neighborhood that existed before redevelopment.[55] In practice, federal authorities gave localities great leeway,

TABLE I.1

Public Housing Developments in New Orleans

Project	Race	Year Opened	Original Units	Mid-1950s Extension	Number of Final Units
St. Thomas	White	1941	970	540	1,510
C. J. Peete (Magnolia)	Black	1941	723	680	1,403
Iberville	White	1941	858	—	858
Lafitte	Black	1941	896	—	896
B. W. Cooper (Calliope)	Black	1941	690	860	1,550
St. Bernard	Black	1942	742	720	1,462
Florida	White	1946	500	234	734
Desire	Black	1956	—	—	1,852
Guste	Black	1963	—	—	993
Fischer	Black	1965	—	—	1,002
Scattered Sites	All	1967–1977	—	—	2,331
Total			5,379		14,591

SOURCE: *Lentz 1978: 212; U.S. House of Representatives 1996: 345;* Times-Picayune, *January 18, 1984*

with New Orleans joining many—but not all—cities that racially segregated public housing. At times the neighborhood composition rule was blatantly flouted in New Orleans, with HANO establishing the all-white Iberville development where the formerly black neighborhood of Storyville had stood. HANO did not begin desegregation of St. Thomas and the rest of its public housing developments until 1965, following passage of the Civil Rights Act of 1964. By the early 1970s, New Orleans public housing complexes were almost entirely made up of low-income African American renters.[56]

New Orleans's African American public housing communities have a tradition of activism that dates to the beginning of the program. The first residents of the St. Bernard development gathered 1,700 signatures and chose a seven-member committee to present them to Mayor Maestri in demand of improved bus services. In 1941, prospective public housing

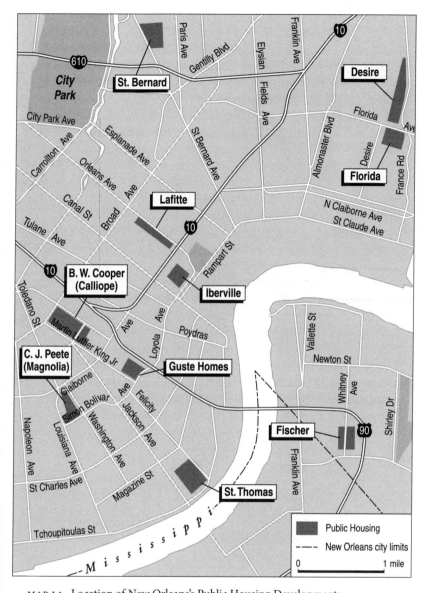

MAP I.1. Location of New Orleans's Public Housing Developments

FIGURE I.1. St. Thomas Public Housing Development, 1941. Photograph courtesy of the Franklin Delano Roosevelt Library and Museum.

residents joined the larger black community to demand that a black manager be named to head the city's first African American–designated public housing development, the Magnolia.[57] In the late 1960s, as the developments became increasingly black, activism increased as residents pressed for improved housing and other public services, decent jobs, and an end to police brutality. This mobilization is perhaps best understood historically as part of a broader, multiclass civil rights/black freedom movement that was taking hold nationally. For example, in 1968 eighty-five residents of the Fischer housing development, mainly female heads of households, many of whom were members of the Algiers chapter of the Welfare Rights Organization, voted to go on a rent strike after the State of Louisiana's welfare agency slashed their Aid to Dependent Families support check—their main source of income—by 10 percent.[58] On April 25, 1969, members of the New Orleans Tenant Organization conducted a two-hour takeover of the office of HANO director J. Gilbert Scheib in an effort—which was eventually successful—to lower rents for welfare recipients.[59] In 1968, HANO's maintenance workers, a workforce that was increasingly composed of African American men, made their first attempt of several at obtaining a collective bargaining agreement with management by working with the American Federation of State, County and Municipal Employees (AFSCME).[60]

The most high-profile example of poor people's resistance to poverty, poor housing conditions, racial discrimination, and police brutality came from a New Orleans chapter of the Black Panther Party, an African American socialist organization that had its base, in 1970, in the city's Desire housing development. In the words of one Black Panther supporter:

> At last, into this hellhole of poverty, came the Panthers like a fresh wind, to start doing what government should have done hundreds of years ago. Free breakfasts, free clothing, donations from merchants (like the churches got [already]); self-respect, self-discipline, community responsibility and authority, the asserting of self-defense against attacks by cops, goons, dogs and spies.[61]

The Panther chapter's political work focused on opposing police harassment of Desire residents; providing social services, such as a children's breakfast program; and demanding improvements to the development's poorly built townhouses and roads, both of which had been compromised even further after the flooding caused by Hurricane Betsy in 1965. After the Panthers had generated a significant following in Desire, however, its leadership was driven from the development by New Orleans city officials through a variety of tactics. These measures included a November 1970 confrontation during which the New Orleans police sealed off the Desire development, parked an armored personnel carrier in front of an apartment where the Panthers were holed up, and unleashed a barrage of fire against them. In addition, authorities employed such soft glove strategies as arranging visits by the clergy and by members of the emerging black political class—among these, Bob Tucker, Sherman Copelin, and James Singleton—to coax them into abandoning their struggle. The HANO board of commissioners, including its first African American member, NAACP attorney A. P. Tureaud, appointed in 1966, and the second black appointee, Reynard Rochon, a rising political star, lauded the police action taken against the Panthers.[62]

Driven from New Orleans continues this story by documenting the activism of public housing residents, particularly from the St. Thomas development, between the late 1970s and the 2000s. But this activism for decent and affordable housing, good schools, jobs, and ending police brutality would not take place, as before, under either a white-controlled, segregationist urban government or a white, racially liberal one, as represented by Maurice Landrieu's administration from 1970 to 1978. Instead, the black public housing activism I analyze operated under the seemingly more favorable conditions of a black urban regime government where the mayor's office and most city council seats, various board positions, and administrative posts were held by African Americans. Complicating this picture was that much of this new black political leadership, along with their white, corporate governing partners, no longer saw public housing as useful, even for warehousing and controlling the poor. Rather, they viewed public housing communities, especially centrally located ones such as St. Thomas and Iberville, as physical and social obstacles to economic regeneration. How these conflicting agendas were managed and settled is the focus of this book.

Sources

Between 2001 and 2004, I drew on—in addition to the knowledge gained from years of working in public housing—a variety of data-gathering methods and sources to understand the fate of St. Thomas. I conducted over thirty interviews with developers, elected officials, government administrators, nonprofit representatives, elected tenant council members, and rank-and-file residents involved in the redevelopment process. I also accessed the archival records of two local nonprofits and those of HANO, as well as consulting government reports and newspaper articles and observing several public meetings. Chapters 6 and 7 are based on four years of participant observation, from 2004 to 2008, of New Orleans's pre–and post–Hurricane Katrina public housing movement. This data was supplemented with documents distributed by activists and lawyers, participation in and study of activist email discussion on Listservs, newspaper articles, and interviews with key participants. The varied sources of data and techniques allowed me to triangulate data in order to confront the study's central questions from multiple angles and, thus, buttress the validity of my observations and claims. Multiple data sources compose, as methodologist Robert Yin argues, "converging lines of inquiry" that increase our ability to make accurate descriptions and convincing claims.[63]

Organization of the Book

Consistent with the multilevel analysis that informs this book, the subsequent chapters examine the broader forces that confronted the St. Thomas community and how, within those constraints, community and tenant activists at the neighborhood level responded and the consequences of those choices. Chapter 1 opens by outlining the unfavorable political and economic context that confronted the St. Thomas community in the 1970s and 1980s. This context is further elaborated through a demographic profile of the community, coupled with a window into the texture of life at St. Thomas through the words of St. Thomas residents. I then turn to how, despite the challenges they faced, including opposition within their own ranks, St. Thomas and other public housing residents, along with their activist allies, were able to mount a collective effort to address their grievances. I conclude by analyzing the consequences of this insurgency and how the St. Thomas case helps us broaden our conceptualization of working-class struggles.

Chapter 2 outlines the expansion, and intertwining, of tourism and gentrification in New Orleans. I identify the primary beneficiaries and supporters, how they promoted their agenda, and the political conflicts it fueled in and around St. Thomas. I then detail and evaluate the effectiveness, in the context of electing the city's second black mayor, of the insider and outsider political strategies St. Thomas residents and their advisers employed to protect their community from the increasing development pressures they faced. Chapter 3 continues a focus on political strategy by addressing how and why the St. Thomas residents and their advisers undertook a dramatic political reversal by forging a partnership with the city's most powerful real estate mogul to redevelop their community and surrounding area.

Chapter 4 begins by moving the analysis to the federal level to explain how public housing policy was neoliberalized in the 1990s, including the ideological role performed by influential social scientists and the expanded use of state coercive measures. The interstate level of analysis is explored by outlining the superficial differences and substantive agreements between Washington and the black-led city administration over public housing reform. Based on the common ground shared by these two parties, the chapter explains how a settlement was reached to oversee what was in their eyes a reform of New Orleans's government-owned, low-income housing stock. Drawing on the concept of the extended state, I outline the crucial role that universities and nonprofit community groups played in legitimating and introducing a public housing privatization plan and framework at the city and neighborhood levels. Chapter 5 chronicles the creation of the final redevelopment plan; the promises broken by developers, the mayor, and housing officials; internal divisions; and the final eviction of the residents. Tenant leaders and community activists—some well compensated, most exhausted, and all now firmly ensconced within the community's nonprofit complex—maintained commitment to the privatization road map, despite the radical departure from earlier promises and bitter denunciations of their leadership by rank-and-file residents.

In the aftermath of St. Thomas's demolition, developers stepped up efforts to demolish the highly prized Iberville development, situated adjacent to the city's tourist center, the French Quarter. Chapter 6 documents how a newly forged interracial alliance of public housing residents and community activists—informed, in part, by a political strategy drawn from this research—stymied those efforts. On August 29, 2005, a month after community activists defeated privatization efforts at Iberville, Hurricane Katrina and the subsequent levee collapse devastated the city. The remainder of the chapter analyzes the post-Katrina movement that challenged efforts by public officials, developers, and nonprofits to sweep away the public housing structures and residents that the floodwaters could not. Chapter 7 chronicles and critiques the intense organizing carried out between late 2007 and early 2008 as local and national authorities moved to demolish four of the city's public housing developments. In the conclusion, I identify the lessons—the silver lining—that the human-made disasters of St. Thomas and Katrina can provide for reigniting a movement for racial and economic justice.

Confronting the New Boss

Struggles for Home and Community in the
Postsegregation Era, 1965–1985

There's hardly anything more important that people can learn
than the fact that the really critical thing isn't who is sitting in the
White House, but who is sitting in—in the streets, in the cafe-
terias, in the halls of government, in the factories. Who is protesting, who is occupying offices and demonstrating—those are the
things that determine what happens.

—HOWARD ZINN

The mayor changed his plans. To defuse tensions following the July 1982
tenant occupation of the Housing Authority of New Orleans's (HANO)
administrative offices, Mayor Ernest Morial held an August 3 "forum
on public housing" attended by a collection of public officials, nonprofit representatives, and cooperative tenant leaders. At the conclusion of
the forum, he led "a cross-section of community leaders and the media
on a bus tour" of the city's housing developments. The initiative was to
show that New Orleans's first African American mayor was concerned
about the city's poor and stigmatized public housing residents, while not
necessarily meeting their demands. To underscore his empathy, Morial
emphasized to the forum attendees that "those who live in the housing
projects are citizens too." He added—in an indication of the racist and
class contempt held by some toward public housing residents—that "they
are human just as you and I."[1] Yet the mayor's effort to posture as an ally
while not implementing any substantive changes was complicated by over
two hundred St. Thomas residents and their community supporters gathering at the development office in order to "greet" the Morial-led bus tour.
When the mayor got word of the gathering, he ordered St. Thomas taken
off the itinerary. Residents responded by occupying the development offices for the next three days to get their grievances heard.

Demands by St. Thomas and other public housing residents for improved housing were not the only political headache this constituency presented the city's first black mayor and the emerging black political establishment. Public housing residents and their allies also regularly raised their voices against police brutality, with their discontent at times arriving literally at the mayor's front door. For example, in September 1980 hundreds of Desire public housing residents protested and clashed with police at the development for two consecutive days over the police murder of one African American man and the beating, the following day, of another. To quell the unrest, local and federal officials held a meeting with residents at the Desire Community Center to reassure them the murder was being investigated. Still, despite the promises, many were not sold that—even with a black mayor—authorities would prosecute the murder of yet another black New Orleanian at the hands of the local police. Therefore, Desire residents and their supporters formed the anti–police brutality group Community Action Now (CAN), forty of whom burst into a September 25 city council meeting, chanting, "We want justice!" CAN member and Desire resident Jesse Turner grabbed the microphone and demanded the council immediately address police brutality.[2]

The Desire confrontation was followed two months later, in November, by the even more explosive protests at the Fischer public housing development, located in Algiers, on the city's west bank of the Mississippi river. After an unknown assailant killed police officer Gregory Neupert near Fischer, twenty members of the police department's Felony Action Squad swept through the development and "kicked down doors, grabbed young men, and with guns marched . . . twenty youths 'like soldiers' through the housing development."[3] The beating and torturing of Fischer residents continued for the next week and culminated in police storming two homes in a neighborhood adjacent to Fischer, where they shot to death three unarmed black residents: James Billy, Reginald Miles, and Sherry Singleton. Two neighborhood residents, after hours of torture by police, had fingered Billy and Miles for the murder of Neupert.

The week-long reign of beatings, arrests, and apartment raids galvanized the community, with Left activists Malcolm Suber and Mary Howell from the Liberation League, Left Black Nationalists Bill Rouselle and Kalamu Ya Salaam of the Police Brutality Committee (PBC), and Michael Williams of CAN joining residents to demand justice. Over 250 Fischer residents rallied with the Liberation League the day after the murders, demanding Mayor Morial fire the white police chief and name, fire, and prosecute the cops involved in the week-long rampage. A multitude of protests and militant actions ensued over the next year, including the Liberation League's picketing of the mayor's home in February 1981 and the PBC's occupying of his city hall office in June, demanding Morial prosecute the police involved in the killings and protect the black community from arguably the country's most brutal police department. These public housing–centered protests were particularly damaging for Morial since they unmasked the central contradiction of his rule: posturing as a defender of the black majority while still being beholden to elite white interests. Though his political base of support was in the black community, Morial was not willing to challenge the powerful white interests that wanted a brutal police force to reign over the city's poor, particularly the 20 percent of the city's black population that then resided in some 14,000 public housing apartments, spread across ten developments and various scattered-site locations.[4]

The political challenges posed by public housing residents, such as those from St. Thomas, Fischer, and Desire, were a major factor in why Morial and other elements of the post–civil rights black political leadership wanted to eliminate these communities. Of course, in his public statements Morial couched his desire to end public housing in benevolent rhetoric. For example, at the August 1982 forum he bemoaned that "residents in public housing are isolated from the mainstream of society, collected together, out of sight of the business community and upper classes."[5] Yet politically, residents were far from marginalized. Indeed, the fact that they were, as Morial put it, "collected together" into government-administered and government-supported housing units facilitated collective mobilization that placed residents—and their demands—in plain view of the city's political and economic power brokers. The now black-led city administration—just like the preceding white regimes—did not prioritize addressing the poor housing, police brutality, and other pressing social problems that confronted New Orleans's poor and black working-class communities. But the political and geographic organization of the black working-class poor into government-administered public housing developments helped galvanize protests that forced their issues onto the political agenda.

Federal government cutbacks to public housing, which resulted in fewer resources to dampen and contain protest, further added to the local political leadership's distaste for the program and support for dismantlement efforts. The Carter administration, following its midterm conservative turn, slashed the Department of Housing and Urban Development's

(HUD) budget—retrenchment overseen by former New Orleans mayor Maurice Landrieu, who headed the agency during the last two years of the one-term president. The Reagan administration continued the cuts to HUD, and by expanding the Section 8 voucher program that subsidized the renting of privately owned apartments and creating the Low-Income Housing Tax Credit (LIHTC) program in 1986 as one of the few sources of funding for new construction of low-income housing, it gave a further boost to the "deconcentration" of residents and the privatization of public housing.[6] Morial recognized, as he explained to attendees at his 1982 housing forum, that "massive federal budget cuts had a tremendous negative effect on public housing."[7] Yet his political instincts were not to challenge federal cutbacks to public housing and other services that were devastating cities at the time but rather to accommodate and help manage their effects at the local level. Morial—who also had national stature as president of the U.S. Conference of Mayors (1985–1986)—echoed the emerging neoliberal political logic that "government cannot do it all; government cannot do it alone" as he encouraged greater cooperation between local government and corporate interests. The Reagan administration's dumping of responsibilities on localities without any funding—what was dubbed at the time as "new federalism"—was to be met by, Morial argued, the "new localism" of private–public partnerships.[8]

The third strike against public housing was the city's turn to tourism and its intertwining with gentrification. The city's public housing, with its concentration of poor African Americans and the proximity of several developments—such as St. Thomas and Iberville—to developing tourist areas, was considered a blight by tourist and real estate interests and viewed as hindering the growth of New Orleans's tourist economy. Adding to the pressure was the return of upper-middle-class whites to some historic neighborhoods, beginning in the late 1960s. This trend was most evident in New Orleans's famous French Quarter, or Vieux Carre, which saw its African American population plummet from 15 to 5 percent between 1960 and 1970 as upper-income whites began to predominate over the city's oldest neighborhood.[9] This racial and class demographic transformation expanded, in a slow and uneven fashion, into neighborhoods above and below the French Quarter, along New Orleans riverfront. These neighborhoods included the city's historic Lower Garden District, adjacent to the St. Thomas public housing project. The white, middle-class urban pioneers (as they called themselves) moving into the area also saw, by all accounts, the St. Thomas project as a blight on the neighborhood and desired its removal.

Thus, considering the political challenges mounted by residents, federal government cutbacks, and the rise of tourism and gentrification, it was no surprise that the city's first black mayor did not see a future for public housing. Indeed, he said as much when he addressed a 1979 meeting of public housing directors. Morial declared that "I hope that you will agree that rehabilitation of large, high-density, low-income projects is not the answer . . . a white elephant with a face lift is still a white elephant."[10] The election of a black mayor would not spare the city's black working-class public housing communities from confronting, by the late 1970s, a new round of "Negro removal." In this chapter, I look at the St. Thomas development and how, in the face of the political, economic, and demographic challenges I have outlined, residents worked to defend home and community.

St. Thomas: A Profile

As a result of the Civil Rights Act of 1964, St. Thomas and other formerly segregated HANO developments were opened to African Americans. The first black family, who moved into St. Thomas on April 28, 1965, was welcomed on their first night in their apartment with a brick through the window. The following night, according to HANO executive director J. Gilbert Scheib, a local white vigilante threw a molotov cocktail at the same apartment. Yet apart from these incidents, there was not much open racial conflict associated with desegregation. The lack of conflict is corroborated by interviews with residents who had moved into St. Thomas in the mid- to late 1960s. As former resident Carol Stewart recalls, when "I moved into St. Thomas in 1965 . . . white people was upstairs and I was downstairs. . . . It was mixed then. . . . We didn't have no problems [with white neighbors]; it was nice then."[11] Calean Smith, who relocated to St. Thomas in May 1969, remembers that "they had a lot of Irish people that lived there then. . . . It was mixed. . . . [Whites and blacks] got along real fine." But she adds, "[Whites] started moving out of there, in 1970 or '71."[12] By the early 1970s, confirming Smith's recollection, most whites had moved out of St. Thomas. Between 1968 and 1972, the percentage of white families at St. Thomas declined from approximately 50 to less than 25 percent. By 1978, there were only eleven such families, with similar declines experienced at the other formerly white public housing developments.[13] One source aiding white flight from the projects was HUD's section 235 program, begun in 1968 to assist low-income people in buying a home. Because of discriminatory real estate practices that continued to block home ownership in the suburbs, the program tended to help mostly poor whites rather than black families.[14]

A profile of the St. Thomas community underscores the economic distress residents faced as it became predominately African American. For example, as Tables 1.1 and 1.2 show, the percentage of black people living in poverty at St. Thomas and in the area immediately surrounding it, from 1970 to 1990, registered between 55 and 80 percent, whereas the unemployment rate ranged between 20 and 45 percent.[15] Looking at this unemployment another way, as Table 1.3 indicates, the labor *nonparticipation* rate—that is, those neither employed nor actively seeking work—ranged among St. Thomas residents from 65 to almost 70 percent for those over sixteen years old. When a community member was lucky enough to get a paid job in the formal sector, they faced a dual labor market that segmented black workers into the lowest-paying jobs. Table 1.4 shows that employed St. Thomas residents tended to be concentrated in New Orleans's nonunionized, low-wage service sector jobs.

Homeplace as a Base of Resistance

The pervasive poverty, unemployment, and job segregation faced by St. Thomas residents represents what sociologist William Robinson calls "permanent structural violence."[16] Structural violence is reinforced and

TABLE 1.1

Black Poverty Levels for St. Thomas Residents, 1970–1990

	1970	1980		1990	
Census tract	81	81.01	81.02	81.01	81.02
Poverty status					
Individuals	77.5	86	64.2	87.1	55.1
Families	76.4	84.7	60.3	86.7	62.6
<125% of poverty level	n/a	91.7	70.3	92.4	72

SOURCES: *U.S. Census Bureau, Census of Population and Housing, Census Tracts, New Orleans, MSA, 1970; Census of Population and Housing, Census Tracts, New Orleans, MSA, 1980; Census of Population and Housing, Population and Housing Characteristics for Census Tracts and Block Numbering Areas, New Orleans, MSA, 1990.*

TABLE 1.2

Unemployment Rates of Black St. Thomas Residents, 1970–1990

	1970	1980		1990	
Census tract	81	81.01	81.02	81.01	81.02
Black men	15.7	37.8	n/a	44.5	34.3
Black women	18.5	25.1	n/a	46.2	32.6

SOURCES: *U.S. Census Bureau, Census of Population and Housing, Census Tracts, New Orleans, MSA, 1970; Census of Population and Housing, Census Tracts, New Orleans, MSA, 1980; Census of Population and Housing, Population and Housing Characteristics for Census Tracts and Block Numbering Areas, New Orleans, MSA, 1990.*

TABLE 1.3

Black Labor Force Participation Rates in the St. Thomas Area by Gender, 1970–1990

	1970	1980		1990	
Census tract	81	81.01	81.02	81.01	81.02
Overall	35.4	34.4	47.8	35.8	31
Men	57.4	44.7	57.8	47.7	28.3
Women	25.3	30.1	41.4	31.4	33

SOURCES: *U.S. Census Bureau, Census of Population and Housing, Census Tracts, New Orleans, MSA, 1970; Census of Population and Housing, Census Tracts, New Orleans, MSA, 1980; Census of Population and Housing, Population and Housing Characteristics for Census Tracts and Block Numbering Areas, New Orleans, MSA, 1990.*

managed, he argues, through regular doses of direct state violence and constant surveillance. In the case of St. Thomas, this direct violence took the form of the local police subjecting St. Thomas's African American working-class community to pervasive and systematic repression and human rights violations. Indeed, New Orleans, along with having some of the highest rates of poverty and inequality in the country, also, unsurprisingly, led the nation in police brutality reports to the Department of Justice.[17] In my interviews with St. Thomas residents, police brutality and

TABLE 1.4

Occupational Distribution of Black Workers in St. Thomas, 1980–1990

	1980 Women	Men	1990 Women	Men
Executive, managerial, and administrative	10	—	15	8
Professional specialty occupations	11	5	23	—
Technicians and related support	20	11	—	—
Sales occupations	28	10	16	14
Administrative support occupations, clerical	66	48	47	—
Private household	27	27	16	14
Protective service	17	4	—	—
Service occupations (food and building services)	211	117	165	45
Farming, forestry, and fishing occupations	—	—	17	—
Precision production, craft, and repair occupations	37	8	—	12
Machine operators, assemblers, and inspectors	44	31	17	6
Transportation and material moving occupations	22	52	8	15
Handlers, equipment cleaners, helpers, and laborers	80	43	38	—
Total employed persons sixteen years old and over	573	356	362	114

SOURCES: *Census of Population and Housing, Census Tracts, New Orleans, MSA, 1980; Census of Population and Housing, Population and Housing Characteristics for Census Tracts and Block Numbering Areas, New Orleans, MSA, 1990.*

harassment is a common theme. One resident, Jacqueline Marshall, who lived at St. Thomas from 1971 until she was forced to move in 2000, argues that although the New Orleans Police Department's (NOPD) cars were emblazoned with the motto "To Protect and to Serve,"

It seemed like it wasn't to protect *or* to serve. . . . They used to beat 'em—they used to beat people. . . . I remember a lot of instances where I'd see the police just jump out of the car, and they'll call . . . to guys and tell them to put their hands on the car, empty out their pockets—well at that time they wouldn't tell them to empty out their pockets, or spread their legs, or nothing! They would kick 'em open, and they would push 'em on the car! They'd go in the pockets and take everything and slam it on the hood of the car. They'll throw them in the car.

You might see that guy coming back, like ten, fifteen minutes later, and he might be beat, you know, . . . right there in front of 'ya. They'll just do what it is they want . . . to do, and if they wanted to let them go, they'd let them go, and if they didn't, they took 'em for a ride, and then they let them go somewhere else. If they wanted to whip them right there, they whipped them right there. It was like they didn't care.[18]

Carol Stewart, a longtime St. Thomas resident, points to wide opposition among residents to placing a police substation in the development, further underscoring the hostilities that existed between the police and the community.[19] Though personal safety was a major concern of residents, many did not look to the police to provide it. The police, who replaced extralegal vigilante terror as the "primary agent of social control of blacks" as African Americans increasingly became an urban people and the civil rights movement gained strength after World War II, were generally not welcome at St. Thomas.[20]

Despite the myriad social problems at St. Thomas and its often negative portrayal in the media, many St. Thomas residents express a strong and positive attachment to their neighbors and the community.[21] For example, Geraldine Moore, a former resident and member of the St. Thomas Resident Council (STRC) who had moved to the housing development in the late 1980s, describes her community this way:

It was a community within a community. I could borrow sugar, flour, whatever from my neighbor. I could walk around the corner, and my stuff would still be there with my door open. I could ask my neighbor to watch my kids while I ran to the doctor's office or went to an appointment with the office of family services. [My neighbors] . . . would watch my children for me. I mean, neighbors two or three blocks down the street would want to know who you are, what are you doing here. . . . If your kids get in trouble, they would come knocking on your door. "I seen your kid two blocks away doing such and such." If my kids got in trouble and they were on Canal Street, somebody in St. Thomas knew my children and somebody working at one of the hotels and would say, "Your kid was down there cuttin' school." It amazed me how people . . . could be miles and miles away, know your children, and come back and tell you, "I seen your kid cutting school." . . . *So, my thing was that we were family and we took care of each other. . . . It was a community within itself. A lot of folks say that we were isolated, but I don't think so.*[22]

This reflection by a St. Thomas resident underscores the depth of the social bonds and networks that tied together this public housing community.

The relationship between two longtime St. Thomas residents, Willie Mae Blanchard and Carol Stewart, further underscores the deep bonds that existed among many residents. Blanchard and Stewart, who lived next to each other for over twenty years, made a pact that they would not move out of the development until HANO had located a place where they could live as neighbors. At the time of my interview, in 2003, they had won their demand, living next to each other just a few blocks from the former St. Thomas project. Nonetheless, while content they were still neighbors, Blanchard and Stewart yearned for the days when they were surrounded by their fellow community members. Stewart, commenting before Hurricane Katrina forced thousands of low-income New Orleanians out of the city altogether, laments that former St. Thomas residents are now "scattered all around" New Orleans. But she adds, "We do see them . . . every now and then, and we be just *soooo* glad." Blanchard, proud of her former community, still defends it when it is defamed: "I spoke to a lady this morning, and somebody said, 'Oh, St. Thomas, St. Thomas doesn't have a good reputation.' But I'm proud I'm from St. Thomas. . . . Other people have given St. Thomas such a bad name."[23]

Another resident recounts the familial support that surrounded her: "That's where all my people was, in the St. Thomas . . . ya, beaucoup family. All my folks were back there." She adds that "everything was all right in St. Thomas" thanks, in part, to the support system she could rely on—a safety net that evictions and demolition untethered.[24] These quotes by former St. Thomas residents Marshall, Moore, Blanchard, Stewart, and Parker underscore the way that St. Thomas residents formed what sociologist Al Szymanski terms a distinct *social class,* or class fraction. The structure of the development and the way that it organized social life helped forge an organic social group—that is, "a socially coherent set of families based on a common class position which share a generally common life-style, social status, traditions, customs and consciousness, and which feel socially comfortable with . . . one another."[25]

In the face of structural and direct state violence, this low-income African American community developed and relied on informal friendship and family-defined networks that played a key role in carrying people through tough times and helped sustain the quality of local life. This pattern at St. Thomas was not exceptional and has been found in other studies of low-income African American communities.[26] Thus, in contrast to what sociologist William Julius Wilson has argued about the withering of social networks in communities of "concentrated poverty," at St. Thomas they were strong, in part, because of adversity.[27] These relationships were central to creating what bell hooks calls "homeplace," which serves not only to provide daily needs but to act as a source of resistance. Home and community became a place where "African American people . . . could strive to be subjects, not objects, where [they] could be affirmed in [their] minds and hearts despite poverty, hardship, and deprivation, where [they] could restore to [themselves] the dignity denied [them] in the public world."[28] St. Thomas, demonized by many, became, despite its problems, a homeplace for residents, a place of family, friends, and nurturing and, therefore, one worth defending. It would also be the base from which residents and leaders would challenge the governmental bodies—HANO, the New Orleans mayor's office, and the city's police department—whose actions directly impacted their lives.

Working-Class Organization

The high levels of unemployment faced by St. Thomas residents may disguise that many who lived in St. Thomas, although often facing long bouts of unemployment, had jobs. For example, many residents worked in hotels located in the relatively close French Quarter and on Canal Street. Carol Stewart, who lived over thirty years in St. Thomas and was a tenant leader, worked in the early 1980s at the New Orleans central business district's Howard Johnson Hotel. While there, Stewart was involved in an unsuccessful union organizing effort, explaining that "we had a few [organizing] meetings, but [management, found out and] told us we would be fired if . . . we were organizing."[29] Others, like St. Thomas's Jacqueline Marshall, oscillated between welfare and work.

> I worked as a short-order cook, day-care provider, assistant at an insurance agency, waitress, whatever I can get cleaning up, anything. I just get me a job, and I work, and if the job ends, then I get on welfare until I find something else, and it was an off and on thing. . . . I worked, I went on welfare, I worked, I went on welfare. It was like a constant thing.[30]

Low pay and employment instabilities must have fallen particularly hard on workers like Jacqueline Marshall, whose earnings came from the secondary labor market. One of the only stabilities in such workers' lives was low-cost public housing, where residents paid 25 percent of their income to cover the cost for both rent *and* utilities.[31]

Within the context of high unemployment and cycles of work and welfare, combined with family responsibilities, the organization and struggles of most St. Thomas residents from the 1970s to the 1990s largely revolved around community concerns, particularly issues associated with housing. The most important organization for St. Thomas public housing residents to voice concerns about the quality and quantity of housing was the STRC.[32] The STRC had a well-earned reputation among residents, city officials, and activists as one of the most combative tenant organizations in New Orleans.

The struggles of the almost all-black St. Thomas community also had a gender dimension. The leadership of the STRC—as well as that of the other tenant organizations in New Orleans—was overwhelmingly made up of African American women. For example, in 1982, of the twelve resident council presidents in the city, only one, Darryl Williams from Fischer, was male.[33] As Table 1.5 underscores, this leadership composition reflected the demographics of the St. Thomas development itself, where single women headed most of the households. Punitive welfare regulations, such as "the man in the house" rule, made it difficult for adult "able-bodied" men to officially live in the projects if their wife or companion was receiving public assistance.[34] Another factor, according to a St. Thomas resident interviewed in the early 1980s, in the lack of male visibility and participation in tenant councils was that "a lot of men are 'on release'—out of jail. . . . They don't want to get involved and attract attention to themselves."[35] Incarceration statistics provide ample evidence that increasing numbers of the city's black men were being shuttled off to public housing in the form of the city and state's expanding jail and penitentiaries. The local jail population exploded from approximately one thousand inmates in the early 1970s to over six thousand by the year 2000. New Orleans and Louisiana by this time had the highest incarceration rate of any municipality or state in the country.[36]

The STRC, along with tenants and tenant leaders from the other public housing developments, led a number of campaigns to improve public housing's living conditions and to press HANO into being more accountable to the community. Fannie McKnight—who, along with Barbara Jackson, was one of the most influential tenant leaders at St. Thomas throughout the 1980s and 1990s—complains that "public housing was not giving us decent, sanitary housing. The roofs were leaking. . . . People did not even have tiles on the floor."[37] The substandard living conditions in public housing, as described by McKnight, affected a large section of New Orleans's working class. As Table 1.6 shows, in the mid-1980s approximately 45,000 New Orleanians, almost all black, lived in the city's ten public housing developments and in the approximately 2,300 scattered-site apartments. On top of this number were those who resided in the developments but were not on a lease and thus not included in official figures. Adding 20 percent to the official figures, to cover the uncounted public

TABLE 1.5

Profile of African American Households in St. Thomas Census Tracts

	1980	1990
Population	6,210	4,580
Ages 5–19 (%)	59	57
Ratio of women to men	2.14:1	2.25:1
Households	1,905	1,276
Female head of household (%)	62	78

SOURCES: *Census of Population and Housing, Census Tracts, New Orleans, MSA, 1980; Census of Population and Housing, Population and Housing Characteristics for Census Tracts and Block Numbering Areas, New Orleans, MSA, 1990.*

TABLE 1.6

African Americans Living in HANO's Conventional Units, 1980–2000

Year	New Orleans population	Black population	Official HANO population (approximate)	Actual HANO population (approximate)	Black population in public housing (%)
1980	557,515	308,149	45,000	54,000	18
1990	496,938	307,728	40,000	48,000	16
2000	484,674	324,675	22,000	26,400	8

SOURCES: Martha Mahoney, "The Changing Nature of Public Housing in New Orleans, 1930–1974" (master's thesis, Tulane University, 1985); House Subcommittee on Housing and Community Opportunity, The New Orleans Public Housing Authority and the Role of the Department of Housing and Urban Development, 104th Cong., 2nd sess., July 8, 1996 (Washington, D.C.: Government Printing Office, 1996), 345; "U.S. Audit Raps HANO Management," New Orleans Times-Picayune, January 18, 1984.

housing residents, creates an estimate of close to 55,000 people who lived in public housing in New Orleans—the vast majority of whom were African American. In testimony before the U.S. Congress in 1987, Jessie Smallwood, then executive director of HANO, put the number of New Orlenians in public housing even higher at 63,000, while other observers placed it as high as 67,000. In any case, in the mid-1980s it can be confidently estimated that nearly 20 percent of the city's black community was living in public housing.[38]

Public Housing and Class Struggle

One of the most dramatic actions taken by New Orleans's public housing residents to force authorities to address their grievances took place in July 1982. With St. Thomas tenant leaders playing a central role, residents organized a protest and eventual sit-in and occupation of HANO's headquarters, then located on Carondolet Street in the central business district. Prior to the protestors' takeover of the HANO offices, the residents had made various attempts to get the city's housing authority to hear and address their grievances. Yet despite frequent petitioning, HANO was unresponsive to their concerns. In response, residents decided to take bolder actions. A key leader in this effort and the eventual takeover of HANO's offices was Crystal Jones, then president of both the scattered-site developments and the twelve-member citywide tenant advisory board, the latter comprising elected representatives from the various public housing developments. From late May through June 1982, Jones, along with Palfrey Johnson, who worked at the St. Bernard (public housing) Community Center, began mobilizing residents, through the leafleting of all developments, for a large protest and occupation of HANO. They also received support from anti–police brutality activist Michael Williams, who ran a youth program at the St. Bernard development, as well as Jim Hayes and Ron Chisom, leaders of the Tremé Community Improvement Association (TCIA) who worked with public housing residents across the city. The mobilization culminated on Thursday, July 1, 1982, when Crystal Jones, along with Palfrey Johnson, led a militant faction of the citywide tenant board and several hundred public housing residents, including a strong contingent from St. Thomas headed by tenant leaders Barbara Jackson and Fannie McKnight, to protest just outside HANO's administrative office.

The protest was not without a glitch. In fact, the protest was opposed by half of Crystal Jones's and Barbara Jackson's colleagues on the twelve-member citywide housing project tenant advisory board. This lack of support, at first blush, seems paradoxical. Why would a notable segment of tenant council leadership reject an organized protest against poor housing conditions in the New Orleans public housing system? The origins of the tenant councils and their relationship to the Housing Authority of New Orleans provide some clues. The reorganization of the New Orleans housing project councils and the creation of the broader citywide tenant council had not resulted from the initiatives of housing project residents themselves. In 1972, HANO itself established these elected bodies, with the city's mayor-appointed Human Relations Committee overseeing the elections. New federal guidelines for New Orleans (and other cities) required the establishment of representative tenant councils to obtain funds for refurbishing existing developments and for various other initiatives, such as summer youth programs.[39] HANO explained the connection between tenant councils and obtaining federal money: "In order to receive funds for many of the HUD programs, it is important that there is full and complete participation by tenants. This participation can be accomplished only through organization that is truly representative of all tenants."[40]

Tenant organizer Ron Chisom confirms this connection between funding and organization, explaining that "what sparked the tenant councils" was the federal government's offering "millions of dollars to modernize [the public housing developments]. In order to get this money, the local housing authority had to make sure they had tenant participation ... , [which meant] you had to have an active tenant council."[41] At the same time, according to Chisom, HANO used its relationship to the tenant councils "to control [the residents]." HANO and the city administration—both of which by the early 1970s increasingly had middle-class blacks in leadership positions—recognized the importance of administratively incorporating black tenant leaders.[42] The increased politicization of African American public housing tenants in the late 1960s drove home to black and white political leaders that the old ways of handling residents would no longer work. As HANO director J. Gilbert Scheib acknowledged in the agency's 1970 annual report, "After more than thirty years of actual operation, and [due to] political and social changes ... it is conceded ... that even greater consideration must be accorded the views and opinions of tenants in the formulation and enforcement of rules and regulations, as well as plans for betterment."[43] Thus although interested in obtaining federal funds, HANO and city officials were also searching for ways in which residents could be steered away from protest and successfully incorporated into the administrative machinery—indeed, this may have been part of the federal government's intentions, as well, when it stipulated tenant "participation" as a prerequisite for obtaining funds for modernization and other programs. One way to keep tenant council leaders—as well as their advisers—loyal to the HANO administration was through the agency's control of tenant council budgets, which were used to fund tenant council office expenses, hire tenants for various jobs, and pay for travel to housing activist conferences, such as those of the National Tenant Organization, as well as to pay fees for housing activists to perform training workshops for tenant leaders.[44] When tenant leaders became troublesome, HANO could cut off funds—as HANO executive director Sidney Cates did to Crystal Jones. In early 1982, before the July takeover, Cates fired the combative public housing leader from her paid tenant liaison position.[45]

With the tenant councils structurally situated as an appendage of HANO administrators, it is not surprising that many tenant leaders distanced themselves from the protest.[46] Emma Del Joseph, then president of the Guste low-rise apartments, went so far as to publically denounce the protest organizers for "misleading the people," adding that Jones was simply "trying to make a name for herself." Criticisms like these from tenant leaders helped to legitimize those being made by HANO administrator

Sidney Cates III. Cates lashed out against Jones and Johnson as simply "two people with their own vested interests" and questioned the legitimacy of protestors' grievances, which he claimed were mostly "half truths and untruths."[47]

The failure to get support from the promanagement tenant leaders did not deter Jones and the protestors. At about one in the afternoon of July 1, 1982, Jones and Johnson, along with St. Thomas tenant leaders Barbara Jackson and Fannie McKnight, rallied about three hundred people, including the children of public housing residents, outside HANO's central office. After a short rally Jones led the protestors, in an orderly manner, up several flights of a narrow stairwell to the HANO boardroom, where the commissioners were about to start their monthly meeting. Some protestors carried anti-Cates signs, while others, altering the lyrics of a then popular call-and-response song by the early hip-hop group Trouble Funk, called for "dropping the bomb on HANO."[48] By "dropping the bomb," the protestors were demanding the dismantlement of what they considered a corrupt, inefficient, and oppressive HANO management, not their homes. The use of these lyrics to oppose HANO management was consistent with the song's confrontational political message, which included the rhetorical question: "Should we drop the bomb on the White House too? Drop the bomb! Drop the bomb!"

Crystal Jones, the spokesperson for the action, demanded that the board—chaired at the time by future HANO director Jessie Smallwood—set aside its agenda and immediately address a list of twenty-four tenant grievances presented by the group.[49] Among the top demands called for by Jones and her supporters were a repeal of the recent rent and utility increases, the firing of the then HANO executive director Sidney Cates III, and the creation of a blue ribbon committee of housing project tenants and of HANO, City of New Orleans, and HUD representatives to review local problems and devise solutions to a host of resident grievances, including poor maintenance and the lack of resident input in decision making.[50] The placard-holding demonstrators (see Figure 1.1) cheered Jones as she read the list of demands, while at the same time several engaged in shouting matches with Guste tenant president Emma Del Joseph, an opponent of the protest.[51]

The protesting residents were, in part, rebelling against the effects of cuts imposed by HUD on New Orleans's housing authority and on others across the country. Localities, particularly New Orleans, had since the early 1970s relied on HUD for their operating subsidies—for example, to pay for

FIGURE 1.1. Protestors at July 1, 1982, HANO board meeting and subsequent occupation of the offices. Residents holding placards are, from left to right, Rosalie Robinson, Jacqueline Gray, and Lillie Holmes. The child in the foreground is Arthur Fondal. Photograph by David Leeson, used with permission of the *New Orleans Times-Picayune*.

the normal upkeep of housing, for which tenant rental payments were not sufficient, and for modernization funds to refurbish aging developments. The increasing militancy among the urban black working class in the 1960s, including public housing tenants, garnered various material concessions, like lower rental charges for public housing and increased federal budgetary responsibility for the program. A major step toward lower rents and greater federal responsibility for public housing occurred in 1969 when Congress passed the Brooke Amendment to the Public Housing Act of 1937, which created additional deductions for calculating gross family income (which rents were based on), set a ceiling of no more than 25 percent of net family income for rent, and allowed for zero-dollar rent for those without any income. The amendment created, in the words of Reynard Rochon, the first African American chair of the HANO board of commissioners, a "financial crisis." By 1972, HANO's average monthly rental charge had been cut in half, dropping from $40 to $20.[52] In 1969, HANO generated $5.4 million in rental income. The following year, it dropped to $4.5 million, and by 1972, it had fallen further to only $3.4 million, a 37 percent decline. Rental income did not exceed its 1969 level until 1976, when the agency collected $5.6 million, although, due to inflation, the real value was much less. As a result, HANO, which had regularly been lauded as a paragon of efficiency and fiscal responsibility, was now running deficits and having to dip into the reserves it had garnered over the previous three decades.[53] To address the ensuing fiscal crisis—with the immediate source being the Brooke Amendment and the underlying one emerging from the black insurgency of the 1960s—Congress, as part of the Brooke Amendment, began providing operating subsidies to compensate for the declining rental revenues.

Yet as Table 1.7 indicates, beginning in the last half of the Carter presidency and accelerating under Reagan's, the HUD budget, particularly the public housing portion, suffered severe cuts. The bulk of these cuts were in the area of new construction: there was simply no federal money to expand affordable public housing. And with operating subsidies and modernization monies remaining essentially unchanged and the increasing costs of materials and labor, cities were not able to keep up with daily maintenance needs or modernize public housing. In addition, by the late 1970s the Target Projects Program had been eliminated. The program was initially developed in the mid-1970s under the Ford administration and had provided millions of dollars to HANO to perform deferred maintenance, as well as for such social service programs as job training. Furthermore, by the early 1980s HUD had severely cut the Urban Initiatives Program, which HANO had received funding from, while simultaneously instituting a Performance Funding System, for calculating subsidies to local agencies, that further reduced funds.[54] Thus, just when the budget of the city's public housing authority was being squeezed and when many of New Orleans's public housing projects were over forty years old—thus requiring more maintenance and modernization—public housing tenants stepped up pressure to improve their living conditions.

HANO's answer to declining federal support for public housing improvements was to squeeze more income out of residents and squelch protest. For example, midway through 1982 HANO—reacting to the Reagan administration's increase in the maximum rental rates that public housing authorities could charge residents—increased New Orleans housing project rents from 25 percent to 30 percent of a resident's gross income. In addition, for the first time since the creation of public housing in New Orleans, HANO began installing meters and charging tenants for utilities.[55]

TABLE 1.7

HUD and Public Housing Funding, 1976–1988, in Billions of
Constant 2002 Dollars

Year	HUD	Public housing	New construction	Subsidies	Modernization
1976	83.6	—	—	—	—
1977	89.5	14.2	8	1.5	1.9
1978	94.3	21.5	16	1.7	2.0
1979	71.3	19.3	13.3	1.6	2.2
1980	74.4	13	7.5	1.5	2.0
1981	64.4	14	7.9	2.0	3.2
1982	36.7	8.8	2.1	2.6	3.1
1983	27.8	7.1	0	2.2	4.3
1984	29	7.3	1.4	2.7	2.5
1985	48*	6.2	1.4	2.1	2.1
1986	24	5.7	1.2	1.7	2.1
1987	21	5.3	.73	2.1	2.1
1988	21.3	5.6	.81	2.1	2.4

SOURCE: Changing Priorities: The Federal Budget and Housing Assistance, 1976–2007
(Washington, DC: National Low Income Housing Coalition, 2002), 22.

*The reason for the increase is that "in 1985 existing public housing debt was converted to
grants to save future interest costs. This apparent increase created no additional public housing
units and the expenditure was actually a cost costing measure of the Reagan administration
that substantially reduced later outlays" (Changing Priorities, 5).

This resulted in a further increase in the cost of living for public housing residents. Furthermore, housing project resident leaders argued that
HANO was making errors in calculating their utility bills. For example,
Selina Ford, a St. Thomas resident who lived on a public assistance grant
of $234 a month, saw her utility bill go from almost nothing to $209 a
month by August 1982. Ford saw other charges increase, as well: security
deposits and repair charges increased for items HANO claimed its tenants

had broken, while HANO's surcharge for each air-conditioning unit in an apartment jumped from $20 to $35 a month.[56]

HANO increased living expenses for residents as the amount and quality of HANO maintenance continued to deteriorate. Edward Williams—a public housing resident and one of the protestors at the July 1 protest outside HANO's administrative office—explained at that time about his housing project: "The grass is so high. The rats are so bad."[57] Overseeing the maintenance cuts that were undoubtedly leading to these conditions was HANO director Cates, whose main qualification for the directorship was having been, in the late 1960s, the NOPD's first high-ranking black police officer.[58] From the perspective of tenant activist Palfrey Johnson, Cates ran HANO "like a police state" and was more concerned with making renovations to his personal office than to the city's over thirteen thousand deteriorating public housing apartments.[59]

When HANO board chair Jessie Smallwood refused to address the tenant protestors' demands during the July 1, 1982, board meeting, Crystal Jones blew her whistle, and on cue, protestors began pulling out their sleeping bags and taking over HANO's boardroom and administrative offices. Fannie McKnight, one of the leading activists at the HANO takeover, describes the occupation this way:

> We didn't intimidate the workers; we just politely asked the workers . . . to leave, [saying,] "We're taking over." The workers just give us the office. There was just too many people. They just took their pocketbooks and walked out and said, "You can have it." We did not touch anything in the housing authority—we didn't touch their papers. We just stood in their office.[60]

The following evening, on Friday, July 2, after several hours of intense and lengthy negotiations held over two days between protest leaders and HANO officials, Executive Director Cates and the board agreed to meet one of the protest leaders' key demands—the formation of a twelve-member blue ribbon committee, which would include four tenants, to hear and act on tenant grievances. Residents placed their hopes in the committee, along with continued organizing and pressure, to obtain their other demands, including the firing of Cates and the rollback of the rent and utility hikes. With these concessions in hand, thirty hours after the protest at HANO had begun, approximately fifty tenant activists filed out of HANO's office, tired but confident, chanting, "The people united shall never be defeated."[61] HUD also included a personal reward for protest leader Jones: she received word, while the occupation was taking place, that HUD had honored her with a scholarship to pursue a master's degree in urban studies at the University of New Orleans. Perhaps, from HUD and HANO's perspective, a move to graduate school might encourage this key tenant leader to take a respite from activism and assume a less combative stance toward her benefactors.[62]

From the Boardroom to the Projects: The Terrains of Public Housing Protest

On August 3, members of the newly created blue ribbon committee, led by Mayor Morial, began a fact-finding tour of several of the city's housing projects. Expecting that St. Thomas would be included in this information-gathering tour, a group of St. Thomas residents decided to welcome the delegation by rallying in front of the project's development office (see Figure 1.2). Hearing that approximately several hundred angry, placard-carrying residents had assembled to greet the mayor and his entourage, Morial ordered that the St. Thomas development be taken off the tour. Protesting residents responded by taking over the St. Thomas project's administrative office.[63]

On the evening of August 3, the St. Thomas Resident Council, while leaving several protestors to maintain control of the project's administrative office, held a mass meeting at the cafeteria of a nearby Catholic elementary school, located a few blocks from the project. At a gathering of over three hundred St. Thomas residents, with advice, support, and encouragement from community organizer and legal assistant Ron Chisom and attorney Bill Quigley—both employed at the time by the New Orleans Legal Aid Corporation (NOLAC)—the residents resolved to withhold rent payments until HANO had met their demands. These demands included eliminating utility bills, improving maintenance, and repairing and reoccupying abandoned and empty apartments. At the time, 6 percent, or 93 apartments out of a total 1,510, were empty, the highest rate among the ten HANO conventional developments. Residents wanted them filled by some of the thousands of families on the HANO waiting list.[64]

The next day, on Wednesday, August 4, while the occupation continued with approximately eighty residents either inside or picketing outside the St. Thomas project office, Barbara Jackson and Fannie McKnight

FIGURE 1.2. St. Thomas residents rally in front of project office during August 1982 occupation. Photograph by David Leeson, used with permission of the *New Orleans Times-Picayune*.

and other representatives of the citywide tenant council held a two-hour meeting with HANO officials at the agency's central business district headquarters. The resident leaders extracted a verbal agreement—which HANO agreed to put in writing and present to St. Thomas residents the following day—to take various measures to ensure that utility bills were correct and that maintenance at housing projects would be improved.[65]

In a mass meeting held outside the St. Thomas housing project office the next day, on August 5, about seventy residents met with HANO deputy director Emilio Dupre to go over the written agreement and to address utility charge inaccuracies and to improve maintenance. To ensure that they could maintain leverage over HANO and guarantee implementation of the agreement, however, the St. Thomas residents decided to continue their rent strike, while at the same time meeting their obligation to pay their rent by placing payments in an escrow account. They used several other levers to keep pressure on HANO and help to ensure that their demands were met. A key legal weapon deployed by residents was a class action that STRC lawyer Bill Quigley filed on September 2 in the U.S. district court arguing that HANO's utility charges were excessive and in violation of federal housing regulations. The suit demanded that HANO return to project residents "all excess utility fees charged" and that the agency be prevented from evicting residents for failing to pay excessive and illegal utility charges.[66] In an effort to counter tenant organizing, HANO sent letters to rent-striking families explaining that their maintenance problems were fixed and, thus, they were no longer able to legally withhold rent. HANO claimed this tactic prompted fifty residents to break with the strike and take their money out of the tenant escrow account. In addition, HANO appeared to have stopped sending new tenants to St. Thomas in a further effort to weaken the community and the strike. For example, between August 1982 and the end of the strike in July 1983, the vacancy rate more than doubled to 13 percent, or almost 200 apartments.[67]

In response to this and other HANO efforts to undermine the strike, tenant leaders attempted to use elected officials, as well as the courts and media, to put pressure on the housing agency and the city. St. Thomas residents successfully lobbied to have the existing Louisiana State Joint Legislative Subcommittee on Public Housing—which included several local state representatives and senators, among them civil rights veteran Rev. Avery C. Alexander and William Jefferson—hold hearings on the problems faced by St. Thomas and other public housing developments. At a public hearing on November 5, 1982—three months into the rent strike—STRC president Barbara Jackson used the gathering as an opportunity to expound before local media and elected officials on the St. Thomas housing project's "wretched living conditions, dilapidated and vacant apartments, fire hazards, and understaffed and lackadaisical maintenance department," as well as on child illnesses due to lead paint.[68] Johnson and others also lambasted Director Cates—who spoke only briefly and then quickly exited the meeting—for his insensitivity to resident concerns and his corrupt and authoritarian leadership style. The fiery meeting concluded with sixty residents taking the legislators on a tour of St. Thomas, where they pointed to the "shattered windows, vandalized vacant apartments, and peeling sheets of paint."[69]

The St. Thomas residents, with the help of their advisers, including lawyer Bill Quigley and community organizers Ron Chisom, Jim Hayes, and Palfrey Johnson, successfully blocked HANO's attempt to use tenant evictions to break the St. Thomas residents' rent strike and intimidate other public housing communities from employing the same tactic. On May 10, 1983, ten months after the rent strike had begun—with HANO threatening to evict a number of St. Thomas residents—U.S. magistrate Eileen Shaver ruled in favor of the strikers. HANO could not evict 62 tenants for failure to pay rent until the housing authority had carried out hearings on each tenants' complaints of excessive utility costs and hazardous living conditions.[70] This decision effectively ended HANO's strategy of using evictions to crush the rent strike.

Quigley, who argued the tenants' case, attributed a great part of the legal victory to the organizing and meticulous record keeping of St. Thomas residents:

> We filed a request for an injunction to stop all the evictions in federal court . . . so we had a very big hearing . . . couple hundred people, [mostly residents were] there. . . . We brought down the files and showed [the residents] were keeping track [of rent payments], they were following the rules, they did have the money. . . . HANO said [that residents] "don't know where the money is, they're just embezzling." So we brought down all the files . . . and the magistrate said, "You couldn't evict them." It was a *tremendous* victory.[71]

Indeed, by July 1983, St. Thomas residents had accumulated in their Liberty Bank escrow account over $250,000. With average rent payments at about $50, according to census figures, this meant that roughly 350 residents, or about 25 percent of the approximately 1,350 St. Thomas households at the time, were participating in the strike. In addition to these hardcore supporters, the rent-withholding action received sympathy from other residents.

Certainly, St. Thomas residents were elated by their court victory. As Fannie McKnight proudly recalled in 2003, twenty years after the poor people's rent strike victory, "Even though many of us didn't even have a sixth-grade education, like myself, . . . baby, we had everything in place."[72] Quigley saw the St. Thomas residents' court victory as the turning point; it led HANO to "sit down and really start negotiating and find some way to" end the tenant dispute.[73] On July 20, 1983, the St. Thomas Resident Council agreed to end its nearly yearlong strike in return for HANO's increasing the utility subsidy by 10 percent for all public housing residents and agreeing to not take reprisals against rent strikers. Eventually, HANO returned to the old policy of not charging for utilities. In addition, HANO dedicated a $21 million modernization grant toward renovations at St. Thomas.[74] Furthermore, in a partial victory, the vacancy rate, which had more than doubled during the strike, was reduced to its prestrike level of just under one hundred apartments—about 6 percent—by October 1984, a year after the conflict had ended.[75]

The strike not only extracted important material concessions from authorities but also increased the political power of the community and their leadership. The strike defined St. Thomas as the most combative housing development in the city and strengthened the bonds and trust between the tenant leadership and residents. As Jacqueline Marshall, a thirty-year resident of St. Thomas, said in 2004, "We had good leaders. . . . We had leaders that cared; they tried and didn't stop. . . . If you pursued it, they'd pursue it with you. So we had good leaders; we really did."[76] Central among such leaders was Barbara Jackson, who came into her own during the rent strike and earned the allegiance of many residents. "Barbara Jackson," as lawyer Bill Quigley reflected, "would stand up and stay standing. [She came] on board [during the strike] and stood up and was a great speaker and passionate. People really loved her."[77]

Gender, Race, Public Housing, and the Reorienting of Class Analysis

By the mid-1980s, St. Thomas, after only a decade as a predominately black community, was facing increasing threats to its continued existence. A major source of this threat came from the federal government, which as part of the first round of neoliberal restructuring, was reducing financial and ideological support for public housing. In addition, the new layer of black public officials in New Orleans—who had faced some of their most intense black working-class opposition from the projects—were willing to be "responsible" and accept "political realities" by imposing the cuts that were coming from Washington. Far from being a line of defense against the renewed war on the poor that emerged in the late 1970s and early 1980s in the United States, the new black political apparatus—the black urban regime—was showing itself to be part of the arsenal the U.S. ruling elite was unleashing against the poorest sectors of the working class.

In this battle for public housing, the primarily black and female tenants showed themselves capable of mounting effective resistance to the neoliberal reform agenda for public housing. Led by activists such as Jackson, McKnight, and Jones, residents organized, oftentimes in opposition to the established tenant council structure, militant direct actions such as sit-ins and rent strikes. These actions were combined with more institutional strategies, such as going to court, to press for a rollback in rent and utility increases, obtain remodeling funds, and democratize the operation of the development and HANO.

The impressive struggles mounted by poor, working-class African American women and their families at St. Thomas underscores the limitations and blind spots shared by many historians, social scientists, and activists over what constitutes work and working-class struggles. "Narratives on working class struggles," as historian Rhonda Williams argues in her study of public housing residents in Baltimore, "have concentrated on the shop floor or labor organizing and therefore, by definition, have excluded discussions of black women as public assistance recipients."[78] Although St. Thomas and other public housing residents did engage in low-wage work, they also performed uncompensated labor in their homes and community and engaged in collective struggles within those terrains. Yet narrow conceptions of class and class struggle that are limited to the paid workplace result in marginalizing the labor and collective struggles that emerge at the household and community levels. These restricted formulations are particularly problematic under neoliberal capitalism, where the attack on public services, such as public housing and welfare, have been a central element of the class struggle from above and have generated significant working-class resistance. Therefore, in theoretical terms the St. Thomas case underscores that although class may be anchored and sustained in production, it is not something that happens only there. Classes extend beyond their bases in the social relations of production, or as sociologist David Camfield puts it, "People do not stop belonging to classes when they leave their workplaces. Class relations [and struggle] pervade all aspects of social life."[79] Employing this broader conceptualization helps to both locate and appreciate the significance of the struggles for homeplace launched by the black, female-led St. Thomas community at the beginning of the neoliberal era and in the context of the post–civil rights black urban regime. The St. Thomas community, their resident council, and the struggles they led were indeed one key part of the labor movement, defined as "the sum total of organizations and activities within the working class that promotes advancement, self-organization and power."[80]

Conclusion

By the mid-1980s, the public housing movement had shown itself to be a formidable political actor in New Orleans. The black female homemakers that made up this movement were at the cutting edge of working-class resistance to neoliberal urban restructuring in this majority black, southern U.S. city. Nonetheless, though resistance had effectively beaten back this first swipe against public housing in the early 1980s, the pressures, particularly against St. Thomas, would intensify in the second half of the decade. The next chapter turns to the mid- and late 1980s, when the opportunity structure deteriorated further for residents as developers increasingly set their sights on the St. Thomas property and government officials moved from budget cuts to attempts at downsizing public housing. How would St. Thomas tenants and their advisers respond? Would they maintain their combative position or try to work out deals with political and economic elites? Would they attempt to expose and deepen the contradictions of the local black political leadership through confrontation? Or would they move to closed-door negotiations to obtain concessions?

2

Undoing the Black Urban Regime

Resistance to Displacement and Elite Divisions, 1986–1988

See, you don't think of all that. You think of living in the home that you're supposed to live in, [one with] safe and sanitary conditions. . . . That's what we were fighting for. We didn't recognize the other stuff in there. We wasn't bothering no one about the land. We just wanted to live and have decent pay—live comfortable.

—FANNIE MCKNIGHT, ST. THOMAS
PUBLIC HOUSING TENANT LEADER

Gentrification is a frontier on which fortunes are made. From the perspective of working-class residents and their neighbors, however, the frontier is more directly political rather than economic. Threatened with displacement as the frontier of profitability advances, the issue for them is to fight for the establishment of a political frontier behind which working-class residents can take back control of their homes: there are two sides to any frontier.

—NEIL SMITH, GENTRIFICATION, THE FRONTIER,
AND THE RESTRUCTURING OF URBAN SPACE

In the post-1970s neoliberal era, all New Orleans public housing developments faced increasing attacks on multiple fronts. Yet two former white-designated complexes, the Iberville and St. Thomas, because of their location, confronted the greatest pressure. Political and economic elites identified these developments and, in particular, the African American communities that resided there as presenting the most serious obstacles to expanding tourism—by now the key engine of the local economy—and gentrifying historic neighborhoods, such as the ones that surrounded St. Thomas. By the mid-1980s, business interests in tourism, banking, and real estate increasingly saw the continued existence of St. Thomas as, literally, a physical obstacle to expanding their two-decade transformation of the built environment on and near the city's riverfront. That is, the white corporate elite demanded the removal of the black St. Thomas community in order to continue transformation of the city's wharves, warehouses, factories, and low-income housing for new productive and consumptive uses in tourism and for upper-income people. Ironically, the responsibility for addressing the "black impediment" to capital accumulation fell on the new black political elite, who were, in part, a product of the 1960s struggle against racial inequality.

In 1985, voters rejected the attempt by Mayor Ernest Morial to change the city charter and run for a third four-year term. Therefore, in the mid-1980s the city's corporate elite looked to New Orleans's second black mayor, Sidney Barthelemy, to address the political obstacles involved in removing the black, low-income St. Thomas community. The 1986 mayoral race pitting two "black" candidates—Barthelemy, a Catholic, Creole, light-complected New Orleans native and William Jefferson, a Protestant, Anglo–African American, dark-skinned northern Louisiana native— underscored the city and state's distinct, tripartite racial structure and politics. The Creoles of Color, who tended to be Catholic, of French-African ancestry, and with long roots in the city, were situated as an intermediary layer in New Orleans and Louisiana's racial hierarchy between "whites" and "blacks." Although there were not any substantive policy differences between the two candidates, Jefferson, backed by former mayor Morial (a Creole), had secured a solid majority of the black electorate. Barthelemy, in contrast, who had clashed with Mayor Morial while a city councilman, had overwhelming white support. Therefore, in an effort to broaden his base and increase his racial legitimacy, Barthelemy sought and successfully obtained the endorsement and support of the city's black, low-income public housing leadership.

Barthelemy's alliance with public housing residents was fraught with contradictions. While needing their political support, the city's second black mayor was, at the same time, committed to a political-economic agenda that threatened St. Thomas and other public housing communities. This chapter addresses how this contradictory alliance was forged and what impact this partnership had on the political power of St. Thomas and other public housing communities. Did political incorporation into the mayor's electoral coalition increase or weaken the power of public housing residents to defend their communities? How was conflict managed and resolved? Before addressing these questions, we first need to examine the economic, social, and spatial transformation of the New

Orleans riverfront and its surrounding neighborhoods that increasingly made St. Thomas, from the perspective of the city's political-economic elite, a major impediment to continued growth. These changes set the context for increasingly sharp and bitter racial and class conflicts that confronted the St. Thomas community. Could a lasting political marriage be forged, in this context, between the St. Thomas public housing leadership and the city's mayor?

Tourism, the Riverfront, and the New Spatial Model of Accumulation

The city's elites have promoted New Orleans, as Kevin Gotham highlights in his work *Authentic New Orleans: Tourism, Culture, and Race in the Big Easy*, as a tourist destination since at least the mid-nineteenth century. Yet beginning in the late 1960s and accelerating in the subsequent three decades, tourism became, unlike in the past, *the* engine of the New Orleans economy. The transformation of New Orleans's riverfront and adjacent warehouse and central business districts, as depicted in Map 2.1, graphically displays the growing importance of tourism. Two anchoring components of the emerging tourist-led economy were the city's first convention center—the Rivergate, opened in 1968—and the Superdome sports stadium, financed by the State of Louisiana and completed in 1975. Thanks to these government-supported efforts, by the mid-1970s major hotel chains, including the Marriot, Sheraton, and Hyatt, either had built or were in the process of constructing large hotels on Canal Street or in New Orleans's central business district. Recognizing the growing importance of tourism to the local economy, a 1978 *Business Week* article noted that New Orleans's "search for a place in the Sunbelt has so far counted very heavily on the expansion of the tourist industry."[1]

The first opening up of the city's riverfront for tourism came in 1976 when the Landrieu administration christened a 410-feet-long, 12-feet-wide boardwalk in front of Jackson Square in the French Quarter, which was called the Moonwalk in honor of Mayor Maurice "Moon" Landrieu.[2] In 1977, the Hilton Hotel opened at the foot of Canal Street. Two years later and a block away, developer Joseph Canizaro built Canal Place, a hotel and high-end retail operation. The 1984 World's Fair, held on eighty-two acres in the warehouse district, was, as developer Pres Kabacoff demurred, "a disaster at the box office, a big loser."[3] At the same time, the influential developer emphasized, the fair, underwritten with generous subsidies

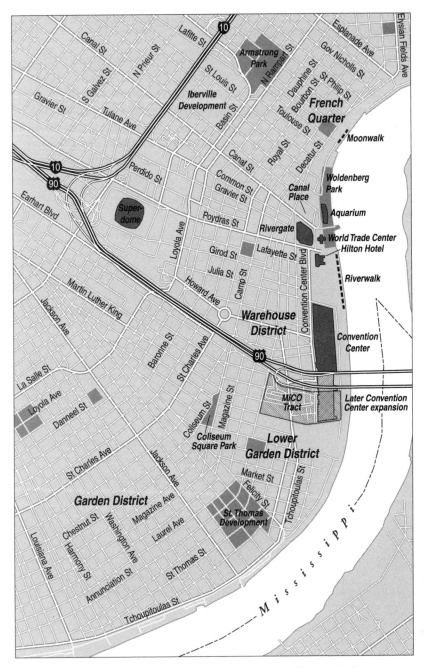

MAP 2.1. Tourist development along New Orleans's riverfront and relationship to St. Thomas and Lower Garden District

from federal, state, and local governments, was a huge success in the way it accelerated the transformation of the riverfront toward tourism. For example, the fair's main pavilion was later turned into the state-and city-run New Orleans Convention Center (later renamed the Ernest N. Morial Convention Center). Two subsequent expansions created a half-mile-long convention facility with over a million square feet of exhibit space, putting the city "plainly . . . in the big time, in the same league with Orlando, Las Vegas, and San Francisco."[4] The World's Fair also accelerated the warehouse district's transformation from light industrial use into con-dominiums, nightclubs, restaurants, and art galleries. Other key additions to the city's tourist landscape were the Riverwalk Mall, opened in 1986, and, four years later, a riverfront park and aquarium built on land owned by the city and the Port of New Orleans.[5]

Gentrification, Tourism, and the Revanchist City

In the 1970s and 1980s, New Orleans's black-led government played a central role in the city's economic and spatial transformation. Yet what political and economic elites framed as a renaissance was seen and ex-perienced by poor black communities as part of what geographer Neil Smith calls a "revanchist" agenda. Smith employs this evocative concept to describe urban policy, as well as the marketing that accompanies it, designed to "take back the city," a "recovery of the city by forces of capital against minorities, the working class, homeless people, the unemployed, women, gays, lesbians, and immigrants."[6] Unlike the original revanchists of post-1871 France, who aggressively worked to bury the revolutionary politics unleashed by the Paris Commune, the New Orleans variant that controlled the local government portrayed themselves as the triumph and institutionalization of the preceding era's social insurgency. Nonetheless, despite their origins, New Orleans's black political leadership was ready to carry out urban displacement by imposing the revanchist agenda de-manded by development interests. James Singleton, the black city council-man for the riverfront area and St. Thomas from the 1970s through the 1990s, has explained the role he and other local officials played in driving urban redevelopment:

> You will see after the 1984 World's Fair there has been great im-provement in the business climate, [and] that was all a strategized plan to get some things done.... We [the city council and Mayor

Ernest Morial] started that earlier.... The big changes came after the World's Fair, but all of the zoning changes to clean it up had started before that, you know, to zone out things. You had flophouses down [in the warehouse district], barracks-style quarters, ... for $2 a night ... no rest room, no showers.... It was an unhealthy situation. This is where we started ... so when you eliminate some of those problems ... get rid of the flophouses ... create the rezoning, [you improve things, but] the vision had to come early on in order to say: "These are things we need to do if we are to improve the city."[7]

The measures that Singleton celebrated, like the closing of single-room-occupancy hotels and other forms of low-rent housing, certainly helped spur development favored by developers. Yet at the same time, they helped to promote homelessness, which had been a rarity in New Orleans before the 1980s but is now epidemic in New Orleans and cities across the United States.[8]

While the New Orleans riverfront and warehouse district were undergoing a transformation, with local government support, the Lower Garden District neighborhood adjacent to St. Thomas was also being gentrified in the 1970s. The process in the Lower Garden District was similar, in some ways, to what sociologist Ruth Glass describes for 1960s London: "Larger Victorian houses, downgraded in an earlier period—which were used as lodging houses or otherwise in multiple occupation—have been upgraded once again." She explained that "once this process of 'gentrification' starts in a district it goes on rapidly until all or most of the original working class occupiers are displaced and the whole social character of the district is changed."[9]

The earlier period for downgrading New Orleans's Lower Garden District began in the 1930s when many large Greek Revival homes were converted into multiple-unit dwellings.[10] The reversal in the neighborhood's fortunes began in the late 1960s and early 1970s as middle-class professionals, many of whom referred to themselves as *urban pioneers*—a name compatible with the revanchist agenda being promoted at the time—began moving into the area, renovating the homes, and displacing the diverse working-class people: blacks, whites, Latinos, and gays.[11] The initial land rush seemed to have been sparked, in part, by the publication in 1971 by local preservationists of *New Orleans Architecture*, whose first edition focused on the endangered architectural gems of an area *the authors* labeled the "Lower Garden District." According to Louis Costa, one of the first arrivals, "It was the publication of this book that convinced me we could do something." He was not alone. Between 1971 and 1973, seventy-five homes were acquired in the neighborhood by "40 young couples and single people" who began restoring them. Many of the arrivals, in addition to their concern with preserving the neighborhood's architecture, also considered themselves politically progressive, especially on race, with several having been supporters of or functionaries in the Landrieu administration. Consistent with this progressive/activist bent, the new pioneers almost immediately organized—through their newly established neighborhood organization, the Coliseum Square Association (CSA)—a successful effort to block the construction of a highway off-ramp for a new bridge through the heart of the Lower Garden District. A key turning point in the neighborhood preservation insurgency was activists' successfully placing the Lower Garden District on the National Register of Historic Places in 1972. This designation created serious obstacles for incoming Governor Edwards and other State of Louisiana officials who supported the original highway blueprints.[12]

Also helping to draw attention to the area were various real estate agents. Of particular importance was realtor Martha Ann Samuel, who promoted the Lower Garden District to young professionals and later opened her own real estate company to market the area. Howard Schmaltz, one of the original pioneers, worked vigorously to get several neighborhood "nuisances," including a machine shop, closed down. He later opened his own real estate company to also market the Lower Garden District. The U.S. Congress aided the efforts of these realtors by passage of legislation in 1976 establishing tax subsidies for the rehabbing of certified income-producing historic properties located within historic districts. That same year, New Orleans established its own Historic District Landmarks Commissions to designate and protect historic structures in the city.[13]

In a further effort to change the social and class image of the neighborhood, the pioneers, individually and through the CSA, organized to officially change the name of the neighborhood. They agitated to have the area bounded by New Orleans's Jackson and St. Charles avenues, the Mississippi River, and a bridge be officially dubbed the Lower Garden District rather than the Irish Channel, which most of the area's working-class residents already called it. This renaming is typical of what critics of gentrification call the *spatial redefinition* game played by real estate interests, which is designed to rebrand a neighborhood as part of an effort to attract a wealthier and—usually—whiter clientele. The neighborhood marketing initiative achieved victory after the Landrieu administration commissioned a study that officially renamed the neighborhood the Lower Garden District. The designation was part of a larger planning project that created 108 distinct neighborhoods, which was later reduced by the Morial administration to 72.[14]

The revival efforts were given a further boost in 1974 with the founding of the Preservation Resource Center (PRC), the city's most important progentrification organization. Crucial financial support for the PRC was initially provided by the Junior League and the local utility company, with the latter's support mirroring the role these entities have played in other gentrifying neighborhoods of the time.[15] The PRC initially focused on the warehouse district, with attention also given to the adjacent Lower Garden District, Irish Channel, and Garden District. As the PRC's first director, Larry Schmidt, explained it, "Our initial goal and role and mission was to bring attention to these neighborhoods, create an environment that people wanted to reinvest, and move back into the city."[16] The local city government—first under a white liberal, Landrieu, and then the first African American mayor, Ernest Morial—used its powers to support PRC's agenda. For example, through new zoning laws and their aggressive enforcement, the city helped to drive out businesses and close multifamily apartments that served low-income people in the Lower Garden District and the other neighborhoods that were targeted. In fact, the collaboration between the city and the PRC in this endeavor was so close that they even had an exchange of personnel. Morial hired Larry Schmidt as deputy director of the Safety and Permits Department in 1978. Schmidt approached the job as a crusade to save, in particular, the "devastated" Lower Garden District. He pushed for new zoning ordinances that would, in words evocative of the frontier metaphor favored by gentrifiers, end the "disincentives for people to move back into [the] *interior* parts" (emphasis added).[17]

In the late 1980s, the PRC gave a further boost to gentrification of the area by the formation of Operation Comeback, a reinvestment campaign backed by local banks and focused on "[reviving] a 24-block area of the Lower Garden District" that included Coliseum Square and other neighborhoods near St. Thomas. Both Councilman Singleton and Mayor Barthelemy spoke at the Operation Comeback kickoff and praised its goals.[18] In contrast, St. Thomas and other low-income residents of the area were not as enamored of the PRC's revival plans, which to them meant evictions, higher rents for privately owned housing, and more pressure to eliminate the neighborhood's public housing. Instead of an Operation Comeback—which St. Thomas resident leaders and their activist allies denounced in a late-1988 meeting with a PRC board member—they called for an "Operation Hold-On," which would allow for neighborhood improvements without displacement of the area's low-income African American residents.[19]

The mid- to late 1980s marked a turning point in the so-called revival of the Lower Garden District and a clear end to what urban scholars have termed the *first wave* or *pioneer* stage of gentrification. The major forces of gentrification during the initial stage that had begun in the late 1960s were, as Lees, Slater, and Wyly found in their study of Park Slope in Brooklyn, an ad hoc collection of "pioneer gentrifiers and neighborhood groups and organizations," historical preservationists, utility companies, and property developers. The initiative of these players, along with various forms of state assistance, "contributed to the revalorization" of the area.[20] While there had been conflict in this initial period, the *second wave* or *anchoring* phase of gentrification would mark a more contentious stage in the neighborhood's social and demographic transformation. As in other parts of the country in the late 1980s—such as the battles in Tompkins Square Park in Manhattan chronicled by Neil Smith—open class warfare began to break out over who had a right to the Lower Gardens District.[21]

The epicenter of the late-1980s conflict was the Lower Garden District's Coliseum Square neighborhood, with a particular point of contention being use of the local public park by the homeless (see Map 2.1). The Coliseum Square Association, whose ranks were made up of recently arrived white, upper-middle-class homeowners, spearheaded the opposition. The CSA was, according to a local minister who served the poor, "militantly opposed to the homeless, who they felt by their very presence reduced home values."[22] In contrast, CSA member Camille Strachan does not see the conflict as class based, as "a question of haves and have nots." Rather, the issue was one of "discipline." She adds, "It's, ahh ... the question of the invasion of space ... [pause] ... by those ... people who are not generally so careful about invasion of space."[23] However they defined the problem, the CSA clearly wanted the homeless out of the park and neighborhood and worked with the local police to accomplish that goal.

> Pam and Keith Casey [heads of the CSA] were the ones leading it. ... I never saw the rolls, but a lot of the middle- and upper-class whites were part of that, and you know they used to have

pitched battles. They'd call the police on people that were sitting on Coliseum Square Park, and the police would come in on horses and beat men and accuse them of not having IDs—all sorts of military-style tactics. And it was a pitched battle in the streets on Sunday afternoons. [There was] a huge police presence and . . . all these neighborhood association people who walked around taking names.[24]

Other components of the CSA's social-cleansing initiative included pressuring churches to stop serving meals to the homeless in the park and calling on the hierarchy of the Methodist Church to remove David Billings, the pastor of a neighborhood church that served the homeless.

Churches would come in from around . . . the larger New Orleans area . . . in their mind to serve a meal to the homeless, and they would get caught up in this neighborhood struggle that was going on. It would take on many dimensions over the years. The Coliseum Square Association would organize very effectively. They would pressure these churches, some of which were out in Metairie [a suburban town]. Eventually, they would put sufficient pressure to have me removed from my position with the United Methodist Church, and I have never returned. That was . . . late 1990 when the bishop ordered me to cease and desist. Not only in those services, but he also said if I was to continue in the United Methodist Church, I would have to agree to not speak out on *any* issue, so I couldn't agree to that, went on a leave of absence, and have been doing other work since then.[25]

Soup kitchens were attracting not only the wrong type of crowd, from the perspective of the CSA, but swing sets, as well. The upscale neighborhood association successfully pressured the city to "take out all the benches and playground equipment from the park so the black kids from St. Thomas could not use them."[26]

David Billings, the Methodist minster that served the local poor, argues that even arson was used by those that wanted to further the class and racial transformation of the area.

A series of fires began to break out in the area [in the late 1980s]. Right across the street from Felicity Church . . . [an apartment

house] burned . . . about eight or nine families were displaced. . . .
We moved some of them into the church. . . . Now that house has
since been totally renovated, with the marble lions out in front.
Again on Camp Street and Felicity, it burned, the house immediately next to Felicity Church, which was owned by this old, can-
tankerous guy. I loved him. He wouldn't sell this huge house, and
part of it burned . . . so we began to say this was part of a process,
that it wasn't accidental, and we began to make those claims.[27]

In the 1970s and 1980s, tax subsidies, zoning changes, police and homeowner harassment of the homeless, political pressure on churches to rein
in radical clergy, dismantling playground equipment, and even arson were
some of the tactics used to drive out the poor from the Lower Garden
District. This revanchist agenda was the prerequisite for continued and
increased flows of investment and relocation of upper-income homeowners to the area. Nonetheless, developers identified the St. Thomas public
housing community as a major physical and social obstacle to further
transformation. In an interview conducted in 1989, developer Pres Kabacoff explains the impediments the St. Thomas community posed for
continued flows of capital into tourism and the up-scaling of housing:

> [The Lower Garden District] is about 400 acres, the same size as
> the warehouse district, the same size as the French Quarter, and is
> the next major development parcel in the city. It is the biggest piece
> of centrally-located *undeveloped ground* in the city. Its importance
> to the city is tremendous. The section which it would connect is
> the strength of our deteriorating city. *The only thing that keeps it
> from developing, keeps it from solidifying, is the 60 acres of the St.
> Thomas development.*[28] (emphasis added)

Thus, by the 1980s Pres Kabacoff and other elements of the New Orleans
black urban regime identified the elimination of the low-income St.
Thomas public housing community as a top priority.[29] The excision
of St. Thomas was essential to realize—in language that reeked of the
frontier metaphors favored by developers—the potential of this "unde-
veloped" section of the city. While not considering the St. Thomas community as "developed," Kabacoff was nonetheless concerned about the
political trouble that residents could generate. In the same 1989 interview cited above, the politically connected forty-three-year-old developer

acknowledged that the removal of St. Thomas would be politically difficult to implement, since "obviously, poor people, when you start talking about dedensifying, are horrified and subject to being scared easily." He argued "courageous" black leadership was critical to gain the residents' consent to redevelopment. "What you really need . . . is a mayor that's going to take on this very sensitive issue."[30]

Forging the Contradictory Alliance

The capacity to take on "sensitive issues," like removing the St. Thomas public housing community, was what the local business class expected of the city's postsegregation era black political class. Managing and removing black impediments to economic regeneration was what they defined as effective governance. In the mid-1980s, members of the business wing of New Orleans's black urban regime looked to Sidney Barthelemy, the city's second black, Creole mayor (1986–1994), to carry out this agenda.

Barthelemy's style of rule differed from that of Mayor Morial. Of course, Morial was, like Barthelemy, a loyal servant of white corporate interests. Yet Morial wanted a procorporate regime in which the mayor played a prominent role in developing the blueprints. He decried the situation where, as Charles Chai found in his 1971 study *Who Rules New Orleans?*, the mayor was not even considered a consequential player in major political decision making. Therefore, as historian Arnold Hirsch argues, Morial's attempt to place the mayor's office at the center of redevelopment efforts, which "was sharply at odds with tradition," helped create his image as a "maverick," as someone hostile to the white business establishment.[31] Morial did, in fact, clash with business interests and the white-controlled Louisiana state legislature when they attempted to strip the Audubon Park Commission from city control, as well as other city agencies. Mayor Morial also fought to secure city government–appointed representation on the municipally subsidized Greater New Orleans Tourist & Convention Commission.[32] Nonetheless, Morial—part of New Orleans's "Radical Creole tradition," as historians Joseph Logsdon and Arnold Hirsch characterize him—was also an enthusiastic supporter of the major probusiness, prodevelopment initiatives that came across his desk. The *appearance* of a "stormy relationship with the business community" is similar to what Adolph Reed describes for Atlanta's first black mayor, Maynard Jackson, also during the 1970s:

Despite the rhetorical tempest, Jackson's record [gave] no reason
to suspect that he ever would have considered breaking the long-
standing public-private marriage ... he unhesitatingly supported
the implementation of the major development initiatives ... he
was an avid proponent of the general framework for downtown
development and revitalization.[33]

Nonetheless, in Atlanta, Jackson's confrontational style, which at times
turned off the business elite, made him, like Morial, attractive to black
voters.

Like Maynard Jackson's successor in Atlanta, Andrew Young, New
Orleans's Sidney Barthelemy also tried to reduce the appearance of being
hostile to business interests. This did not go over well with black voters,
so Barthelemy, who became mayor anyway, did not get the majority of
the black vote in his 1986 race. Whites, rather than blacks, composed the
majority of his electoral coalition. Therefore, to garner some level of racial
legitimacy (and votes), Barthelemy campaigned—successfully—to obtain
the support of public housing activists Ron Chisom and Jim Hayes. They
worked, in turn, to get public housing leaders, including the combative
St. Thomas leadership, to endorse Barthelemy in his 1986 race. The organized power of the public housing residents, as tenant organizer Chisom
explains, led political leaders like Barthelemy to pay attention:

> We had a chance to talk to all [mayoral candidates] because we
> had a big strong tenants group. . . . We were always turning two
> hundred people to a HANO meeting . . . then they really started
> talking with us. But before . . . they thought we were a bunch of
> radicals. They would play us off, but when they saw us consistent-
> ly, and saw the leverage we had . . . they treated us as somebody
> you had to reckon with.[34]

Fannie McKnight, a longtime St. Thomas resident council officer, said that
she, along with Chisom, helped to broker a meeting between Barthelemy
and activists from several of the housing developments. Recognizing the
importance of the black working class within New Orleans's political system, McKnight emphasizes, "There was a mayor's race, so the politicians
had to come to us."[35] Yet the drawback was that to the extent public housing residents were more closely incorporated into the black regime—due,

in part, to their political activism—they tended to lose their freedom to disrupt, a key source of their strength.

In exchange for their support, residents demanded that Barthelemy hire Jessie Smallwood, then a HANO board member, as the executive director of the housing agency. As a HANO board member, "Smallwood," St. Thomas tenant leader Fannie McKnight argues, "joined [with] the residents, and she let the people know that the residents were paying her way. She understood us, and she worked with us." Chisom and other tenants, as McKnight's statement indicates, saw Smallwood, a native New Orleanian, a former public housing resident, and a graduate of the University of California–Berkeley's master's program in urban planning and public health, as the most competent and the most sympathetic to tenants' interests. Nonetheless, though Smallwood appeared as an ally, relying on sympathetic faces in the local government to achieve tenant demands further distanced resident leaders from their historical sources of power rooted in mass mobilization.

Shortly after taking office, Barthelemy did make good on his promise to hire Smallwood. In July 1986, the newly installed mayor successfully put pressure on the HANO board to fire Executive Director Cates, the longtime bête noire of the St. Thomas leadership. Following Cates's dismissal, Barthelemy met with tenant leader Barbara Jackson and other members of the Tenants' Fight Back Organization, a new group she had formed with the help of organizers Ron Chisom and Jim Hayes, to receive input on selecting the new HANO director and future board members. This group had been formed as a counterweight to the official citywide tenants council, led by president of the Magnolia development and HANO board member Augusta Kerry. Jackson criticized Augusta Kerry and other tenant leaders linked to city government for "not representing the tenants . . . for not [knowing] what's going on in the developments." In a response reminiscent of the attacks on tenant activist Crystal Jones a few years earlier, Augusta Kerry and HANO board chair Harry Ladas questioned the legitimacy of Barbara Jackson's leadership, arguing that the St. Thomas president was not "representing the wishes of HANO's residents."[36]

The People's Institute as Regime Intermediary

Why was Ron Chisom able to gain the trust of the public housing leadership and act as an intermediary with the mayor? Chisom, as briefly discussed in the previous chapter, had worked in New Orleans with various poor people's struggles since the late 1960s. Together with Jim Hayes, Chisom had formed the Tremé Community Improvement Association (TCIA) in 1968, which involved them in a host of community issues, from helping drug addicts to dealing with abusive landlords to running a rummage store to serve low-income residents.[37] Yet by the early 1970s, as Chisom and Hayes began to make contacts with the National Tenants Organization (NTO)—the leading national public housing tenants organization from the 1960s through the 1980s—they became increasingly focused on working with public housing residents and issues. NTO trainings educated these organizers about "all the laws on public housing modernization, . . . the Senator Brooke amendment, all that stuff, and we learned so much." Chisom and Hayes soon concluded that "people were more protected in public housing than in private housing." Public housing offered the best opportunity to politicize low-income people and, therefore, as Chisom explains, "give us some strength . . . [and] build our base."[38] Thus as Chisom points out, public housing—compared with private sector housing—provided a more favorable environment for political mobilization. The rights enshrined in public housing, which the struggles of the civil rights and poor people's movements of the 1960s helped to expand, created an ideal by which the state could be held accountable.[39]

Initially, Chisom and Hayes began working with the Iberville and Lafitte developments, but they eventually forged relationships with all New Orleans's housing developments following the establishment, in 1972, of a citywide public housing tenant council. To fund the TCIA, Chisom and Hayes were forced, at times, to seek resources from the same organizations they were fighting. For example, HANO allowed TCIA to use an apartment in the Lafitte project as an office, for which the group paid only nominal rent. HANO contracted with Chisom and the NTO to conduct leadership training workshops for members of the tenant councils. In addition, Chisom and Hayes turned to support from city hall. For instance, the federal government's Comprehensive Employment and Training Act (CETA) and Manpower employment programs, which were disbursed through the mayor's office, allowed them "to hire a large staff."[40] The TCIA also regularly turned to the then mayor Ernest Morial, whom they had endorsed in his first run for mayor in 1977, for funds and consulted with him on various issues.[41] The relations with Morial were so close that, in 1979, the mayor named Chisom to the HANO board, for which Chisom served only one year, stepping down well before his five-year term had expired because, as Chisom explains, "I was becoming co-opted."[42] Other activists agreed that Chisom's and Hayes's ties to city hall had affected the stances that they could take. For example, a leading activist in the grassroots campaign to prosecute the police officers involved in murdering four unarmed black people in 1980—while Ernest Morial was mayor—said that Chisom and Hayes would not get involved in the campaign, because of their close ties to the mayor: "When we asked for their support they told us, 'you know, we can't touch it.'"[43] Thus, as the evidence indicates, these advisers to city government, even though associated with public housing causes, also served contradictory interests. On one side, they allied with the public housing residents in support of their demands, while on the other they supported the procorporate black urban regime, many even taking government posts and receiving financial support from that regime for their pro–public housing organizations. As Chisom and Hayes' case shows, their political and material ties limited what they could do to oppose the regimes' activities. Their influence with public housing residents, and with the broader black working class, was precisely what made them important to the new black political elite, This same influence within the New Orleans black urban regime constrained the types of black working class challenges and insurgencies that Chisom and his public housing group could support. It could be said that the same contradictions that existed within the regime—to both promote accumulation and maintain class and racial harmony—extended to the regime's community activist allies.

In 1980, Chisom and an African American sociologist, the late Jim Dunn, founded the nonprofit activist-consulting business the People's Institute for Survival and Beyond (PI). The PI's primary activity since the organization's founding has been to conduct workshops for a variety of organizations, especially social change and social service organizations, to develop strategies for identifying and "deinstitutionalizing" racism. They identify racism as *the* key stumbling block for building effective social movements for progressive change.

In the mid-1980s, local black community activists Barbara Major and Crystal Jones and David Billings, a white Methodist minister active in local community struggles, joined Chisom and Dunn and Dunn's wife, Diana, as core PI antiracism trainers. The formation of the PI's inner circle of trainers would impact their relationship with St. Thomas residents and the future fate of the development in two important ways. First, the PI was the body that tied these actors—Chisom, the Dunns, Billings, Major, Jones, and, to a lesser extent, Hayes—together. Although they had known and worked with each other in the past, the PI brought them together as a team with a shared political outlook, regular interaction, and mutual business interests. They now had an organizational vehicle for developing a common strategy, tactics, and approach to issues, including the future of the St. Thomas public housing development. Their close ties were reflected in how Chisom distributed the political patronage he had earned by swaying public housing leaders to endorse Barthelemy: Barbara Major and Crystal Jones garnered appointive positions in the new administration due to the political acumen of the PI cofounder.

The second important aspect of the PI network and the antiracism workshops they conducted was that it helped strengthen the authority these activists wielded with public housing tenants, social service agencies, and local community and political activists. The workshops, attendance at which became almost de rigueur for many local social service representatives and activists, further burnished the PI's credentials.[44] Therefore, the position the PI took on local issues—such as redevelopment at St. Thomas—influenced people's perceptions, especially those within the social service and activist milieus. PI support provided a certain antiracist imprimatur for any initiative and would therefore not be something a self-identified progressive antiracist would want to oppose. The workshops, at which St. Thomas leaders occasionally made appearances, also helped further solidify ties between the PI cadre and public housing residents.

Political Courage, Black Elected Officials, and the Rochon Report

The alliance between Mayor Barthelemy, tenant leaders, activists associated with the PI, and HANO director Smallwood began to collapse following the administration's release of its *Housing Plan for New Orleans,* better known as the Rochon Report. Although the report was released in early 1988—a year and a half after Barthelemey took office—developer Pres Kabacoff argues its origins date to a meeting he called the previous year: "I called everybody in the room, [and told them,] 'This thing [St. Thomas and public housing] doesn't work.'" Prominent among the meeting attendees was Reynard Rochon, an influential political consultant and the first African American chairman of the HANO board of commissioners.[45] Following this meeting, in April 1987, the Barthelemy administration quietly appropriated $100,000 for Rochon and his company—Rochon and Associates—to develop a housing plan for New Orleans.[46]

The report, released in early 1988, dealt with housing in general, but the component of the report that raised the most concern and interest was the recommendations about public housing. The report called for eliminating HANO, privatizing management of the developments, and cutting the number of public housing units in half. Regarding St. Thomas—the first project discussed in the report—Rochon recommended stopping the second phase of a planned $23.6 million rehabilitation and reducing the number of units there from 1,510 to 750.[47]

Mayor Barthelemy was very supportive of Rochon's recommendations. He argued, using some of the language popularized by sociologist William Julius Wilson and invoked by New Orleans developer Pres Kabacoff, that "the recommendations made a lot of sense."

> Part of the problem was the *concentration of poverty*. And then, most of the poor people were concentrated in public housing; it was *too dense*. And it needed to be *dedensified* . . . or the density reduced. And that was [the Rochon Report's] recommendation, but I had made a commitment to all the resident committees and councils that we were going to have hearings.[48] (emphasis added)

Other black elected officials, such as Councilman Jim Singleton, were equally supportive of the report and eager to begin moving his poor, black working-class constituents out of St. Thomas. According to architect Davis Jahnke, Singleton bluntly told him that "the best thing that could happen to St. Thomas would be to drop a bomb on it and to annihilate it."[49]

Black working-class public housing residents did not share the enthusiasm of black political functionaries and consultants. Just as Edward Goetz found in his study of public housing displacement in Minneapolis, residents did not clamor for a mixed-income community or for dedensification. Rather, St. Thomas and other residents of New Orleans's public housing, in a pattern representative of other low-income, working-class communities in the face of gentrification, emphasized "priorities of stability, affordability, and improvements without displacement."[50] The Rochon Report was roundly condemned by public housing residents, and the St. Thomas leaders were the most vehement in their opposition. Yet as the former mayor points out, tenant leaders were not monolithic. Augusta Kerry, the longtime leader of the C. J. Peete development—a development also targeted for downsizing under the Rochon Report—was more open to discussions about the plan.

I think it was Barbara Jackson and Fannie McKnight who I
had several meetings with to try and convince them to let us
go through with the hearings, but they didn't want to [almost
inaudible]. Those were the most [difficult tenant leaders]. But
Ms. Kerry [from the C. J. Peete development] wasn't. She was . . .
she wanted to have the hearings and stuff. She might have even
had one. I don't remember all the details.[51]

Barthelemy was also able to entice a longtime community activist and
lawyer—Endesha Juakali, formerly known as Michael Williams—to lend
his legitimacy to the plan. Juakali, who grew up in the St. Bernard Project
and, before law school, had run a youth program that served his childhood community, had in the past worked in cooperation with People's
Institute activists. He now broke with his erstwhile allies and defended
Barthelemy's proposal before a packed city council hearing on February 18, 1988, as he pleaded with residents to reevaluate their position and
"try to make peace, before you make war."[52] Neither Juakali's nor Bathe-
lemy's pleas were heeded: "The plan was scorned," as *Gambit* editor Clancy
DuBos, a strong supporter of the Rochon Report, lamented, "by many
public housing residents, who jammed a City Council Chamber meeting. . . . [W]hen Barthelemy presented the plan, [residents] boo[ed] and
shout[ed] [at] him repeatedly." St. Thomas leaders Barbara Jackson and
Fannie McKnight were among those leading the charge.[53]

PI organizers, including Barbara Major, Crystal Jones, and Jim Hayes,
also broke ranks with Mayor Barthelemy and spoke out at the hearing
against the Rochon Report's recommendations.[54] Figure 2.1 shows PI organizer Jim Hayes, report in hand, haranguing Mayor Barthelemy at a
city council hearing. This photo visually captures the gulf separating the
neoliberal agenda of the black political leadership on one side and public
housing residents and their PI supporters on the other. It became impossible for Barthelemy's PI allies to maintain their status as defenders of
public housing residents while at the same time lending support to a plan
that would demolish half the public housing stock. This balancing act was
particularly difficult for Major and Jones, who held posts in Barthelemy's
administration. They had to choose sides. As Barbara Major explains, the
decision to denounce the Rochon Plan at the city council led to a de-
finitive break with their employer and erstwhile political ally: "When he
released that report, Crystal [Jones] and I went to the city council and
ragged him. And boy it was on then. Sidney basically said we would make

no money in this city, and that was cool."[55] Thus, the Rochon Report led to a major split between the black political leadership and some of their former public housing activist allies in the PI.

HANO director Smallwood was, for her part, also a supporter of downsizing public housing, though she "wanted ... to look at pairing down gradually."[56] Nonetheless, although supporting neoliberal reform of public housing, Smallwood opposed the Rochon Plan, since she saw it as a thinly disguised land grab by developers. In Smallwood's mind Mayor Barthelemy was plainly working on behalf of developers:

> [Developers] pressured the mayor, Barthelemy. In fact, that was the reason I was fired, because I said, "Over my dead body," so they made sure I was a dead body.... I'm talking about Pres Kabacoff, to a degree [former mayor] Moon Landrieu, who was involved at the time, another guy who is dead and who was a key partner with Pres Kabacoff. They saw the value of the land, and they convinced Barthelemy—who didn't take very much to convince—that that was a very sought after piece of land and just having it wasted with a few people in it [was insupportable].[57]

Due to Smallwood's bureaucratic resistance to the Rochon Plan—which was, in great measure, a product of resident opposition to the plan—a war raged between February and June 1988 over control of HANO. The Barthelemy administration worked feverishly to engineer Executive Director Smallwood's removal. The basis of the conflict, from the perspective of the Barthelemy administration, was simply—as *Louisiana Weekly* reporter Norbert Davidson commented—that "Smallwood would not give up public housing."[58] Yet the HANO director's intransigence and willingness to challenge the mayor cannot be understood in isolation from the pressure coming from her vocal public housing resident allies, particularly the St. Thomas Resident Council.

An initial attempt by Barthelemy and his top city housing specialists, Shelia Danzy and Larry Jones, to get the HANO board to fire Smallwood at the March 1988 board meeting failed miserably. After receiving an independent investigative report that praised her management, the HANO board gave Smallwood a vote of confidence rather than a pink slip. The board's decision was also impacted by "fifty angry tenants at the meeting who supported Smallwood [and] intimidated" them from following Barthelemy's orders.[59] In response, the mayor removed HANO board chair

FIGURE 2.1. Housing activist Jim Hayes, with study in hand, denounces the Rochon Report at a city council hearing, February 18, 1988. Mayor Sidney Barthelemy is in the foreground. Photograph by Bryan Beateaux, used with permission of the *New Orleans Times-Picayune*.

Charles McGilberry and worked to stack the board by appointing two close allies, attorney Endesha Juakali, whom Smallwood called a "trouble-maker, ruthless to the core ... [who] was always trying to trip me up," and black businessman Zachary Ellis, to finally remove her. Smallwood, despite intense pressure from Barthelemy and his aides, refused to bow out quietly: "I said, 'Oh no, I'm not going to resign. You're going to fire me, and you're going to do it publicly. And then I'm going to tell the world why.' And they really thought I was a pain in the ass. But I didn't [resign], [I said,] 'I'm not just stepping down.'"[60]

To put further pressure on Barthelemy, Smallwood, working with Jim Hayes, Ron Chisom and with the support of St. Thomas's and other tenant leaders, organized a plan to send out 5,000 letters to black Republicans who were preparing to meet in New Orleans for the 1988 Republican National Convention. The letter requested black attendees not to support Barthelemy's plans to demolish public housing and relocate residents and instead "convince HUD officials and the Republican Party to develop and implement programs to properly house our people."[61] The mass mailing effort, which was squashed when Juakali made an unannounced visit to the HANO central office while the letters were being prepared to be sent out, deepened Barthelemy's resolve to remove Smallwood, whatever the cost.[62] Finally, at the June 14, 1988, HANO board meeting, the commissioners, including the two public housing tenant members, Augusta Kerry of Magnolia and Donald Jones of St. Bernard, voted six to one to remove Smallwood. Residents, who had filled the boardroom, were enraged over the decision. After the vote they began singing the popular civil rights song "Ain't Gonna Let Nobody Turn Me Around." Several public housing residents embraced Smallwood. Fannie McKnight, then vice president of the St. Thomas Resident Council, screamed at the HANO board, "Why was she fired? Give us the reason!"[63]

Black Political Elites Can't Deliver: Residents Force Retreat on Public Housing "Reform"

Despite Barthelemy's successful effort to remove Smallwood, his larger goal of public housing downsizing and privatization was not achieved, at least in the short term. The opposition from St. Thomas residents and other combative tenant councils and their allies resulted in the Rochon Plan officially being dropped. As Barthelemy recalled, regarding the Rochon Plan's fate,

> I think they probably had a couple of [Rochon Plan meetings]. But after that, we sort of dropped the Rochon Report because the residents just . . . did not want to do it. It was just too controversial

with all the other issues that we were dealing with. So I went directly to HUD, you know, [and asked,] "How do we resolve some of the problems," and one of [their solutions] was the private management [of public housing]. And that's when we moved to private management.[64]

Therefore, in late 1988, HANO and HUD did sign an agreement to provide for a private management team to run the New Orleans housing authority.[65] The larger-scale privatization of public housing envisioned in the Rochon Report had been beaten back, however, by resident protest. Barthelemy himself acknowledged that without resident support his downsizing and displacement efforts would fail:

Basically, the approach was to get the public housing residents to be supportive. And then you would approach HUD and try and work the issue through with HUD. *But if you didn't get it done on the local level, there was no way you could go to HUD and get dedensification talked about.*[66] (emphasis added)

A December 9, 1988, letter from Barthelemy to STRC president Barbara Jackson confirms the former mayor's recollection of the Rochon Report's fate. In that letter he makes a commitment to "not permit, during my administration, any wholesale destruction or demolition of units in the St. Thomas Housing Project," obviously a commitment at least in part nurtured by tenant pressures.[67]

Another business-led effort, from 1988 to 1989, which included an array of nonprofits and university consultants, to gain resident cooperation in privatizing the Iberville development also collapsed, even though it had attempted to solicit resident collaboration and cooperation.[68] At the same time, while public housing residents dealt the Rochon Plan a setback, a demolition by neglect seemed to gain momentum at St. Thomas. By February 1990, the vacancy rate was at an all-time high of 29 percent, or 435 of the complex's 1,510 units.[69] Such units were increasingly vandalized or taken over for drug use and sales, conditions that further nurtured arguments that disparaged public housing.

Panic set in as residents began hearing rumors that "they were going to take the project. . . . They was going to rent the projects as apartments, but only to whites. . . . [St. Thomas] was not gonna be for blacks anymore."[70] Resident leaders did not think these rumors were unfounded. Rather, they believed, according to the resident's longtime lawyer, Bill Quigley, that the increased vacancies and the drug activity and vandalism were part of a plan to allow the development to deteriorate in order to justify demolition.[71] Nevertheless, by beating back the Rochon Plan, St. Thomas residents (and other public housing developments) still had their communities and the power to improve and defend them. They could fight another day.

Public Housing Residents' Powers of Political Destabilization

I have elaborated how the forces of housing gentrification and tourism were dramatically changing the city's built environment. A new spatial model of accumulation, based in tourism and upscale housing, was emerging along New Orleans's Mississippi riverfront; the city's main thoroughfare, Canal Street; and the central business, warehouse, and Lower Garden districts. The new business elite in tourism, real estate, and banking needed the new black political elite to play a role in facilitating the transformation into a tourist-friendly environment, into creating a "new" New Orleans. Governing under these conditions meant using local political authority and resources to assist and subsidize the corporate revitalization agenda and removing any obstacles to this agenda. In the eyes of New Orleans's white corporate elite, one of the central political, social, and physical impediments to continued urban revitalization, particularly by the mid-1980s, was the city's public housing developments and poor black people in general. The Iberville and St. Thomas developments were particularly problematic, since they were located near the French Quarter and Canal Street and the rapidly developing riverfront, respectively. A city-commissioned 1989 Urban Land Institute (ULI) report raised concerns over "the presence of large numbers of minority shoppers on Canal Street." In a 1998 report, the ULI adds that "both residents and tourists [were] intimidated by the presence of large groups of young [black] people on Canal Street . . . and the concentration of poverty–level residents in the Iberville public housing project" only contributed to the problem.[72] The same could be said of St. Thomas and its stymieing of riverfront development. The job of New Orleans's black political elite was to deal with the perceived nuisance of poor blacks who represented an impediment to elite-defined revitalization efforts.

In lieu of demolition and displacement, New Orleans's black leadership stepped up what Cook and Lauria call the city's "spatial containment" strategy.[73] Police patrols were beefed up, especially around centrally located public housing developments. Mayor Barthelemy rerouted the city's annual Martin Luther King Jr. parade—the largest annual African American celebration/political protest, which regularly brought out tens of thousands of people. Beginning in 1989, the parade ended at Armstrong Park on North Rampart Street, rather than continuing several blocks further to Canal Street, which had been the site of important sit-ins by civil rights activists in the 1960s. The precipitating event for the change in the route of the MLK parade was the *alleged* punching of pedestrians and breaking of windows on Canal Street by black youths following the 1988 parade.[74] Nonetheless, the move also addressed a number of long-held concerns, delineated in the previously cited ULI reports, about the negative impact on the city's image posed by the very presence of large numbers of poor and black people on Canal Street, New Orleans's signature street. In addition to these measures, failing to repair and fill apartments, particularly the St. Thomas public housing development, also cast a dark shadow over public housing and increased calls for its demise.

Nonetheless, despite these measures the main thrust of the black urban regime's agenda—to destroy and displace poor black communities—still fell far short of its goals. Barthelemy's inability to successfully introduce public housing reform was not a result of his electoral alliance with poor blacks. Indeed, it could be argued that the confidence that came with this electoral bloc was what emboldened the Barthelemy administration to undertake a neoliberal reform initiative of public housing. The real stumbling block for the city's political elite and allied developers came when public housing residents broke from their political incorporation into the Barthelemy-led black urban regime. The vocal opposition of residents split the black urban regime from within, below, and above. For example, Executive Director Smallwood, a functionary within the local government, could not lend her full support to the Rochon Plan, despite being a supporter of privatization. Clearly, strident resident opposition encouraged Smallwood to break with her fellow black petty bourgeois colleagues' blatant subservience and catering to white corporate interests—most prominently represented by Barthelemy and Rochon. Whatever role Smallwood played during the 1987–1988 historical juncture, her acting to undercut neoliberal transformation of New Orleans was a product of residents' actions. The protests unleashed by public housing residents, such as the outburst at Smallwood's firing, helped to expose the regime's class and racial contradictions, as they played out at the local level. From below, public housing resident protests helped sever the Barthelemy administration's alliance with the nonprofit PI activists, an outfit that had provided a source of racial and class legitimacy for the Barthelemy administration. Finally, defeat of the Rochon Plan led to the business community's disillusionment in Barthelemy's capacity to govern—that is, to impose the corporate agenda on the black working class.

Key to isolating residents from their powers of disruption were the nonprofit PI activists. By advocating an alliance with Mayor Barthelemy, the public housing residents were incorporated into the regime and, consequently, lost their ability to mobilize and exploit their powers of disruption. The elite pact between resident leaders and Barthelemy undermined or reduced their willingness to exercise their class-specific forms of power. Rather than benefiting public housing communities, the elite pact only emboldened Barthelemy and led him to introduce the draconian plans laid out in the Rochon Report. It was only when residents broke with the alliance that they could exercise their collective power and deal the Rochon Plan a defeat.

The elite pact also undercut possibilities of residents' allying with other sections of the black working class to increase their power and achieve their demands. For example, in the mid-1980s, as I can attest, having been a local labor organizer at the time, the alliance among residents, the PI, and Barthelemy isolated tenants from HANO workers, who were trying to gain collective bargaining rights. The attempt to forge a worker–resident alliance was foreclosed by the pact that the PI helped broker with the Barthelemy administration and Smallwood.

Thus, isolating residents from their indigenous sources of power and other working-class allies in exchange for an alliance with regime elites did not gain residents increased protection. Indeed, it increased their vulnerability. Although the pact eventually collapsed, the experience did show the local political leadership that if public housing residents could be enticed into an elite alliance, their powers of mobilization could be undercut. By eliminating their powers of disruption, public housing communities could be dismantled and dispersed consensually. With the help of nonprofits and university advisers, regime elites attempted to isolate the Iberville community and work out a privatization scheme in the late 1980s.[75] This attempt failed, but a much more sophisticated effort at St. Thomas in the 1990s, one in which nonprofits played a central role, was successful.

3

Neoliberalism and Nonprofits

Selling Privatization at St. Thomas, 1989–1995

> There has been a change in me. . . . You better change. Shit, you
> can't change racism in the new millennium just using old sixties
> tactics. . . . Some people are just stuck in the sixties.
>
> —BARBARA MAJOR

> It seems that ever since the Negro has been free some founda-
> tion has watched over his destiny. Right after emancipation the
> Peabody fund was giving him wrong advice. Then later on the
> Rosenwald Fund corrupted his leaders.
>
> —E. FRANKLIN FRAZIER

By late 1988, intense opposition by St. Thomas and other public housing
residents forced Mayor Barthelemy and his real estate allies to shelve their
downsizing plan for New Orleans's public housing. The city's political and
economic elite had presented the Rochon Plan, which would have literally removed the obstacle of public housing—and its ten complexes, 14,000
apartments, and around 60,000 low-income black residents—as a way
to revitalize the city. Barthelemy's plan placed particular attention on the
St. Thomas housing development, situated, as a city-commissioned study
emphasized, "in the center of the city's politically supported growth area."[1]
Nonetheless, developers and their African American backers in city government did not get their way, despite the importance they placed on removing
the St. Thomas and other public housing developments. The public housing movement forced the Barthelemy administration to withdraw its plan.
Opponents identified the initiative as simply a new form of the old policy
of "Negro removal," only now it was being promoted by the new post–civil
rights African American political class. Intense opposition from the public

housing wing of New Orleans's black working class, with St. Thomas in the lead, forced the black political leadership and their white corporate allies to retreat from this initial foray into rolling back public housing.

The battle over St. Thomas was a concrete expression, a manifestation, of the deep class and racial lines dividing New Orleans. Arrayed on one side of this conflict were the white real estate and the other corporate interests, white upper-middle-class homeowners in the Lower Garden District, and black elected and appointed officials. Although having their own internal divisions and tactical differences, they were nonetheless united in their effort to eliminate St. Thomas. This proneoliberal alliance confronted a female-led black working-class community that wanted to defend and improve, not demolish, the St. Thomas public housing development. Tenant leaders and advisers advocated what they called an Operation Hold-On plan for the neighborhood rather than the gentrifying Operation Comeback advocated by the PRC and others committed to an elite-defined renaissance of the area.

Despite this seemingly intractable divide, by the early 1990s these erstwhile adversaries had become partners. In 1992, the St. Thomas tenant leadership and their leading advisers agreed to collaborate with New Orleans's most powerful real estate developer, Joseph Canizaro, in a privatized planning effort, strongly supported by public officials, to redevelop St. Thomas and the surrounding area. By middecade the tenant leaders, along with Canizaro and middle-class homeowners, had enthusiastically accepted a plan drawn up by an influential real estate industry think tank to significantly reduce the number of public housing apartments and privatize the development. How did this happen? How did this transition from confrontation to cooperation take place in support of privatization and poor people removal? My argument is that nonprofit organizations, a generally understudied area of contemporary U.S. urban politics, are critical for explaining the political transformation at St. Thomas in support of privatization. Nonprofits are particularly important under a black urban regime form of city government, divided as they are between an elite *governing coalition* primarily composed of black political officials and white corporate leaders, on one side, and an *electoral coalition* rooted in the black working class, on the other. As political scientist Adolph Reed notes, underscoring the deep, underlying tension in these political formations, "The relationship of their two principal components is or is very nearly zero-sum in many important policy areas."[2] This certainly points to public housing. The nonprofits allied to the regime played an indispensable role, within the context of a race- and class-polarized social structure, in legitimizing and gaining the support of key tenant leaders for a policy that deepened the city's entrenched patterns of inequality.

The transformation of community activists and their organization into nonprofits and their embrace of developers and the privatization agenda was not an overnight affair. This chapter identifies the various stages, or acts, from 1988 to 1994 that led to this dramatic political, ideological, and organizational transformation. Rather than representing a one-time, simplistic selling out, the transformation of the St. Thomas tenant leadership and their activist allies was a progressive process that built upon and deepened in each successive stage.

Act I: From Class Struggle to Self-Help

A key demand of the public housing insurgency in New Orleans and across the country in the late 1960s and 1970s was for greater control of developments by residents. This demand was linked to the larger issue of community control—from schools to businesses to police—that some in the black liberation movement advocated.[3] The Ford Foundation, a central element of what sociologist William Domhoff calls the ruling class's nonprofit "policy-formation network," responded in the early 1970s to these demands by promoting tenant management corporations.[4] The Ford Foundation, following its support of a 1975 pilot program in St. Louis, collaborated with HUD in establishing the National Tenant Management Program in order to promote tenant management corporations or, as Ford officials characterized them, "real estate holding companies." To develop a tenant management pilot program for the Calliope (B. W. Cooper) development, in 1976 HANO received an $8.5 million grant jointly funded by HUD and the Ford Foundation. The program was later expanded to include the St. Bernard development, as well, although the initiative was later disbanded.[5]

Mayor Ernest Morial was, for his part, a major proponent of tenant management, arguing it would aid in dismantling, as he explained in a 1979 speech to a meeting of public housing directors, the "old developments" that "isolate large numbers of people." Tenant management would provide public housing residents, Mayor Morial explained, with "the social and psychological benefits of *self-determination* and the acceptance of responsibility" (emphasis added) and would therefore help wean them off government dependence.[6] This line of thinking was wholly consistent with the racialized self-help ideology that increasingly took hold in the 1980s in the context of Reaganite retrenchment. The message to African Americans was clear: the solutions *and* sources of the social problems they faced—such as lack of jobs and housing—were rooted in their communities. This self-help ideology "facilitated," argues political scientist Preston Smith, "the corresponding growth of a new *black privatism* [ideology and political practice] exemplified by an increased faith in the capacity of private institutions and voluntary actions . . . to improve black social conditions."[7] Morial's tying of self-determination rhetoric to government retrenchment presaged how grassroots activists would place a progressive spin on self-help, neoliberal solutions to public housing.

HANO director Smallwood, although opposed to the radical downsizing proposed by the Barthelemy administration, was a strong advocate of tenant management and promoting, as she explains, "self-sufficiency" among residents (i.e., getting by on less support from the government). To promote self-help efforts, Smallwood, after taking over as director in 1986, hired People's Institute trainers Crystal Jones and Barbara Major to "help build the capacity of tenant groups."[8] As part of this capacity-building effort, Jones and Smallwood brought tenant activist Kimi Gray, the tenant manager of a Washington, DC, housing project, to address HANO tenant leaders in December 1986. Gray was then a darling of the mainstream national media and of many influential public officials, as well, such as Republican congressman Jack Kemp, later HUD secretary in George H. W. Bush's administration, who regularly trotted her out as "a showpiece for the 'success of self-help.'"[9] Unsurprisingly, during her New Orleans speaking engagement Gray preached the gospel of self-help and tenant management schemes as she counseled residents to create nonprofit organizations and, through these entities, obtain financial support from the government, foundations, and corporations to run their developments. Gray's directives were made in anticipation of passage of the Community Housing and Development Act of 1987, strongly supported by Kemp and the Reagan administration, which provided money and training for resident management corporations (RMCs).

The support for resident management gained steam locally as a chief disseminator of local elite thinking, the *Times-Picayune*, came out strongly for it in a 1988 editorial, while the Amoco Corporation, as part of its national program, began giving out grants to support the program locally.[10] Underscoring the growing political importance of RMCs in New Orleans at this time was the emergence of public housing resident Cynthia Wiggins as the dominant force on the citywide tenant council and the most politically influential tenant representative on the HANO board. Wiggins, who organized and was the CEO of the Guste public housing development RMC, became a player at the national level, as well, eventually becoming president of the National Association of Resident Management Corporations in 2000 after the death of Kimi Gray, who headed the organization for its first ten years. HUD, which invested $22 million in over three hundred RMCs between 1988 and 1993, helped to create a political force and entrepreneurial layer among residents who had a material stake in privatizing public housing. Wiggins, who set up a whole series of nonprofit and for-profit corporations as part of her operation, is a prime example of this new class and unsurprisingly became a fervent supporter and advocate of RMCs.[11]

Self-Help Efforts at St. Thomas

Consistent with the self-help, tenant management trend, in 1987 the St. Thomas Resident Council, following Gray's visit and with support from HANO officials, created a nonprofit entity, the St. Thomas Economic Development Corporation (STEDC). The STEDC mission was to promote and implement self-help efforts, such as creating microenterprises, obtaining private-funding sources, and, eventually, running the development. In January 1988, HANO did award the STEDC a small contract to "cut grass and trim trees on apartment yards."[12] Yet despite this initial support, in mid-1988 HANO (after Smallwood's firing) rejected STRC leader Barbara Jackson's grant application to develop a tenant management program at St. Thomas.

Part of the reason behind HANO's denying funding to St. Thomas appeared to be the willingness of Barbara Jackson and the other STRC members to maintain their relationship with organizers from the People's Institute. As discussed in chapter 2, the PI was a nonprofit organization formed in 1980 by a cadre of local, mainly black community activists that provided what they called Undoing Racism training sessions for, primarily, social service agencies and even businesses. The PI activists had also been longtime advisers to St. Thomas and other public housing tenant councils and had joined with residents in backing Barthelemy in his 1986 mayoral race. Yet after Barbara Major, Crystal Jones, Jim Hayes, and other activists associated with the PI joined residents in denouncing the Barthelemy administration's public housing demolition plans outlined in the

Rochon Report, in early 1988, the city cut off funding to these disobedient community activists and pushed Jones out of her post in city government. (Major had already resigned before the fallout). Nonetheless, despite their allies falling from grace with the Barthelemy administration, the STRC leadership wanted to continue their relationship with the PI and their promotion of self-help initiatives. As Barbara Major explains:

> [STRC president] Barbara Jackson and them said they wanted [the PI] when [HANO] cut the money. . . . We [Major and Jones] still wanted to work with the [tenant] organizations because we knew the potential that we were dealing with. But we only worked with groups that invite us in. St. Thomas said, "I want to work with you all," but the other [public housing tenant] groups said their money was hinging on [the mayor]. . . . [But] Barbara [Jackson] understood; she understood some of the things that had to hap-pen and so she and her resident council said, "We want to work with you all. . . . We want to do what ya'll talking about doing, about building that capacity for leadership and taking direction from the people."[13]

Jones and Major, as key advisers to the STRC, obviously had differences with Mayor Barthelemy over the pace of restructuring public housing. Nonetheless, PI activists tended to support the same self-help initia-tives and solutions proffered by mainstream political officials. Self-help ideas resonated with the tenant leadership, as well. The struggle was no longer, for both STRC leaders and PI activists, about building a tenants movement to place demands on the state. Rather, the issue was about em-powerment, about taking over responsibilities that had been previously provided, albeit inadequately, by the government. The goal was, as Major explains, "developing tenant leadership to really take charge of all of what was going to happen to them"—that is, to accommodate rather than chal-lenge privatization of the St. Thomas development.

Laying the Institutional Foundation for Neoliberal Reform

In 1988, Barbara Major, Crystal Jones, and Dave Billings accepted the in-vitation of the STRC to work full time with this low-income, black com-munity. To achieve what she termed "self-determination," Barbara Major argued that residents needed to focus on how they could take control of the development rather than simply pressure the government for concessions. Furthermore, as part of "really being in charge," St. Thomas residents needed to reach out to nonprofit agencies and institutions outside the development. This was difficult for residents, Major explains, because "there was such a suspicion made of the outside."[14]

The engagement process with surrounding churches and nonprofits began in 1988 when St. Thomas tenant leaders and advisers began participating in a dialogue initiated by the nearby Trinity Episcopal Church, whose congregation was drawn from a primarily white, upper-middle-class stratum. The meetings brought together homeless providers, St. Thomas residents, and upper-income homeowners to work out differences over the use of Coliseum Square Park (as discussed in chapter 2). The STRC and its advisers participated in these discussions and believed they were a positive start in the process of St. Thomas's developing relationships with the surrounding community. Nonetheless, the relationship continued to be hampered, from the perspective of the STRC and the PI, by inequality and paternalism. A key component of an equal, respectful relationship meant residents's control of the money spent by local churches and nonprofit agencies on behalf of St. Thomas. David Billings calculated that the budget of agencies serving St. Thomas was over $8 million annually. But without control over these resources, many social service agencies were, in the opinion of the PI and STRC, "poverty pimps"—that is, people and institutions making money and a career managing the community's oppression.[15]

To change this unequal relationship, STRC president Barbara Jackson sent, in June 1989, a letter to thirteen social service agencies in the Irish Channel/Lower Garden District area adjacent to St. Thomas. Jackson demanded their attendance at a meeting to discuss their relationship with the St. Thomas community and the issues that divided them.[16] The content of the letter and how it emerged further underscores the influence that PI organizers exercised at St. Thomas. As Major explains:

> One of the things we did a real good job at was helping the [St. Thomas] community understand that they had a right to evaluate those who were supposed to be serving them. And that's what they did. That letter was basically to say, "An evaluation has been done, and we're not satisfied, and we need to talk and renegotiate the relationship" ... an evaluation in terms of "you're serving me but I'm still here pulling this shit, so we need to rediscuss this, you

getting all this money." And that was from the resident council, the leadership. So all they asked was [for the PI activists] to draft this letter—no problem.[17]

After some further prodding by the PI and the STRC, representatives from various churches and social service agencies agreed to attend the meeting. At the initial and subsequent gatherings, which David Billings and Barbara Major chaired, the STRC advisers argued that the power relations between social service agencies and St. Thomas had to change. The agencies had to become accountable to the community. The nonprofits could undergo this transformation, PI and STRC organizers argued, by joining and taking direction from an organization dedicated to the self-determination and liberation of the African American St. Thomas community. The organization—eventually named the St. Thomas/Irish Channel Consortium but better known by its acronym, STICC—would be the guarantor that agencies operating in the community were accountable to the people they allegedly served. STICC's founding statement, which drew heavily from PI ideology, defined what an accountable relationship between nonprofits and the St. Thomas community would be:

> The acceptance of a role that fits within a cultural, political, and social perspective that leads to the liberation of peoples of color from racism, oppression, and cultural subordination. It requires a commitment to the vision of African American and other oppressed people to assume *self-determination over those areas deemed by them to directly affect their lives.*[18] (emphasis added)

STICC became the guarantor that organizations working with St. Thomas residents fulfilled their appropriate role by adhering to this definition of accountability. As Major explains the enforcer role:

> People often say the acronym was STICC, and STICC carried a big *stick.* But I think the reality is the community does have to carry a stick in its initial relationship with institutions, because institutions do what institutions do, and that is protect themselves at all costs, at the expense of the community if allowed. So there was a struggle there, but . . . agencies [also] knew something had to change, not to say they were willing to move easily, but people were open.[19]

While STICC, composed of the STRC, PI activists, and various social service agencies, was technically the enforcer, the PI ideology and cadre dominated the organization. Thus, the latter, in reality, had great influence in
determining what, concretely, constituted support for self-determination
at St. Thomas. Further strengthening the group's ideological influence
and authority was STICC's requirement that all its members or whoever
worked in the community had to go through a People's Institute–led Undoing Racism workshop.[20]

Key to achieving self-determination, from the perspective of STICC
and the PI, was gaining control over the private and public funds coming
into the community. To enable STICC to handle grants, members voted
to incorporate the organization as a nonprofit in April 1990 with the State
of Louisiana and, later that year, obtained a 501(c)(3) designation as a tax-
exempt nonprofit from the IRS. STICC's first major grant was a three-year
$1 million award from the New Orleans–based Institute of Mental Hygiene
(IMH) to work on teen pregnancy. STICC obtained the award after challenging an application by the local office of Planned Parenthood. Barbara
Major, who was elected STICC's first president, and other PI cadre argued
that the Planned Parenthood grant application for an anti–teen pregnancy
program was a prime example of nonprofits' obtaining resources to work
in oppressed communities without the consultation or approval of the
presumed beneficiaries—in this case, the African American St. Thomas
community. In response, acting in its enforcer role STICC wrote a letter
to the IMH asking that the grant be given not to Planned Parenthood but
rather to a consortium of groups led by STICC. The foundation heeded
their call. With the grant, STICC was able to set up the Kuji Center, the
name being taken from the abbreviated version of the Swahili word for
self-determination. The center, located at a city-owned gymnasium and led
by PI activist Crystal Jones, housed STICC's teen pregnancy program and
other social service programs.

The IMH grant was the first of several awards from public and private
sources that STICC garnered (see Table 3.1). One of the most generous
supporters was the Annie E. Casey Foundation. Consistent with what
political scientist Nikol Alexander-Floyd critiques as the "black cultural
pathological paradigm," the influential foundation identified the "family
as the fundamental influence in the lives of children." The foundation
diagnosed "concentrated and persistent poverty" in cities as the major
threat to the "competence and confidence" of families and therefore committed resources "toward helping challenging neighborhoods become

places where children and their families can flourish." In practice, this supposedly profamily initiative provided grants to nonprofits embracing or at least amenable to the deconcentrating poverty agenda of demolishing public housing.[21]

The foundations, consistent with their channeling role, contributed to a new political orientation among St. Thomas tenant leaders and their advisers that represented a subtle but important accommodation to privatization. Increasingly, the focus became one of finding private sources of support, rather than placing responsibility on the state, to address the pressing housing, educational, employment, and other social needs of the St. Thomas community. Instead of confrontation with developers and public officials, cooperation became the watchword. Under these conditions self-determination came to mean control of private funding sources, weaning people from dependence on the state, and, as we will see, collaborating with developers in neighborhood transformation.

Regime Intellectuals at Work

STICC meetings were held, at minimum, once a month but often more frequently. The gatherings began to gain the attention and the interest of not just board members and member agencies but people across New Orleans. David Billings explains what he terms the "STICC phenomena," "At the high point of the energy level in the community and consortium— I mean we would have 120 people at a board meeting—it was incredible there for a while. People from all over would come in to just watch the process." Part of this excitement, according to local journalist and activist Orissa Arend, who attended as an observer in the early years of STICC, was that "the money was flowing in, which is why I think a lot of people were around the table."[22] In addition, she and others attended the meetings, which were dominated by the PI cadre, because it was interesting to see "a laboratory for Undoing Racism" in action. In fact, as PI trainers went around the country and performed antiracism workshops, they would tout STICC and their involvement as a model for community organizing and empowerment.[23] Underscoring the dominance of the PI within STICC, Arend found that

> for the meetings, you know, Ron [Chisom] and Barbara [Major]
> and Diana [all PI trainers] would all provide technical assistance

TABLE 3.1.

Selection of Grants Received by STICC, 1990–2000

Private foundation	Years(s)	Amount	Public agency or program	Year	Amount
IMH	1990–1993	$1 million	CDBG (federal money through city)	1998	$45,000
GNOF	1992	$10,000	Louisiana Office of Public Health	1998	$58,000
Annie Casey	1993–1996	$1 million	—		
Mott	1997–2000	$300,000	Great Expectations (city program)	1997	$111,345
Mid-South	1997	$15,000	HANO	1997	$160,000
Wisner	1999	$20,000	Job Training Partnership Act, through Orleans Private Industry Council	—	n/a
Public Welfare	1998	$50,000	TOP grant from HUD (for STRC)	—	$100,000

SOURCES: *STICC Funding, STICC file, St. Thomas Redevelopment box, Hope House archives; Housing Authority of New Orleans, The New St. Thomas/Lower Garden District HOPE VI/Application (New Orleans: HANO, 1996), 2; Crystal Jones, "The Bottom-up Approach to Collaboration for Social Change: A Case Study of the St. Thomas/Irish Channel Consortium,"* (master's thesis, University of New Orleans, 1993), 130; Author's interview with Don Everard, November 10, 2003, New Orleans; Author's interview with Dave Billings, November 18, 2003, New Orleans.

for what should be the agenda, who should speak, what should be the questions answered, and just got us all to think real strategically about everything. It was very intellectually stimulating to be there.

Former St. Thomas resident Tammy Fleming-White, who was employed in the Kuji center's sex education outreach work and regularly attended STICC meetings, also highlighted the important influence of PI leadership:

They say they took leadership from us, but a lot of times that
was just being said. That is my opinion, because we did not consider ourselves the experts. We did not consider ourselves the
professionals. Yes, we came to meetings. But they would inform
us, and most likely whatever they were telling us we were like,
we would be like, "Oh, that does sound good." So it depended
on the presentation. *If it sounded like something they were for,
because we trusted them and believed in them, we went with it.*[24]
(emphasis added)

Therefore, the PI, whose organizers and ideology had clearly gained leadership over and dominance within STICC, acted, in the Gramscian sense, as
key intellectuals for the black urban regime. Through their ideas and moral
authority gained from years of struggle—that is, by consensus over force—
they helped "channel issue-articulation and agenda-formulation processes
in black politics . . . in ways that reflect the regime's common sense."[25] In
practice, their definition of self-determination came to mean reliance on
and collaboration with elite private foundations and local notables, instead
of organizing tenants to place demands on the state. Yet as Walter Adamson
has argued in a critique of the Gramscian consensus and coercion dichot-
omy, it is better to conceive of these concepts as "endpoints of a continuum
that includes such intermediate positions as constraint (e.g. fear of unemployment), co-optation, and perhaps even Arendt's category of 'authority.'"[26]
Thus the increasing constraints faced by tenants—a form of coercion—
including decreasing government funding and ideological attacks on public
housing, strengthened the ideas of the regime's intellectual deputies and the
course of action they advocated. Further bolstering PI's influence among
residents were the "material bases of consent," the jobs, social services,
trips, and other perks, that foundation grants provided.[27]

Nonetheless, the hegemony, the influence of PI-led STICC over the
"direction of society," was not written in stone.[28] As Stuart Hall emphasizes, "Hegemony is not a state of grace which is instilled forever. [And
neither is it] a formation which incorporates everybody."[29] The next
major challenge was how STICC would deal with what STRC leader Fannie McKnight called "the land issue." That is, how would STICC, whose
"initial agenda was to protect the public housing development from what
everybody could see as a future attack," respond to the growing pressures
by developers?[30] What would self-determination mean under these conditions? The need to address these questions intensified in September

1991, when developers bought seventy-two acres of riverfront property close to the St. Thomas public housing development.

Act II: Riverfront Redevelopment and the Search for Racial Legitimacy

Joseph Canizaro, a banker and real estate developer, has been a key part of the corporate-governing wing of New Orleans's black urban regime since the early 1970s. One example of his political influence is the key role he played in founding the Downtown Development District, the nation's first assessment-based Business Improvement District, created by the State of Louisiana in the mid-1970s.[31] In addition to sitting on various advisory boards and being a generous donor to local and national politicians, he had an especially close relationship with Mayor Maurice Landrieu (1970–1978), who worked for Canizaro's real estate company both before and after leaving office. In fact, Senator William Proxmire's inquiries of Landrieu during his confirmation hearings as HUD secretary in 1979 raised doubts whether he had ever stopped working for his former boss, even while mayor. The land swap deals the city negotiated under Landrieu that generously rewarded Canizaro raised serious questions for the senator from Wisconsin. A further cause for concern was a previously undisclosed real estate deal that Landrieu entered into and maintained with Canizaro while in office, which resulted in a profit of $58,000 for the former mayor after investing "the relatively nominal sum of $300."[32]

Canizaro defended these and other pay-to-play practices, arguing that "you have to participate in this government if you want to get something out of it."[33] These thinly veiled bribery practices did not tarnish Canizaro's image among the city's business class or close off access with elected officials in New Orleans, Baton Rouge, and Washington. He continued to be a central player, as exemplified by his role, along with other leading locally based corporate leaders, in founding the influential, fifty-member New Orleans Business Council in 1985. The business council was an attempt by New Orleans's power elite to create a peak business organization that could dominate city policy making as thoroughly as their counterparts in Central Atlanta Progress.[34] Although Canizaro worked both sides of the political aisle and was particularly close to Democrats in New Orleans, where the party held sway, he was nonetheless most closely connected to the Republican Party. He raised hundreds of thousands of dollars for the GOP, including $200,000 for George W. Bush's 2004 reelection campaign, placing him in the President's elite Ranger fundraising list and providing him regular access to the White House.[35]

In 1991, Canizaro and his company, Columbus Properties, partnered with two other investors to form the New Orleans 2000 Partnership. This consortium, with Canizaro holding a controlling interest, acquired seventy-two acres of riverfront property from the Missouri Pacific Railroad (the MICO tract) on September 10, 1991, for $11 million (see Map 2.1 [p. 32]). The developers envisioned their venture, dubbed the River Park Project, as a way to turn dilapidated wharves and warehouses into hotels, restaurants, upscale housing, convention space, and other high-end uses that would increase the value of the property.[36]

Initially, Canizaro sought out and received support for his project from progentrification interests such as the Coliseum Square Association, other middle-class homeowner associations, and the residential real estate interests allied with them. The ability of Canizaro to cultivate support among small-scale real estate players was exemplified by the enthusiastic reception his plans generated from a lawyer, resident, and owner of several properties in the Lower Garden District, which was adjacent to the River Park Project.

> Life in the inner city gives you lots of [business] opportunities. Whatever comes along I was just interested. . . . I really like development. And I was interested in the proposals. I was interested in watching Canizaro, who is hugely energetic. Interesting, bright man.[37]

With affluent white homeowners on board, Canizaro and his partners now faced one remaining obstacle to realizing their redevelopment plans: the St. Thomas project. Nathan Watson, who Canizaro hired as the coordinator for the River Park Project, explains the obstacle the African American St. Thomas community presented:

> We spent some time . . . working with [non–St. Thomas] neighborhood groups, realizing the other obstacles we faced were the deteriorated neighborhood around it. There was a lot of good things, a lot of good potential there, but there was a lot of [pause, searching for tactful language] ugliness and a lot of deterrent to development. *And it would be difficult to attract out-of-town developers with the kind of blight that we had around the property,*

immediately, and also with the St. Thomas public housing develop-
ment five or six blocks away, half empty, and perceived as a hot bed
of crime.[38] (emphasis added)

How would developers remove the "blight" of St. Thomas? This was no
easy task. Public housing developments, as geographers Christine Cook
and Mickey Lauria note, "present a more intractable barrier to regeneration strategies" than do privately owned low-income neighborhoods,
which do not require as much government intervention to muscle out the
poor.[39] This political problem was further complicated by St. Thomas's
history of combativeness and the fact that the black political leadership
legitimated itself as the voice and defender of the city's black majority.
Urban regeneration efforts could not simply be justified by invoking
the jobs, taxes, and tourism mantra. Consent would have to be won at
St. Thomas. Canizaro soon realized this.

> [Canizaro] probably brought some [white, middle-class groups]
> into his office to meet with them. That is exactly right. He did bring
> some into his boardroom for a meeting and had about twenty
> people there, from various neighborhood people. . . . [But he soon]
> realized that this was only half of the picture, that it wouldn't get
> done. *There would be too many political obstacles to get anything pos-*
> *itive if it didn't include everyone. So it wasn't going to work if we just*
> *had the preservationists, just the ahh, the ahh, the ahh, the white folk*
> *there at the table. We needed more than that.*[40] (emphasis added)

As emphasized by Nathan Watson, Canizaro's project coordinator, developers deemed the participation and consent of the black, working-class
St. Thomas community as critical for success. Watson added that "we
probably could have pushed it through" without the participation of St.
Thomas, but "it would be a whole lot easier if it was handled in an efficient
manner." These sentiments seem to be standard among modern urban
elites when imposing racially charged urban restructuring. For example,
financier Felix Rohatyn, an important part of New York City's power elite,
explains the rationale behind many business leaders' supporting the city's
first black mayor, David Dinkins, back in the early 1990s.

> On balance people in the business community think that re-
> duced tension has to be the highest priority; that it's impossible

to govern with any requirement for *sacrifice* unless the people who are being asked to sacrifice *feel* they are being treated fairly.[41] (emphasis added)

Political scientist Adolph Reed, consistent with Rohatyn, has argued that black urban regimes are attractive to progrowth coalitions precisely because of their ability to create this feeling, because of "their peculiar skill at derailing opposition to developmental initiatives and cultivating loyalty or acquiescence of the growth machine's victims"—of whom working-class African Americans tend to be the largest component.[42] Nonetheless, as the St. Thomas case demonstrates, we must also appreciate the role of the nonprofits, in addition to black elected officials. The former are critical for explaining the power of the regime to successfully "sacrifice"—to use Rohatyn's words—its most loyal supporters at the altar of contemporary urban redevelopment.

James Singleton, the African American city councilman whose district encompassed St. Thomas and the Canizaro-owned riverfront acreage, also agreed that the project had to be accomplished in what Watson characterized as an "efficient" manner—that is, with the consent of the St. Thomas community. He conveyed this message to Canizaro, as well. Underscoring the close relationship between black political officials and the white corporate elite—a hallmark of black urban regimes—Singleton causally says that Canizaro and he were "close friends." Singleton explains the directives he gave Canizaro on how the project should be approached politically:

When he came in and talked about what he wanted to do . . . he talked to me before he bought it and we talked . . . after he bought it. One of the requirements I had with him, with anything he wanted to do, he had to involve the neighborhood. And not just St. Thomas . . . but the entire neighborhood, and that's why the coalition was kind of put together. That's why they give him a lot of credit for working with [the community] and doing things, *but behind the scenes that was something I insisted.* . . . I always did feel that strongly. Citizen participation, citizen input, and *black participation in particular* is something that had been ignored all those years, and that was one of the agreements we had . . . that he was going to have to do that. Otherwise, when he came back to get something down at the city council, I was going to be looking the other way. . . . *We had a general agreement that was there, and is still there, in order for him to work.*[43] (emphasis added)

Others, such as the late Mildred Young, a black, middle-class civic activist, "let Canizaro know that he could not ignore this group [STICC and STRC]: 'they're too close to where you want to do your stuff and they can, *they can wreck you,'*" she implored.[44]

As these quotes point out, Canizaro, Singleton, and their advisers were in agreement that the removal of St. Thomas had to be dealt with carefully. Their approach to this conflict was consistent with Mary Jackman's argument, made in her study of contemporary forms of racial, gender, and class relations, that "groups who dominate social relationships strive to keep hostility out of those relationships, not in order to foster equality, but rather to deepen and secure inequality. They have learned that persuasion is better than force."[45] Indeed, Larry Schmidt, who was later hired by Canizaro as part of an effort to cultivate community support for the project, explains that real estate developers have put these theoretical insights, outlined by Jackman, into practice:

Joe [Canizaro]. . . was interested in redeveloping his land and *he knew he had to get consensus.* . . . These days [post–civil rights era] developers don't just come in off the street and develop something in isolation . . . it has to be very transparent and Joe knew that. . . .[46] (emphasis added)

To eliminate or at least contain what Jackman called "hostility" and to build what Schmidt identified as the all-important "consensus" on redevelopment, regime elites needed a peace partner. Councilman Singleton, who would play the key role in bringing the two sides together, was confident that he could find a reasonable partner at St. Thomas. Singleton points to his long relationship with the St. Thomas Resident Council leaders, their key adviser Barbara Major, and their growing maturity for his positive assessment:

You get to know people like Barbara Major, who is very articulate, very smart, *who used to be a rabble-rouser much more than she is now.* [Laughs]. You just get to know those people over time, and you develop those relationships. And when you know what they're doing in the community, you always . . . they do many things.

If something comes up and I should know about it, somebody
would call me up and let me know. And if something was going
on in their community, then I would always try and maintain
that relationship, and that open dialogue, so they could know and
participate. (emphasis added)

Judging from their recent work, Singleton no longer considered the St.
Thomas leaders and their activist allies, including Major, irresponsible
and unreliable radicals. Rather, he now viewed them as "mature" community leaders who were ready to face reality and "recognize that if you
are going to survive in New Orleans and improve, then the businesses had
to survive and improve."[47] That is, the nonprofit leaders accepted the key
nostrum of growth politics, that local governments must, above all, "enhance the economic attractiveness of their locality . . . and entice mobile
wealth to enter their boundaries."[48]

Constructing the Black Urban Regime from Below

How did the relationship between Canizaro and STICC first begin? That
is, what were the concrete steps involved in developing a relationship between the governing elite, the nonprofit sector, and black public housing residents to push through redevelopment? Barbara Major, the STICC
president, explains how Councilman Singleton played the key role in bro-
kering a 1992 meeting with Canizaro, which was attended and supported
by city and HANO officials:

Apparently, Jim Singleton knew Canizaro and the fact that he was
meeting with the folk that had money and stuff. . . . And Jim Singleton said to [Canizaro and his white, middle-class allies] that maybe
we need to talk. But I don't know if they listened—apparently
not. . . . So Jim said to us, "These folk are meeting"—because we
didn't know they were meeting—"and ya'll need to be a part of
those conversations." So we wrote a letter—as chair of the consortium I wrote a letter—to the city and every developer that I even
heard of to say that it is imperative that you be at this community
meeting because if you doing something in this community without the community, it ain't going to happen. And so they all came.
It blew my mind. That's the meeting at the Lyons Center.[49]

In April 1992, STICC hosted a public meeting between Canizaro and the St. Thomas leaders and their allies. The STICC board, without much debate, supported this initiative spearheaded by Barbara Major and the two key tenant leaders, Barbara Jackson and Fannie McKnight. "It only made sense" to meet with and try to collaborate with developers, argued a leading STICC board member, a sentiment that reflected the prevailing opinion of board members. Class cooperation was the prevailing "sense held in common" of the social service agencies that made up STICC.[50]

Approximately seventy-five people attended the meeting, including members and representatives of the Coliseum Square Association, the Preservation Resource Center, HANO, HUD, and the city planning commission; Councilman Singleton and other city officials; St. Thomas residents; and STICC members. Barbara Major opened the meeting, stating, "We understand ya'll got big plans for us up here. But none of ya'll talked to the people up here. So we want to know ... what ya'll got planned." Canizaro, the private developer and center of attention, gave his presentation, in which he made clear that "he wanted to make money" but added that he would cooperate with the community in the process and accommodate their needs, as well.[51]

After the meeting, Major, other PI activists, and the STRC leadership met and discussed their reaction to the presentation. Unlike another developer, Pres Kabacoff, who made it appear that he was "coming to help save all these pitiful poor people," Canizaro was open about his agenda.

> Canizaro said, "I'm here to make money." So we said, "You know what? He's more honest." ... But all this other bullshit, "ya'll want to help all the poor people," that was a bunch of crap. If you want to make money, just be honest with us. We know it's not always going to work out, but at least we know where you're coming from. *And that's when the relationship between Barbara [Jackson], Fannie, and the resident council and Joe Canizaro began.*[52] (emphasis added)

Working to coordinate the interests of public housing tenants and developers was accepted as the only realistic course of action. The STICC board concurred, ratifying Major's and the STRC's decision.

Following the STICC and STRC decision to collaborate, a series of meetings were held between Canizaro, the STRC, David Billings, and Barbara

Major. Canizaro would meet them both at his office and even at the STRC office, located in the St. Thomas development. The willingness of Canizaro to venture into St. Thomas and hold meetings—a no-go zone for many whites and blacks, let alone the city's most powerful developer—impressed tenant leaders. David Billings further explains Canizaro's skill at gaining trust and developing rapport with both the resident council leaders and Major:

> One of the first meetings I remember with Canizaro . . . was a smaller group . . . [with only] the resident council and STICC [members]. . . . At the end of the meeting, he would spend a lot of time . . . just get to try and know who the resident council was, what is the resident council. So at one meeting, after the meeting he would get kind of personal and say, "You know, a lot of people think I'm connected, because I'm Italian, to organized crime," and I remember someone saying, being kind of humorous, "What we're afraid of is not organized crime. It's the disorganized crime." . . . And we'd go back and forth, [and] he would say, "You might hear I'm a Mafioso," and then someone, maybe Barbara Major, said, "Well, you might hear we're communists," and he said, "I did," and she said, "Well, let's just see where this leads." That kind—he took a lot of time. He would spend a lot of time to get to know the resident leadership and . . . so Canizaro was very compelling in that way.[53]

On the surface these interactions were playful bantering. On another level these exchanges were deeply political. They were part of the critical work of constructing the black urban regime from below. The exchanges between Canizaro, Major, and the other STRC leaders was part of building the relationships, the bonds of trust, necessary for a consensual subterfuge for "Negro removal." Canizaro built on these initial meetings to further develop his personal ties among influential St. Thomas residents. He began to spend time, "much more than you thought he would," Billings remarks, with not only Major but STRC leaders, particularly Fannie McKnight. According to resident council member Louise Franklin, Canizaro became the "godfather" to many residents: "If you needed something, he would get it. . . . There was just something about him. . . . He was just too nice. My grandfather always warned me to watch out for those that want to befriend you. . . . There was always something about him."[54] Canizaro, remarks another STRC officer, "would be there for residents . . . and was particularly generous at Christmas time."[55] Fannie McKnight, who became the dominant force on the STRC after longtime tenant council president Barbara Jackson reduced her activity drastically in the summer of 1992 after her son was murdered, developed a particularly strong bond with Canizaro. McKnight underscores the allegiance and support that Canizaro was able to cultivate among key resident leaders:

> I don't care what nobody say about Joe Canizaro! I don't care what they call him. I don't care if he's going to get a little money. He was straight-up forward with me. He was straight; he was true to me. He was real with me. He told me what he was about.... He came up to me and let me know he was going to make money one way or the other. But he was honest enough to help me to bring my process what I want for my people.[56]

By 1993, Canizaro was successful in developing a relationship and even trust with St. Thomas, particularly among key leaders such as McKnight and Major. His ability to gain access to the community without being denounced was due in great part to the change in thinking by Major and her collaborators that Councilman Singleton had highlighted and praised. The PI activists had come to the conclusion that they had to accommodate themselves to the neoliberal economic and political realities rather than resort to knee-jerk protest: "For us, we know change is going to come. You can either be a part of it or not. You know what I'm saying. *For some of us it's going outside of ourselves*" (emphasis added).[57] Therefore, due to this newfound realism and the material benefits Canizaro, private foundations, and the local government were able to deliver, New Orleans's leading real estate developer was able to extend his base of support. From his initial beachhead of white, middle-class homeowners, small businesses, and professionals in the Irish Channel/Lower Garden District area, he could, by mid-1992, count among his allies the St. Thomas leadership and their most influential advisers. The next section examines how this alliance and the new ideologies and nonprofit organizations that undergirded it were maintained as they worked out a class, racial, and spatial restructuring plan.

Act III: Nonprofits, Consultants, and Forging Agreement on the "Roadmap"

Initially, the STRC, Major, and Billings wanted discussions about redevelopment plans for St. Thomas to be conducted under the umbrella of

STICC. Canizaro and the middle-class homeowners objected, however. As STICC member Don Everard explains, "Some of the other groups were not willing to take part in STICC ... so that, like the Coliseum Square Association, going to workshops with the resident council was just not going to happen." Major concurs, arguing that white homeowners and businesses "weren't ready to join an organization like STICC and certainly not ready to deal with leadership of color. So why would we want to fight with them and have them there?" STICC conceded. This was a major concession. STICC's raison d'etre was to guarantee that St. Thomas residents would determine what the future of the neighborhood would be. Nonetheless, the leadership, both of the STRC and STICC, compromised on this important point, the first of many compromises they would make.

In June 1992, the STRC, STICC, HANO, Canizaro, and middle-class neighborhood association representatives held a follow-up meeting to the historic April gathering. At this summit the participants agreed to form another nonprofit, the Community Resource Partnership (CRP), to coordinate the redevelopment plans of the neighborhood. STICC would be able to send representatives to the CRP, and in turn the CRP would join STICC. Nonetheless, the discussions regarding land redevelopment and housing—issues critical to St. Thomas's future and ones that gave rise to STICC—would be dealt with by the CRP.

The key issue that divided the CRP, composed as it was of homeowner and small business associations, Canizaro, social service agencies in STICC, and the STRC, was the future of the St. Thomas public housing development. Canizaro, who appointed himself chairman, presided over the CRP meetings, and bankrolled the group for the first couple years, did not openly state his views on the topic but rather tended to sit back and act as the "honest broker."[58] Yet the white homeowners and businesses at the meetings were clear that they wanted St. Thomas to come down. St. Thomas tenant leader Fannie McKnight's reflection underscores the depth of the racial and class gulf separating black public housing residents and white homeowners: "The thing was we had a big battle going on between knocking them down and renovating. The residents ... were part of the ones for not tearing them down, for renovating."

To settle the differences, Canizaro, the mediator, who enjoyed increasing legitimacy with the STRC, offered the good offices of the Urban Land Institute (ULI), a think tank and lobbyist for the real estate industry. The irony of using the ULI, founded in 1936 to, in part, oppose the construction of St. Thomas and other public housing developments then emerging, did not seem to bother the CRP chairman, who was also, incidentally, a past chairman of this national real estate organization: "Joe said he had an organization, the land institute, and he said, 'How about I bring this organization down to see, ask everybody how they feel' ... so he brought his people."[59] Due to the goodwill and trust Canizaro had developed with the STRC and STICC, these organizations gave the green light to the ULI study. Canizaro arranged for the ULI to send in a ten-person team—with the tab picked up by Canizaro, Freeport McMoran Corp, Gulf Coast Bank, and Trinity Episcopal Church—to meet with the CRP members and lay out a redevelopment plan for St. Thomas and the surrounding neighborhood. The initiative was part of ULI's Inner-City Building Program, begun in 1993 "to involve the private sector more extensively in inner city issues and bring resources of ULI's membership to bear on urban problems."[60] "Inner city" was code for poor black communities, particularly public housing. With new federal legislation just coming on line to open up valuable "inner-city" public housing property (as further explored in chapter 4), the ULI's Inner-City Building Program was to help capitalize on these new opportunities. Thus, through Canizaro's intersession, STICC and the STRC helped legitimate ULI's agenda of opening up public housing to the private real estate market.

Vince Lane, then director of the Chicago Housing Authority and a nationally recognized supporter of public housing privatization, chaired the ULI delegation, all of whose members were drawn from banking and real estate.[61] Through five days of group meetings or "charrettes," as the delegation called them, the ULI panelists met with over two hundred residents, advisers, homeowners, and public officials to take their comments. Tenant leaders gave tours of the project for panelists, further solidifying their commitment to the privatization process and bonds with Canizaro (see Figure 3.1). The ULI followed up their five days of intensive meetings with a report on what should be done to St. Thomas and the surrounding area. The report's key recommendations were "intended to serve as a *roadmap* for CRP's actions and activities over the next few years" (emphasis added).[62]

The ULI report on St. Thomas called for downsizing the development from 1,510 to 950 units, with half of these reserved for families making below 30 percent of the area median income (the income level of over 90 percent of residents). Expansion of homeownership programs and use of the Section 8 voucher program were recommended to deal with displaced residents. In addition, the report recommended that the new development be privately owned, with residents holding a 51 percent interest in a

FIGURE 3.1. Building the black urban regime from below. St. Thomas Resident Council vice-president Fannie McKnight, in the center, leads Urban Land Institute panel members and others on a tour of the St. Thomas project as part of their privatization study in December 1993. To the right of McKnight is developer Joseph Canizaro. Second from the right is the chairperson of the panel and the then chairman of the Chicago Housing Authority, Vincent Lane. In the background, behind Canizaro, is key tenant advisor David Billings. Panel member Lewis Bolan, a real estate consultant, is to the right of Lane. Photograph courtesy of the Urban Land Institute, used with permission.

"joint venture" with a private developer. To finance the redevelopment, the report advised applying for a HOPE VI grant, the then new federal government program, and Low Income Housing Tax Credits. These public sources of funding would help developers leverage private sector borrowing. Finally, in further support of privatization, the ULI emphasized that the CRP "must be in charge of the process of community renewal," which would be achieved by obtaining governmental "discretionary authority over zoning, historic preservation and neighborhood revitalization."[63]

The report was a classic neoliberal document that outlined both the rollback or destructive phase of neoliberal state reform, as well as the second, rollout or creative stage.[64] The redevelopment would drastically retrench the low-income portion of the development (rollback), while creating a new mixed-income component with market-rate units (rollout) financed through public–private financing mechanisms. A voucher program would deal with the displaced. The ULI privatization plan also included a populist or what Gary Teeple would label a "people's capitalist" veneer by including tenants as co-owners and managers of the new development, although details were kept vague.[65] Finally, in one of the most important yet understudied parts of neoliberalism, the ULI emphasized that the redevelopment process should be insulated from democratic pressure. The nongovernmental Community Resource Partnership would usurp the role of the city council, HANO, and other governmental agencies and thus move "governance out of the routinized channels of the formal state," where opportunities for popular input are greater.[66] New Orleans's local black political leadership had overseen and supported the privatization of the planning process by turning it over to Canizaro and the foundation-funded CRP and STICC. The ULI, by awarding greater powers to the CRP, wanted to push the process even further.

Securing and Maintaining Consent to Privatization

To ensure strong support for the ULI recommendations among the tenant leadership, Canizaro hired Vince Lane while he was still head of the Chicago Housing Authority.[67] Lane came to national prominence in the late 1980s, imposing an authoritarian rule, which received bipartisan support in Washington, over black public housing residents. Under his so-called Operation Clean Sweep, he ordered security guards to "root out gangs and squatters" by making raids on apartments—what he called "emergency inspections"—and by regularly stopping and frisking "suspicious" residents. Lane could rely on support from Washington, first from President George H. W. Bush's HUD secretary, Jack Kemp, who lauded him as "one of the most progressive public housing leaders in the country," and later from Henry Cisneros, President Clinton's appointee for the post.[68] Underscoring Lane's growing national prominence, the Bush administration in 1989 appointed the Chicago Housing Authority director as cochair of the National Commission on Distressed Public Housing. Organizations composed of residents and allies, such as the Campaign to End the CHA Lockdowns, as well as the American Civil Liberties Union, protested in the streets and challenged in the courts Lane's policies that flagrantly violated the constitutional rights of public housing residents. Yet Lane was also able to cultivate some support among residents for his policies. His political abilities impressed New Orleans developers like Joe Canizaro and Pres Kabacoff, who wanted to dismantle and remove public housing as part of their neoliberal urban redevelopment agendas.[69]

By 1994, as sociologist Mary Pattillo observed, Lane had become a fervent advocate of demolishing public housing.[70] Aware of his background and political skills, Canizaro touted the Chicago Housing Authority head to the St. Thomas tenant leaders, Billings, and Major and personally chose Lane to be part of the New Orleans ULI delegation.

> [Canizaro] was saying that these people are coming in from this group that he is a part of, and which we would learn as the ULI, and he would mention names like Vince Lane as having all this expertise in the public housing wars. . . . [Lane] had this experience in hearing what the residents wanted and [what] they were dreaming about, and then they would put the plans to paper.[71]

The white elite, especially in real estate, as this quote suggests, are constantly looking for and promoting new "talent" to legitimate and help impose racially charged redevelopment. "Whites need blacks," as Stephen Steinberg has argued in his critique of the role played by the conservatizing Bayard Rustin, "to provide ideological cover for their regressive policies."[72] In the post–civil rights era in particular, developers see placing a black imprimatur on their plans as crucial to success. Though the People's Institute organizers were important in this respect, Lane provided added legitimacy. He helped win residents, as David Billings explains, to his new vision of public housing, and what an ally he could be:

> I remember meeting [Lane] in Ms. McKnight's kitchen. . . . He would begin to talk about this innovative housing program that was coming down the pipe, that was the best piece of housing legislation that he had ever seen, and he had had a part in it. He had been brought in by the Clinton administration . . . and he had been on the cover of *Newsweek*. . . . Lane was at that time kind of a guiding light . . . in bringing out all the possibilities embedded in federal language that the residents could possibly obtain through HOPE VI. . . . *So the residents began to move to a vision of a whole*

new neighborhood, a whole new neighborhood ownership pattern,
that the residents would comprise all that sort of thing and that
there would be a mixed-income area. (emphasis added)

Camille Strachan, a white member of the CRP and owner of several properties near St. Thomas, also appreciated the legitimacy and political cover
Lane provided.

Vince Lane is a very charismatic person. I can remember him
standing in the middle of St. Thomas saying things had to change.
And I think coming from Vince Lane it was more convincing
than coming from [pause] any homeowner in the Coliseum
Square [Association].

Partly due to the work of Lane, whose involvement Barbara Major, David
Billings, and other members of STICC did not oppose, the STRC came
out strongly in support of the ULI plan. At the CRP's April 1994 meeting,
members unanimously endorsed the ULI recommendations.

Although the leadership of the STRC was fully on board with redevelopment, there was much more reticence among the some eight hundred families that still called St. Thomas home in 1994.[73] Therefore, the challenge,
from the perspective of the tenant leadership, was, "How do we get people
to buy into this? You know, How do we get people to be a part of this process?"[74] To help garner broader support for the redevelopment plans, the
STRC and their advisers employed STICC's social service apparatus. For
example, STICC's Plain Talk program to prevent teenage pregnancy had
a team of outreach workers, called "walkers-and-talkers," that informed
residents about various social services available to them.[75] These outreach
workers, who "moved through the neighborhood . . . passing out information on one hand about STDs," David Billings explains, were also used
as "organizers that would say, 'Hey, you know we got a meeting Monday
night?' and would try to go into homes and talk about the *dreams of St.
Thomas* and get people's ideas—you know, different kinds of things" (emphasis added). In addition, the "home health parties" that walkers and
talkers organized to discuss sex education, were also used as an opportunity to explain the on-going re-development plans, and inform residents
about future meetings to discuss the "New St. Thomas."

There were other efforts at outreach. Organizers used the St. Thomas youth newsletter, *What's Happening,* published with support from the STRC and Hope House, a local Catholic social service agency, to sell redevelopment. Fannie McKnight would often go through the development with a bullhorn to announce various meetings that the STRC and STICC were holding regarding the "New St. Thomas." Nonetheless, despite the best efforts to use the STICC social service infrastructure to sell redevelopment, many residents remained skeptical. David Billings's recollections emphasize the difficulties STICC and STRC officials had in getting buy in among many St. Thomas residents:

> We had just constant development-wide meetings, you know. . . .
> There was a lot of, kind of, [a] combination of . . . residents that
> were very hopeful, that maybe this can work, but there was a lot
> of hopelessness, too. They had been betrayed many times, and
> you know there was cynicism, but at various times there was . . .
> community meetings that were sometimes very well attended,
> other times not very well attended.

Fannie McKnight also acknowledges significant distrust with the "roadmap":

> The residents wanted it. They wanted everything we said. . . .
> They had a few kinks in it, you know, they didn't . . . [They felt] it
> wouldn't go nowhere. It wasn't going to 'mount to nowhere. But
> we still took their voice into it. All they wanted . . . is for housing
> to fix up their apartment.

Many did not buy the merits of the cross-class alliance advocated by the STRC and their advisers. Consent to redevelopment had only gone so far.

Theorizing the Role of Nonprofits

Studies informed by black urban regime theory are concerned with how, within the context of a majority black city and black-led political system, "entrenched patterns of racialized inequality" are legitimated and reproduced.[76] For example, in his study of Maynard Jackson, Atlanta's first black mayor, political scientist Adolph Reed points to the discursive powers and racial legitimacy of black mayors as key to obscuring the real winners and losers of the procorporate neoliberal agenda. Central "to cementing blacks into the pro-development coalition," Reed argues, was the ability of Maynard Jackson and other black office holders to shift

> black response to policy debate away from substantive [material] concerns with potential outcomes and toward protection of racial image and status, as embodied in the idiosyncratic agenda of the black officials. In this way it becomes possible for black officials to maintain support from both their black constituents and the development elites that systematically disadvantage them.[77]

This study, examining development conflicts in the 1990s, after twenty years of black mayors in New Orleans, and the deepening of the neoliberal agenda, provides new insights into how inequality is reproduced. The St. Thomas case suggests that in addition to the elected political leadership, nonprofit, grassroots organizations allied to a regime also perform a vital function. The critical role nonprofits play in governing is underscored in the three turning points over the 1988–1994 period: (1) the ideological and organizational changes, (2) the political alliance forged with developers, and (3) the approval of a privatization and downsizing plan. In all three periods nonprofits helped cultivate critical black working-class support, or at least acquiescence, to the procorporate neoliberal development agenda. It was not so much the black elected and appointed officials but rather the nonprofits who were the crucial mediators who helped convert the concerns of the black public housing residents "into forms that fit into—or at least [posed] no threat to—the imperatives of larger . . . pro-business, pro-growth priorities."[78] Marrying free market ideas of privatization with those of self-determination and empowerment, the nonprofit leaders helped to sell support for privatization that was key to the regime's redevelopment agenda.

Geographer and urban theorist David Harvey has argued that capitalist elites have employed both coercive—including military dictatorships—and consensual measures and techniques to impose and implant key neoliberal reforms, such as the privatization of public services. Central to the success of the latter strategy has been the ability of the neoliberals to package their agenda as progressive by drawing on one of the central ideological strains of the 1960s—the demand for greater individual freedom. Neoliberal ideologues have effectively captured, as part of the battle of ideas, the "ideals of individual freedom" while ditching the other fundamental demand of the 1960s—social justice—and used them as an ideological battering ram "against the interventionist and regulatory practices of the [welfare] state."[79] In the case of public housing privatization at St. Thomas, the nonprofits and real estate interests, in a prime example of what geographer David Wilson describes as the "contingent . . . improvisational nature of urban neoliberal governance," were able to draw on another important element of the 1960s libratory movements, as well, that of self-determination for African Americans.[80] But rather than the formulators of neoliberal ideology being elite think tanks, it was instead supposedly grassroots nonprofits who helped forge a hybrid form that combined pro-market ideas with antiracist notions. These two ideological strains were, in the case of St. Thomas, complementary rather than contradictory. Indeed, the free-market agenda was required to operationalize self-determination in this poor African American community through tenant ownership and the management of St. Thomas.

This ideological packaging developed at St. Thomas and, by extension, its intellectual purveyors became a political—that is, a material—force in the way they "[oriented] and set limits on human action by establishing codes of conduct which [organized] entire populations."[81] This ideology helped to *structurate* the action of residents toward developers and the nonprofits and away from building alliances with other tenants, HANO workers, and antiregime community and labor groups. The political choices made by the nonprofit and tenant leadership worked to obscure rather than make transparent the racial and class biases of privatization and the black-led city government supporting neoliberal public housing reform. Tenant leaders and advisers followed the path of inter-class collaboration, guaranteeing that privatization would take place in what Canizaro aid Nathan Watson and Councilman Singleton deemed an all-important "efficient" manner. Consensually introducing reforms avoided the disruption that could have doomed the project, in particular, and destablized the political system in general.[82] The process became an efficient one because by entering into the elaborate planning procedures, the tenants and their advisers were "[guided] . . . into a narrowly circumscribed form of political action, and precisely the form for which they [were] least equipped."[83] Being effective in these types of negotiations, as Francis Fox Piven argues in her critique of advocacy planning, requires "powerful group support, stable organization, professional staff and money—precisely those resources which the poor do not have."[84] In the St. Thomas case, though, residents and their advisers were able to garner these resources. Nonetheless, the grants, technical support, and relationships with developers, foundations, and local government were predicated on being responsible—in other words, on maintaining support for privatization and elite-defined redevelopment, albeit with a progressive, antiracist veneer. If residents and advisers had failed to be "politically mature," their elite sponsors would have quickly cut off funds and political support. Thus, through entering negotiations, the St. Thomas tenant's movement, historically the city's most combative, was diverted from the types of political action that had been most effective in gaining real material concessions and power—disruption in the streets and boardrooms. By entering into the planning process, the residents conceded, on the counsel of their advisers, this key resource that they controlled.

Foundations, Nonprofits, and Neoliberal Capitalism

The foundations, who Joan Roelofs calls the "planning and coordinating arm" of the nonprofit sector, provided the key financial support for STICC. Unlike during the 1960s, when the federal government took the leading role in funding a whole series of antipoverty community organizations, foundations play a more pivotal role in pacification efforts under neoliberalism. The foundations, as evinced in the symbiotic relationship established with nonprofits at St. Thomas, are indicative of the so-called third sector. The nonprofits and foundations that compose this sector "essentially function," as Joan Roelofs argues, "as a protective layer of capitalism." One key element of this prophylactic role is the third sector's capacity to co-opt, "to provide jobs and benefits for radicals willing to become pragmatic."[85] In the *Communist Manifesto,* Marx and Engels, in the section "Conservative, or Bourgeois Socialism," identifies these actors and the role they play in capitalist societies:

> A part of the bourgeoisie is desirous of redressing social grievances, in order to secure the continued existence of bourgeois society. To this section belongs economists, philanthropists, humanitarians, improvers of the conditions of the working class, organizers of charity ... hole-and-corner reformers of every imaginable kind.[86]

Under the neoliberal stage of capitalism, the bourgeoisie has not dispensed with these "hole-and-corner reformers." Rather, in their progressive, antiracist form, the bourgeoisie increasingly relies on them to stabilize their rule. In the context of expanding privatization, poor people displacement, and state social service dismantlement, we can expect that foundations and their nonprofit acolytes will play an increasingly important role in helping to smooth the way for neoliberal restructuring and managing the social fallout.

4

No Hope in HOPE VI

*Dismantling Public Housing from the
Nation to the Neighborhood*

> If you break the law, you no longer have a home in public housing,
> one strike and you're out. That should be the law everywhere in
> America.
>
> —PRESIDENT WILLIAM CLINTON, MARCH 23, 1996

> We need . . . to send a message to public housing tenants that
> we are going to make their neighborhood safe, and if anyone
> is involved in drugs in those neighborhoods, they are going to
> forfeit their right to public housing.
>
> —MAYOR MARC MORIAL, JANUARY 23, 1996

> Penal expansion in the United States . . . is at bottom a *political
> project*, a core component of the retooling of public authority
> suited to fostering the advance of neoliberalism.
>
> —LOÏC WACQUANT, *PUNISHING THE POOR:
> THE NEOLIBERAL GOVERNMENT OF SOCIAL INSECURITY*

"The era of big government is over," proclaimed President Clinton at his
1996 State of the Union address. He meant business. In his speech Clinton
demanded that Congress finalize a bill to scale back welfare—which he
signed that same year—and reaffirmed his commitment to further budget
cuts. Yet in the same speech, the Democratic Party leader underscored that
"more police and punishment [was] important" as he highlighted the suc-
cesses and continuing commitment to reaching his administration's goal
of 100,000 federally financed police on America's streets and expanding
the policing and prosecutorial powers of law enforcement to stop, search,

arrest, charge, and imprison. One of the new weapons Clinton unveiled for prosecuting the war on crime was the so-called one strike and you're out policy for public housing residents—and not other recipients of governmental assistance—merely accused of committing a crime. While Clinton touted his shrinking of the social service arm of government, his "'tough on crime' policies resulted in the largest increase in federal and state prison inmates of any president in American history."[1]

New Orleans mayor Marc Morial (1994–2002) was in the House of Representatives chamber at the U.S. capitol to hear the president announce his crime and public housing initiatives. The attendance by New Orleans's third consecutively elected African American chief executive and eldest son of the city's first black mayor underscored that the federal government and the black-led urban regime in New Orleans were, for the most part, on the same page with regard to public housing. Both Clinton and Morial agreed that the "era of big government" in the form of public housing needed to end. Furthermore, Morial concurred with the president's get-tough policy with public housing residents. Morial's hearty endorsement, cited in the chapter epigraph, highlights their support for strengthening the coercive powers of government to facilitate the downsizing of public housing. Indeed, although the Reagan administration authorized one-strike public housing evictions in 1988, "the sad fact is," Clinton lamented at the March 1996 One Strike Crime Symposium he hosted at the White House, "that in most places in this country, one strike has not been carried out."[2] He aggressively worked to change that, as his HUD secretary, Henry Cisneros, put real teeth into enforcing one strike. The administration would not encounter any opposition to this policy from Marc Morial or other elements of the U.S. post–civil rights black urban political leadership.

While Clinton and Morial were both in agreement on the need to dismantle public housing, they still had to figure out *how* they would reach their goal, both nationally (Clinton) and locally (Morial). How, politically, would they sell and implement their agenda? How could they legitimate a displacement policy whose major targets would be low-income African American households, one of their most loyal constituencies? They could not rely solely on coercion. Both the country's "first black president"— a title awarded to Clinton by renowned African American author Toni Morrison—and New Orleans's third black mayor had to somehow package the plan to downsize public housing as a benevolent measure. What, therefore, would be the specific policy measures—the mix of coercion, concessions, and ideological obfuscation—employed in the dismantle-ment and dispersal process? Further complicating the process were intra-state conflicts. Although New Orleans and Washington were in agreement on the aims of public housing reform, there was still contention over what level of government would control the process. How would conflict be managed and authority be divided? Finally, while the national and local government erected the scaffolding for dismantling public housing, there was still the question of how it would play at the neighborhood level. How would a final redevelopment plan be worked out on the ground at St. Thomas? Would residents and their nonprofit allies finally sign off on and legitimate a privatization deal?

HOPE VI and the Reform of Public Housing

The Clinton administration's HOPE VI program became the key vehicle for downsizing and dismantling public housing in the 1990s. The Clinton initiative, which would find a receptive audience in New Orleans, was consistent with the main thrust of federal public housing policy since the 1970s, which had been one of cutbacks, privatization, and "devolution of both authority and funds from the federal government to local authori-ties."[3] The specific origins of HOPE VI date back to 1989, when the U.S. Congress passed legislation to establish the National Commission on Se-verely Distressed Public Housing to ostensibly address what they termed "severely distressed" public housing. In its final 1992 report, the commis-sion—cochaired by Vince Lane, then chairman of the Chicago Housing Authority—estimated that approximately 86,000 units, or 6 percent of the nation's 1.4 million public housing stock, could be termed severely distressed. The commission's report defined severely distressed public housing developments very broadly as complexes with residents that had low levels of earned income, high crime levels, "management difficulties" such as high vacancies and move-out rates, and excessive scale or density.[4]

To address the unclearly defined distressed developments—a number that would continue to increase from the original estimates—the com-mission recommended creating mixed-income communities to replace "concentrations of poverty." The new developments, as opposed to the old public housing model of allocating housing to only low-income resi-dents, would include a mix of tenants paying market and subsidized rates. To institute this restructuring, the commission outlined three key neo-liberal reforms: (1) public–private partnerships to finance redevelopment,

(2) for-profit and nonprofit management arrangements, and (3) providing the secretary of HUD with the "flexibility" to waive public housing rules that blocked restructuring.[5]

In 1992, Congress passed the Housing and Community Development Act to implement the commission's recommendations. The legislation provided for the creation of competitive annual federal grants—which the Clinton administration dubbed with the uplifting moniker HOPE VI—to redevelop so-called distressed public housing developments. HUD, consistent with its proprivatization direction, encouraged public housing authorities to use HOPE VI grants to "leverage other funding sources and form partnerships with the private sector" to redevelop and subsequently own and manage developments.[6]

With a Republican majority taking control of both houses of Congress in the fall of 1994, the Clinton administration, consistent with actions in other policy arenas, accelerated the scaling back of federal support for public housing and protections for residents. In 1995, the third year of the program, HUD began reducing the size of HOPE VI grants, further guaranteeing private sector control of redeveloped public housing and necessitating increases in the number of market rate units in the new developments. Reduced funding accompanied a shifting of the original, stated goals of HOPE VI away from tenants and more toward promoting economic development. For example, HUD increasingly, in its grant evaluations, placed emphasis on how a redeveloped public housing development under HOPE VI could spur economic growth in the surrounding neighborhood, rather than emphasizing benefits that would accrue to tenants. The Clinton administration's 1995 suspension of the one-for-one rule—a long-established rule that required the rebuilding of any demolished public housing apartment either on the original site or in another location—further morphed HOPE VI into an economic revitalization program. The Quality Housing and Work Responsibility Act of 1998 (QHWR), which amended the original Housing Act of 1937, eliminated the rule. To further facilitate demolition and push residents toward HOPE VI, Section 33 of the QHWR codified a policy, begun in 1996, requiring public housing authorities to close down a development and provide residents with Section 8 vouchers if it is deemed less expensive than revitalization. At the same time, QHWR eliminated HUD's public housing modernization program, which had provided funds for rehabilitation.[7]

The QHWR's amending of the Housing Act of 1937 highlighted the neoliberal retrenchment of the state's social service arm. The 1937 act, which established public housing, emphasized that it was the responsibility of the state "to remedy the unsafe and unsanitary housing conditions and the acute shortage of decent, safe, and sanitary dwellings for families of lower income." In contrast, the 1998 amendments excised the outdated Keynesian language as it emphasized "that the federal government cannot through its direct action alone provide for the housing of every American, or even a majority of its citizens" (emphasis added). Instead, consistent with neoliberal principles, the role of government was to "promote and protect the independent and collective actions of private citizens," through such vehicles as nonprofit and for-profit corporations, "to develop housing and strengthen their own neighborhoods."[8]

Legitimating Negro Removal in the Postsegregation Era: The Role of Sociology

To garner a HOPE VI grant, public housing authorities, who were the only entities allowed to apply, had to show that the particular development or developments for which the grant was written met at least one of the four criteria of severe distress: high poverty, crime, density, or poor management. Yet with the definition of distress so broad and vague, various critiques of the program have concluded that it is almost meaningless, since "virtually any public housing development can meet the definition of 'severe distress' for HOPE VI purposes."[9] In practice, the program has overwhelmingly targeted developments and surrounding neighborhoods where African Americans comprise large majorities.[10]

Of course, any program to demolish public housing was bound to place a heavy burden on African Americans. Although comprising less than 15 percent of the population, blacks made up 48 percent of all the public housing residents—66 percent in larger cities—where officials targeted HOPE VI. But even taking these numbers into account, poor African Americans bore an especially high burden. Between 1996 and 2007, HUD and local public housing authorities demolished 394 projects, encompassing over 163,000 apartments (110,227 were occupied). Approximately 350,000 people were displaced, 82 percent of whom were black, and in half of the demolished developments—such as St. Thomas—blacks made up 95 percent or more of those forced to leave their homes. Further adding to the trauma was that only 14 to 25 percent—less in some cases—could ever expect to return and only after years of displacement. In addition to the direct displacement achieved by destroying occupied public housing apartments, there is evidence of HOPE VI redevelopments' fueling indirect displacement as the surrounding neighborhood becomes gentrified, forcing out even more low-income and black residents. In other cases, black gentrification has been the result as affluent African Americans displace the poor while retaining the racial demographics of the area.[11]

Therefore, considering that African Americans have again borne the brunt of displacement, how could the Clinton administration frame this post–civil rights era urban renewal program as one of hope? The racialized displacement and exclusion of the 1990s differed, to be sure, from the past. In the Jim Crow era, blacks were explicitly denied FHA housing loans or excluded from newly built public housing developments, even at times when constructed on land on which they had formerly resided. In contrast, the national and local authorities administering HOPE VI in the 1990s did not overtly target poor African American families. Nonetheless, in practice, they still ended up being disproportionally marked for removal. Communities such as New Orleans's St. Thomas development were evicted while the new mixed-income replacements rarely provided enough affordable housing for the former residents to return. In addition, strict readmission criteria, often arbitrarily enforced, were used by public housing authorities and their private developer partners as another weapon to block the return of former residents. While local and national housing authorities were busy pushing minority residents from public housing, they did little to strengthen the enforcement of fair housing laws or confront other barriers, such as exclusionary zoning ordinances, that limit private housing market options for low-income African American renters. How then, in the face of this record, could the Clinton administration still market HOPE VI as a progressive, antiracist, and antipoverty initiative? To address this question, we need to turn to the role that American sociology and some of its leading practitioners played in legitimating HOPE VI.

HOPE VI: The Bill Clinton–Bill Wilson Connection

By all accounts of both supporters and detractors of public housing dismantlement, the research of renowned African American sociologist William Julius Wilson informed the HOPE VI program.[12] The central, stated goals of HOPE VI—the creation of mixed-income communities, the dedensification of existing developments, and the deconcentration of poverty—find inspiration in Wilson's works. In various celebrated books, he has identified social isolation and the concentration of poverty as key for understanding—and addressing—the problems of inner-city African American communities. He argues that the concentration of very poor people—with public housing being a prime example—leads to the decline in social organizations, defined as formal institutions (churches, political parties), voluntary associations (block clubs, parent teacher associations), and informal networks (marital and parental ties, neighborhood friends). As a result of this "breakdown," a "ghetto specific culture and behavior" of teenage child bearing, drug abuse, welfare dependency, violent crime, and other social ills arise.[13] Wilson does recognize the importance of what he considers impersonal structural forces, particularly deindustrialization, as limiting the economic opportunities of poor inner-city African American communities. Yet overwhelmingly, his analytical focus is placed on the black poor's alleged cultural characteristics, albeit structurally produced, which become intergenerationally transmitted obstacles to economic advancement. Thus class, understood in Weberian terms as an individual's collection of skills and cultural attributes, rather than race becomes the key obstacle for the underclass, a racialized construct that almost invariably refers to poor blacks and, in some cases, Latinos.[14]

Wilson, it is important to emphasize, unlike conservative critics of the welfare state, posits that the key sources of inequality and poverty lie outside the ghetto. Yet as political scientists Larry Bennett and Adolph Reed emphasize in their critique of the social science underpinnings of HOPE VI:

> By *giving analytical primacy* to the role of social isolation and the effects of concentrated poverty, Wilson ... present(s) a picture in which very poor people suffer most immediately from bad individual behavior stemming from moribund social networks. *From this perspective, improving people's conditions requires altering their patterns of behavior and interaction by, among other ways, dispersing them throughout neighborhoods in which very poor people do not predominate—in which ... more affluent residents can act as social buffers against disorganization and as role models discouraging pathological behavior.*[15] (emphasis added)

Thus, Wilson's writings helped to justify and legitimate public housing dismantlement, privatization, and poor-people dispersal as an antipoverty initiative. President Clinton himself, who oversaw the downsizing of the welfare and public housing components of the nation's social safety net, acknowledged the role of the former American Sociological Association president in this endeavor. At a 1999 White House ceremony, he lauded "William Julius Wilson whose work has deeply influenced what I have tried to do as President," as he awarded the Harvard University sociologist the National Medal of Science.[16] Wilson's ideas provided support and justification not only for government officials but also for private developers who wanted to eliminate public housing developments. For example, developer Pres Kabacoff, whose company eventually won the contract to redevelop and privatize St. Thomas, found inspiration and validation in Wilson's work. "The biggest impact I ever got," Kabacoff explains, "was [from] the Julius Wilson book, *Truly Disadvantaged*." This book drove home to Kabacoff the detrimental impact of

> the loss of role models, *and [that] we just got to break this stuff [poor black communities] up*. That influenced me in everything that I'm doing, and I think I'm one of the few people [that got it]. . . . I guess what they don't understand in this town . . . what ten housing projects, 50,000 people concentrated in an area, [what] that meant for a city. So . . . that's my background.[17] (emphasis added)

Political scientist Adolph Reed further elaborates how developers and public officials employed Wilson's work to legitimate the seizure of valuable real estate and institute a new round of "Negro removal" in U.S. cities.

> In fact, the HOPE VI program, the main vehicle that Clinton's Department of Housing and Urban Development used to displace poor people from inner-city locations attractive to developers, has drawn its perverse legitimation as an antipoverty strategy largely from Wilson's [work]. . . . *The Chicago Housing Authority explicitly cited Wilson as justification for its plan to displace residents from the Cabrini-Green low-income housing project and raze the site for construction of upscale housing. Other housing authorities, and even private developers, evoke his formulations in their proposals.* Just as "blight" and "slum clearance" sanitized the destruction of poor people's housing as humane social policy under urban renewal a half-century earlier, Wilson's "concentrated poverty" and "isolation effects" now provide similar rhetorical lubricant for a

yet more concerted and more surgically extensive effort to remove poor people from desirable central city locations and to replace them with upper-income occupancies.[18] (emphasis added)

In defense of Wilson, it can be argued that he and other academics cannot control the way politicians and others use their works. Yet, Reed retorts, despite his prominence as a Democratic Party policy adviser, "Wilson has never deigned to object publicly to the way his wrong-headed theories are borne out on the backs of poor people."[19] Indeed, he proudly received presidential honors such as the National Medal of Science. Thus, Wilson's work, written ostensibly in the service of improving the lives of the inner-city black poor, was harnessed by state officials and developers to legitimate the 1990s and 2000s revanchist agenda against public housing communities.

Although Wilson's ideas have been important in legitimating racialized public housing policies, they are, it must be remembered, not novel. Other academics have also pointed to structurally produced cultural deficiencies to explain black poverty. For example, in the mid-1960s Daniel Patrick Moynihan argued that slavery had produced a weak family structure and permissive black culture that was at the root of black poverty, crime, and welfare dependency. Likewise, Douglas Massey and Nancy Denton, writing three decades later, argued that government housing policies and real estate practices that foster residential segregation have produced a violent, pathological black ghetto culture. One key public policy prescription that flows from their analysis is, as with Wilson, the dismantlement of public housing projects.[20] Indeed, Doug Massey and Shawn Kanaiaupuni, writing just as HOPE VI was beginning, indict public housing as a key cause of "concentrated poverty" and provide legitimacy for emerging state dismantlement efforts.

> Public housing thus represents a federally funded, physically permanent institution for the isolation of black families by race and class, and it must be considered an important structural cause of concentrated poverty in U.S. cities.[21]

Why, then, place so much attention on Wilson when other social scientists are making similar arguments? The critical difference between Wilson and the other writers is not so much the message but the messenger. In short, as Stephen Steinberg argues, the ability within the U.S. political context to legitimate an objectively racist policy is much greater if advocated by an African American authority.

> Here we come to the delicate but unavoidable issue concerning the role the race of a social theorist plays in determining what Alvin Gouldner refers to as the "social career of a theory." Not only was Moynihan white, but he wrote at a time of heightened racial consciousnesses and mobilization, both inside and outside the university. As a white, he was susceptible to charges of racism. . . . Even the voluble Moynihan was reduced to silence when it came to parrying the charges leveled against him by black scholars and activists. . . . Wilson too, had his critics, but at least he was immune to the charge of "racism."[22] (emphasis added)

Steinberg's critique of Wilson provides insight into how racial inequality continues to be normalized and legitimated in the post–civil rights era. Employing symbolically antiracist gestures, such as naming an African American—or other racial minority—to endorse or head a substantively racially inequitable practice, initiative, or institution, has become routine. This stratagem is employed by liberals and conservatives alike.[23] Invoking the authority of William Julius Wilson or Vince Lane—the latter being the African American head of the commission that crafted the outlines for the legislation creating the program—provided HOPE VI advocates added protection from charges of racism. Indeed, Wilson's work could be used not simply as a prophylactic against accusations of racism but as an offensive weapon. Opponents of deconcentrating poverty advocates could, armed with Wilson's ideas, charge their opponents with advocating the continued warehousing of the black poor.

The Centaur State: Expanding Repression in Support of Privatization

The Clinton administration combined HOPE VI and its attendant underclass ideological underpinnings with a whole set of coercive mechanisms to facilitate the downsizing of public housing. This combination of "downsizing the social-welfare sector of the state and the concurrent upsizing of its penal arm are," sociologist Loïc Wacquant argues in his study of the politics of neoliberalism, "functionally linked." They represent, he emphasizes, "two sides of same coin of state restructuring in the nether regions of social and urban space in the age of ascending neoliberalism."

Thus, under neoliberalism, we get a bifurcated centaur state that has a liberal head that lifts all controls in the pursuit of profit and a "brutally paternalistic and punitive" body to contain opposition and manage the social fallout.[24]

The Clinton administration took various measures to strengthen the repressive body of the centaur state to facilitate the further shredding of the U.S. safety net in the form of public housing. In 1988, President Reagan signed the Anti-Drug Abuse Act, which provided for one-strike evictions of all tenants of a public housing apartment if the leaseholder, another household member, or even a guest was merely charged with a criminal offense. Nonetheless, as mentioned, the Reagan administration did little to enforce the measure. HUD secretary Jack Kemp, under the Bush Sr. administration, did step up evictions by reducing the rights of tenants to fight evictions. Yet the real expansion of one-strike evictions took place under the Clinton administration. As part of the Housing Opportunities Extension Act of 1996, the administration toughened the 1988 legislation by requiring eviction of an entire public housing household if either anyone on the lease or a guest was *accused* of criminal or drug-related activity on or off—that is, anywhere—as opposed to on or near, a public housing development. The 1996 legislation also struck the word *criminal* from mandatory lease provisions, so any activity by a leaseholder, household member, or guest that threatened the safety of residents could lead to eviction. The bill further expanded the centaur state's powers of coercion and surveillance by ordering closer cooperation between the FBI's National Crime Information Center and the local police. Both agencies were required to provide criminal conviction and arrest records to public housing authorities for the purpose of applicant screening, lease enforcement, and eviction.[25]

To ensure local implementation, the Clinton administration through HUD established penalties, in the form of budget cuts, for housing authorities that did not aggressively enforce the new rules and work more closely with the police. The annual ratings of public housing authorities would be partially based on how effectively they implemented these new rules. In 1998, under QHWR, Congress and the Clinton administration further toughened rules on eviction and provided for mandatory work requirements for some public housing residents. In 2002, the U.S. Supreme Court in *HUD v. Rucker* upheld HUD's one-strike rule, holding it was constitutional to evict innocent tenants for a violation another household member or guest committed, even when they knew nothing about the alleged wrongdoing. New Orleans activist Malcolm Suber denounced the decision as legalizing "collective punishment."[26]

Complementing the stepped-up and expanded enforcement of one-strike evictions was a federally financed expansion of local police forces and drug war efforts. The major targets of this initiative were poor and black urban communities. The "criminalization of the poor," as political scientist Ed Goetz notes, became the de facto U.S. urban policy in the 1990s as spending on domestic social programs faced cutbacks. Indicative of these developments, in 1994, as part of the Violent Crime Control and Law Enforcement Act, President Clinton created the office of Community Oriented Policing (COPS). The new initiative provided grants to local police departments and other agencies, including public housing authorities, to hire more police. By 2000, COPS reached its goal of placing 100,000 federally financed police on U.S. streets.[27] Oftentimes, as in New Orleans, these officers were used to beef up police presence at public housing developments and other poverty areas of cities. In addition, the federal government's weed and seed program, begun under Bush and continued by Clinton, funded more local police and promoted greater collaboration between local and federal law enforcement agencies, community organizations, businesses, and social service agencies in so-called high-crime neighborhoods. Like COPS, weed and seed prioritizes and promotes closer civilian–police relations, including developing police informants in the community as a prerequisite to accessing the seed aspect of the program—the delivery of social services. Adding to its punitive nature, the program authorized the creation of special law enforcement zones where "offenders [could] be prosecuted under more stringent federal laws."[28]

Strengthened eviction powers and an increased and expanded police presence, both legitimated as part of the war on drugs, were critical to dismantling public housing communities. In addition, stepped-up evictions were strategically used in some cases, such as Chicago, "as a displacement tool to reduce the number of public housing tenants in projects slated for HOPE VI," further trimming the number of residents for which the government needed to find replacement housing. Finally, authorities could and did use selective eviction enforcement to target vocal opponents of HOPE VI, thus eliminating another roadblock to privatization.[29]

The Clinton administration, HUD, local housing authorities, and developers relied primarily, as I have argued, on underclass ideology to legitimate HOPE VI. Likewise, the state's coercive apparatuses that oversaw the increased use of repression directed against public housing residents required an ideological justification for their actions.[30] Key to legitimation was the reinforcement—to which sociology's underclass ideology certainly contributed—of "the sacred border between commendable citizens and deviant categories, the 'deserving' and 'undeserving' poor." Through "language and representation," as Kenneth Saltman argues in his study of privatization, authorities were able to "produce the conditions ... for the implementation of direct coercion."[31] The pervasive use and coupling of drugs, criminality, and blacks by both government authorities and the media to describe public housing residents laid the racialized groundwork for the reasonable-sounding one-strike, zero-tolerance, weed and seed, and other counterinsurgency-like measures deployed against public housing tenants. Thus, this demonization simultaneously constructed a normal subject that as a prerequisite for this categorization, had to consent and, at times, collaborate with the unleashing of repression against the racialized, deviant other.[32]

National and Local-Level Cooperation to Downsize and Privatize Public Housing

The first half of the 1990s was a period of intense conflict and jockeying between HUD and the city government over control of New Orleans's public housing authority. Yet the differences were not so much over the main thrust of federal policy—privatizing and downsizing public housing—but rather over who would control it. Once a local–national power-sharing agreement was signed, one that further limited democratic input of residents, local officials eagerly worked to exploit all the new federal government–provided tools to accelerate privatization.

As mentioned in chapter 2, in 1988 the Barthelemy administration agreed to accept federal recommendations that a private consulting firm take over management of HANO.[33] Nonetheless, under the accord, the HANO board maintained significant powers, including the selection of a consulting firm to administer the agency, the approval of major contracts, and the confirmation of the executive director selected by the company. HUD began to increasingly challenge these prerogatives. In 1991, HUD, charging mismanagement, pressured the mayor and HANO to replace the African American–owned management contractors and Executive Director Larry Jones. Later, in September 1991, HUD ordered Mayor Barthelemy to remove the entire seven-member HANO board for allegedly mishandling $500,000 in federal money.[34] A newly contracted white-owned management company, C. J. Brown Management Corp., which ran HANO from 1991 to 1994, did not improve conditions, either, according to HUD. In a 1994 audit, the first one since 1983, HUD found in a survey of 150 apartments that not one met minimal federal quality standards. In addition, the audit criticized the board for politicizing contracts by awarding them to firms linked to former board members or city hall instead of the lowest bidder and filling administrative positions based on patronage. HUD's solution for what it considered one of the worst-managed authorities in the country was not democratization but instead recommending that "the entire operation of the authority should be privatized."[35]

The incoming Morial administration and his new board, which now included developer Joseph Canizaro, who headed up HANO's strategic planning committee, called for a sweeping overhaul of the agency that would go far beyond private management schemes. In August 1994, Mayor Morial's handpicked HANO board, following the recommendations of the Canizaro-controlled committee, selected a consulting company owned by an African American political associate of Mayor Morial, Robert Tucker, to develop a detailed reorganization plan. Canizaro worked closely with Tucker—who sat on the board of directors of the developer's bank—"influencing the direction of the plan."[36] Tucker's $500,000 study, in line with HUD and federal government thinking—and the interests of developers like Canizaro—called for privatizing and dismantling HANO. The St. Thomas, Iberville, Guste, and Lafitte projects, located on the most valuable real estate, would be managed under the plan by a partnership of residents and private interests, with remaining developments run by nonprofits or tenant management. A new entity, New Orleans Works, made up of businessmen and chaired by the mayor, would enforce strict tenant rules and acquire private sector money for redevelopment. HANO and its workforce of eight hundred civil service employees, almost all African American, would be downsized to only fifty, with workers being either laid off or transferred to the privately managed developments.[37]

The seven-person HANO board unanimously endorsed the Tucker recommendations in May 1995. Influential public housing resident manager Cynthia Wiggins—one of four public housing resident board members appointed by Mayor Morial, whom he pointed to as evidence of his support for resident empowerment—joined Canizaro, along with a black lawyer and a black minister, in a united front that reflected the larger race and class components of the black urban regime. In an effort to assuage the concerns of some skeptical residents, the resolution endorsing the report included a clause—a promise—that assured HANO would protect resident control. Despite the reassurances, the report's recommendations were essentially a rehash of those made by another influential African American consultant, Reynard Rochon, seven years earlier. The key difference was that Morial, unlike his predecessor, did not encounter opposition from the city's historically most combative tenant council after unveiling his neoliberal reform plan for public housing. Instead, following a half decade of nonprofit–private sector collaboration, STRC leader Fannie McKnight joined with Canizaro in strongly backing the privatization agenda. At a press conference to introduce the plan, McKnight declared that "this is a good deal and we don't want to lose this deal." No opposition was heard from STICC or the PI organizers, as well. Former radical activists had become realists and accepted the austerity and privatization agenda. The plan and its backers did face opposition from some residents and HANO employees. Yet importantly, the black political leadership, allied black contractors like Tucker, and white developers such as Canizaro enjoyed willing collaborators at the St. Thomas public housing project—one that occupied a strategic piece of real estate that New Orleans's black urban regime elite deemed as crucial for realizing their redevelopment agenda.[38]

Tulane University and the Brokering of a National–Local Power-Sharing Agreement

The Morial administration, to further show HUD that it was serious about reform, conducted a national search for a new HANO director in late 1994. In February 1995, the new executive director, Michael Kelly, assumed power with a clear mission: to drastically reduce the number of public housing units in New Orleans. The Clinton administration greatly facilitated New Orleans's public housing downsizing by lifting the one-for-one rule, which required one new unit of public housing for every unit destroyed.[39] Washington's elimination of this protection of poor people's housing did not encounter opposition from African American officials in New Orleans. In fact, far from objecting, Kelly, Morial, and the HANO board *hailed* Clinton's executive order. As Vincent Sylvain—a trusted Morial adviser and head of the city housing department—underscores, the one-for-one rule had constrained the black-led municipal government's public housing redevelopment plans. Sylvain laments that, for example, the initial redevelopment blueprint for the Desire project did not, because of the one-for-one rule, call for a "reduction in units. . . . It was just a reconfiguration of the units that were currently there." With the removal of the Keynesian-era protection, the Morial administration was freed from federal constraints in their effort to carry out a neoliberal makeover of public housing.[40]

With full political backing from city hall and cooperative housing officials in Washington, Director Kelly moved aggressively on demolition. By August 1995—six months after taking the helm—he obtained HUD approval to use modernization money dedicated for refurbishing apartments to demolish almost one thousand apartments across four "too crowded, too dense" public housing developments and several scattered-site housing locations. A year later, in late August 1996, Kelly received HUD approval and funding to bring down another 954 apartments, including 168 St. Thomas apartments, 66 of which were occupied. This measure, one St. Thomas resident explains, "sent a message that they were all going to come down."[41] Kelly's demolition measures, along with an initiative to create a public benefit corporation to oversee the Florida and Desire developments, were part of his effort to "dismantle . . . the HANO empire. . . . [of] delivering a major promise [of] moving toward a leaner, meaner, more decentralized operation."[42]

Thus by 1995, Washington and New Orleans were on the same page. Both agreed on the need to reduce and privatize public housing for New Orleans's black working class. Nonetheless, differences still continued over who would control this process. The parties involved reached a compromise in February 1996 when a cooperative endeavor agreement between the city, HANO, HUD, and Tulane University was worked out and signed. The agreement abolished the HANO board, replacing it with a HUD appointee who acted as a one-person board to enforce the agreement. Tulane University's first and only African American senior vice president, Ronald Mason, would act as the "executive monitor of this agreement," with the responsibility for overseeing HANO's daily operations, including the work of Executive Director Kelly, "subject to [HUD] oversight."[43] In addition, HUD, HANO, and Tulane University signed a "memorandum of understanding," which initially allocated $2 million to Tulane for its oversight responsibilities.[44] Furthermore, HANO awarded the Tulane–Xavier Initiatives (TXI)—the agency created by Tulane and the historically African American Xavier University—a no-bid contract to work with residents, while HUD funded the Community Action Program (CAP) to work in the C. J. Peete housing development. The mission of

TXI, CAP, and the sociologists and other academics that staffed the operation was to oversee and facilitate the displacement of residents in the name of promoting "economic self-sufficiency among residents." On February 10, 1996, in a meeting that violated Louisiana's open-meeting law and was held in an isolated ninth-floor room of the city hall rather than the agency's office, the HANO board endorsed the agreement and voted itself out of existence.[45]

Police and Privatization

Following the February 1996 signing of the cooperative endeavor agreement, HANO diligently worked to implement the new coercive measures developed at the national level. The new administration altered leases to prove, as HANO deputy director Brenda Drain-Williams explains, that they were "serious about enforcing the Clinton administration's one strike policy."[46] Results followed. Under the new policy, HANO evicted forty-one residents for being charged with crimes between April and September 1996. Evictions continued to increase, with a 1998 report from HUD's Office of Inspector General—an agency that historically had been very critical of HANO—praising the authority for increasing evictions in 1997 by 67 percent when compared with the previous year.[47]

In a further embrace of federal directives, the new HANO management and Mayor Morial also strengthened cooperation with national and local law enforcement agencies. This partnership between the social service and coercive sides of city government was embraced by new police chief Richard Pennington, as well. Hired by Morial in 1994 after a national search, the former assistant police chief of Washington, DC, prioritized increasing the city's police presence in public housing. "You have to be out there in the street making one-on-one contact with people," Pennington emphasized, and for the new police chief, the streets of primary importance were those in and around public housing.[48] The one-on-one contact with public housing residents promoted by Pennington often came through broader use of the stop-and-frisk policing tactic. This practice, which flouted Fourth Amendment protections, allowed officers to stop individuals without probable cause. The NOPD–HANO collaboration was run through the police department's Police and Public Housing Liaison Section, which deployed federally funded officers hired under the COPS program to patrol all public housing developments.[49]

In another example of local and national cooperation, the city, HANO, and the NOPD obtained, beginning in 1996, multiyear funding from the federal government's Department of Justice for a weed and seed program. The NOPD and HANO worked in partnership with the U.S. attorney's office and other federal agencies, such as the DEA and the ATF, to police a zone that included the Lafitte and Iberville developments.[50] Typifying this collaboration was the task force HANO formed in 1996 with the ATF, the NOPD, the Orleans Parish district attorney's office, and HUD investigative officers to crack down on crime in public housing developments and to share information.[51] ATF and NOPD officers in the late 1990s, advised by a lawyer from the DA's office, conducted twice-weekly surveillances of various housing developments, between 4:00 P.M. and 12:00 P.M. The targets, according to the DA's representative on the task force, were young black men.

> Basically [we would] go and address young black men that looked suspicious and were hanging out in the courtyards and on the corners.... If we saw individuals standing in a corner, in a conspicuous way ... if they were in conversation with other people, we jumped out and investigated them.... We had a lot of leeway.[52]

When the team made arrests, information was handed over to HANO, who could then use it to evict residents.

The aggressive policing strategy recounted here, which was primarily directed against New Orleans's poor, working-class black communities, resulted in an enormous expansion of people funneled into the criminal justice system. For example, the number of prisoners in the city jail exploded from an already historical high of over 3,600 prisoners in 1991 to 6,381 in 2000, while the number of people processed annually through the local jail jumped from 40,000 to 72,000 between the mid-1990s and 2000.[53] Increasing numbers of juveniles were also ushered into the system after Mayor Morial pushed through the city council, in 1994, one of the most stringent juvenile curfew laws in the country. Chief Pennington aggressively enforced the curfew, which led to the arrest of approximately 4,000 juveniles a year. This massive expansion of the criminal justice net directed against New Orleans's poor greatly expanded the number of opportunities—including juveniles arrested under the curfew law—for HANO to employ one-strike provisions to evict residents.[54]

The aggressive enforcement of one strike by HANO, combined with weed and seed sweeps, the COPS program, and aggressive policing, had a noticeable impact at St. Thomas in the latter half of the 1990s. As one resident notes,

> The one strike and you're out thing, the zero tolerance policy . . . they started increasing. . . . There were like a lot of people who got evicted for maybe because their sons were convicted of a felony or something like that and you could lose your lease . . . even if they are not on your lease but if it's a person that's been by your house.[55]

Geraldine Moore, an STRC officer, notes the link between increased evictions under one strike and closing down the development:

> They had a big incident where there was this young lady and her boyfriend, and he knew the young lady, and he would come and visit her. And he got caught with drugs, but he didn't live there, but he knew her. And [HANO] figured, well . . . one strike, you're out. . . . *That's their way of shrinking down the waiting list of families to get back into St. Thomas.* (emphasis added)

In another case, Moore highlights the injustice and biases of the collective punishment aspect of one strike:

> They had a grandmother that fought that case after her grandson got picked up for drugs. . . . It can be anybody. For instance, if I'm angry with you, I could say I'm visiting so-and-so's house . . . and I'm caught with drugs. They figured I bought the drugs in my apartment. It was crazy. . . . I figured they should apply it across the board. If they're going to apply [the one-strike rule] against us, then HANO should abide by it, too. We're not going tolerate you guys not coming around and fixing stuff.

In dramatic fashion, St. Thomas and other public housing residents were firsthand witnesses to—in fact, the most direct targets of—the remaking of the state under neoliberalism. On one side, they faced, to use sociologist Loïc Wacquant's phraseology, the "Malthusian retraction of the social wing" of the state. This retraction came first in the form of cutbacks and disinvestment and later through demolition of the solid brick government-owned and government-operated apartments that for decades had provided an important safety net for New Orleans's poor. At the same time, St. Thomas and other public housing communities confronted "a gargantuan enlargement of the penal clutch of the state" in the form of one-strike evictions, zero-tolerance policing, and the creation of the largest prison population per capita in the entire country and, indeed, the world.[56] These trends were not in opposition to one another but part of a holistic approach to demolishing the welfare state. To end the era of big government, President Clinton and his willing collaborators in New Orleans needed some help from the permanent institutions of the state in the form of the police, courts, and prisons.

Resident Collaboration and the HOPE VI Grant Application

By 1996, the conditions for dismantling the St. Thomas development looked promising. President Clinton's 1995 executive decree lifted the one-for-one rule that had posed an obstacle to mass demolition and displacement of residents. Furthermore, local and national authorities had worked out a power-sharing agreement and now had a new policy mechanism to implement redevelopment in the form of HOPE VI. Ostensibly designed for distressed developments, in practice the new initiative could be used for any site authorities saw as an obstacle to local regeneration efforts. The next step was gaining the support of St. Thomas leaders and advisers in applying for a HOPE VI grant to carry out the redevelopment plans.

Maintaining cooperation was of concern for developers and, in particular, their allies in city hall. The black political leadership, which legitimated itself as representatives of the black community, was engaging in an initiative that threatened the housing security of the 15 to 20 percent of black New Orleanians that still called public housing home. Therefore, resident consent, particularly from the always difficult St. Thomas tenant leadership, was critical for providing the political cover needed by the local black political leadership to support a HOPE VI application.

The federal government also encouraged gaining local support, particularly among public housing residents. For example, participation in HOPE VI was not mandatory but did require the initiative of the local public housing authority. Residents did not have, of course, as St. Thomas and other residents across the country bitterly discovered, specific veto power over HOPE VI plans. As a HUD-funded study lectured, "This [lack of veto power] has not been well understood by residents."[57] Nonetheless, at both the local and the federal levels, it was apparent that authorities desired cooperation and took measures to entice residents into supporting redevelopment initiatives. For example, as mentioned, the HANO board emphasized—early on in the process—that in carrying out redevelopment, it would not take action that threatened resident control. Later, St. Thomas residents received assurances that the "the housing authority could not turn the [HOPE VI] grant into HUD without the permission and support of the resident council."[58] Further underscoring the importance federal authorities placed on consent was HUD's wording of its 1996 Notice of Funding Availability (NOFA) criteria for HOPE VI, the year HANO applied for a grant for St. Thomas.

> HUD encourages full and meaningful involvement of residents and members of the communities to be affected by the proposed activities. *HUD will consider the extent of resident consultation in shaping the application, (including the designation of the development that is the subject of the application),* the level of resident support for the proposed activities, the continued involvement and participation by the affected public housing residents, and the proposed involvement of residents in management of revitalized or replacement units.[59] (emphasis added)

HUD provided a maximum of 30 points, out of 235, if the resident participation criteria, *including consent from residents for the housing authority to apply for the grant,* were met. Nonetheless, as a report critical of HOPE VI concluded, "Rules . . . are soft on involvement *after* a grant is awarded" (emphasis added).[60]

In the end, it still came down to the nonprofit and tenant leaders' consenting to participate, thereby legitimating the process. The STRC and STICC agreed, working to fit residents' demands within the interstices of the procorporate development agenda. The nonprofit's role at this juncture again underscores the crucial task they perform in managing and implementing urban neoliberalism.

Consistent with the ULI's recommendations, which advocated a privatized and insulated planning process, HANO in 1996 hired a well-known corporate consulting firm, Wallace Roberts & Todd, to develop and write the HOPE VI grant. The tenants and advisers—assisted with grants of $100,000 from HUD and one of $50,000 from a private foundation—worked closely with the private consultants in developing the application. STICC's David Billings headed up the tenants' planning efforts and received support from various STICC members, as well as Vince Lane, who had been retained as a consultant.[61] Residents also participated in the process, attending planning meetings and conducting a survey from which consultants culled data for preparing the HOPE VI grant application.[62] Resident involvement in the planning meetings, which included the key leaders in the community, was more symbolic than substantive. The nonprofit advisers and consultants made the major decisions and wrote the reports. Nonetheless, participation in "the elaborate planning procedures," in these "prestigious rites," was important, since it removed residents from the terrain of struggle in which they could significantly influence the direction of redevelopment.[63]

HANO, consultants, and the nonprofits used the participation of residents to frame and legitimate the application as a resident-driven process. The first sentence of the HOPE VI application, delivered to HUD on September 10, 1996, reads: "This is a resident and community directed program." The introductory page, which includes a prominent photo of STRC leader Fannie McKnight, goes over the origins of STICC. The formation of the nonprofit—according to the history constructed by David Billings and other authors of the application—arose out of the STRC's desire to ensure service providers were accountable to the community, to "address institutional and individual racism," and to realize the "dream" of self-determination. The HOPE VI application was couched as a continuation of that process and agenda. The document, importantly, harmonized the progressive, self-determination goals of the black St. Thomas community with the deconcentrating poverty agenda. "Take St. Thomas out of the box!" Fannie McKnight exclaims in the application, which emphasizes that the "goals [of residents] are consistent with the goals of HOPE VI." To further show resident ownership of the document, the grant application includes a resolution, signed by the ten-member STRC board, fully supporting the "HOPE VI revitalization efforts."[64]

The document also makes clear that a resident-driven process would include the willingness of tenant leaders to distinguish between the deserving poor like themselves and their undeserving, unrehabilitatable, underclass neighbors. The section entitled "Tough Screening Requirements" leads with the quotable Fannie McKnight announcing that "some people gotta go!" The report emphasizes that "residents recognize the need for 'good neighbors' who obey the law." Consequently, the application underscores, residents are "eager to develop a strict new lease" that will include vigorous enforcement of the "One Strike You're Out" clause.[65]

The populist gloss placed on the revitalization plan could not obscure the fact that it did not even guarantee housing for the current residents, let alone protect all of the public housing units at St. Thomas. For example, the grant application calls for drastically reducing the original 1,510 apartments to only 775. Of this number, only a small portion would be considered public housing, in which residents would pay 30 percent of their income for rent. Furthermore, unlike the existing public housing apartments, rent payments would no longer cover utilities but would have to be paid by the tenant. Therefore, even the existing 776 poor families then living at St. Thomas were not guaranteed a slot at the New St. Thomas, since "*clearly they cannot all be accommodated in the proposed new mixed-income, lower density development*" (emphasis added).[66] Thus, although over 90 percent of the 776 families at the half-filled complex were extremely poor (i.e., below 30 percent of the median area income), only 240 units would be provided for this income level. In another reversal of a long-held position of the STRC, the resident leadership signed off on a plan to demolish rather than refurbish most—1,310 of the original 1,510—of St. Thomas's sturdy brick apartments and buildings.[67] These solid structures, which were a source of pride for residents, provided not only housing but a secure refuge from hurricanes, including for many of their friends and family who flocked to the "bricks" at St. Thomas and other developments as storms approached.

Table 4.1 shows the number of apartments and income levels planned for the "New St. Thomas." Always emphasizing consensus, the authors of the HOPE VI application explain that the numbers were arrived at "over a week-long session" by the STRC, STICC, the CRP, HANO, and the HOPE VI planning team.[68] As mentioned, only 240 apartments would be available for extremely low-income families, a reduction of 84 percent. In addition, 150 apartments, for those between 30 and 50 percent of the median area income, would round out the public housing component. The next 195 apartments would be Low-Income Housing Tax Credit (LIHTC) units that could rent to tenants who earned up to 60 percent of the area median family income. The LIHTC apartments were to be priced at below-market rates, but unlike the public housing units, the rent would not vary based on the occupants' income. Furthermore, developers would be required to keep LIHTC units affordable for only 15 to 20 years, after which time they could opt out of the program and charge market rates. The final piece of the New St. Thomas, the 190 homes, would be sold at market rates.

Another key element outlined in the proposal is private management. Promoting the ideological message that private is inherently better and

TABLE 4.1

Proposed Income Mix by Units and Percentage in HOPE VI Application

		Proposed in HOPE VI grant		Existing	
Type	Income as % of median	Mix (%)	Number of units	Mix (%)	Number of units (occupied)
Rent	<30	30	240	91	706
Rent	30–50	20	150	9	70
Rent	>50	25	195	0	0
Own	>50	25	190	—	—
Total			775		776

SOURCE: *Housing Authority of New Orleans,* The New St. Thomas/Lower Garden District HOPE VI/Application *(New Orleans: HANO, 1996), 11.*

more efficient than public control, the "Operation and Management Principles" section of the grant opens with the public confession that "HANO recognizes its weaknesses." The solution, therefore, was for "St. Thomas to be managed under a wholly new private structure." Consistent with the hybrid racial-empowerment/neoliberal ideology that residents and advisers synthesized during the 1990s, the HOPE VI proposal presents a "people's capitalism"—to use sociologist Gary Teeple's term—form of privatization that is compatible with the idea of self-determination. The "development of the rental units and their ownership" of the New St. Thomas—as tenant leaders and nonprofits began to call their "dream"— would be "*a private partnership of developers with residents and the St. Thomas Irish Channel Consortium*" (emphasis added). Nonetheless, the details of what the application calls a "unique partnering opportunity," including ownership percentages and powers reserved for residents (a term left undefined) and STICC, are not delineated.[69] The ensuing years would underscore the problems arising from this lack of clarity and, especially, the absence of any enforcement mechanisms for tenant ownership and the other provisions outlined in the proposal.

As the plans emerged—ones that diverged from earlier assurances that no one would be displaced—some elements within STICC dissented.[70]

Robert Mayfield, one of the grant writers, explains the conflict over the limited number of units:

> The sticky point . . . was a struggle over the number of low, low–income units that were going to be built. That was a sticky point. . . . At that point [when the HOPE VI proposal was unveiled] I felt as though the community was not informed sufficiently, that there was only going to be such a minimal number of low, low–income units.

Mayfield was taken by surprise when the final numbers came out and believed that Billings and Major, the key STRC advisers, had made some decisions behind the scenes.

> I was at a meeting when the architects presented the numbers in terms of what would be the income for such units and . . . the numbers. . . . When that was presented, I thought all hell was going to break loose, because I was in shock, but nobody said nothing . . . *so at that point I knew there had been meetings where I had not been included. . . . Well, David definitely was in the loop. Barbara Major was definitely in the loop.* . . . But I was savvy enough to know that if at that point people weren't standing up and scream-ing, there were decisions that had been made, because [HANO and the consultants] would never have presented it that openly in front of other folks without at first getting an endorsement from folks that it would pass without any opposition. (emphasis added)

Others were incredulous, as well, when the number of planned public housing units were revealed. An outreach worker employed by the STRC and leader of the Kuji Center–supported Black Men United for Change ex-claimed to Mayfield, in private: "What is going *on?* . . . This is not good!"[71] STICC leaders invoked the TINA (There Is No Alternative) argument to manage the contradiction between what they had been promising and the actual plans they were signing off on. More broadly, TINA became the key rationalization employed to justify neoliberal accommodationism; it allowed these social justice advocates to maneuver between their public persona as advocates for economic and racial justice and their involve-ment in a privatization and displacement effort directed against a poor, black community that would primarily benefit white developers. STICC member and Hope House director Don Everard's evaluation of the limited number of public housing apartments included in the HOPE VI application captures the dominant thinking of the time among nonprofit and resident leaders:

> I was OK with the thing with the way they wrote it, although I knew there was ... *I knew a lot of people would lose housing*, but it was like ... the environment, the physical and social environment of St. Thomas was so devastated that something, something realistic had to happen, and it was pretty well understood that that was the only vehicle that could be used to make something happen. *So they didn't have much choice but to go for it.*[72] (emphasis added)

Everard's reflection underscores the way that neoliberalism, as geographer Jason Hackworth argues, "has become naturalized as the 'only' choice available to cities in the United States and elsewhere." Clearly, as Hackworth points out, neoliberalism from above has greatly impacted the decision of St. Thomas and other neighborhood leaders to collaborate with rather than resist various neoliberal redevelopment plans. The rolling back of the Keynesian state at the national level, particularly public housing, the constraints placed on cities by bond rating agencies, and the rise of a government failure ideology that sees government intervention—with the exception of state subsidies and support for private profit making—as creating "inefficiency, inequity and corruption" all weighed heavily on local actors at St. Thomas and other urban neighborhoods.[73] But to understand the ready embrace of neoliberalism at St. Thomas and other public housing developments—a "key arena," as Brenner and Theodore emphasize, "in which the everyday violence of neoliberalism has been unleashed"—we have to look not simply at how acceptance was imposed from above, as Hackworth does, but also at how it was assembled from below, as well, in the form of St. Thomas's nonprofit complex.[74] This complex built over the course of a decade (the social relationships, material rewards, daily practices, and ideologies) made cooperation with the neoliberal agenda, however harsh it was, the "default position of common sense."[75] From below, the nonprofits—not only the pressures coming from Washington, city hall, the academy, and the police—helped to "naturalize neoliberalism" at the St. Thomas public housing community and thereby fit this low-income black community into "the programmatic frameworks and priorities" of the black urban regime.[76]

The Post-Civil Rights Black State

The black urban regime, conceptualized as a local apparatus of the U.S. state, emerged in part out of elite efforts to contain the growing militancy of black workers and communities in the post–World War II period.[77] Underscoring this assessment is the central role that the new black petty bourgeoisie has played in staffing and leading the local black state and how this layer has emerged. The rise of an expanded black petty bourgeois stratum was largely a product of what Patricia Hill Collins calls a "politically mediated" process that emerged in response to the civil rights/black freedom movement of the 1950s and 1960s.[78] One element in the politically mediated construction of this class was the opening up of professional schools and management-level jobs in the private and public sectors that had historically been closed or severely restricted for African Americans. Another important factor in this class formation process was the "creation of a cadre of [moderate] black political leaders" in the 1960s, which as Jill Quadagno and Cedric Johnson emphasize, the federal government played a key role in creating through its antipoverty programs. "In the wake of civil rights mobilizations and urban riots," Johnson explains, "a wide range of governmental initiatives … mobilized certain sectors of local black communities around a moderate form of political subjectivity that was amenable to system preservation."[79] Daniel Patrick Moynihan provides support for Johnson's observation regarding the crucial role the national state played in cultivating this new conservative political class. The then presidential adviser argued in 1969 that "*very possibly, the most important long run impact of the community action programs of the 1960s will prove to have been the formation of a urban Negro leadership echelon* at just the time when the Negro masses and other minorities were verging toward extensive commitment to urban politics" (emphasis added).[80]

These new leaders, such as James Singleton, who entered politics in the 1960s through the local federal antipoverty agency Total Community Action, began to take political control of various majority black cities such as New Orleans in the 1970s and 1980s. These new local black states (as well as the national state) in turn assisted, through jobs and contracts, to further nurture the ranks of the new black petty bourgeoisie. This new black political class and the broader black petty bourgeoisie that emerged in this era have generally played, as Sharon Collins argues, a conservative role that does not reverse but rather helps "preserve inequality while it [carries] out its role in reinstating social order."[81]

The assessments of Johnson, Collins, and Moynihan aptly captured the trajectory and role of the new black political class in New Orleans. They began to take control of the local state in the late 1970s at the intersection of two important structural changes: (1) a dynamic wing of the local white bourgeoisie, composed of and tied to large mobile capital and real estate, began to assert its dominance and (2) the U.S. national state began its neoliberal restructuring agenda.[82] The response of the black political leadership and the larger black petty bourgeoisie to these structural changes was to act as a junior partner with the new white bourgeoisie. This partnering relationship and their accommodation to neoliberalism were understandable because the new black petty bourgeoisie was largely a product of state intervention and because of the various ways this class was tied to large, white corporate interests. Thus, this layer is best conceptualized as a comprador or what sociologist Mary Pattillo calls a "middle(wo)man" class that, through its control of the local state, helps to impose and manage the neoliberal agenda while accruing some benefits from it.[83] Consultant Robert Tucker, a close ally of African American mayor Morial and a business associate of white developer Joseph Canizaro who made $500,000 providing plans justifying and legitimating public housing privatization, exemplifies this post–civil rights era sociological phenomenon.

The Local State, Nonprofits, and Achieving Consensus on Privatization

The work of geographers Gordon Clark and Michael Dear, who conceptualize the local state as a "consensus seeking sub-apparatus of the state," provides a useful schema for appreciating and understanding the relationship of nonprofits to the local state. The state's primary mission, according to Clark and Dear, is threefold: (1) securing class-wide consensus on the social contract, (2) securing conditions of production, and (3) integrating subordinate classes. To assist in achieving these objectives, the local state often relies on "para-apparatuses" that, while linked to the state, possess substantial "operational autonomy." A leading variety of these "consensus seeking para-apparatuses" are those led by business and concerned with promoting corporate-centered economic development models.[84]

Tulane University, in its public housing role and in solving local–national state conflicts, operated, as well, as a para-apparatus of the local state. The city's most prestigious and wealthiest private university played a key role in mediating intrastate conflicts and in both legitimating and implementing critical reforms, such as public housing privatization, seen as critical by the local dominant class. Compared with business organizations, universities may be more effective as para-apparatuses, since non-profit institutions and seats of higher learning appear as objective players solely interested in serving the public good rather than in securing profits. Though Tulane's role was important, the preeminent consensus-seeking para-apparatus in the local state's public housing privatization effort was STICC and the STRC. Tulane did not have the long history and deep roots the STICC and STRC cadre enjoyed at St. Thomas, which along with Iberville, was the most valued piece of public housing property in the city. These relationships were important and needed by the city's economic and political elite. Privatizing St. Thomas was central to the redevelopment of the riverfront and the promotion of tourism, the key engine of the local economy. Yet politically, implementing a redevelopment plan was a challenge. St. Thomas historically had the most militant leadership and the capacity to mobilize tenants and other working-class allies. STICC and the STRC could have destabilized the local regime and its racially inequitable development project with a militant, class-wide movement of noncooperation. Instead, they took the path of collaboration and helped to solve the local black petty bourgeois leadership's main dilemma: "how to appear to be progressive in addressing the needs of the black community and yet meet the needs of the major business interests."[85]

Considering the critical role the nonprofits played in securing consensus on redevelopment, it is not a surprise that the president of STICC, Barbara Major, was named New Orleanian of the Year by *Gambit*—a local newspaper whose owner was a fervent supporter of downsizing public housing—in 1996, the year the HOPE VI agreement was signed. From the perspective of the local governing elite, Major richly deserved the award, since she helped manage "their" city's central contradiction, as it was played out at St. Thomas. She helped accomplish this feat by forging a new state apparatus that managed to package an objectively racist, post–civil rights state policy as not simply racially neutral but one promoting black liberation and self-determination.

The concept of *consensus-seeking state apparatuses* is useful for understanding the central role nonprofits played in privatizing public housing. Nonetheless, the emphasis on consensus should not obscure the fact that the state simultaneously developed, at both the local and the national levels, a vast array of coercive measures to implement its restructuring agenda, as well. As discussed, weed and seed, one-strike eviction policies, and the more invasive zero-tolerance policing techniques, also introduced to New Orleans in the 1990s, were part of the state weaponry used against black working-class people to push through privatization. In addition, abolishing the HANO board, violating open-meeting laws, and making changes to federal public housing through administrative fiat rather than legislative debate were further coercive, antidemocratic measures used to close avenues that black working people could exploit to oppose privatization.

Attention to both the expanding consensual and repressive state apparatuses and mechanisms developed in the process of public housing privatization sheds light on the sources of state transformation and the centrality of the black working class. As Simon Clarke has argued, under capitalism the state and its transformation are a product of the class struggle:

> If there were not class struggle, if the working class were willing to submit passively to their subordination to capitalist social relations, there would be no state. The development of the state is an essential aspect of the development of the class struggle, and has to be seen as an essential form of the struggle.[86]

This dialectic clearly was at work in New Orleans. The construction and development of a whole array of new state apparatuses and mechanisms, from the nonprofits to one strike to the local black state itself, is a testament to the centrality of the black working class for understanding political and economic development in New Orleans. The local state has evolved to contain the organizations and resistance thrown up by this combative class, particularly the black public housing faction. By the mid-1990s, the local black state and its para-apparatuses had indeed made advances in overcoming popular opposition to public housing reform at St. Thomas. Nonetheless, more work still lay ahead.

5

When Things Fall Apart

From the Dreams of St. Thomas to the
Nightmare of River Gardens, 1996–2002

The dreams of St. Thomas started to become part of our organizing vernacular. People began to dream about, not only about the
problems that existed in a place like St. Thomas, but what might
it look like.

—DAVID BILLINGS

The whole thing is, I think we was railroaded. The whole thing is,
I think they want the land.

—JACQUELINE MARSHALL, ST. THOMAS RESIDENT

"I was the last one to move out, in June [2001]," recalls Geraldine Moore,
a former member of the St. Thomas Resident Council. She had been at a
tenant leadership training seminar in Washington, DC, when she began
receiving frantic calls from HANO employees charged with relocating
(i.e., evicting) St. Thomas residents: "I had to get back to New Orleans. . . .
They were going to put my stuff out." In June 2001, almost a year past its
original deadline, HANO was making a final push to remove the remaining St. Thomas residents. "I got back home on a Saturday," Moore explains,
"and that Monday morning I was going to work as usual, and everybody
that I knew from HANO was knocking on my door and telling me I had
to be out."[1] That day, Moore joined the ranks of hundreds of other African
American families forced out of the historic sixty-year-old St. Thomas
development over the preceding eighteen months. Those evicted included
St. Thomas's longest-residing African American tenant, Evelyn Melancon,
and her forty-two-year-old disabled son.[2] Melancon (see Figure 5.1), who
raised her seven children at St. Thomas, "never believed this day would

come." She moved out a few days before Moore. Marjorie Crocket, another thirty-plus-year resident, needed, like many of the elderly, family members to persuade her to vacate. Her son Carlos explains why leaving St. Thomas was so traumatic for his mother: "She had raised her children there.... It was, despite all the negative publicity about St. Thomas, *a home*. ... We maintained a normal family life even though the news media portrayed it as a violence-tarred community."[3]

In the early 1980s, St. Thomas was home to some 1,300 African American families. In the summer of 2001, a few weeks after Geraldine Moore and the other families had left, the historic St. Thomas public housing development was history. Bulldozers from Durr Construction—a company praised by HANO and the *Times-Picayune* for employing some seventy for-

FIGURE 5.1. Evelyn Melancon, who also took care of her disabled son, was forced from her home of over three decades. Abandoned apartments are in the background. Photograph by Michel Varisco.

mer residents in the bulldozing of their own community—finished razing most of the remaining structures (see Figures 5.2 and 5.3).[4] The only lasting physical memory of the St. Thomas public housing development were 5 of the original 161 two- and three-story walk-up apartments that had been protected as a sop to the historic-preservationist community. The bulldozing of St. Thomas's brick apartments and the eviction of the last black resident underscored the seriousness of Bill Clinton's declaration made a few years earlier that—at least for poor people—the era of big government was over. St. Thomas's opening sixty years earlier, as part of the first wave of public housing, was a physical representation of the new welfare state. Likewise, its demise at the hands of the neoliberal centaur state, which literally clears the ground of any impediments to profit making, provided a very visual end to New Deal–era policies.

FIGURE 5.2. Bulldozers finish leveling the sixty-year-old St. Thomas public housing development as former residents look on. Photograph by Michel Varisco.

Not only was St. Thomas gone by the summer of 2001 but so were the earlier promises and agreements. Developers and housing officials shattered key parts of what tenant and nonprofit leaders had sold as the dream of St. Thomas, such as residents owning and managing the development, resident-run microenterprises, a community and daycare center, and the right of return for those displaced. In its place was a corporate-owned and corporate-managed development with a minuscule number of affordable apartments, numerous obstacles to return, and residents scattered all over the city in other high-poverty neighborhoods, including some who became homeless. The private developer, with full backing from HANO, even eliminated the name that residents and nonprofits had chosen for their dream—the New St. Thomas. In a final effort to erase and extirpate any memory of the previous African American working-class community, the developer, Historic Restorations Incorporated (HRI), unilaterally renamed the development River Gardens.

How and why did this happen? Why did the residents and their advisers continue to cooperate with the redevelopment process even after government officials and developers abrogated earlier agreements? Why

FIGURE 5.3. A boy stands on the ground of his former home at St. Thomas.
Photograph by Michel Varisco.

did they agree to leave their homes without any assurances that they
could return? If there was resistance, what were its forms, and how was
it contained? The key for explaining the consensual removal of hundreds
of poor, black working-class families was the nonprofit structure of conciliation. This structure was not a thing independent of the city's power
structure but rather a relationship that tied public housing residents and
their advisers to the corporate and political governing elite. This relationship was not static and frozen in time but rather a dynamic one that was
continually tested and remade at various critical junctures. This chapter addresses how this crucial component of New Orleans's black urban
regime—one that ensnared public housing residents in a pact with white
developers and black public officials—was maintained as the privatization plan began to veer substantially from its initial promises. The final
stages of the St. Thomas saga—from 1996, when local leaders celebrated
the awarding of a HOPE VI grant, until the eviction of the last St. Thomas
resident in 2001—highlight the crucial role played by nonprofits in maintaining support for a "roadmap" that led to displacement and privatization.

Nonprofits and the Structuring of Conflict

On October 8, 1996, leading members of New Orleans's black urban regime and their nonprofit allies gathered, as a *Times-Picayune* reporter described it, with much "fanfare and high expectations" in front of the STRC's office. Attendees included Mayor Marc Morial, HANO director Michael Kelly, developer Joseph Canizaro, Elizabeth Julian, who represented HUD secretary Henry Cisneros, Vince Lane, Barbara Major, STRC officers Demetria Farve, Fannie McKnight, and Felton White, and other STICC and STRC members. Standing among his governing partners, the mayor proudly announced to the local press that HUD had awarded a $25 million HOPE VI redevelopment grant for the St. Thomas public housing development and $7.2 million for relocation. Morial praised the federal government initiative as the "radical change" needed for public housing. STICC president Barbara Major, for her part, celebrated a "heaven of a victory," adding that "the new St. Thomas won't have people piled up on top of each other in rundown apartments." HUD representative Elizabeth Julian, along Major's lines, emphasized that the "sheer density of public housing has undermined its ability to be a viable community." The issue of density raised by Major and Julian represented the new way removal of black people under HOPE VI was discussed. The nonprofits and the local and national state not only were in agreement on privatization but used some of the same euphemisms to justify the removal and displacement of black people.[5]

Despite the euphoria, HANO actually received $15 million less than the original $40 million requested in the grant. The shortfall meant that more private sector funding than originally anticipated would have to be raised, thus jeopardizing construction of even the limited number of public housing units proposed—and not guaranteed—in the HOPE VI application. Further complicating redevelopment was the simultaneous mid-1990s "reorganizing and downsizing [at HUD that] . . . left [it] with fewer resources for overseeing HOPE VI grants."[6] Fewer staff and less resources at HUD meant a slower approval process of St. Thomas and other redevelopment efforts taking place across the country. Nonetheless, while HANO and HUD slowly proceeded on the reconstruction plans, they hurriedly worked to begin demolition. In March 1997, six months after awarding the HOPE VI grant and before approving a developer or final revitalization plan, HUD granted permission to HANO to demolish all but 200 of St. Thomas's original 1,510 apartments.[7] A HUD representative justified the demolition order by pointing to President Clinton's 1995 executive order—the rescission ruling—empowering HUD "*to approve [St. Thomas's] demolition application without a plan for providing replacement housing*" (emphasis added).[8] Although residents kept the wrecking ball at bay, for the most part, until 1999, the rescission rule was another weapon wielded by HANO and developers against residents.

In May 1997, seven months after receiving the HOPE VI grant, HANO finally issued bids—called a Request for Qualifications (RFQ)—for a private, for-profit "development partner for the St. Thomas Housing development." HANO also prepared an eight-member panel, composed of four people selected by STICC and the STRC, three by HANO, and one by the mayor, to review the RFQ applications and select a developer from among those submitting their credentials.[9] Two months later, in July 1997, HANO announced the panel had chosen a Florida-based company, Creative Choice Homes (CCH), as the developer over ten other competitors. Nonetheless, CCH's next hurdle—gaining approval from HANO and HUD on a revitalization plan required before construction could start—proved difficult. In November 1997, representatives from HANO, STICC, CRP and CCH held a two-day retreat to establish a closer working relationship to help break the logjam in negotiations.[10]

Negotiations, despite the November 1997 summit, continued to be deadlocked into 1998. The chief stumbling block to signing a deal appeared to be the development fees that CCH—and its development partner, the STRC—demanded from HUD and HANO.[11] The STRC worked vigorously to support CCH's position. STRC president Barbara Jackson—who had recently regained her long-held position after displacing Demetria Farve—wrote letters on January 15 and February 11, 1998, to HANO's federally appointed executive monitor, Ron Mason, and on March 4 to HUD representative Kevin Marchman protesting HANO's unnecessary delays and asking for help in bringing the redevelopment negotiations to a close.[12] To pressure HANO into accepting an agreement, STRC president Barbara Jackson, former Chicago Housing Authority director Vince Lane, who was now employed by CCH, and Felton White, a former STRC member hired by Lane, moved from letter writing to mobilization. On March 11, 1998, White and Jackson led a march, accompanied by a traditional New Orleans brass band, through the St. Thomas development that ended at the nearby school gymnasium. At the gym Jackson and White chaired a meeting of 400 residents and community supporters, with Lane and Rev. Torin Sanders, the successor to Barbara Major as STICC president, at their sides. The leaders threatened to march on HANO and city hall if an agreement was not quickly signed with CCH. The pressure bore fruit, with HANO, CCH, the STRC, and Ron Mason finally signing—eight months after awarding the contract to CCH—a development agreement and sending it off to HUD on March 27, 1998.[13]

Although negotiations between the STRC–CCH partnership and HANO were contentious, they nonetheless stayed within the framework of privatization. Preserving St. Thomas's badly needed 1,510 apartments for low-income black families in the center of the fast-developing riverfront tourist corridor and mobilizing a mass movement to achieve this goal were no longer fathomable for the STRC and STICC. In fact, the STRC–CCH development plan included the same miniscule numbers proposed in the HOPE VI grant for the New St. Thomas—775 units divided between market-rate, tax credit, and generously defined public housing. These numbers represented a further reduction in affordable units from the 900 that had been proposed in the ULI study five years earlier. Underscoring the extent to which the STRC and STICC had distanced themselves from the concerns of low-income black renters and embraced a neoliberal logic was their major sticking point in negotiations with HANO—the developer fees they and their development partner, CCH, would get under the deal. The nonprofit structure, including the real material benefits it provided for tenant leaders and activists, once again helped to channel conflict in ways that were compatible with the larger procorporate development model.

The improving fortunes of former STRC officer Felton White illustrated the benefits to being "realistic" and cooperating with the dismantlement of St. Thomas. White was hired by CCH project director Vince Lane to help build support for the company's position among residents. In addition, he and several other STRC members actively involved in the redevelopment process obtained homes on generous terms from the Canizaro-led CRP, which had acquired properties along a street adjacent to the St. Thomas development. With some resident leaders, including longtime firebrand Fannie McKnight, moving into private homes, a feeling that the resident council was out for itself began to take root. As Geraldine Moore, a former STRC member concludes, their obtaining those homes, whether justified or not, "didn't look good at all. [Residents] thought [the leadership] had sold out. They thought Fannie McKnight had sold the community out."[14] Thus, cynicism and distrust increased. Longtime resident Irma Ricardo sums up this widespread sentiment:

> The people that were supposed to be helping out got their own houses. We're renting, and they got their houses.... The resident council is for themselves, not for us. All of it was about a scam. They represented themselves; they didn't represent me.[15]

Possibly adding to the cynicism was that as some of the STRC leaders were getting homes, advisers David Billings and Barbara Major began to scale back their involvement in STICC and the redevelopment process they had advocated since the early 1990s.[16]

The Class Loyalties of the Black Political Leadership

The STRC–CCH victory was short lived. On July 10, 1998—nearly two years after HANO received the HOPE VI grant and a year after awarding the redevelopment contract to CCH—HUD representative Elinor Bacon informed HANO there were irregularities in the developer selection process, and therefore, it had to be redone. Officially, Bacon based her decision on HUD's Office of Inspector General report, which found that residents had too much influence over the panel that selected the developers, that they were not "qualified" to choose a developer, and that an "inherent conflict of interest" existed, since the developer was expected to hire public housing residents.[17] In rebuttal, the STRC and its advisers argued that residents' involvement and the promise of jobs were how HUD and HANO had sold HOPE VI to residents. Furthermore, the STRC emphasized that consultants hired and approved by HUD and HANO—Abt & Associates—trained public housing residents for the selection process and approved their participation on the panel.[18] The real issue was, from the STRC's perspective, that Mayor Morial wanted to award his politically connected campaign contributor developer Pres Kabacoff, the CEO of HRI, who had not been able to obtain the contract during the first round of bidding. Bacon provided support for the claim of a backroom deal when she met in July 1998, following the decision to reprocure, with tenant leaders, advisers, and HANO officials. At an emotional meeting held at the HANO office, Bacon claimed, according to one of the attendees, that the real reason for reopening the contract was pressure from Mayor Morial.

> It was a deal that was already cut by [Morial] and the powers that be to gentrify St. Thomas, to let this developer [HRI and Pres Kabacoff] do what he wanted at all costs, and this was said on

this tape. . . . And just a lot of ugliness that happened out of Elinor Bacon's mouth. That it wasn't about residents—it was about making money. Sister Rose . . . vivid in my mind . . . stood up and told her, "How could you do this to poor people? I thought that public housing was supposed to be for the have nots, and for you to say that it's not about them, this is a travesty," and they actually started crying (Bacon and Sister Rose). And Elinor Bacon said, "I never made a nun cried," and you know, she tried to make a joke out of it. And so, uhh, we got up and we left.[19]

It may be that the combined influence of Democratic mayor Morial and the longtime Democratic Party supporter Kabacoff led the Clinton administration's new HUD secretary—Andrew Cuomo—to revoke CCH's contract. Nonetheless, whether Mayor Morial's influence played the key role in HUD's decision to throw out the CCH contract is not the critical issue for discussion of the class allegiances of the black political leadership. Neither is accepting the self-serving analysis that the CCH-led redevelopment effort would not also fuel gentrification. What is critical is that resident leaders wanted to work with CCH rather than HRI. Nonetheless, following HUD's decision the mayor undertook—against the expressed wishes of the St. Thomas leadership—various measures to ensure that HRI and several black-allied professionals and entrepreneurs obtained the contract.

Following the July 1998 meeting with Bacon, the St. Thomas tenant leaders and advisers tried to retain CCH as their private development partner. Barbara Jackson sent letters to HUD secretary Andrew Cuomo in August and October 1998 asking him to reconsider his agency's decision to "reprocure the HOPE VI grant." She argued the decision to restart procurement was the result of a "backroom deal" to award Kabacoff and HRI at the expense of CCH and St. Thomas residents.[20] HANO, despite objections by STICC and the STRC—the latter deciding to boycott the new selection process—proceeded to form a new panel, under guidelines laid down by HUD, to review anew the ten original proposals submitted in June 1997.[21] Nonetheless, despite HUD's directive to simply select a new panel to review the existing proposals, HANO and Morial took various measures that provided support for the STRC's assessment that the "fix was in" to award HRI the St. Thomas contract.[22] For example, the new selection panel was composed of government employees controlled directly or indirectly by the mayor. The mayoral appointee was Vincent Sylvain, a Morial confidant and director of the city's Department of Housing and Neighborhood Development, while Michel Kelly, an ally of the mayor and the HANO director, selected the four others. Thus, even if the STRC had agreed to participate and had filled the three other posts of what had been an eight-person panel, the public housing representatives would still have been in the minority. Mayor Morial further conveyed his sympathies to the panel by writing a recommendation letter for HRI—the only applicant to enjoy this—while Kelly provided one of HRI's five references.[23]

Further changes to HRI's application, which included several local African American contractors, investors, and professionals as part of their development team, in apparent violation of the HUD directive, also suggest why the mayor favored the New Orleans–based developer. The additions included Gregory St. Etienne, a vice president with the black-owned Liberty Bank and a former STICC board member. HRI also replaced the white-owned architectural outfit named in their original proposal with the black-owned Billes/Manning architectural firm, the latter being a "major Morial campaign contributor."[24]

The Billes/Manning firm, formed by African American architects Gerald Billes and Raymond Manning in 1985, was a good example of the petty bourgeois professionals and entrepreneurs that obtained real benefits through their relationships with the black-controlled local state. For example, thanks to the help of Mayor Barthelemy, Billes/Manning became the first black-owned firm to receive a major architectural contract with the city-owned airport, leading to several other government contracts, as well. This is not to say that the black leadership steered contracts only to African American firms. The bulk continued to go to large, white-dominated corporate interests such as HRI and national consulting firms like Wallace Roberts & Todd, who made millions churning out studies justifying privatization. Nonetheless, the black state certainly worked to nurture the development of black entrepreneurs through public sector contracts, as well as aid their white corporate allies. These contractors reciprocated with HRI and its partners, including Billes/Manning, contributing over $44,000 to Morial in his 1994 and 1998 campaigns.[25]

Political support, solidified through campaign contributions and long-held relationships with New Orleans's post–civil rights black political class, meant that HRI had a lock on the St. Thomas contract. Even though the panel ranked HRI's proposal low on the objective written portion, its subjective oral presentation widely surpassed its nearest competitor and allowed the locally based firm to obtain the contract.[26] The panel's decision demonstrated the class bias of the black political leadership and shed new light on why the mayor worked so hard to maintain local control over the agency. Morial used his power over HANO not to shield residents from a federal government bent on dismantling public housing but rather to better reward his elite governing allies, both black and white. Conditioned on the awarding of some favors to black contractors, Morial delivered for friendly white corporate capital at the expense of black public housing tenants. The STRC and nonprofit leadership were shunted aside rather than rewarded for their years of cooperation in the redevelopment process. Of course, Morial, the head of the local black urban regime, had periodically met with and supported the efforts of STICC and the STRC to cooperate with developers and HANO in the privatization effort. He "always expressed real support," David Billings explains, "and real appreciation of the way in which the resident council pulled this off. And he would help from time to time." This posturing by Morial was part of his job to "appear to be progressive," to appear to be concerned about the interests of the black poor.[27] Nonetheless, Morial provided no help when black tenants and their nonprofit allies requested his support after HUD eliminated their preferred private sector development partner.

> Marc Morial would be very supportive behind closed doors in the meetings with the resident council but, ultimately, would not be supportive, would not be there at crucial times when, in fact, the residents needed him.[28]

He not only was not there but was working to award the contract to a firm black tenant leaders and most of their nonprofit allies did not want. The St. Thomas leadership was behaving itself, from the perspective of the black urban elite, by cooperating with the corporate agenda. Nonetheless, when a conflict emerged regarding the particular form corporate redevelopment would take, Morial had no qualms about sacrificing the interests of his electoral base to satisfy the needs of his white and black business allies. The other black petty bourgeois leaders acted no differently. Ron Mason, the executive monitor and university official; Vincent Sylvain, the city administrator; Michael Kelly, the HANO director; and Gregory St. Etienne, the black banker and STICC member all played their parts in wresting the contract away from CCH despite the pleas of many in the St. Thomas community. The role this layer played underscored their structural position as a comprador class. They represented a distinct social layer that was hostile to the interests of the black working class and whose role was to impose neoliberal reforms for white capital while extracting some material rewards in the process.

Nonprofits and Backroom Meetings

The STRC and their advisers, in response to awarding HRI the St. Thomas contract, began to return—briefly—to confrontation. On October 30, 1998, the day HANO officially awarded HRI the contract, the STRC marched "to protest the selection process for the development of their community."[29] About forty activists barged into the HANO boardroom, as Kabacoff recollects, "singing songs and objecting." Barbara Jackson, in echoes of the STRC protest actions of the 1980s, denounced the whole process: "I submit there is a conflict of interest now. We refuse to be part of this scam. There's a strong smell of backroom deals here, when the tenants want something different from the politicians/dealmakers." Kabacoff re-assured those in attendance that "I can fully understand their view; these are their homes." He committed himself to "intense collaboration" with residents "to make it work."[30]

The resident leadership was not buying Kabacoff's peace overtures. According to Bill Quigley, in a 2004 reflection on this crucial period in St. Thomas's fate, Barbara Jackson and other STRC leaders wanted "to go back to confrontation, to rent strikes, to things that had worked for them in the past." While the longtime tenant adviser supported a return to militancy, Vince Lane, who was increasingly influential, counseled tenant leaders "*not* to be bold, to not lay down the gauntlet."

> Vince, HANO, and all these people kept telling them you can't do that. [HOPE VI and privatization are] your last best hope to try to hold onto this project, or else otherwise it's just going to be demolished, and you're never going to get any houses, and all that stuff. This is a way to hold onto your houses to renovate and to take care of people to get jobs.[31]

Also joining or, at least, not opposing Lane in encouraging residents and their advisers to step back from throwing down the gauntlet and return to insider negotiations was lawyer Bart Stapert. The towering six-foot-seven Dutch human rights lawyer—who already had a law degree from the Netherlands—attended a local law school in the mid-1990s to fulfill his burning desire to serve as a poor people's attorney in New Orleans. Underscoring the hegemony of the nonprofit model, after graduating in 1997 he immediately set up the nonprofit St. Thomas Community Law Center to serve this low-income black community. By 1998, he had become the tenants' key adviser following the exit of Barbara Major and David Billings. In a December 1998 memo to fellow nonprofit advisers and resident leaders, Stapert explains the decision to collaborate with HRI:

> After HUD ordered a re-procurement, the STRC and its advisors studied our different options, including legal action. *Guided by what is ultimately in the best interests of the residents of St. Thomas, we decided not to sue, nor to throw up roadblocks, but to see if we could work in an honest and equal partnership with HRI, HUD and HANO.* So we come to the table prepared for business.[32] (emphasis added)

The strategy advocated in the letter is a classic example of what Joan Roelofs critiques as the nonprofits' crucial hegemonic role in neutralizing dissent. The linking of "partnership" and "the best interests of the residents" delegitimates a confrontational strategy as simultaneously extremist and self-defeating. Stapert normalizes collaboration with a neoliberal reform agenda by presenting the "views and practices" of himself and other nonprofit leaders as "'this is the way the world is,' as the 'normal' framework of reference."[33]

Why was Vince Lane, the most influential advocate of insider negotiations, still in New Orleans after his last employer, CCH, lost the St. Thomas contract? The largesse of developer Joseph Canizaro, who initially brought Lane to the city in 1993 to head up the ULI study, was the answer. The STRC obtained Lane's services in late 1998 after tenant president Barbara Jackson requested and obtained funds from Canizaro, whom she praised for his "assistance through the years . . . in our efforts to revitalize the community."[34] In fact, Lane became the key "development and revitalization consultant" for resident leaders and their advisers as they entered into negotiations with HRI and HANO in late 1998. HANO and HRI senior management—including Kabacoff—initiated negotiations with a goodwill gesture by attending, with St. Thomas tenants, a two-day Undoing Racism workshop led by PI trainers Barbara Major and David Billings.[35] This confidence-building measure was not enough to bridge the gulf separating the housing needs of residents and the profit-making and the class- and race-removal agendas of HRI. The new developer, as negotiations began, demanded concessions and abandonment of the people's capitalism components of the original plan, including (1) resident ownership and managerial control over the new development, (2) the number of public housing apartments, (3) the right of return for St. Thomas residents and resident control of the admissions process, (4) resident-owned microenterprises, and (5) STICC control of the self-sufficiency component of the HOPE VI grant.

The HRI Strategy: Disrupt, Misdirect, Discredit, and Neutralize

HRI implemented a two-pronged approach to support their bargaining position. First, they developed a parallel nonprofit structure and a layer of community supporters to undermine the power and question the legitimacy of STICC and the STRC. Vince Lane was central to HRI's delegitimization campaign. After the money Canizaro had provided dried up in mid-1999, Lane "sold the residents out" and went to work for HRI. Lane made his move while the STRC was in the midst of divisive negotiations with HRI and, therefore, was able to bring with him all the intimate knowledge he had about the STRC, their advisers, and their plans.[36] Lane—who three years earlier had been forced out as head of the Chicago Housing Authority and in 2001 would be convicted for banking fraud and sentenced to two and a half years in federal prison—also worked to sow further division in the community by collaborating with former STRC member Felton White to form a rival tenant council to challenge the legitimacy of longtime tenant leader Barbara Jackson. In an effort to develop White's patronage powers and, thus, influence in the community, HRI began contracting with his own newly created nonprofit—St. Thomas Community Vocations Inc.—to provide residents jobs for the demolition. STICC was also destabilized as some member agencies, particularly those that received financial support from Kabacoff, either openly backed HRI or stayed neutral in the real estate company's disputes with the STRC.[37]

The second part of HRI's strategy involved hiring two former local high-level African American government officials—ex-mayor Sidney Barthelemy and his former housing administrator and HANO director under private management Shelia Danzy. HRI commissioned Danzy—whom Kabacoff described as a "tough-love kind of person" and residents, who had dealt with her a decade before while she advocated for the Rochon Plan, called a bulldog—to lead negotiations with black public housing tenants.[38] Danzy aggressively pushed HRI's position and was very demeaning and condescending with St. Thomas's black, female tenant leaders—a behavior that may have been less socially acceptable if evinced by a white corporate official. STRC president Barbara Jackson's rebuke of Danzy for questioning her intelligence and savvy illustrates the aggressive and abusive behavior she faced from one of HRI's top African American officials:

> Maybe by you being in the corporate world, you have forgotten about African American definitions of certain words. I know what role our attorney plays and what he is supposed to do.[39]

Danzy's role at HRI exemplified what sociologist Sharon Collins calls the racialized position of blacks in the corporate structure, whose role is to appease and contain black constituencies. This post–civil rights era pattern of placing a black middle-class face on an agenda that worsens the material conditions of black working-class people also informed Tulane University's, the Urban Land Institute's, and developer Joseph Canizaro's relations with black public housing residents. While HRI unleashed Danzy to deal with black public housing tenants, the real estate development firm employed former mayor Barthelemy to woo black public officials. Barthelemy used his influence with public sector administrators and elected officials, such as Emmett Moten, to advocate for the position of HRI, the firm that was now his official employer. Moten, a former colleague of his when they both worked in the Landrieu administration as part of the first generation of middle-class blacks incorporated into the local state machinery, had been hired by HANO executive monitor Ron Mason to serve as his point person for the St. Thomas redevelopment. Barthelemy's lobbying apparently bore fruit, as developers Kabacoff and Canizaro praised Moten for helping to fast-track negotiations.[40] Thus, while HRI placed both Danzy and Barthelemy, to varying degrees, in the same racialized corporate positions, they were simultaneously positioned in separate class boxes and consequently forged distinct types of interaction with their respective clienteles.

The Limits of the Insider Strategy

The strategy of the STRC and STICC leadership in the face of HRI's intransigence to meet their bargaining demands was to appeal to Joe Canizaro for financial and political help. They wanted Canizaro to put pressure on Kabacoff—"[who] was just jamming stuff down their throat"—to be more reasonable in negotiations. In addition, STRC lawyer Bart Stapert petitioned and received funding for his law clinic from Canizaro.[41] On one level, considering HRI's immense financial resources, compared with those of STICC and STRC, turning to the city's most powerful developer, particularly after eschewing protest and disruption, seemed plausible. Yet this strategy was problematic, since Canizaro's interest was, as it was with Kabacoff, for residents to accommodate so that construction could start. Increasing the value of Canizaro's riverfront property required the removal of St. Thomas. Indeed, by 2000, when the last residents were leaving St. Thomas, Canizaro had made $71 million from the sale of sixty-four of the original seventy-two acres, and he still had a pending deal to build the city's largest hotel, with substantial public subsidies, on part of this property.[42]

Making an alliance further problematic were business ties with Canizaro's First Bank and Trust, which acted as HRI's chief banker.[43] Thus, at the request of STICC and the STRC, Canizaro would periodically intervene between 1999 and 2001 to help end negotiating deadlocks with HANO and HRI. Nonetheless, Canizaro, while making some efforts to support the position of residents, would not have tolerated residents' returning to disruption to gain their demands. Therefore, the STRC and their advisers began to be caught in their own contradictions. Obtaining influence and resources through elites like Canizaro simultaneously undermined their ability to employ their own powers of disruption.

Nonprofits, Evictions, and Everyday Forms of Resistance

In late 1999, HANO commenced relocating—evicting—the almost six hundred families then living at St. Thomas, and demolition began in July 2000. Documents relating to the redevelopment consistently identify HANO, working with the STRC, as having the authority and responsibility of removing residents.[44] This agreement, signed early in the redevelopment process, was one that HANO, with HRI's full support, strictly adhered to and fulfilled. The STRC dutifully met its responsibilities, as well. "The whole board was," as former STRC member Geraldine Moore explains, "involved in that [eviction] process" as part of the tripartite HANO-STRC-HRI relocation committee.[45] Moore bitterly recounts how the STRC not only helped sell privatization but became part of the state machinery to remove their ostensible constituents and neighbors:

I can admit I was part of that process, going to people houses,
giving them notices, saying you have to come in so that we
can talk to you to see what your needs are and have you go
down to HANO and make the decisions whether you wanted
to go into Section 8 or back into public housing, which was
a joke.

The evictions, begun in the fall of 1999, were divided into three consecutive phases covering different parts of the development. The eviction process started when a resident received a three-month notice in her or his
rent bill, accompanied with an invitation to meet with STRC and HANO
representatives to review the household's housing options.[46] The relocation alternatives presented to residents were to (1) move to another public
housing development; (2) use a Section 8 rental voucher, in which residents paid 30 percent of their income to rent a private sector apartment,
with the housing authority covering the other portion; or (3) move to a
private sector apartment without any government support. HANO also
offered assistance with moving costs and security deposits, although the
agency did not cover utility deposits.[47]

Between November 1999 and May 2000, HANO sent out 585 notices to
the remaining families, which had dropped by approximately 200 families
since the STRC signed the HOPE VI agreement in 1996.[48] The St. Thomas
residents that did attend STICC- and STRC-led counseling meetings,
which normally involved ten to fifteen residents, were often very bitter at
the tenant leadership and their advisers. A common response, according
to STRC member Geraldine Moore, was, "'You sell outs; you sold us out.'
We never did anything for them. All kinds of stuff." Resident Irma Ricardo
told STRC leaders during her meeting that "it was all about a scam." She
concluded that "they represented themselves; they didn't represent me."
Other residents, particularly the elderly, evinced subtle forms of opposition and disgust with the evictions.

Lot of them, especially on the old side, a lot of senior citizens lived
on that side. We had the hardest time convincing them that they
had to move. We had to call in family members, ministers, pastors,
I mean everybody to come in. This one particular family, her son
from California had to come and tell her that "you have to move
out of here, you can't stay here, they're going to tear it down." She
just couldn't leave.[49]

In another act of defiance, young people repeatedly knocked down the fence that HANO placed around St. Thomas as demolition began. "It was so funny because every time they put the fence up, people would go back there and knock it down. It was really hysterical."[50] The denunciation of the STRC, the foot dragging by the elderly, and the St. Thomas youths' vandalizing of the fence were all examples of what James Scott calls "everyday forms of resistance" and Robin Kelley terms "infrapolitics"— the region of daily confrontations and evasive actions by the oppressed. Yet as Adolph Reed has argued in a critique of these concepts, there is a qualitative difference between everyday forms of resistance and a political movement that collectively and consciously confronts the sources and institutions of power and oppression.[51] The political transformation of the STRC and their radical advisers created an obstacle to making this qualitative transformation from simple resistance to "a historical ... agent ... active and taking the initiative."[52] The nonprofits, through their incorporation of St. Thomas's "organic intellectuals," served as a political and structural barrier to the emergence of a conscious political force to challenge the black urban regime's neoliberal agenda. Due to the effectiveness of the nonprofit collaborationist structure, the grievances and justified anger of the black St. Thomas community could not find political expression. Instead, residents internalized the pain and anger of being deconcentrated. "A lot of people took sick; they just haven't been right. You know we lost a lot of people like that, older people. That happens," as displaced St. Thomas resident Willie Mae Blanchard sagely concludes, "when you uproot a person."[53]

Relocating, Not Deconcentrating Poverty

Many residents felt pressured by HANO to relocate to a conventional public housing development. The public housing option provided a relatively easy solution for HANO, as compared with the private market, in which, as a 1996 study by the Greater New Orleans Fair Housing Action Center found, "77 percent of the time African Americans were discriminated against when trying to find an apartment."[54] The case of St. Thomas resident Emilie Parker highlights the limited housing choices many tenants had and the emotional toll displacement inflicted. Parker was content with St. Thomas, since, to her, "everything was all right. ... That's where all my people was, in the St. Thomas ... ya, beaucoup family. All my folks were back there." She received a call from STRC president

Barbara Jackson, who told her, "You know, everybody's moving," and that she had to attend a relocation counseling session. Jackson advised her against taking a Section 8 voucher, because of the added expense of utility bills, which Parker did not have to pay at her St. Thomas apartment. Thus, Parker chose public housing when given a survey and then later received a notice from HANO telling her to move to the St. Bernard public housing development. Yet Parker says, "I turned that letter down."

> I just didn't want to go to St. Bernard. I just don't like that project. Too much going on out there, [but] I didn't have no choice. [It was] St. Bernard, Section 8, or just be on the street. So that's when I didn't have no choice. . . . So I just took St. Bernard. I just took it anyway to prevent my children from being on the streets.[55]

The reticence of residents, due to safety concerns, to relocate to St. Bernard and other developments was confirmed by STRC member Geraldine Moore. While counseling residents about their options, she found that "a lot of folks just didn't want to move into certain developments because they were beefing (killing) at the time, over turf."[56] In the absence of any larger political movement to oppose demolition, the forced march of families from one poor community to another underresourced one led to conflicts, particularly among the youth. Some turned deadly. Similar scenarios have played out in other cities where mass public housing demolition, neighborhood school closures, and displacement has taken place, such as in Chicago.[57] But because of the limited options facing poor St. Thomas residents, many, like Emilie Parker, assented to relocating to another public housing development.

Proponents of HOPE VI trumpeted it as a method to deconcentrate poverty. Nevertheless, at St. Thomas poor people were for the most part simply reshuffled. As Table 5.1 shows, HANO simply relocated St. Thomas residents to another public housing development in over 80 percent of the confirmed cases as of January 2001. Evelyn Stevens, HANO's director of admissions, acknowledged that many people from St. Thomas, as well as residents being simultaneously evicted from the C. J. Peete and Desire public housing developments, were being forced back into public housing "because they just couldn't find anything else." She admitted "that is not the ideal situation. It is not how the program was supposed to work. The idea was to decentralize public housing developments, not repopulate them."[58] The intended vehicle for deconcentration—the Section 8 program—ran into problems, since HANO was unable to find enough "landlords ... willing to participate in the program."[59] Even when a family was able find an apartment with a Section 8 voucher, the demographics of the neighborhood were oftentimes similar to those of public housing. For example, the Greater New Orleans Fair Action Housing Center found that 75 percent of New Orleans's public housing residents relocated to a Section 8 apartment in the late 1990s moved to a census tract that was over 80 percent African American and had high rates of poverty.[60] Other studies of HOPE VI have similarly concluded that "not much deconcentration is taking place ... too many of the relocatees wind up in other seriously distressed high-poverty neighborhoods."[61] In a scathing indictment of HOPE VI, housing policy analysts Rosenbaum and Deluca concluded:

> Thousands of families are being moved out of public housing projects across the country. In their haste to empty buildings, many officials are not giving much thought to where families are moving. Officials contend that these moves will improve resident's lives, but ... families are being moved into low-income, mostly black areas, which are very similar to the neighborhoods they left ... rapid willy-nilly moves out of public housing seem to be merely displacing families into equally bad neighborhoods that will have little benefit.[62]

Similar results at St. Thomas led residents to dub the program "homeless opportunities for people everywhere" and to "hope that HOPE VI would never come back to haunt anybody."[63]

St. Thomas: From Public Land to Private Hands

The final reconstruction plans developed by HRI and HANO extended and deepened the privatization and downsizing of St. Thomas first outlined in the 1993 Urban Land Institute study and the 1996 HOPE VI application. As Table 5.2 shows, only 176 on-site public housing apartments—defined as units in which low-income renters paid 30 percent of their income for rent—were planned. Of the 176 apartments, only 70 would be reserved for those making 30 percent or less of area median income—the income level of most former residents. In addition, on land just adjacent to the St. Thomas, 67 one-bedroom apartments for the elderly were to be built through HUD's 202 Grant program.[64] This was not well received,

TABLE 5.1

Housing Replacement for Displaced St. Thomas Residents
as of January 29, 2001

Housing replacement	Phase 1	Phase 2	Phase 3	Total
HANO development (confirmed)	89	42	30	161
HANO development (planned)	—	2	26	28
Section 8 (confirmed)	28	3	3	34
Section 8 (probable/planned)	52	58	165	275
Private (includes evictions)	22	22	43	87
Total	191	127	267	585

SOURCE: *St Thomas Relocation Report as of 1/29/01, Housing Authority of New Orleans, Eviction Process file, St. Thomas Redevelopment box, Hope House archives.*

since many of St. Thomas's elderly took care of children and preferred family-sized rather than efficiency apartments. Also categorized as affordable were 15 of the planned 73 privately owned homes, whose price, nonetheless, were out of reach for most residents. Further limiting housing for former residents and increasing private over public power were the privately administered admission criteria for the new development. HRI, a subsidiary of which would manage and own the buildings while receiving a ninety-nine-year ground lease, had a list of criteria, from lack of employment to bad credit, a criminal record, and even housekeeping deficiencies, that could be used to weed out former residents.[65]

The market rate component of the new development included 414 apartments initially projected from $850 to $1,400 per month, along with 58 homes selling from $200,000 to $425,000. All these prices have subsequently increased (see Table 5.2). These apartments and homes would round out the HOPE VI development, which was divided into two parts, called CS (Construction Site) I and CS II. In addition, a luxury 312-unit retirement center and condominium that required an initial payment of between $250,000 and $350,000 and $3,000 a month in fees and a 100-unit condominium selling between $300,000 and $400,000 would be included as part of the overall redevelopment of the area. HRI would build the 12- to 18-story retirement center in collaboration with Tulane and

TABLE 5.2.

Affordable and Market Rate Housing at River Gardens and Off Site

Affordable Housing	Number	Cost
Low-income, on-site apartments (1, 2, and 3 bedroom[s])	176*	30% gross income, plus utilities
Elderly on-site apartments (1 bedroom)	67	30% gross income, plus utilities
Low-income, off-site apartments built and run by nonprofit agency (3 and 4 bedrooms)	100	30% gross income, plus utilities
Affordable homes	15	$100,000**
Total	358	
Market level	**Number**	**Cost**
Apartments	414	$850–$1,400/month
Continuing care retirement community or luxury elderly	312	$3,000/month or one-time payment of $250,000 to $300,000
Luxury condominiums	100	$300,000 to $400,000
For-sale homes	58	$200,000 to $425,000**
Total	884	

SOURCES: Brod Bagert, "St. Thomas and HOPE VI: Smoke, Mirrors, and Urban Mercantilism" (master's thesis, London School of Economics, 2002), 22–23; St. Thomas Revitalization Plan (New Orleans: HANO, 2002); Greg Thomas, "New Phase to Start in June at Former St. Thomas Site," New Orleans Times-Picayune, March 30, 2005.

*Allocation: <30% AMI, 70 units; <50% AMI, 35 units; <60% AMI, 71 units.

**By March 2006, developers had raised the cost of market rate homes to between $280,000 and $450,000 and the number to be constructed to sixty, whereas the price of the nominally low-income homes rose to between $130,000 and $140,000 while the number to be constructed stayed the same at fifteen (Greg Thomas, "Homes Planned Near CBD," New Orleans Times-Picayune, March 23, 2006).

Loyola universities. In total, there would be 1,144 units on the former site, of which 884 units or <u>77 percent of the total would be for upper-income renters and homeowners.</u> The deal also involved selling—privatizing—approximately fifteen acres of the original forty-nine-acre development to pave the way for private homes, condos, and a Walmart. Finally, as mentioned, to erase the memory of this former black working-class community and reinforce who had the real power, HRI unilaterally <u>changed the development's name from the planned New St. Thomas to River Gardens.</u>

Walmart, HRI, and the White Upper Middle Class: From Friends to Foes

In a front-page news story on July 21, 2001—a month after HANO and HRI evicted the last St. Thomas resident—the *Times-Picayune* reported that HRI had welcomed Walmart to open a store as part of the commercial component of the River Gardens redevelopment. The only obstacle to this plan, part of the world's largest corporation's strategy of entering urban markets, was several regulatory hurdles. The primary hurdle was city council approval of a special sales- and property-taxing district—a Tax Increment Financing (TIF) and property tax–based Payment in Lieu of Taxes (PILOT)—comprising the new development and the store. The tax revenue from this district would be redirected from the city's general fund and used to pay off over $20 million in long-term twenty-year bonds needed to finance HRI's for-profit redevelopment deal. In essence, tax revenues themselves would be privatized. HRI justified the special taxing district and Walmart as crucial to financing 100 three- and four-bedroom public housing apartments to be built off site and run by a nonprofit.[66]

The upper middle class, predominately white homeowners and small businesses of the area had been enthusiastic supporters of Kabacoff and HRI's efforts to demolish St. Thomas and prevent as many low-income, black working-class families from returning. Indeed, they benefited materially from St. Thomas's demolition and the ensuing gentrification of the area. Between 1999 and 2000, home values in the Lower Garden District soared 32 percent, the largest gain of any neighborhood in the metropolitan area.[67] Yet at the same time, this largely upper-middle-class demographic was vehemently against placing a big box store like Walmart in their neighborhood, even if it was backed by Kabacoff. Indeed, they felt betrayed by their erstwhile ally—who, in a Machiavellian maneuver, waited until after evicting the last St. Thomas resident before unveiling his plan. They would have been content, Kabacoff remarked, with "a cutesy little shopping center, . . . but they don't like Walmart, they *hate* Walmart. It's like waving a flag in front of a bull (laughs)."[68] To express their displeasure, this class, represented by residential organizations such as the Coliseum Square and Irish Channel neighborhood associations, preservationists and gentrifiers at the Preservation Resource Center, and small business groups such as the Historic Row Magazine Association, mobilized over the next year to stop Walmart. Reflecting the concerns of small businesses, furniture store owner Herbert Halperin denounced Walmart at a special November 2002 city council meeting, regarding the project as a "predator that will suck business away" from nearby stores.[69] Camille Strachan of the Coliseum Square Association says her organization and historical preservationists reacted with "shock and horror" when they heard about the Walmart deal. "It's totally inappropriate. It's too big. It generates too much traffic. . . . There are innumerable reasons."[70] She and other historical preservationists and homeowners filed several lawsuits in their unsuccessful effort to block the store.

Geoff Coates and Edward Melendez of the Urban Conservancy, the then recently formed nonprofit preservationist group dedicated to preserving New Orleans "historic urban fabric," joined Strachan, the CSA, and small businesses in vociferously opposing Walmart. At the same time, the Urban Conservancy officials were, like Kabacoff, fervent supporters of deconcentrating poverty through public housing demolition. Although they advocated for the "wise stewardship" of New Orleans's unique "built environment and local economies," their concern did not extend to preserving St. Thomas's historic structures and community. Instead, they lectured that "the St. Thomas residents were in need of a . . . rejuvenation." They then went on to explain that the St. Thomas community was a menace and, therefore, their removal was for the best:

> Crime, chronic underfunding and government mismanagement created an environment that threatened all residents of the Lower Garden District. Observers have noted a reduction in crime in the area after the destruction of the housing.[71]

Even with a united front, the middle-class forces were no match for the key elements of the governing and electoral wings of the black urban regime that HRI had garnered to support its position. The New Orleans

Chamber of Commerce and the New Orleans Business Council unsurprisingly emphasized the need for economic development and sending the right messages to justify their support for Walmart. The intervention of one of their chief spokesmen, Ron Foreman, the director of the Audubon Institute, a local, quasi-state agency, followed this trope. "New Orleans is dying," Foreman intoned at a city planning hearing as he urged passage of the Walmart deal "to show our children they have a future here."[72] The tact taken by Foreman to legitimate the growth coalition agenda exemplifies what geographer Kevin Cox calls a "territorial ideology ... [that] postulates interests at a local level which marginalizes divides of class, race and gender, and accentuates those defined by locality."[73]

In addition to white-dominated business groups, a number of black ministers and community activists backed the Walmart plan, with most having received contracts and other material rewards from HRI. For example, one vocal backer, Rev. Marie Galatas, and her company, Broadway Rehab, was the beneficiary of a $35,000 contract from HRI as part of the St. Thomas redevelopment.[74] In contrast to white business organizations, the ministers portrayed their support for the tax and zoning changes needed by the largest corporation in the world and its local real estate allies as one of promoting black self-determination in the face of elitist white opposition. Rev. Charles Southall, at a press conference in front of city hall, cried, "The time has passed when preservationists can tell predominately African-American neighborhoods what can be built and cannot be built." In addition, the ministers defended black councilman Oliver Thomas, a fellow supporter of the project, in the face of intimidation from rabid, white Walmart opponents. Their message was also conveyed through a full-page ad in the *Times-Picayune* paid for by the white-owned public relations firm Katz/Columbus. The agency received $55,000 from HRI for this and other media initiatives.[75] From the perspective of Kabacoff, these expenses were simply the cost of doing business and were a drop in the bucket compared with the several million dollars that he and real estate partner Darryl Berger would make from the land deal with Walmart alone.[76]

The approach taken by the black ministers to lend their support to the Walmart deal is an example of what Adolph Reed has termed the "reinvention mechanism." When employed in the context of the black urban regime, it often takes the form of black public officials staking out some position that appears to be progressive but which still allows them to back the development initiative demanded by the white-dominated corporate power structure. In the Walmart case black ministers stood in the role usually performed by black elected officials. Nonetheless, the same principle and logic were still operative: "to shift the basis for black response to policy debate away from substantive concerns with potential outcome and toward protection of racial image and status, as embodied in the idiosyncratic agenda of the black official."[77] Just as with their white corporate allies and white petty bourgeois opponents, the ministers did not demand decent pay, job quotas, or the workers' right to organize as a prerequisite for their support. Instead, the focus was on black image, with some attention to the trickle-down impact of the project thrown in for good measure.

For her part, STRC president Barbara Jackson came out in support of the regulatory changes, arguing they were necessary to build the 100 off-site public housing apartments.[78] The STRC, which had shaken the city in the 1980s, had now become harmlessly incorporated into the black urban regime. HRI, a leading member of the local black urban regime and growth coalition, had been able to coordinate the interests of black public housing tenants with its profit-making agenda. Indeed, even the last concession came at no cost—at the time of this writing, a decade later, HRI had still not built any of the promised off-site apartments.

Drawing Conclusions on the Reproduction of Class and Racial Inequality

This chapter began by recounting the great fanfare that accompanied HUD's awarding of a HOPE VI grant to the St. Thomas public housing development. That story ended ignominiously with the community expelled, past promises unilaterally broken, no right of return for residents, and every attempt to wipe away any remembrance of the African American community that called St. Thomas home for thirty-five years. In a further act of humiliation, African American resident leaders and their advisers even joined with HRI and the company's corporate allies to support tax changes from the local government. This support was in exchange for a commitment—a promise never fulfilled—for the construction of some off-site apartments that would have not nearly made up for the numbers lost due to demolition. Yet as exemplified by the collaboration with HRI in support of tax changes, the privatization at St. Thomas was not simply imposed by big, powerful developers in alliance with local and national state authorities. Rather, the governing elite of New Orleans's black urban regime gained the cooperation of leading community activists to privatize the St. Thomas public housing development. Although there was significant conflict, it always stayed within acceptable parameters. It was never *if* St. Thomas would be privatized but rather *how*. Furthermore, even when the how began to deviate from what had been promised, the nonprofit advisers and tenant leaders stayed committed to negotiations. They never took actions—such as refusing to leave and therefore requiring authorities to use force—that may have exposed or made transparent the central racialized class contradiction that the black urban regime embodied.

How do we understand and characterize the consensual introduction of neoliberal state reforms at the level of the black urban regime and the role of nonprofits? Sociologist Michael Burawoy's concept of "hegemonic despotism," which captures how capitalists have wrenched huge wage, benefits, seniority, and labor control concessions from U.S. manufacturing workers since the late 1970s, is useful. "Hegemonic despotism," Burawoy argues, is driven by "the 'rational' tyranny of capital over the *collective* worker." Under this form of despotic control, "the fear of being fired is replaced by the fear of capital flight, plant closure, transfer of operations, and plant disinvestments."[79] At St. Thomas tyranny came in the form of disinvestment in the 1980s and the threat of public housing flight in the 1990s. HUD and HANO's threats of "getting out of the housing business"—as some tenant leaders phrased it—increased the coercive power of the state and their real estate partners to privatize and seize the land of the St. Thomas community. But St. Thomas's demise, as with the labor union bureaucracy used to introduce austerity and concessions at the workplace, was a hegemonic process, since the state harnessed the existing tenant representation structure, as well as the new nonprofit one, to introduce privatization and austerity consensually. The nonprofit structure served not as a defense from the depredations of capital and the state but rather as an abettor, as a mechanism to "command consent to sacrifice."[80] Working within the conciliation apparatus, advisers like Vince Lane effectively used fear to encourage resident leaders to be "realistic" and work out a deal at the margins, much like the United States' AFL-CIO union bureaucracy has done.

The removal of the "negative anchor" of St. Thomas that prevented "anything from happening"—as Vince Lane phrased it—represented a qualitative new move in handling black impediments to corporate-defined economic regeneration efforts.[81] The "spatial containment strategy," as described by geographers Cook and Lauria, was giving way to what Mike Davis and others have called "racial cleansing." This solution, as discussed in chapter 6, underwent a dramatic expansion in the aftermath of Katrina. But as this study of St. Thomas underscores, the precedent had been well established before the levees broke.

6

Whose City Is It?

Hurricane Katrina and the Struggle for New Orleans's Public Housing, 2003–2008

> We finally cleaned up public housing in New Orleans. We couldn't do it, but God could.
>
> —CONGRESSMAN RICHARD BAKER, BATON ROUGE

> They can put me in jail. . . . I'm seventy years old, and I wanna come home. If I got to die, let me die in New Orleans!
>
> —GLORIA "MAMA GLO" IRVING,
> ST. BERNARD PUBLIC HOUSING RESIDENT

"What do we want? . . . Our Homes!" This was the heartfelt call-and-response chant invoked by a contingent of St. Bernard public housing residents and supporters marching toward a driveway that led into their now-shuttered community. On April 4, 2006, the thirty-eighth anniversary of Dr. Martin Luther King Jr.'s assassination and seven months after being forced out by Hurricane Katrina's floodwaters bursting of the city's decaying levees, displaced public housing residents were making it clear that they were coming home. The marchers—led by seventy-year-old, wheelchair–propelled Gloria "Mama Glo" Irving—were greeted by a phalanx of HANO and New Orleans police and a recently erected chain link fence. The protestors were undeterred. In her wheelchair, Mama Glo—pushed by former St. Bernard resident and HANO chairman Endesha Juakali and ignoring orders from HANO police chief Mitchell Dussett to stop—burst through the police line and led the marchers into the development.[1]

Why did St. Bernard and other public housing residents have to fight the police and face arrest simply to return home? How could national and local authorities selectively block public housing residents—and not other displaced New Orleanians—from exercising their right of return in the wake of a human-made disaster? Indeed, the UN Guiding Principles on Internal Displacement and other treaties to which the United States is a signatory codify the right of return, making it the responsibility of governments to facilitate—not block—the return of displaced people.[2] Public housing authorities did raise concerns of contaminated soil to justify the continued closure of developments, but this danger was no greater than that faced by other displaced New Orleanians who were allowed to return. Likewise, the damage sustained by public housing structures could not explain why residents were barred from their homes. In fact, several located in the center of the city—Iberville, Lafitte, and C. J. Peete—faced little or no flooding. While the first—but not second and third—floors of B.W. Cooper and St. Bernard did flood, the brick-and-cement outer structures and interior plaster walls came through the storm in much better shape than those of much of the city's flooded private housing stock. The mops and other cleaning material that protestors brought to the April 4 protest underscored that many of the apartments simply needed a thorough scrubbing in order to be made habitable.[3] The black women that lived at St. Bernard and other developments were willing and prepared to do the necessary cleaning if only authorities would lift the legal and physical barriers. Yet they were portrayed as lazy "soap opera watchers," as black city councilman Oliver Thomas smeared them in a calculated attack in February 2006 after an initial rally demanding the reopening of St. Bernard.

The obstacles public housing residents faced were not accidental or due to government foul-ups or inefficiency. Rather, they were intentional and made perfect sense in light of the blueprints drafted by political and economic elites for a new New Orleans in the aftermath of Hurricane Katrina. "Those who want to see this city rebuilt," New Orleans Business Council leader James Reiss explained to the *Wall Street Journal* only a week after the flood, "want to see it done in a completely different way: demographically, geographically and politically." Developer Joseph Canizaro was confident the vision of his fellow council member could be realized. "I think we have a clean sheet to start again," the city's most powerful developer and a major financial contributor to President Bush told the *Wall Street Journal*, "and with that clean sheet we have some very big opportunities." The pronouncements and actions taken by Reiss, Canizaro, and other powerful political and economic actors in New Orleans, Baton Rouge, and Washington in the immediate aftermath of Katrina made it clear that public housing communities were not part of the "completely different" city they were imagining.[4]

The city's public housing communities had faced an unrelenting attack over the three decades preceding Katrina. Yet Hurricane Katrina and the forced displacement of residents provided an opportunity to fast-track the revanchist agenda—to drown public housing in a fully human-made "neo-liberal deluge" and finally rid the city of these concentrations of poverty.[5] Therefore, it was no surprise that the Bush administration–controlled public housing authority, with full support from the city's Democratic African American mayor, seized the moment and closed most of the developments immediately after the storm.

But public housing was not the only target of the reenergized revanchist agenda that was spearheaded by state and corporate officials and cheered on by a host of think tanks, academics, and newspaper columnists. The city's primarily poor, black working-class population, the public sector on which they relied for jobs and services, and the political power this provided were all on the post-Katrina hit list. This unprecedented disaster and the suffering it caused for the survivors would not deter authorities from taking advantage of what former New Orleans city planning director Kristina Ford called a "*horrible opportunity* . . . to think about things that in the past were unthinkable" (emphasis added).[6] Indeed, the horrible displacement of the city's poor, black majority was precisely what created the opportunity to carry out the unthinkable—to rapidly and massively impose a neoliberal restructuring plan. This opportunity was at the heart of what *Wall Street Journal* and *New York Times* columnists Brendan Miniter and David Brooks, among others, meant when they referred to Katrina's silver lining.

Therefore, with a silver lining mind-set prevailing among leading government, business, and opinion leaders, it was not surprising that Democratic governor Kathleen Blanco ordered Charity Hospital, the main source of health care for the city and region's low-paid workforce, closed three weeks after the storm. Blanco and her top hospital administrator, Donald Smithburg, shuttered the impressive art deco 2,000-plus-bed hospital built by the Public Works Administration (PWA) in the 1930s, despite facing little damage and while the Oklahoma National Guard, foreign volunteers, and the hospital's staff were preparing to reopen it. The governor followed this action by ordering a state takeover of almost the entire 120-plus schools that composed New Orleans's primary and secondary public education system. With little opposition from the local school board, state authorities fired over 7,000 mainly black teachers and support staff and abrogated their collective bargaining agreement. Of those the state allowed to reopen, most were operated as nonunion, privately run, and publically subsidized charter schools. Not to be outdone, New Orleans mayor Ray Nagin fired over half of the city's 6,000 mainly black municipal workforce a little over a month after the storm.

This was the hostile political environment that public housing residents and their allies faced in their battle to return home. Government officials and their business partners—whether national or local, Republican or Democrat, white or black—were prepared to employ police repression or flout international law to carry out an agenda author Naomi Klein has termed "disaster capitalism"—the "orchestrated raid on the public sphere in the wake of a catastrophic event."[7] But force, "shock" in Klein's terminology, was not the only strategy employed in post-Katrina New Orleans to open up sectors, like public housing, schools, and hospitals, that had been closed off to profit making. As political economist Doug Henwood has argued in his critique of Klein's celebrated work *The Shock Doctrine: The Rise of Disaster Capitalism,* the singular emphasis she places on coercion to explain the post-1973 global imposition of the neoliberal model "skirts the difficult question" of how popular consent and legitimation for this agenda was won.[8] Addressing this omission is of particular importance for understanding how the disaster capitalism agenda in post-Katrina New Orleans was imposed and the challenges it generated. Force and coercion were not the only obstacles confronting public housing residents attempting to exercise their right of return. The other, less obvious barrier came in the form of the post-Katrina deluge of foundation-backed nonprofits that helped to consensually introduce the privatization of public housing and other core components of the neoliberal agenda.

The partnership between the nonprofit industrial complex and state and corporate officials to carry out the neoliberal agenda in post-Katrina New Orleans took both direct *and* indirect forms. The direct variety was the most obvious and transparent. Some nonprofits, such as the New Orleans Neighborhood Collaborative and the Archdiocese of New Orleans's Providence Community Housing, directly privatized public housing developments in partnership with either another nonprofit or a for-profit corporation. Another variant was the Rockefeller Foundation's fellowship program that, in collaboration with the University of Pennsylvania, assigned young professionals to various nonprofits either privatizing public housing or vying for the opportunity.

The critical indirect role played by nonprofits in facilitating privatization was channeling or "manufacturing"—as Michel Chossudovsky terms it—dissent that did not present a serious obstacle to the post-Katrina neo-liberal agenda. This "controlled form of opposition" took various forms.[9] One variant was nonprofits and their foundation funders helping to literally construct a nonprofit alternative to public housing and other public services. Nonprofits, whether conventional like Habitat for Humanity or supposedly radical like Common Ground Relief, channeled hundreds of thousands of volunteers into repairing and constructing homes and providing other services rather than incorporating them into a movement to defend public housing and advocate for a public works program to rebuild New Orleans and the gulf. Likewise, Brad Pitt's much-ballyhooed Make It Right Foundation channeled hopes that Hollywood stars and corporate backers would come to the rescue of the city's battered Lower Ninth Ward. This initiative, while obviously appreciated by the relative handful that have benefitted, has nonetheless helped to further foster the illusion that philanthropic efforts could rebuild the city. Promoting this illusion—a characterization that will not be negated even if Pitt does eventually deliver on all of the promised 150 homes, none of which are rentals—provided further political cover for the government's abandonment of this low-income black community.[10] Paltry, private initiatives such as these will not reverse the nearly 150,000-person population decline the city suffered between 2005 and 2010. The decline in the black population—118,000—represented over 80 percent of the loss.[11]

A second form of channeling was through foundations and various levels of government funding a variety of advocacy organizations that narrowly addressed one particular injustice or oppression. This layer of single-issue groups acted as a bulwark against "the articulation of a cohesive common platform and plan of action" to challenge the larger neoliberal agenda in post-Katrina New Orleans.[12] The now-defunct Association of Community Organizations for Reform Now (ACORN), for example, which received generous funding from HUD and foundations, did challenge some inequitable policies directed toward low-income neighborhoods, but it studiously avoided any involvement in the struggle to defend public housing. Other foundation-backed nonprofits, when they did get involved in defending public housing, undermined direct action protests and kept the movement from directly challenging the authority of the state to destroy public housing communities.

Despite confronting these hard and soft forms of power, a formidable social movement emerged both before and after Katrina to challenge the neoliberal solution to public housing. How did this movement emerge?

What obstacles did the movement confront, particularly from the non-profits and foundations? And how were they managed? Why did the movement succeed in achieving some goals and not others? What lessons can be drawn from the New Orleans public housing experience for others struggling for an egalitarian urban future? These questions direct the accounts of New Orleans's pre- and post-Katrina public housing struggles examined in chapters 6 and 7. The story begins in the pre-Katrina aftermath of St. Thomas's demolition and remaking as River Gardens as a grassroots movement emerged to stymie efforts of emboldened developers to privatize the Iberville public housing development, located just outside the city's famed French Quarter and main thoroughfare, Canal Street. Chapter 7 concludes two and a half years after Katrina as the dust—both figuratively and literally—settled on years of protest and the demolished remains of some five thousand little-damaged and badly needed public housing apartments. At the same time, the over eight hundred red brick apartments at Iberville, despite intense pressure from developers and government officials, continued to provide affordable housing for low-income Katrina survivors.

I was a leading participant in the pre- and post-Katrina public housing defense campaign analyzed in these chapters, and therefore, I write about my own involvement where needed. My participation facilitated my "understanding," as Leon Trotsky argues in his firsthand account of the Russian Revolution, "not only of the psychology of the forces in action, both individual and collective, but also of the inner connection of events."[13] At particular points in the narrative, I draw on my insider knowledge to provide a detailed account of events in order to elaborate concepts and support and substantiate my broader arguments. Nonetheless, my participation in these events does not relieve me of the necessity to base my analysis on verified documents. Therefore, this account of the 2004–2008 campaign to defend New Orleans's public housing and the role of nonprofits relies not only on my memory but also on a variety of primary and secondary sources, including my observation notes.

On to Iberville!

By 2003, in the aftermath of St. Thomas's demolition, the dispersal of residents, and the makeover as River Gardens, New Orleans's real estate developers, bankers, and assorted entrepreneurs began setting their sights on the Iberville public housing development. In undertaking this initiative, the corporate wing of New Orleans's black urban regime would have to work with some new public sector partners. Ray Nagin, the city's fourth consecutively elected black chief executive, now occupied city hall. Nagin, a millionaire former executive with the local Cox Cable operation (a TV, Internet, and phone provider) who was derided as Ray Reagan during the campaign because of his sympathies with the Republican Party, won the 2002 mayoral race. Nagin, like Sidney Barthelemy a decade and a half earlier, was the preferred candidate of the white business elite and, also like the city's second black mayor, won a first term without garnering a majority of the black electorate.[14] There were changes at HANO, as well. In early 2002, the Bush administration broke the accord that Mayor Morial had crafted with a cooperative Clinton White House to maintain local control over HANO and imposed a series of HUD-appointed administrators to run the agency. Despite the change of faces, electoral coalitions, and political party affiliations, these public officials were as eager to enter into public–private partnerships to redevelop Iberville as their predecessors had been with St. Thomas.

There were other similarities between the Iberville and St. Thomas cases. Iberville was also located in highly valued real estate—in this case, just outside New Orleans's old-city tourist destination the French Quarter and a block away from the Crescent City's major thoroughfare, Canal Street. As with St. Thomas, developers and local officials were crafting grand schemes for redeveloping the entire area, with the removal of Iberville being critical to their vision. For example, in 2003, Mayor Nagin commissioned the Downtown Development District (DDD)—a Business Improvement District established by the Louisiana state legislature in 1974, whose board was dominated by real estate interests—to oversee the preparation of a new vision and implementation strategy for redeveloping Canal Street. Released in early 2004, the plan called for incentivizing the creation of upscale housing and new hotels, attracting high-end retailers, expanding an existing medical/biotech corridor, and creating a family-friendly entertainment district. Just as Canizaro's aid had designated a low-income, black public housing community as, quote, a "deterrent to development" along the riverfront, so did those attempting to "revitalize" Canal Street. "The presence of the Iberville Housing Development has had a profound [negative] effect" on Canal Street, lamented the authors of the *Canal Street Vision and Development Strategy*, a report subsequently endorsed by the DDD and the mayor. "A high concentration of households with low to very low incomes . . . and welfare dependence," the report went on with a litany also reminiscent of St. Thomas, "has proven a formula for community instability throughout urban America, and New Orleans with Iberville is no exception. Fear of crime, generated either by those who live there or those who prey on its residents, has had negative impacts in all directions."[15] Not to be overshadowed, Pres Kabacoff came out with his own revitalization plan in late 2004, with its recommendations mirroring, with a few additions, those made in the DDD-commissioned report. Just as with the DDD study, Kabacoff held that "the single most important linchpin to making this happen"—to realizing his "vision of the city" along Canal Street—was dealing with Iberville.[16] To solve the Iberville problem, both Kabacoff and the DDD drew on the tried-and-true St. Thomas formula—a mixed-income, privately run development that would slash the number of public housing apartments and drive out most residents. The black, low-income Iberville community had to go, but it would have to be done, as Canizaro's aid Nathan Watson emphasized at St. Thomas, in an "efficient" (i.e., consensual) manner. "Controversy," Kabacoff stressed, "will derail any discussion of rebuilding Iberville" and had to be avoided at all cost.[17]

Hands Off Iberville

In 2004 as the drive to redevelop Iberville gained steam, local antiwar organization Community, Concern, Compassion, better known as C3, initiated a campaign in defense of the besieged community. Local activists, including myself, formed C3 after the terrorist attacks of September 11, 2001, in New York City and Washington, DC, to resist a U.S. military invasion of Afghanistan and Iraq. While opposing the war abroad, activists in this grassroots non-501(c)(3) organization always linked the foreign assault with the domestic war at home on poor and working-class communities. The Iberville struggle offered an opportunity to concretely connect these two fronts. As with many antiwar coalitions around the country, the size of meetings and protests had dwindled by 2004, after the unprecedented mass mobilizations the year before had been unsuccessful in stopping the Bush administration's drive to invade Iraq. When C3 decided to focus on Iberville (while not abandoning antiwar work), more activists, uncomfortable with taking on public housing, drifted away. A core group, including three white activists—Mike Howells, Marty Rowland, and myself—as well as legendary African American civil rights activist Andy Washington, continued on. At the same time, as C3 expanded the issues it addressed, the organization became more diverse as more female, African American, and low-income members began participating. These new activists included a white woman, Elizabeth Cook, black community activist Randy Mitchell, and three black Iberville residents—Cody Marshall, Delena Moss, and Cary Reynolds. These eight to nine activists, constituting the core of C3 before the storm, were regularly joined by a wider group of public housing residents, students, and other community activists for the group's weekly meetings and protest actions.

The first action where C3 explicitly drew parallels between the wars abroad and at home was during the March 2004 demonstrations marking the first anniversary of the Iraq war. C3 activists led a march that stopped at the local public hospital—Charity—and Iberville to highlight how the United States was simultaneously leading a war of pillage in Iraq for oil and one at home against public services. The other core C3 members and I performed outreach work, before and during the march, to Iberville residents in order to show support for defending the development and opposing demolition or any loss of units.[18]

After Pres Kabacoff announced his own grand plans for Iberville in late 2004, C3 decided to prioritize the defense of Iberville. Taking advantage of the power embedded in public housing's geography, I secured the St. Jude Community Center to hold C3 meetings, conveniently located for Iberville residents only a few blocks from the development. C3 activists, as part of their outreach, began regular leafleting and door knocking at Iberville to explain their support for defending Iberville and invited tenants to the weekly meeting to help organize a movement in defense of the community that would unite residents and nonresidents, blacks and whites. Invitations were also given to the tenant council to join the defense campaign. Iberville tenant council president Ollie Pendleton did not accept the offer, but she did begin to monitor the gatherings by standing at a nearby street corner to observe, argued Iberville residents, who and how many of her constituents were attending. Citywide public housing tenant council president Cynthia Wiggins—who by the mid-2000s was drawing a comfortable salary of over $70,000 as CEO of the nonprofit corporation that managed the Guste public housing development—was invited, as well, but never returned phone calls.[19]

The first public demonstration taken by C3 activists and supporters since placing Iberville at the center of their work was on February 12, 2005. Under the new name C3/Hands Off Iberville, which underscored the group's forceful and unapologetic defense of public housing, a few dozen protestors gathered in front of the development. Led by Iberville tenant Delena Moss, activists challenged the common sense that Iberville would follow the same fate as St. Thomas. Moss, others that spoke, and I called for not only saving Iberville but recovering the thousands of public housing units lost over the last decade. In contrast to the St. Thomas experience, where nonprofits helped mask the contradictory class and race interests at play in public housing redevelopment, the grassroots, non-foundation-supported Hands Off Iberville worked to make them transparent. Instead of being cowed by developers and city hall and accommodating to the neoliberal reform agenda, it was defiant and announced support for defending and expanding public housing. The initial demonstration, in addition to attracting new members, including Iberville resident Cody Marshall, helped create the controversy so feared by developers by making it clear there was a pole of opposition to demolishing Iberville. A free local newspaper geared toward the black community, *Data Weekly,* helped fuel the controversy by emblazoning "Hands Off Iberville: The Community Strikes Back" across its entire front page in its coverage of the protest. The local paper of record, the *Times-Picayune,* a longtime supporter of public housing demolition, did not cover the protest. Instead, two days after the rally, New Orleans's only daily newspaper came out with a front-page article in the metro section that appeared designed to quell the brewing controversy by placing redevelopment in a positive light. The article, entitled "HANO to Start Housing Blitz," touted the new housing that would be shortly built at four demolished public housing developments.[20]

Throughout the winter and spring of 2005, C3 continued to use various venues and forums to denounce attempts to demolish Iberville and expose the contradictions of New Orleans's black urban regime. For example, a ten-person C3 delegation spoke at the city council's televised April housing committee meeting and later, after continual requests and pressure, before the entire council in June. The speakers contrasted their agenda of expanding Iberville and public housing with that of developers, which was described by activist Mike Howells, in a strategic attempt to dramatize the two opposing poles, as one of "ethnic and class cleansing." Similar messages were regularly delivered at HANO's monthly board meetings. Activists also organized an April 12 Night Out against Gentrification demonstration in front of a former department store, located near Iberville on Canal Street, that developers were converting into high-priced condominiums.[21] Yet in C3's effort to broaden support for Iberville, the grassroots activists failed to garner the backing of nonprofit groups, even those that identified as activist, antiracist, and prolabor. One of these was Community Labor United (CLU), found and led by a retired African American labor organizer whose ostensible mission was to connect labor unions with community-based struggles for racial and economic justice. Nonetheless, despite repeated invitations, CLU—which at the time was busy obtaining funding for its nonprofit think tank, the Louisiana Research Institute for Community Empowerment (LaRICE)—failed to mobilize support for Iberville.[22] The group INCITE! Women of Color against Violence, which held its third Color of Violence conference in New Orleans in March 2005, also declined an invitation, made by a young African American women active in C3, to route their planned march to Iberville. C3 argued that the attack on Iberville was a concrete, local expression of structural violence directed against primarily African American women and would be an ideal way for the organization to connect with local struggles. INCITE!, a 501(c)(3) nonprofit at the time, was not swayed.[23]

C3's last major initiative before floodwaters swamped the city was spearheading the defeat of a HOPE VI application for Iberville. In late May a local legal aid attorney sent me an email explaining that the new HANO director, Nadine Jarmon, despite earlier assurances to the contrary, was planning to submit a HOPE VI application for Iberville. But before submitting the required annual *Public Housing Agency Plan* to HUD—which outlined the agency's plans for Iberville and other developments for the 2005–2006 fiscal year—HANO had to hold a hearing at the end of June to take public comment. HANO could then revise its plan in the light of public feedback before sending it to Washington, DC, in mid-July.[24] Over the next month C3 members, including tenants Delena Moss, Cary Reynolds, and Cody Marshall, mobilized through phone calling and door knocking to inform residents and supporters about HANO's plan and encourage attendance at the crucial June 30 hearing. As part of a strategic effort to expose collusion between developers and public officials and increase the controversy that developers wanted to suppress, I handed, during my testimony before the city council on June 16, a public records request to city councilwoman Jacquelyn Clarkson, whose district encompassed Iberville. I demanded at the televised hearing that she come clean about her meetings with developers. After Clarkson produced the documents, C3 distributed a flyer exposing the meetings she had concerning Iberville with HRI CEO Pres Kabacoff and his top lobbyist, former mayor Barthelemy.[25]

Although little headway had been made getting nonprofits on board the campaign, on June 30, dozens of grassroots activists, including key Iberville resident leaders Cary Reynolds, Delena Moss, and Cody Marshall, descended on the HANO boardroom. The HANO police—a force that dramatically expanded as the agency simultaneously downsized its housing stock in the 1990s and 2000s—ordered protestors to discard their placards before entering the building. These heavy-handed tactics, far from squelching the protestors, seemed to only raise their ire further as a series of speakers rose to the mic to denounce any plans to demolish Iberville. Delena Moss exposed the class issues at stake: "It's about the land. They're trading lives for money." Creating controversy worked. Officials were put on the defensive, as they claimed—in contradiction to their written report—that they had no plans to demolish Iberville. Jarmon, in a subsequent mid-July meeting with C3, agreed to eliminate the HOPE VI request from the annual plan. Carmen Valenti, who acted as HANO's one-person HUD-appointed board, tried to defuse the situation by portraying the HOPE VI plans for Iberville as a misunderstanding: "It should have never been included in the agency's plan. It caused some embarrassment."[26]

Is There an Alternative? Lessons from Iberville

While the defeat of the HOPE VI application by no means permanently protected the Iberville from the designs of developers, it nonetheless was an important poor people's victory. HANO's decision validated both Pres Kabacoff's concerns that controversy could derail his redevelopment initiative and, conversely, the hopes of grassroots activists that, in contrast to the reigning TINA ideology, their efforts could have an impact. Other urban scholars have found, as well, a rational basis for both concern and hope regarding contemporary urban redevelopment initiatives. As sociologist Joe Feagin argues, neoliberal policies such as demolishing public housing "do not develop out of an inevitable structural necessity but rather in a contingent manner. They result from conscious actions taken by individual decision makers." The actions taken by local government and corporate decision makers are, adds Pauline Lippman, "conditioned by the relative strength and mobilization of social forces (e.g. organizations of civil society, working class organizations, popular social movements) and the political culture of specific contexts."[27]

What helped create the popular mobilization and power at Iberville that Lippman identified as crucial for defeating contemporary urban neoliberal initiatives? A key source of the movement's power was the freedom that came from activists operating outside the nonprofit complex. This independence enhanced the ability to forge power from below to challenge the urban neoliberal agenda in two ways. First, as an independent, grassroots organization, C3 was not limited to issues outlined in grant applications or constrained by directives of foundation officers. Operating outside the government-sanctioned and foundation-funded third sector provided the organization the freedom to democratically decide what organizing campaigns to initiate and when. This independence allowed activists to quickly respond to moves by developers and state officials rather than wait for permission from funders or for the following year's grant cycle. Furthermore, independence from foundations provided the flexibility to move beyond single-issue activism and begin to connect, theoretically and concretely, with other struggles. As Michel Chossudovsky has argued, corporate funding of advocacy groups tends to "fragment the people's movement into a vast 'do it yourself' mosaic," and as a result "dissent has been compartmentalized. Separate 'issue oriented' protest movements (e.g. environment, antiglobalization, peace, women's rights, climate change) are encouraged and generously funded as opposed to a cohesive mass movement."[28] In contrast, the Iberville campaign was able to move beyond these strictures and build greater power by linking the war abroad to cuts in social programs at home and the activists involved in these struggles.

The second source of strength that arose from C3's organizational independence from the nonprofit complex was that it allowed the group to undertake an aggressive campaign that could exploit the race and class contradictions of the black urban regime's development agenda. The elite's attempt to privatize Iberville and displace this low-income black community was a clear manifestation of the accumulation–legitimation contradiction at the heart of the black urban regime. A critical source of power for working-class organizations therefore is their ability to highlight and exploit this pressure point within the local power structure. As Mark Purcell argues, neoliberal regimes "creak under their contradictions," but he adds, "it takes active, organized, and committed resistance to bring about a collapse."[29] Nonprofits, as analysts have noted, are, however, ill equipped for this job, tied as they are to a "pragmatic" agenda of "reasonable goals" obtained through "negotiations with state officials via sympathetic politicians."[30] In contrast, the grassroots Iberville insurgency, though not having large numbers, nonetheless had the political and financial independence to use various terrains—from HANO hearings and televised city council meetings to street protests and press conferences—to dramatically and forcefully expose the regime's class and race contradictions. A final strength the Iberville movement enjoyed arose from the political-geographic organization of residents in public housing. The concentration of residents in one geographic area, under a single state authority, facilitated organizing and collective consciousness. This source of power took a major blow, however, a little over a month after the poor people's victory at Iberville when Hurricane Katrina roared into the Gulf Coast.

Public Housing and Hurricane Katrina

For many low-income African Americans in New Orleans, public housing historically provided not only a source of affordable housing but hurricane protection, as well. With over a third of the city's African Americans living in poverty and without cars, the costly privatized evacuation system was not a realistic option. Thus, as Katrina approached many of the poor turned once again to the city's two- and three-story brick-and-cement public housing buildings for protection. The "bricks" successfully spared them, as they had in the past, from the Category 2 hurricane that hit New Orleans on August 29, 2005. Then, after floodwaters breached the federal government's inadequately maintained levees—dramatically unmasking just one piece of the country's severely eroded infrastructure—public housing became a secure base for residents to organize an evacuation after their abandonment by all levels of government. As St. Bernard resident Gloria Irving explains, "I was on the third floor with my flag waving for them, but they never stopped," in reference to helicopters circling the city. "They were passing by, but they didn't help anybody." It was "our men," Irving and other survivors explain, who "were our heroes."[31]

Irving's firsthand account of post-Katrina New Orleans contrasts sharply with reports that emanated from mainstream media outlets at the time of the disaster. The airwaves were filled with unsubstantiated reports of black men carrying out rapes and other atrocities at the convention center and the Superdome, the city's two main evacuation centers, and shooting at rescue helicopters, while attempts to obtain food, water, and other necessities were indiscriminately labeled "looting." These claims of wanton violence, which were later debunked, were also given credence by the city's African American mayor, Ray Nagin, and police chief, Eddie Compass. Before national and international audiences in the week after

Katrina, they repeatedly reported that "hooligans" among the overwhelmingly black survivors at the Superdome and convention center were beating, killing, and raping people.[32] Governor Kathleen Blanco furthered the demonization and criminalization of survivors as she hailed the "landing" in New Orleans of "troops fresh from Iraq, well trained, experienced, battled tested." As she coldly announced, "[The troops] are ready to shoot to kill, and they are more than willing to do so if necessary, and I expect they will."[33] While this vilification campaign was going on, the African American men at St. Bernard were helping ferry children and the elderly from the St. Bernard development to a nearby highway overpass at a time when authorities had effectively abandoned these folks. Most had to wait for days, camped out on the asphalt and under the broiling sun, before finally being evacuated. Many, to the chagrin of former first lady Barbara Bush, ended up in Houston.[34]

While St. Bernard and other public housing residents were dealing with their trauma, tracking down loved ones and figuring out where they could obtain food and housing, their affluent city brethren had other concerns. They were busy gathering, as *Wall Street Journal* reporter Charles Cooper entitled his September 6 article, to "plot the future" of the city. Joseph Canizaro was, of course, at the center of these deliberations. Members of the New Orleans Business Council—with Canizaro calling in orders from his vacation home in Utah—met in early September with Mayor Nagin in Dallas to lay out a post-Katrina framework for reconstructing the city. Out of this and subsequent meetings and discussions came the Bring New Orleans Back Commission (BNOB), which the mayor authorized to develop a rebuilding blueprint. Canizaro sat on the BNOB's critical urban planning committee. Barbara Major, another familiar face from St. Thomas and close associate of Canizaro, was named—ostensibly by the mayor—as the BNOB cochair. In another page from St. Thomas, the first decision of the seventeen-member BNOB was to invite the Urban Land Institute to develop a plan delineating which parts of the city should be rebuilt. The ULI experts called for a "smaller footprint" through "green spacing"—not rebuilding—certain sections of the city. These areas overwhelming were black neighborhoods.[35]

Like the BNOB, a variety of activists also began, in the wake of the storm, to plot the challenging of the closure of public housing, the green spacing of other low-income neighborhoods, and a range of other regressive plans then being rolled out. Nonetheless, the post-Katrina landscape presented serious obstacles to C3's resuming their defense of Iberville and other public housing communities. Cody Marshall had taken a job with a cruise line before the storm (he would later return), while Delena Moss and Randy Mitchell decided not to return to the city, and it would be several years before Cary Reynolds reappeared. Andy Washington, Marty Rowland, and I had evacuated, although within the first few months we were back periodically and were in regular contact with each other, as well as folks in New Orleans. Thus in the first few weeks and months after the storm, much work fell on Elizabeth Cook, who lived in the city's unflooded west bank and returned home shortly after the storm, and Mike Howells, a holdout who never evacuated. They took the lead in challenging the claim made by HANO officials and repeated by the *Time-Picayune* that the developments, including Iberville and Lafitte, both of which received little flooding, were "ruined," "decimated," and "not habitable" and, thus, could not be reopened.[36] They took photos of Iberville and other developments showing that the buildings faced little or no damage and could be reopened. On September 10, Howells led Amy Goodman, the host of the nationally syndicated radio show *Democracy Now,* and journalist Christian Parenti of the *Nation* to the Iberville to show the little damage it had incurred.[37] In addition, both Cook and Howells regularly went to the developments to meet residents who were returning to check on their belongings.

In contrast to the frequent claims in the mainstream press that most poor African Americans had no interest in returning, Cook and Howells repeatedly encountered residents who desperately wanted to return home. For example, Cook met future public housing activist Sam Jackson while he was visiting his apartment at the B. W. Cooper development in October. She worked with Jackson to organize a press conference to underscore that he and his family wanted to return and for HANO to stop blocking them. In addition, they called upon local authorities to end the looting of public housing families' apartments, which plagued New Orleans after it was reopened in mid-September.

Though C3 activists demanded the reopening of all public housing developments, their efforts in the first few months after Katrina centered on Iberville. Residents were on the front lines of this struggle as many took direct action to reclaim their homes. For example, one couple, Paul and Shantrel Martin, moved back with their children and used a generator to provide electricity, since HANO had cut off utilities in an effort to keep people out. Even an eighty-plus-year-old resident, whom C3 activist Marty Rowland assisted, was one of several Iberville residents who reoccupied their homes without official permission. As in the past,

C3 used public forums, including the city's first post-Katrina city council and HANO meetings, both held in October, to vociferously call for the reopening of public housing and to offer counterarguments to those used to justify its continued closure.

By early October Howells and Cook had resumed the weekly Thursday public housing meeting, and they eventually returned it to the St. Jude Community Center. The group was then joined by other activists, including some connected to the Peoples Hurricane Relief Fund (PHRF)—the successor organization to Community Labor United—and Common Ground Relief, a group formed after the storm by former Black Panther Malik Rahim. Common Ground was a nonprofit that attracted volunteers from across the country and world to provide a number of services for Katrina survivors, from a free health clinic to house gutting and repair to the development of organic gardens and the opening of a low-income apartment complex. While the bulk of their efforts, as I critique later, were directed toward self-help and nongovernmental social service efforts, some of the young people involved with the group did get involved in the defense of public housing and renters' rights. C3, Common Ground, the PHRF, and other activists helped form the new housing coalition New Orleans Housing Eviction Action Team (NO-HEAT). The group focused on reopening public housing and stopping the post-Katrina evictions of private sector renters by landlords trying to get higher-paying tenants as rents soared after the storm. On December 3, NO-HEAT held a march in front of Iberville demanding the reopening of public housing. Shortly afterward, the movement won its first major victory when HUD announced it would reopen Iberville. The controversy created before Katrina, the protests after the flood, and the direct action taken by residents had forced HUD's hand. As Iberville resident Annette Davis puts it, HUD "wanted to keep the low-income people away" and give Iberville to developers, but because of the protests and media attention, officials "got scared" and "gave in."[38] As the late Rev. Marshall Truehill, a politically connected black minister with access to the mayor, confirmed, "[C3's] protests made a difference." Also important, the protests impacted the calculations of HUD secretary Alphonso Jackson, who had the final say on reopening Iberville. Underscoring the extent to which the pre- and post-Katrina public housing movement had created a controversy around Iberville that raised the political costs of keeping it closed, Jackson told housing advocate James Perry that "I know people want to do [Iberville] as a land grab, and it's not going to happen on my watch."[39]

Nonprofits, Identity Politics, and Ideological Struggle within the Public Housing Movement

As the new year began, the housing movement celebrated some victories, including the reopening of Iberville and the defeat of the BNOB's greenspacing scheme to block the rebuilding of mainly black neighborhoods. Vehement denunciation of the proposal and Joe Canizaro—who led the BNOB's urban planning committee, which unveiled and advocated the plan—forced Mayor Nagin to withdraw support for the initiative.[40] Nonetheless, despite these victories four other traditional developments (St. Bernard, Lafitte, C. J. Peete, and B. W. Cooper), hundreds of scattered-site units, and two Ninth Ward developments (Florida and Desire) that had been turned into mixed-income communities before the storm remained closed. Furthermore, with most public housing residents now scattered across the state and country and federal and local authorities intent on taking advantage of their displacement in order to rid the city of these concentrations of poverty, the obstacles confronting NO-HEAT's efforts to reopen public housing were formidable. In addition to these external challenges, internal ideological conflicts, rooted in questions of legitimacy and identity, confronted and divided the city's post-Katrina public housing/right of return movement. C3 activists, as they had before the storm, emphasized the importance of an interracial class struggle and confrontational strategy, what William Sites has called the "militant" or "community resistance" tendency in neighborhood and community battles.[41] C3 combined calls for reopening public housing developments, public schools, and Charity Hospital with a larger demand for a mass, direct-government employment program, funded by ending foreign wars and taxing the wealthy, to rebuild New Orleans, the Gulf Coast, and the entire country.[42] With the displacement of most public housing residents, Mike Howells argues, "It was more important than ever for white and other non–public housing folks to raise their voices." In contrast, some activists, usually those affiliated with nonprofit organizations, criticized white members of the multiracial C3 for taking a lead role in the public housing movement. For example, Mayaba Liebenthal, an organizer with Critical Resistance, a nonprofit prison abolitionist group, argues in a March 2006 posting on the NO-HEAT Listserv that "the white folks at C3 need to back off."

> Dealing with racism isn't your life's experience, I would never presume to speak on behalf of white people, could one of you show me and other people of color the same respect. . . . This habit on

speaking on behalf of those "less fortunate" is becoming more
than just comically irritating but offensive and damaging to actual
change . . . for me this [is] about very practical issues, organize
from where you personally and actually are.[43]

An antiracist trainer with the People's Institute disrupted a March 2006
C3 meeting to level a similar criticism. Liebenthal's critique articulates central elements of identity politics, a postmodernism-informed worldview
and theory of organizing that has risen in tandem with neoliberalism. Ex-
ponents of identity politics place emphasis on "differences as the central
truth of political life" and therefore stress, to cite Liebenthal's manifesto,
organizing "from where you are."[44] That is, organizing should be based on
a particular racial, gender, sexual orientation, ability, or other oppression
(or privilege, depending on where you stand). This form of organizing is
rooted in a key epistemological assumption of identity politics that "only
those who actually experience a particular form of oppression" are able to
understand and fight against it. Thus if, as Liebenthal explains, "racism isn't
your life experience," if you don't "actually experience a particular form of
oppression," then you are not "capable of fighting against it."[45]

With most public housing residents still in exile, Liebenthal and other
identity politics advocates effectively were demanding quiescence while
authorities proceeded to demolish the homes of low-income, black Katrina
survivors. In fact, if identity politics logic is followed consistently, even
African Americans who were nonetheless not public housing residents,
such as Liebenthal, would not have had the legitimacy required to take
a leading role. The following critique by political scientist Adolph Reed
captures the demobilizing impact the identity politics debate had on the
public housing movement:

> [Identity politics's] focus on who is not in the room certainly does
> not facilitate strategic discussion on how best to deploy the re-
> sources of those who *are* in the room, and its fixation on organiz-
> ing around difference overtaxes any attempt to sustain concerted
> action.[46]

As was the case in New Orleans, the immobilizing debates on legitimacy,
identity, and difference undermined attempts to assemble the resources
activists did have to confront the powerful forces bent on doing away with
public housing and all public services.

It was not surprising that an identity politics critique of the public housing movement emanated from the nonprofit world. This milieu provides, Joan Roelofs argues, a "fertile soil" for the promotion of an IP form of organizing that focuses on a particular oppression, with only those most directly impacted eligible to participate. While identity politics ideology did strike a chord with the nonprofit sector, it did not enjoy much resonance among public housing residents. In fact, in late January 2006 several displaced St. Bernard public housing residents then living in Houston began calling C3 activist Elizabeth Cook after finding her number on an Internet post announcing a Martin Luther King Jr. Day march that the public housing movement had organized from the Lower Ninth Ward.[47] They desperately wanted to return home. After several weeks of networking with residents, I was designated by C3 members to take a bus to Houston, rent a van, and bring back the residents for a Valentine's Day action to demand the reopening of the development.

A brief discussion of my experience organizing the trip helps elaborate the opportunities and constraints confronting antineoliberal challenges that operate outside the nonprofit sector. On one level, independence from the nonprofit complex provided flexibility on what issues C3 addressed and the tactics and strategies employed. Yet operating outside the reach of the foundations left activists bereft of the financial support that was at times needed for organizing. To address this contradiction, I reached out for support from various Left activists based in Houston who had been involved in post-Katrina solidarity work. Activists with the Revolutionary Communist Party (RCP), whose party members have been active in other cities, particularly Chicago, in defense of public housing, were the only group that responded to my request.[48] I was picked up in the bus station by an RCP member and brought to the airport, where I rented a van. Again, since C3 had no significant financial resources, I charged the rental to my credit card with the expectation that we would then raise money to get reimbursed. I then followed my guide to the apartment complex in south Houston where I had arranged to pick up the residents. About ten displaced women from St. Bernard, including seventy-year-old Gloria "Mama Go" Irving, who had called me repeatedly to confirm that I would pick her up, boarded the van in the early hours of February 14 for the six-hour ride through the Louisiana bayou and back to New Orleans.

We arrived in the early afternoon for what C3 dubbed the Have a Heart, St. Bernard Must Restart rally and press conference. Among those in attendance was antiwar activist Cindy Sheehan, who helped connect the antiwar and the New Orleans right of return struggles by pointing out the contradictions between the resources spent on the war in Iraq and the lack of support for low-income Katrina survivors. St. Bernard residents Gloria Irving and Stephanie Mingo, depicted in figures 6.1 and 6.2, made it clear they wanted to return home. Their moving but forcefully delivered message broke through the dominant narrative, propagated in various human interest stories of displaced New Orleanians, that the city's poor had found opportunity in the diaspora and had no desire to return to their impoverished city.[49] The response of the African American political leadership to their pleas was, though, to either place responsibility for the matter in HUD's lap or denigrate public housing residents as unworthy burdens that the city could not accommodate. "We don't need soap opera watchers right now," bellowed Councilman Oliver Thomas at a city council meeting a few days after the rally as Stephanie Mingo called for reopening St. Bernard. This African American Democrat conjured up the racialized and gendered welfare queen stereotype, pontificating that "we're going to target the people who are going to work . . . at some point there has to be a whole new level of motivation, and people have got to stop blaming the government for something they ought to do."[50] HANO responded to resident's pleas by placing a metal fence, topped by barbed wire, around the development.

Despite these attacks, the movement to reopen public housing—the closure of which crystallized the class and race biases of what historian Lance Hill calls the post-Katrina "exclusionary" agenda—began gaining traction. Endesha Juakali, a former chair of the HANO board who grew up at St. Bernard, joined the fight to reopen his childhood community after the February 14 protest. Juakali, as explained in chapter 2, had lent support, as HANO chair in the late 1980s, for Reynard Rochon's plan to massively downsize public housing. Nonetheless, Juakali, in the aftermath of Katrina, supported the demand to reopen all apartments at St. Bernard and other developments. At a C3 meeting in late March, Juakali proposed that activists organize a caravan of displaced residents from Houston for an April 4—the anniversary of Martin Luther King Jr.'s assassination— action to force the reopening of St. Bernard. C3 members endorsed the plan, and I volunteered to join Juakali for this second Houston mission. After four days of phone calls and meetings, with Gloria Irving's apartment serving as an organizing center, we joined thirty or so residents in two vans and several cars in a caravan back to New Orleans. To cover the costs, Juakali and I turned for help from the PHRF, an organization

FIGURES 6.1 AND 6.2. Stephanie Mingo and Gloria Irving (seated) speaking to the press at the February 14, 2006, press conference and rally to reopen St. Bernard.

that emerged after Katrina as the successor to the CLU. The PHRF, whose donations were routed through its 501(c)(3) fiscal sponsor, the Vanguard Foundation, had raised over a million dollars after the storm. In contrast to other nonprofits, the PHRF saw itself as spearheading a radical grassroots fight for the right of return and against the racist exclusionary agenda. Nonetheless, the PHRF's leaders, Malcolm Suber and Kali Akuno, who were then in the midst of a nasty internal fight with a faction led by CLU founder Curtis Muhammad that would lead to a splinter group, did not deliver on our request. Therefore, I was forced to charge the costs of two vans and a car rental to my credit card and hope, as happened in the last trip, to be reimbursed through subsequently collected donations.

The April 4 attempt by St. Bernard residents to reclaim their community and the repressive response this generated graphically exposed the contradictions of New Orleans's black urban regime and the U.S. state. On the anniversary of King's death, the locally controlled police and federally directed HANO cops lined up to physically block attempts by displaced black women and their families—and their black and white supporters— to clean and reclaim their apartments. The phalanx of police contrasted sharply with both the claims of the local black leadership to be a defender of the black community and that of the U.S. state to be *the* beacon of human rights. Residents and activists were undeterred by the show of force. Armed with mops and brooms and led by the wheelchair-propelled Gloria Irving, marchers burst through the police lines and entered into the development. Residents proceeded to go into their apartments and collect personal items and mementos, and although they were not ready to mount a permanent reoccupation, they vowed to return. The pace of events accelerated as the bold action taken by St. Bernard residents spurred on others. In late April, C3 led a march of Iberville residents to the local HUD office to demand quicker action on reopening apartments and addressing a myriad of other problems tenants faced. Then, on May 3, hundreds of residents and supporters converged to shut down the monthly HANO meeting, declaring there would be "no business as usual" until the people came home.

The new offensive proposed by Juakali was to launch a Survivors Village tent encampment in front of St. Bernard and his nearby home and office. By this time, the NO-HEAT coalition had collapsed, but activists with C3 and Common Ground enthusiastically supported Juakali's plan and helped clean his home of debris as part of the preparations. The encampment, which was to open on Saturday, June 3, would be used as an

FIGURE 6.3. Public housing residents and supporters rally before beginning the march and reentering the St. Bernard development on April 4, 2006, the anniversary of Dr. Martin Luther King Jr.'s assassination.

organizing base to push for the reopening of St. Bernard. Indeed, as the event neared, Juakali announced the June 3 action would culminate with a march and reoccupation of St. Bernard. Residents were emboldened and ready. "Guess what?" declared St. Bernard resident Karen Downs while addressing the city council housing committee a few days before the weekend launch of Survivors Village, "Saturday and Sunday, we're going to tear it [the fence] down." The pressure from below was even forcing conservative citywide tenant leader Cynthia Wiggins to make bold pronouncements, as she declared at the same city council meeting: "Come June 3rd, we're not going to wait.... We're going to move forward to getting our complexes open."[51]

Spirits were high as the movement approached a potential turning point. As civil rights historian Lance Hill wrote at the time, "The elite group that engineered the plan to prevent the poor from returning" had been able to carry out this agenda, until now, "without fear of social disruption or civil disturbances." The June 3 action promised to change this

FIGURE 6.4. St. Bernard residents and supporters clash with police as they attempt to reenter their apartments and community. Photograph courtesy of *Workers Vanguard.*

calculus, as residents were, Hill observed, ready "to defy the law and take back their homes."[52] Of course, there had been protests, police clashes at St. Bernard, and individual, unauthorized reoccupations at Iberville, but June 3 promised to ratchet up considerably the level of disruption against the silver lining agenda. It was not to be. As residents and supporters marched to the development on June 3, Juakali unilaterally decided that the march would not, as previously announced, culminate with an occupation. A larger march on July 4 was also ordered to stop short of retaking the community. When the public housing movement did not follow through on its promises, HUD retook the initiative. On June 14, HUD secretary Alphonso Jackson announced that the four remaining traditional developments—St. Bernard, Lafitte, C. J. Peete, B. W. Cooper—would be demolished and transformed into mixed-income communities along the lines of St. Thomas. Jackson reassured participants in the teleconference announcing the decision—one lauded by Mayor Nagin—that "public housing [residents] will be welcomed home."[53] This promise—one

FIGURE 6.5. St. Bernard residents, including Linette Bickham (center) and Sharon Jasper (far left, white shirt), after reentering St. Bernard on April 4, 2006.

that public housing residents were used to hearing but was infrequently fulfilled—was belied by the rebuilding numbers submitted by developers subsequently selected by HUD. Of the over 5,000 public housing apartments at the four original developments, developers planned to rebuild only 669 in their new mixed-income communities.[54] In another contradiction that further raised skepticism among residents, authorities claimed their redevelopment plans were designed to deconcentrate poverty, yet they failed to reopen hundreds of the smaller scattered site apartments built three decades earlier with that very goal.

Nonprofits and Privatization

A few months after the June 2006 demolition announcement, HUD began awarding contracts to redevelop public housing. These contracts went, unsurprisingly, to for-profit developers such as McCormack, Baron, and Salazar, whose CEO, Richard Baron, sat on the 1989 national commission that laid the groundwork for HOPE VI. Baron's outfit won the contract to redevelop C. J. Peete, with Goldman Sach's Urban Investment Group acting as the major investor.[55] But nonprofit organizations were included, as well. For example, HUD named the New Orleans Neighborhood Collaborative (NONC)—headed by Orleans Parish school board member Una Anderson, who fully supported the post-Katrina dismantlement of the public school system and collective bargaining—as a partner with McCormack and KAI architects to lead the redevelopment of the C. J. Peete complex. Providence Community Housing, an arm of the Catholic Archdiocese of New Orleans, received the contract to oversee the redevelopment of the Lafitte public housing complex.

New York Times architecture critic Nicolai Ouroussoff termed the demise of the little-damaged 900-unit Lafitte complex—with its "handsome brick facades, decorated with wrought-iron rails and terra cotta roofs" built by WPA-employed Creole artisans and modeled after the French Quarter's 1850s-era Pontalba apartments—"a human and architectural tragedy of vast proportions."[56] Partnering with Providence in this tragedy was Enterprise Community Partners, who operate on a national level, providing "capital and expertise for affordable housing and community development" initiatives.[57] The collaboration at the neighborhood level by the nonprofit Ujamaa Community Development Corporation, run by an activist priest at the local Catholic parish, and the embracing of the plan by Emelda Paul, the head of the tenant council, and Leah Chase, a civil rights veteran and owner of the landmark restaurant Dooky Chase, located next to Lafitte, provided a grassroots veneer to the initiative. The actual selling of the Lafitte redevelopment was a classic example of what Michelle Boyd has called the "Jim Crow nostalgia" approach to gentrification. Redevelopment was framed by neighborhood elites and their foundation and church backers as a way to recapture an idealized, racially unified, "authentic" blackness from the neighborhood's past. This packaging helped obscure the reality of an elite-driven "economic development strategy that ultimately privileged homeowners over low-income and public housing residents."[58]

Other nonprofits connected to the Lafitte initiative even included ostensible defenders of public housing. For example, Shelia Crowley, president of the National Low Income Housing Coalition (NLIHC), whose organization receives generous funding from large foundations and banks, served on the board of trustees of Enterprise, a key player in the Lafitte plans. During a weekly conference call coordinated by the National Housing Law Project and with participants from the NLIHC and other national and local housing advocates, C3 activist Elizabeth Cook and I repeatedly called on Crowley to denounce Enterprise's role in demolishing Lafitte and to resign from the board if they refused to pull out. Neither Crowley nor key staffer Diane Yentel—who represented NLIHC on the calls and later went on to work in HUD's public housing division under the Obama administration—even deigned to respond to these repeated requests.[59]

The AFL-CIO's investment arm, the Housing Investment Trust (HIT), also wanted to participate in the Lafitte redevelopment, but when the Archdiocese's Providence Community Housing refused to use union labor, they pulled out. The following year in the spring of 2007, HIT teamed up with a recently formed nonprofit that Survivors Village leader Endesha Juakali helped form—the St. Bernard Housing Recovery & Development Corporation—to obtain the contract to redevelop St. Bernard. Unfortunately for the AFL-CIO bankers and Juakali, HUD had no intentions of nixing the deal they had already made with the nonprofit Bayou District Foundation and their development partner, Atlanta-based Columbia Residential, which enjoyed close business ties to HUD secretary Jackson.[60] Though unsuccessful at winning the contract, Juakali's nonprofit initiative did succeed in pulling residents for a time toward insider negotiations, as happened at St. Thomas, and away from the terrain of protest where they could exercise power.

The Rockefeller Foundation Redevelopment Fellowships program, which was administered by the University of Pennsylvania's Center for Urban Redevelopment Excellence (CURE), also buttressed privatization of public housing. Fellows were assigned to various for-profit and nonprofit corporations involved in privatizing New Orleans's public housing, including Enterprise, NONC, Urban Strategies, Providence Community Housing, Columbia Residential, and HIT. CURE was an appropriate interlocutor for the program, with their board of directors filled with private and public sector officials who played major roles in dismantling public housing. This list included developer Richard Baron, as well as Bruce Katz of the Brookings Institution's Metropolitan Division, who promoted and oversaw HOPE VI redevelopment schemes as a high-ranking Clinton HUD official in the 1990s. The well-known and then New Orleans–headquartered community organization ACORN also received several fellows. Though not directly involved in privatizing public housing, the organization studiously avoided any contact with the antidemolition movement. Contributing to this reticence must have been the almost

$1 million in grants ACORN obtained from HUD—the agency ordering and overseeing demolition—for work in post-Katrina New Orleans.[61]

In addition to ACORN, a whole host of nonprofit, foundation-funded advocacy, or activist, organizations either emerged or expanded in the aftermath of Katrina to address various social justice issues related to post-Katrina New Orleans. The newly created NGOs included the Peoples Hurricane Relief Fund (the successor to Community Labor United) and a later split off, the People's Organizing Committee (POC); the Workers' Center for Racial Justice; and the Louisiana Justice Institute. Preexisting nonprofits that expanded included Advocates for Environmental Human Rights (AEHR), the People's Institute, and the criminal justice reform groups Safe Streets, Friends and Family of Louisiana's Incarcerated (FFLIC), and Critical Resistance.[62]

In addition to the advocacy variety, a slew of nonprofits emerged post-Katrina to provide relief services, from housing to health care, rather than defend public services. These outfits included the well-known home-building nonprofit Habitat for Humanity—which acquired some public housing properties—as well as the locally based St. Bernard Project, which operated in the neighboring parish, not the public housing development, and was founded by two Washington, DC, transplants in 2006.[63] Another variant in this direct-service trend was nonprofits founded by self-identified radical community activists who framed their conventional social service work in radical-sounding language. A prime example was, surprisingly, the local chapter of INCITE!, an organization that published an influential book critiquing the conservatizing role of foundations and nonprofits. While nominally supporting the reopening of Charity Hospital, INCITE! activists nonetheless directed most of their energies toward opening a nonprofit health clinic. Common Ground was organized by former Black Panther Malik Rahim after Katrina to provide, as he and his collaborators explained, "solidarity, not charity." Indeed, some of the youth associated with Common Ground did solidarize and participate in the public housing movement and played a leading role in reopening the Dr. Martin Luther King Elementary School in the Lower Ninth Ward.[64] Nonetheless, despite the radical rhetoric, Common Ground funneled most of their volunteers—mirroring how the traditional social service nonprofits used the *hundreds of thousands* of volunteers who flocked to the area—into creating a nonprofit alternative to the public sector rather than a social movement to challenge the post-Katrina revanchist agenda.[65]

These supposedly activist NGO groups collectively received millions of dollars in funding from foundations such as Rockefeller, Ford, and Open Society (Soros) and local ones such as the Greater New Orleans Foundation (GNOF). The GNOF, in addition to doling out its own funds, also operated as what sociologist Darwin Bond-Graham calls a "capture foundation" by acting as a distributer of funds from larger foundations, such as the Gates Foundation and the Bush–Clinton Katrina Fund, to local groups. For example, one GNOF-managed fund was the Community Revitalization Fund (CRF), a $25 million endowment provided by ten major foundations, including Rockefeller and Gates, and other fervent supporters of privatization. Cathy Shea, a program officer at the Rockefeller Foundation and a "key coordinator in the creation of the fund," made it clear that the CRF initiative was to fund replacement housing for "failed" public housing.[66]

The local activist nonprofits not only received funding from foundations but in some cases became incorporated into the governing structures of their financial backers. For example, after Katrina the Rockefeller Philanthropy Advisors created the Gulf Coast Fund for Community Renewal and Ecological Health, dedicated to supporting "local organizing" focused on "social justice concerns and movement building." The Rockefeller Philanthropy Advisors—an arm of the same Rockefeller Foundation that supported the demolition of public housing—sat many local activists, including Shana Griffin of INCITE!, Steve Bradbery of ACORN, Monique Harden of AEHR, and Angela Winfrey of the People's Institute, on the fund's advisory board. The major concern of many activist nonprofits in post-Katrina New Orleans was not that they were becoming incorporated into the nonprofit foundation complex. Rather, as expressed in an open letter signed by representatives of various local nonprofits, they were dismayed that foundations and other nonprofits had not delivered enough financial support to the local nonprofits on the ground in New Orleans. This level of criticism is typical, argues Joan Roelofs, of nonprofit leaders "who do not object to the hegemonic role of foundations"—that is, to the way they use their financial power to channel and contain movements. Rather, "they complain that large 'progressive' foundations are not giving enough."[67]

Organized labor, operating in the form of a social movement unionism that links labor with community struggles, could have served as a political and financial counterweight to the influence of the foundations, yet U.S. labor unions, both locally and nationally, were not prepared to lead a larger fight against the post-Katrina disaster capitalism agenda. In fact, as mentioned, the major initiative of the AFL-CIO was through its banking arm, underscoring the extent to which financialization of the economy has penetrated even ostensibly working-class organizations. Instead of leading a fight against privatization, the union's bankers were prepared to sacrifice public housing for a profitable investment deal. The local American Federation of Teachers (AFT) and their national affiliates did fight to regain collective bargaining rights that had been abrogated by state and local officials. Nonetheless, the AFT was neither willing nor prepared to lead a larger fight to defend the public sector, one that could have incorporated the struggle to defend public housing, health care, and myriad other issues facing black and working-class Katrina survivors.

C3 activists, for their part, criticized foundation funding, but at the same time, the group was incurring costs for transporting displaced residents and volunteers and was overstretched. On behalf of the organization, I reached out, unsuccessfully, for funds from two unions with a social movement unionism tradition—the local chapters of the International Longshoremen's Association (ILA) in Charleston, South Carolina, and the International Longshore and Warehouse Union (ILWU) in San Francisco. C3 did obtain small donations from the local bricklayers' unions and a Unitarian church in Ithaca, New York. Then, just after the PHRF refused to pay for the vans rented for the April protest, I was invited by the Unitarian Universalist Service Committee (UUSC), who had established a fund to support social justice initiatives in New Orleans and the Gulf Coast, to apply for a grant. C3 researched the UUSC and concluded that it shared more similarities with what Joan Roelofs has called radical "social change foundations" than with liberal foundations, such as Ford and Rockefeller, that were bankrolling most of the nonprofits.[68] The group therefore voted to apply for a $20,000 grant to pay for transportation and other costs, as well as a modest stipend for an organizer, but made it clear that we would return the money if the UUSC undermined our independence. C3 received, in total, $40,000 from the UUSC that allowed me and, then, Elizabeth Cook to work as paid organizers for about a year. The funds, which were handled by a church-based nonprofit, were exhausted by May 2007.

In the Streets and Courts

Despite failing to reoccupy St. Bernard during the summer of 2006, the public housing movement continued to mobilize. In mid-June 2006, for example, Survivors Village and C3 organized a march to Audubon Place—a wealthy gated community on exclusive St. Charles Avenue, located next to Tulane University. The marchers' lead banner read "Make this Neighborhood Mixed-Income," in reference to the justifications used to demolish public housing neighborhoods but, of course, never invoked to make uniformly wealthy ones more diverse. As St. Bernard resident Pam Mahogany quipped at the time, "We could mix in their community, [but] are they sure that's what they want?" In late June and again on July 1, activists marched from the Iberville development through the French Quarter, as a warning that we were willing to disrupt the tourist industry if public housing residents were not allowed to return home.[69]

The public housing movement also began pursuing a legal strategy to block demolition. New Orleans–based human rights attorney Bill Quigley and Tracie Washington, along with lawyers from a large Washington, DC–based nonprofit, foundation-backed advocacy law firm—the Advancement Project—filed a class action in June 2006 against HUD to stop the demolitions (*Anderson et al. v. Jackson*). While welcoming the intervention, some activists raised concerns that the suit would lead the movement to look to the courts and professionals, rather than our own self-activity, as the key motor of change. The allure of the courts is particularly strong, civil rights advocate and litigator Michelle Alexander argues, in racial justice struggles "where a mythology has sprung up regarding the centrality of litigation," particularly in flawed interpretations of the civil rights movements.[70] To address these threats, activists such as Mike Howells emphasized in meetings that judges were simply "politicians in robes," and others criticized efforts by some of the lawyers to drive a wedge between the plaintiffs—the residents—and the activists who did not live in public housing.[71] Nonetheless, despite these damage control efforts, the suit did lead some residents to step back from protest and may have contributed to the failure to reoccupy the St. Bernard in June and July, as previously announced.

By the summer of 2006, with Iberville and a section of B. W. Cooper having been reopened as a result of protests, increasing numbers of public housing residents began returning to New Orleans. Although the Lafitte, C. J. Peete, and St. Bernard developments remained closed, some of their displaced residents were able to use Section 8 vouchers to locate an apartment in New Orleans. Among returning public housing residents, a core group emerged, including the late Patricia "Sista Sista" Thomas and D. J. Christy from Lafitte; Gloria Irving, Sharon Jasper, her daughter Kawana, and Stephanie Mingo from St. Bernard; Sam Jackson from B. W. Cooper; sisters Bobbie and Gloria Jennings and Rosemary Johnson and Diane Allen from C. J. Peete; and Cody Marshall (after completing his offshore employment) from Iberville. This group played a leading role in the public housing and right of return movement.

For the first-year anniversary of Katrina, the public housing movement used the renewed spotlight on the city to highlight the government's failure to reopen viable public housing while thousands of New Orleanians continued to be displaced. The contradiction was maybe most transparent at Lafitte, a well-crafted, little-damaged development situated, like Iberville, close to the French Quarter. To help draw attention to the issue, Soleil Rodrigue, the Common Ground liaison to the public housing movement, organized a spoof press conference with the Yes Men, a self-styled "culture-jamming" media activist team, and displaced Lafitte tenant Patricia Thomas. Posing as a HUD assistant secretary, the Yes Men and Thomas staged a ribbon-cutting ceremony at Lafitte where they announced that the agency had reversed its policy and was reopening all of the little-damaged public housing developments. Simultaneously, but not coordinated with the Yes Men event, C3 activists and several volunteers associated with Common Ground aided a displaced Lafitte resident in removing the metal doors that sealed off his apartment and reoccupying his home. The action led to several of the activists, but not resident D. J. Christy, being arrested by the New Orleans police for trespassing. The Loyola University legal clinic, run by activist attorney Bill Quigley, took this case and those of the scores of other activists arrested during the 2005–2008 fight to defend public housing. With the support of the People's Organizing Committee, several C. J. Peete residents did later reoccupy their apartments in February 2007, but were persuaded to end their occupation under threat of arrest.[72]

Despite the failure to reopen the city's four closed developments, the New Orleans public housing movement did show its ability to scale up and go national by garnering concessions in Washington.[73] Congresswoman Maxine Waters, in 2006, introduced and shepherded legislation through the House of Representatives—HR 1227—that guaranteed one-for-one replacement of public housing and the immediate reopening of 3,000 public housing units. The bill, which the House passed in March 2007 and was sent to the Senate, clearly was won through the struggles on the ground in New Orleans and not simply the lobbying by Washington-based advocates. At the same time, the Bush administration, with the full support of Mayor Nagin and the city council, moved forward with their demolition plans of the four developments. But the public housing movement was not cooperating. HANO officials had barely started their "Vision for Redevelopment" PowerPoint presentation before residents and supporters chanting "No demolitions!" took over the November 29, 2006, hearing, which was held at a packed high school auditorium.[74] More confrontation followed as the movement introduced a new tactic—marching on the homes of local politicians supporting demolition. The first target was Mayor Nagin, who was paid a holiday visit in mid-December 2006. St. Bernard resident Sharon Jasper, who was emerging as the face of the public housing movement, played a leading role. She told the assembled crowd that

> It's only just begun.... We're going to fight.... Residents will keep on pushing. We're *going* back....We're going to take St. Bernard back.... They're going to have to demolish it with us in it because we're coming back.[75] (emphasis in original)

She added, underscoring the social gulf separating the black public housing residents fighting to get home and the black political leadership standing in the way, that "you're living in luxury while we're suffering."

The following month, on Martin Luther King Jr. Day 2007, the public housing movement followed through on its earlier promise to take back St. Bernard as hundreds of residents and supporters broke down the fence and reentered the long-shuttered community. People were exhilarated by what was the public housing movement's largest mass action to date. Residents went into their apartments and retrieved belongings while others began cleaning up one of the three-story brick apartment buildings that had housed a day care center.[76] C3 helped organize and build the MLK Day action, but the key role was played by Endesha Juakali of Survivors Village and Soleil Rodrigue, the Common Ground liaison to the public housing movement. Unbeknown to C3 or other participants, Juakali and Rodrigue had coordinated with two activists—Jamie "Bork" Loughner and Curtis Rummil—to occupy one of the apartments in the building housing the former day care center.[77] They then proceeded to barricade the doors and windows to hold off any attempt by the police to enter. The organizing plan, as Loughner explained to me, was for Juakali to later announce their presence and build a major rally to defend the occupation. The secrecy was understandable, since organizers did not want to

FIGURE 6.6. Public housing residents prepare to march on Mayor Nagin's home, December 2006.

FIGURE 6.7. March to Mayor Nagin's home, December 2006. C. J. Peete resident Rosemary Johnson is in the foreground.

tip-off the police—who were monitoring the movement—and the initiative clearly was consistent with the tactics and goals of the public housing movement. The problem was not the secrecy but the failure of Juakali and Rodrigue to follow through on the plan of announcing the occupation and building political support—the most logical and opportune occasion being MLK Day while hundreds of activists were at St. Bernard. Part of this hesitancy may have been from the lawsuit HANO and HUD filed against Juakali and ten residents for illegal trespassing and damaging property during the MLK Day reoccupation of St. Bernard. Whatever the case, during their two-week stay nothing was done to build public support until, on February 1 at two in the morning, a heavily armed SWAT team raided the apartment and arrested the two activists at gunpoint.[78]

The influence of identity politics was partly to blame for the reoccupation fiasco. Juakali, despite his past role in supporting the Rochon Report, was deemed by Rodrigue and other activists as the authentic African American voice of the public housing movement. Thus, it was difficult,

FIGURE 6.8. MLK Day 2007 march to reopen the St. Bernard development. From left to right is public housing resident Rose Kennedy, holding the banner, and C3 activist Mike Howells. In the wheelchair is Gloria Irving, pushed by Paul Troyano, and on the far left holding a sign is Andy Washington. Photograph by Roy Blumenfeld.

FIGURE 6.9. Elation as protestors break through the chained gate at St. Bernard, MLK Day 2007. Photograph by Roy Blumenfeld.

even after learning about the occupation a few days before the raid, to mobilize a defense without Juakali's approval, since St. Bernard was considered his turf and any challenge would be a sign of disrespect. This undemocratic environment also facilitated Juakali's ability to unilaterally forge a partnership with the AFL-CIO investment arm. This deal violated the movement's earlier agreed-upon principle of reopening all the units and maintaining them as public housing.[79] After forging an alliance with the AFL-CIO in the spring of 2007 and further moving into the non-profit camp, Juakali became increasingly hostile to protests. For example, in April 2007, C3 began targeting U.S. senator Landrieu for her failure to push for passage of Congresswoman Maxine Waters's public housing bill, which had already passed the House, and her Republican counterpart, Senator David Vitter, for his open hostility to the legislation.[80] As the larger public housing movement had done with Nagin and city councilwoman Stacy Head, C3 organized protests at the homes of both Landrieu and Vitter to force the former to push for the bill and the latter to quit blocking it. Among the new participants in these actions was Homeless Pride, an organization that emerged out of an encampment that homeless

FIGURE 6.10. Reoccupied building at St. Bernard, January 15, 2007.

people had set up in the summer of 2007 in front of city hall. But now, Juakali joined vetted tenant leader Cynthia Wiggins and minister Marshal Truehill in criticizing protests targeting Landrieu and argued against residents' participating.[81] Juakali's about-face was not surprising, considering his deeper embrace of the nonprofit world. His St. Bernard Housing Recovery & Development nonprofit corporation and the AFL-CIO badly needed Landrieu's support in their desperate and ultimately futile bureaucratic, insider effort to force HUD to reassign the St. Bernard contract to their consortium. Loud protests at Landrieu's home were, from this perspective, now a problem.

Drawing Lessons from New Orleans's Public Housing Movement

Naomi Klein's shock doctrine theory explains, in part, the unfolding of the elite-engineered assault on public housing and other public services in post-Katrina New Orleans. The storm's shock power—abetted by the long-term disinvestment in the public infrastructure, the racialized urban

FIGURE 6.11. Sharon Jasper speaks to the press before leading the march to retake the St. Bernard public housing development, January 15, 2007.

pauperization, and the criminalization of survivors—led to the displacement of a large chunk of the city's black working-class majority. Public officials and their corporate partners seized on this "clean slate" to institute a wide-ranging "accumulation by dispossession" that opened up "new fields for capital accumulation in domains hitherto regarded off-limits to the calculus of profit making."[82] Schools, housing, and hospitals were closed down or handed over to private interests, and any kind of obstacles to profit making, such as union contracts, were lifted.

But shock tactics only partly explain the implementation of the disaster capitalism agenda in post-Katrina New Orleans. Authoritarian and coercive measures were accompanied by more consensual apparatuses and practices in the form of the nonprofit complex. The nonprofits, for example, partnered with corporations to fill "the vacuum in social provision left by the withdrawal of the state" from activities such as public housing.[83] The nonprofits therefore helped to legitimate further state retrenchment and abdication of responsibility and thus acted, as Tina Wallace has argued in her trenchant critique, as the "Trojan horses of global neo-liberalism."[84] But the nonprofit contribution to privatization was not one-dimensional. In addition to the openly collaborationist role, these organizations also facilitated privatization by manufacturing dissent that did not seriously challenge the post-Katrina revanchist agenda. One expression of this role was the funneling of the compassion and energy of thousands of volunteers into rebuilding homes and providing services and away from a social movement challenge to the neoliberal agenda. In fact, this form of voluntarism not only failed to present a challenge to the post-Katrina neoliberal agenda but actually legitimated the radical downsizing of local public services. The post-Katrina media hoopla surrounding, for example, the construction of affordable housing by various nonprofits, including Habitat for Humanity and Brad Pitt's Make It Right foundation, helped foster the illusion that volunteerism could provide the affordable housing needed in the storm-devastated Gulf Region.

The role played by black community activist Endesha Juakali represents a classic, and tragic, example of how insertion into the nonprofit world undermines the strength of poor people movements. The charismatic and talented organizer initially played a critical role in galvanizing disruptive protests to challenge the exclusion of public housing residents from post-Katrina New Orleans. He articulated his "no justice, no peace" organizing philosophy just before leading public housing residents and supporters to reopen the St. Bernard community on April 4, 2006. "Oliver Thomas said if you are not willing to work then don't come back to New Orleans," Juakali began in response to invective directed against public housing residents by an African American city councilman. "I say if you are not willing to fight, then don't come back to New Orleans." He reiterated the philosophy in a June 2006 march and rally in front of a swanky gated community in uptown New Orleans, explaining that "we're miserable and suffering" and, therefore, "we're going to go uptown and make them miserable, and we'll all be miserable together" until the New Orleans elite relented and reopened public housing.[85] But as he moved further into the nonprofit world, disruption was deemphasized as the parameters of the conflict were redefined in a manner that did not threaten the neoliberal agenda. The struggle was no longer to reopen public housing; rather, the competing poles of dissent now ranged between the "people's capitalism" plan of the AFL-CIO and his new nonprofit and a "bad capitalism" represented by private developers and nonprofits selected by HUD secretary Alphonso Jackson. Instead of escalating demands and confrontation, such as calling for the reopening of St. Bernard and other public housing developments as part of a new mass public works program and mobilizing mass support for the 2007 Martin Luther King Jr. Day reoccupation, dissent was tamed. The struggle was diverted into how—not whether—public housing would be privatized. Consequently, disruptive protests, like those at the homes of "friendly" Democratic politicians that AFL-CIO bankers were trying to woo in order to win a contract or militant occupations designed to reopen public housing, now had to be reined in. The result of being realistic by trying to work out a deal within the interstices of neoliberalism proved to be as much a disaster for St. Bernard as it had been at St. Thomas.

Despite the obstacles presented by the nonprofits, a public housing movement did emerge that presented a real impediment to fully realizing Katrina's silver lining. The clearest-cut victory was at Iberville, where organizing before the storm, reoccupations by residents after Katrina, and street demonstrations forced the reopening of the development. This success was the product of an organizing strategy that rejected the strictures of identity politics. The Iberville movement united a broad layer that uncompromisingly fought against the special oppression faced by public housing residents while simultaneously raising demands for a public works program that addressed the interest of a wide swath of middle- and working-class people. While the other four developments (except for a section of B. W. Cooper) were not reopened, the movement, for over two years, stymied efforts by authorities to proceed with demolitions. The failure to demolish public housing reflected the movement's ability to question the dominant neoliberal common sense that public housing simply represented concentrations of poverty that, for the benefit of poor people and the larger community, had to be broken up and replaced with mixed-income communities. But as the movement commemorated the second anniversary of Katrina, it became increasingly clear that the courts would not block the Bush administration–controlled housing authority's plans. The only force that then stood between thousands of viable and badly needed low-income apartments and the bulldozers ready to wipe them away was the public housing movement. How would they respond?

7

Managing Contradictions

The Coalition to Stop the Demolitions

> The Coalition to Stop the Demolitions in New Orleans has
> put itself in a contradictory position. It's a coalition to stop the
> demolitions that has decided to withdraw its opposition to the
> one demolition that has already begun.
>
> —CARL DIX, FOUNDING MEMBER OF THE
> COALITION TO STOP THE DEMOLITIONS

The period between November 2007 and March 2008 was one of intense struggle over the fate of New Orleans's public housing. The battle lines were clear: reopen the developments and maintain them in the public sphere to meet the housing needs of low-income residents or privatize and demolish the developments and dispossess black working-class communities of their homes and land. This fight was taking place within what David Harvey has posited as *the* key terrain of the class struggle and the ascendant mode of accumulation in the neoliberal era, that of "accumulation by dispossession." Harvey places a wide array of processes and practices under this rubric, but what ties them together is that capitalist accumulation occurs through the redistribution of wealth and income upward from the working class to the capitalist class rather than the generation of new wealth through the exploitation of labor and extraction of surplus value (expanded reproduction). The state, much more than is normally the case in struggles at the workplace and similar to what Karl Marx describes in his analysis of "primitive accumulation," is usually the central player in directing dispossession and containing dissent.[1]

Thus, seen through the prism of accumulation by dispossession, the popular challenge to state officials' redistributing public housing away from residents and to for-profit and nonprofit corporations was a deeply racialized and gendered *class* struggle and conflict. This chapter analyzes how this struggle unfolded at both the interclass and, in particular, the intraclass levels during the months between late 2007 and early 2008. The latter level of analysis is a crucial part of the post-Katrina public housing story, since as sociologists Maurice Zeitlin and Judith Stepan-Norris emphasize:

Every class struggle is simultaneously an *intra*class struggle. For no class is infallible about its interests. What are the real interests, immediate or historical, of a class? What is the class struggle really about? Indeed, *is* it a *class* struggle? These questions are always at issue among the contending factions and parties of a class as they struggle to define its interests and what has to be done to protect and advance them. *The process of self-organization of a class, then, involves concrete political struggles within it—and within its organizations—over what its class interests are and who should organize and lead it.* Classes do not simply organize themselves. They become organized in a particular way and by particular leaders, factions, or parties, with particular theories, social objectives and political/organizational strategies.[2] (emphasis added)

The types of political struggles that emerge among sections of the working class, within the terrain of either dispossession or exploitation, do not take place, of course, on a blank slate. Rather, the actions of class actors are constrained by the "existing historical situation and social relations (political, economic and cultural)" in which they operate.[3] In the case of New Orleans's public housing movement, the mass displacement of residents post-Katrina, combined with decades of racist and gendered housing, employment, and criminal justice policies, placed real limits on—but did not determine—the range of political struggles that could be mounted to defend public housing. Thus, operating within these structures, I examine how the public housing struggle unfolded, including the factions at play; the intraclass conflicts over demands, framing, and strategy; how different factions engaged in the interclass struggle; and the consequences of these struggles.

The Coalition to Stop the Demolitions?

On November 15, 2007, U.S. federal district court judge Ivan Lemelle dismissed large portions of the class action *Anderson et al. vs Jackson*, which challenged HUD's plan to demolish four New Orleans public housing developments. The ruling removed any illusion that somehow the courts would come to the rescue and save public housing. Rather than provide protection, the federal courts gave the green light for housing officials to drive poor black people from the city, an agenda that crystallized the racial, class, and gender inequities of post-Katrina New Orleans and openly violated the right of return championed by many in the progressive nonprofit milieu. How would the progressive NGO sector and all those inspired to activism by the racial and class injustices and inequalities that Katrina laid bare respond?

A November 13 protest C3 held at the federal courthouse—a few days before Judge Lemelle's then-pending decision—and a subsequent meeting both brought in scores of new activists and signaled people were willing and eager to challenge demolition. Symbolizing this renewed determination was St. Bernard public housing resident Sharon Jasper, who came to the courthouse protest carrying a hangman's noose. Brandishing this symbol of Jim Crow racist terror had a double meaning. One was to evoke and show solidarity with the then recent struggles in Jena, Louisiana, against the hanging of a noose from a tree in the school yard, which was designed to intimidate black students who had had the temerity to sit under the school's unofficial "white tree." The other was to make clear that the public housing movement would not countenance the placing of a collective noose around the necks of poor and displaced residents and communities. "Take the noose from around the poor and working-class people!" she thundered at the rally.[4]

After Lemelle gave the green light to demolition on November 15, human rights attorney Bill Quigley, who was well respected locally and nationally among social justice activists, convened a meeting of all public housing defenders in late November at the Loyola law school, where he taught. Out of the initial and subsequent meetings emerged the Coalition to Stop the Demolitions. The coalition included C3, Survivors Village, Common Ground, and Pax Christi (a Catholic peace organization) activists that had long been involved in the public housing fight, as well as those who previously had played a less active role or none at all, including members of the PHRF, Critical Resistance, the RCP, the New Orleans Workers' Center for Racial Justice, Amnesty International, AEHR, European Dissent and the Anti-Racist Working Group (two white antiracist groups mentored by the People's Institute), INCITE!, and Safe Streets, a criminal justice reform group that was also the local affiliate of the national antigentrification alliance Right to the City (RTTC). ACORN, which had received generous funding from HUD for work in post-Katrina New Orleans, was invited but did not participate.[5] At a November 24 meeting, the coalition voted unanimously to resist demolition through various means, including direct action sit-ins and other forms of civil disobedience to block the bulldozers.[6]

Key to swaying support for direct action against demolition was the strong endorsement of public housing residents Sharon and Kawana Jasper, Rose Kennedy, Stephanie Mingo, Sam Jackson, and Cody Marshall. This group formed a public housing leadership council within the coalition, to which it deferred for major policy decisions. This leadership council—as opposed to HUD and HANO's prodemolition, vetted tenant leadership—heartily endorsed direct opposition to demolition, as long as it was nonviolent. They also endorsed the coalition's making a local and national call for volunteers to join the protests. "We have been marching and talking, but now," Sharon Jasper declared, "we have to show we're serious."[7]

Although the initial meeting ushering in the coalition was called by Quigley, the African American coleader of the PHRF, Kali Akuno, began to chair the gatherings. Before coming to New Orleans after Katrina to head up the PHRF, Akuno had worked in San Francisco for an offshoot of the nonprofit Ella Baker Center, founded by lawyer, author, and, later, member of the Obama administration Van Jones.[8] Although Akuno was a relative newcomer to the city and previously had participated in few public housing actions, he was, due to the weight of identity politics, chosen to lead the meetings. Adding to his stature and intersecting with identity politics was that the PHRF had the most prestige and influence nationally among Left and activist groups—ones the coalition hoped to draw on for support. Further bolstering his résumé was that Akuno, along with other nonprofit leaders, such as Monique Harden of the AEHR, had represented New Orleans before the UN Human Rights Council, where they indicted the U.S. government for violating human rights agreement by their treatment of Katrina survivors, including public housing residents. Human rights was the key framework and discourse used by many of the progressive advocacy organizations to critique the inequities of post-Katrina New Orleans. Although a rights talk had its place, it did not negate Karl Marx's insight, made in his magnum opus, *Capital,* that when two rights come into conflict, "force decides" the issue.[9] Many of the nonprofit human rights advocates, such as AEHR, were comfortable making their cases before international bodies and organizing visits of human rights officials. They were much more reticent about confronting and opposing the state's exercise of its prerogatives with direct-action resistance.

On November 26, the coalition's direct action committee met at the PHRF office to plan the national call out to activists to join the protests to stop demolition. Although the coalition had unequivocally come out for direct action and for issuing a call for volunteers, PHRF coleader Malcolm Suber expressed his reservations, explaining that he "didn't just want to have white radicals coming from outside" and that "we didn't have enough public housing residents" involved, which questioned our legitimacy. In contrast to the others at the meeting, Suber and Akuno placed great strategic importance on swaying the city council members, particularly the three black representatives—Cynthia Willard-Lewis, James Carter, and Cynthia Morrell—in order to stop demolition. Willard-Lewis—who had sponsored ordinances, demanded by black middle-class homeowner associations, to ban the construction of low-income multifamily housing in her New Orleans East district—had explained to Suber that "we need [to see] new faces,... old faces don't impress" the council.[10] The focus on swaying the council rather than building the power needed to confront the bulldozers increased when attorney Tracie Washington discovered that the council had to vote to allow demolition to proceed. Akuno, Suber, and Washington subsequently spent much time behind the scenes in a fruitless effort to sway the three black members and a decisive fourth one—either white city councilwoman Shelly Midura or city council president Arnold Fielkow, both considered swing votes, at times—to vote against demolition.

A central part of the NGO's strategy of swaying the council was winning over respectable church-affiliated groups like the Southern Christian Leadership Conference (SCLC), All Congregations Together (ACT), and the Jeremiah Group to the no demolition cause. Others in attendance at the coalition's direct action committee meeting, including myself and fellow C3 activist Mike Howells, Carl Dix and Paul Stets with the RCP, and Sharon Jasper, argued that although the coalition should try to garner the greatest support to stop demolition, it should not become paralyzed if groups such as the local SCLC did not join. In fact, garnering the support of these leaders, such as SCLC head Rev. Norwood Thompson, was highly unlikely, because of their close relationships to the black political leadership. Thompson and others were not ready to sacrifice political access and financial perks by siding with the public housing movement. The focus should be, we argued, on building a determined group of people, both nationally and locally, to stop the bulldozers, which is what the coalition voted to do. Carl Dix added that it was important to get the support and endorsement of residents to stop the bulldozers, but because of their vulnerability to losing their housing support, they didn't necessarily have to participate in occupations.

On November 27, the day after the committee meeting, the coalition issued a national call for activists to converge on New Orleans by December 10 to prepare for direct action against the bulldozers, which HUD announced would begin on December 15. Although the call was issued in the name of the coalition, activists under the direction of the PHRF wrote the letter and issued it by email, and prospective volunteers were required to register through a process they controlled. PHRF, which was clearly ambivalent about building a direct action campaign, would be in charge of the volunteers who had been told, in the call letter, that they would simply "act as allies, and *not to be part of major decision making*" (emphasis added). The PHRF would be giving the orders.[11]

The coalition's first public action was a November 30, Friday morning, press conference on the steps of city hall, entitled "Calling on the City Council to Oppose Demolition and Support the Right of Return." The next day, December 1, Akuno and Tamara McFarland of the Workers' Center for Racial Justice chaired the coalition meeting, but no concrete plans were made to confront the impending bulldozers. Instead, Akuno unsuccessfully tried to establish a steering committee that would, more than had already happened, place control of the coalition into the hands of the PHRF and himself. On Thursday, December 6, several dozen coalition activists addressed the city council, denounced plans to demolish public housing, and demanded the council state their positions on the issue. PHRF leaders Akuno and Suber had a few days earlier assured the coalition that Councilwoman Willard-Lewis would introduce a resolution against the council's issuing demolition permits and call for a vote.[12] She did not. Instead, Willard-Lewis tried to placate the coalition by promising to meet with them at "a later date." The group was in no mood to wait. They began yelling, "Yes or no?" and, "Stop the demolition! Stop the demolition!" as the city council members fled the chambers. After occupying the chambers for about an hour, the group tried to go to the mayor's office on the second floor, when attorney Bill Quigley was grabbed by a police officer, aggressively thrown against a wall, handcuffed, and charged with disturbing the peace.[13] The rough treatment faced by someone of Quigley's stature was a clear message that anyone opposing demolition would not be safe from police repression. That would become increasingly clear in the subsequent days and weeks.

Over the next two weeks, following the December 6 city council action, the pace of events accelerated. At the coalition's Saturday, December 8, meeting, the fifty or so assembled activists discussed plans by lawyers to file a suit to force the city council to vote on demolition and to pack a meeting of the city's Housing Conservation District Review Committee, which would vote Monday, December 10, on whether to support demolition.[14] The coalition also planned a Sunday march to the mayor's home, a December 15 rally at St. Bernard, and the reception of out-of-town activists that responded to the call, mostly from the new Students for a Democratic Society (SDS), who would begin a three-day training program on Monday. Yet the coalition still had no firm emergency plans on mobilizing protestors, on short notice, to confront the bulldozers. Although HUD had announced December 15 as the beginning of demolitions, the coalition was still not sure when they would actually begin or, also important, at which of the four developments.

After the Sunday march to Nagin's home, the coalition mobilized over a hundred activists who packed what the *Times-Picayune* called a "raucous three-hour meeting" of the housing conservation committee to press the board to oppose demolition. The board voted against allowing demolition of Lafitte but gave the go ahead for the C. J. Peete and B. W. Cooper developments.[15]

The Betrayal

On Wednesday afternoon, December 12, I received an urgent call from Luisa Dantas, a filmmaker who had been documenting the public housing movement for over a year: the wrecking balls had arrived. Dantas breathlessly explained that contractors were moving demolition machinery into the Cooper development, part of which had been reopened after Katrina, while the rest of the over 1,000 apartments were not occupied. I immediately called three leading members of the coalition's public housing leadership council—Sam Jackson, who lived at Cooper, Sharon Jasper, and Cody Marshall—and C3 activists Mike Howells and Elizabeth Cook. I explained what was happening and told them to send out a message for everyone to immediately converge on Cooper. I asked Sam Jackson to meet me at the office on Canal Street where the out-of-town activists were undergoing civil disobedience training. Sam and I sounded the alarm.

Yet shockingly, Akuno and Critical Resistance activist Mayaba Liebenthal said they would *not* join the protest nor authorize the participation
of the SDS activists, who as mentioned, came as allies and were to have
no decision-making power. Akuno and Liebenthal argued a view shared
by Survivors Village leader Endesha Juakali that since the Cooper tenant
council supported demolition, they could not join the protests.[16] Even
after Sam Jackson—a Cooper resident and member of the coalition's public housing leadership council—told Akuno and Liebenthal that he endorsed the action and requested their support, they still refused to budge.
This decision flagrantly violated the coalition's earlier agreement to confront demolition through direct action and to follow the lead of the public
housing leadership council, who had all endorsed the measure. Efforts by
Jackson and myself to rally the SDS activists fell flat, as well. Apart from
their earlier agreement to take marching orders from the PHRF, the fact
that SDS itself was organized along identity politics lines also contributed to the young activists not disobeying their New Orleans mentors. SDS
members are organized into caucuses based on a particular oppression
(class, race, gender, sexuality, and various combinations of these) and a
corresponding auxiliary group that does not "face the specific oppression
of a caucus." "It is the responsibility of auxiliary members," according to
SDS organizing principles, "to take [an] active role in not practicing oppressive behavior *as well as actively supporting the leadership of caucus
members*" (emphasis added).[17] Thus, following the directive of the local
black caucus leadership made perfect sense for the SDS auxiliaries. The
urgency of getting to Cooper made it impossible to engage the students in
an extended discussion into the contradictory position that their identity
politics principles had taken them.

Despite this sabotage, several dozen coalition members were able to
mount a picket line at Cooper, with public housing resident leaders Sharon
Jasper, Sam Jackson, and Cody Marshall in the forefront, to stop the bulldozers (see Figures 7.1, 7.2, and 7.3). Protestors held the line all afternoon
and into the early evening, even after Akuno showed up at the event trying
to coax protestors to abandon their posts. Common Ground representative Sakura Koné, who in contrast to other NGO activists, was steadfast
in his support of direct action, was incensed when he was encouraged to
leave the line:

> They tried to break the line, but we refused. . . . I had people com-
> ing to me, whispering, "When the bulldozers arrive, break the

line." But I said, "Wait a minute. I've been going to the meetings, and we didn't discuss this as an option." And they didn't have a response. They actually thought I would cut and run.[18]

While the picketers blocked the bulldozers, two activists, Angela Jaster of C3 and Paul Stets of the RCP, sneaked into the development and hid in one of the apartments. Their supporters made plans to announce their presence the following day, which would force HUD and their demolition contractors to stop the bulldozing and give us further time to build a larger blockade.[19]

At this point it was clear that many of the NGO groups in the Coalition to Stop the Demolitions had no intentions of living up to the name. The same Wednesday afternoon as the pickets went up at Cooper, the NGOs issued a call for a march the following day from city hall to the HUD office a few blocks away. Officially, the march was to protest both HUD's demolition of public housing and the Fifth Circuit Court of Appeals's throwing out the movement's latest legal maneuver.[20] More fundamentally, this blow-off march represented an attempt to manage the contradictions of the coalition's foundation-funded NGO members. This layer, while ostensibly members of the Coalition to Stop the Demolitions, nonetheless had, as coalition member and RCP leader Carl Dix critiqued at the time on the national Black Left Unity Listserv, "decided to withdraw its opposition to the one demolition that has already begun."[21] A North Carolina activist, writing on the same Listserv, was also confused by the stance of Akuno and others, since "[it] looks and sounds like people on the ground want to defend public housing in New Orleans." Akuno attempted to address the paradoxical situation.

> Maintaining the Coalition has and will remain a challenge. . . .
> There is also intense internal debate regarding the action taken by the Coalition Wednesday in defense of B W Cooper. . . . The overwhelming majority of the coalition now believes it was a critical mistake. . . . *But, this decision has placed the coalition in an obviously weird, and somewhat contradictory position.*[22] (emphasis added)

Of course, there had never been a vote by the coalition to reverse its earlier agreement to oppose demolition through direct action—a fact underscored by the public housing leadership's leading the action. Nonetheless, despite the attempts at obfuscation, Akuno acknowledged the

FIGURES 7.1 AND 7.2. Blocking demolition at B. W. Cooper. Photographs by Edwin Lopez.

FIGURE 7.3. From left to right is Cody Marshall, Sam Jackson (with bullhorn), and Sharon Jasper. Photograph by Edwin Lopez.

contradictory position the NGO radicals had created for themselves. This is the context in which the so-called militant Thursday, December 13, march must be understood. The defiant rhetoric on the steps of city hall, the subsequent unpermitted march to HUD, and the angry kicking of the federal building's glass doors all allowed the NGOs and their followers to appear as if they opposed demolition. At the same time, they were relieved of having to physically confront the national and black-led local state's negation of the right to housing—a right that the NGOs, in forums at home and abroad, had repeatedly declared as sacred. The performance represented a further iteration of Reed's "reinvention mechanism" that was on display in the conflict over building a Walmart as part of the St. Thomas redevelopment. The twist this time was that activists rather than middle-class ministers led the diversionary initiative.

At the NGO's Thursday morning, December 13, city hall rally, Mike Howells, Carl Dix, and I tried to sway—unsuccessfully—Malcolm Suber of the PHRF, who acted as the leader of the action, to follow up the HUD action with a march to Cooper to stand in solidarity with the occupation (activists Jaster and Stets were then hiding in a Cooper apartment awaiting our arrival before they announced their presence). The betrayal of Suber was particularly demoralizing and underscored the extent to which the "NGOization of the left"—the term used by David McNally in a recent book—has progressed under neoliberalism. Suber had come to New Orleans in the late 1970s with a Far Left group that was part of what Max Elbaum calls the "New Communist Movement," a collection of parties inspired by variants of Maoism and third-world Marxism.[23] Suber and the party's mass organization that he led—the Liberation League— played the leading role for over two decades in New Orleans organizing against police brutality, as well as other struggles. Suber was unrelenting and eloquent in exposing the black political leadership's alliance with the white ruling class to repress the black working class and betray the aspirations of the 1960s black freedom movement. But as he became incorporated into the nonprofit sector—first, before Katrina, with an educational nonprofit and then later with the PHRF—his politics also underwent a transformation. The role Suber played in leading a march against demolitions and simultaneously channeling protestors away from taking direct action against demolition reflected his political metamorphosis and the contradictions of NGO organizing.

Despite the lack of support from the NGO wing of the coalition and their SDS allies, C3 and the RCP, with support from Sakura Koné—the independent-minded Common Ground representative—were able to rally about a dozen supporters to hold a press conference that afternoon. As Mike Howells announced their presence to the press the two activists occupying the Cooper apartment simultaneously unfurled a banner from their second-story apartment. Although there was not a large number of people, the occupation did force demolition work to stop for the rest of the day. A detachment of police, including a heavily armed SWAT team, roped off the area and forced supporters to gather several blocks from the development. The SWAT team then arrested, at gunpoint, Jaster and Stets, who were charged with misdemeanors.

Part of the strategy behind openly confronting the bulldozers was to make Washington and New Orleans pay the highest political price possible for demolishing the homes of poor Katrina survivors. Allowing demolition without any fight would have only further emboldened the forces pushing the post-Katrina neoliberal revanchist agenda and demoralized those fighting for an economically and racially just reconstruction. "The absence of dissent," as Patricia Hill Collins has argued, "makes it easier for dominant groups to rule," since silence "suggests that subordinate groups willingly collaborate in their own victimization."[24] The messy protests made it impossible, despite the best efforts of state officials, developers, and the official tenant leadership, to package demolition as a consensual affair. But activists were not simply content with registering their opposition. They also theorized that mounting a dramatic physical defense of public housing in post-Katrina New Orleans had the potential of stopping demolitions and forcing the reopening of the badly needed apartments. A heroic direct-action defense of public housing presented an opportunity to create a public space, in a manner similar to what would take place a few years later in the Middle East and across the United States, that would form a physical and political challenge to not only the destruction of public housing but the broader inequities of post-Katrina New Orleans's neoliberal reconstruction agenda. The taking of a public space could act as a magnet to attract more local—including from the thousands of volunteers involved in purely self-help work that may have become politicized—and out-of-town activists and create an arena for democratic self-organization and debate.

A dramatic defense of public housing could have also inspired solidarity actions around the country. In fact, solidarity protests did take place in several cities, including Minneapolis, Washington, DC, Chicago, Raleigh, and New York City, and the mainstream press was beginning to take note. The demolitions had become such a national issue that even the then presidential candidates John Edwards and, later, Hillary Clinton—but not Barack Obama—felt compelled to call on HUD to stop the demolitions, as did the House and Senate's leaders.[25] This support could have grown even further if the coalition had followed through on its earlier commitment and used all its resources to confront the bulldozers. If this type of protest had been mounted, it would have been much more difficult for the Bush and Nagin administrations to proceed. But of course this did not happen, which further underscores the indispensable role these organizations play in facilitating the implementation of regressive neoliberal reforms.

C3 and other members of the coalition continued to advocate taking action at Cooper—the only development where demolition had begun. They challenged the pretext invoked by Akuno and his allies on the coalition that a "clear majority of the residents," including the tenant council leadership, at Cooper were in favor of the demolition.[26] Direct action advocates pointed out that the coalition had committed to oppose demolition on principle and that our own resident council leadership within the coalition, including Cooper resident Sam Jackson, supported it. Furthermore, they provided evidence from their canvassing of the development that most residents were in fact opposed to demolition. Nonetheless, many residents were, they explained, hesitant to join the protests because of threats from HANO, often delivered through tenant council members, that they would be evicted and banned from public housing for life if they spoke out against the demolitions. Even after two other Cooper residents, Rebecca Glover and Theo Moore, attended a coalition meeting to encourage protests, the NGO faction was not moved. In fact, by this time, after the confrontation at Cooper, some of the NGOs had dropped all pretense of opposing demolition by ending their participation in the coalition altogether. Interestingly, defections even included Safe Streets, whom the national antigentrification, foundation-funded Right to the City coalition had previously knighted as its local affiliate.[27] In addition, as Sakura Koné observes, the infighting caused by the NGO leaders' intransigence in actually opposing demolition led some activists to drift away. "Those meetings went on, and they really drained a lot of people. I remember when they were huge, and then they were dwindling in numbers because people were getting so frustrated with the arguments ... debates and so forth." For Koné the arguments underscored that "there was a class issue going on," since "a part of the coalition who represented a certain class interests"—namely the NGOs—"wanted to run from the bulldozers."[28]

The tact taken by the PHRF and the other remaining NGOs in the coalition was not to drop out entirely but to continue maintaining a pretense of opposition to demolition, without actually having to confront the bulldozers. Emblematic of this Goffmanesque front-stage performance was the Saturday, December 15, blow-off action held at St. Bernard, where demolition had not yet started. Although there was no attempt to occupy St. Bernard, the cops stepped up their aggressive tactics as they ran a cruiser into the middle of the march and arrested three activists, including J. R. Fleming (a public housing activist from Chicago) and Sherri Honkala, who was with the Poor People's March for Economic Rights, based in Cleveland (see Figure 7.4). For their part, several members of the antiracist working group were arrested after chaining themselves to the gates in front of the HANO office—safely away from the Cooper demolitions that the self-appointed coalition leadership had ruled off limits—on December 14.

Despite the coalition's betrayal, C3 and others continued to take action at Cooper. Before sun up on Wednesday, December 19, three white working-class women—Jamie Loughner, Elizabeth Cook, and Joy Kohler—broke through the wire fence, avoided guard dogs, and chained themselves to a fire escape and an apartment window. Supporters from C3, the RCP, May Day New Orleans, Sakura Koné from Common Ground, and others then called a press conference and rallied support for the occupation, which resulted in shutting down demolition operations for the second time in a week. Police responded again with a heavily armed SWAT team, as well as a police deployment even larger than the previous occupation's, and harsher penalties. For the first time in the fight to stop demolition, authorities leveled felony charges against activists for their nonviolent direct-action activism (see Figures 7.5 and 7.6).[29]

The December 20 City Council Battle: Heroic Resistance and Lost Opportunities

On Thursday, December 20—the day after the three arrests at Cooper—the battle moved back to the city council chambers. The week before, civil district court judge Herbert Cade brokered a consent decree between coalition lawyer Tracie Washington and HANO that required the city council

FIGURE 7.4. Arrest of Sherri Honkala at December 15, 2007, protest at St. Bernard. Chicago housing activist J. R. Fleming, who was also arrested, is pictured on the left.

FIGURE 7.5. Joy Kohler chained to apartment window at B. W. Cooper to stop demolition.

to approve demolition permits—a responsibility they had tried to duck—for Lafitte, C. J. Peete, and St. Bernard, while allowing demolition to continue at part of B. W. Cooper. The vote was a fait accompli, with all seven councilmembers making it clear before the meeting that they would vote for demolition.[30] Nonetheless, the remaining parts of the public housing movement, even those not willing to confront the bulldozers but who had not exited completely (such as the nonprofit leaders at Safe Streets), were intent on registering their opposition before the city council. But instead of preparing for democratic input, the city began to further criminalize dissent and deepen its bunker mentality and preparations—a response the post-Katrina movement continually confronted but which had been taken to a higher level following Judge Lemelle's decision to approve demolition a few weeks earlier. The NOPD mobilized and deployed over 150 officers for the meeting, including the department's Special Operations Division, which housed the sixty-officer SWAT team and the bomb squad, as well

FIGURE 7.6. From left to right is Jamie "Bork" Loughner, Elizabeth Cook, and Joy Kohler, following release from jail after being arrested for blocking demolition, December 19, 2007.

as the intelligence division, district officers, and mounted police. Underscoring the military metaphors and framing that had taken hold, a police commander of the operation recounted that "10 SWAT officers *took up positions* inside the council chamber to protect the council members" (emphasis added). The morning of the hearing, SWAT leader Lt. Dwayne Scheuermann—who was later indicted and tried for involvement in the killing of an unarmed civilian in the aftermath of Katrina—commented, "Something bad is going to happen.... I can promise you that," which underscored that the police, with the full backing of the political leadership, had gone into combat mode and were itching for a fight.[31]

This siege mentality and heavy police presence was what greeted attendees as they began lining up for the 10:00 A.M. city council meeting. Conflict soon erupted when police tried to prevent public housing resident Sharon Jasper and PHRF organizer and rapper Darrel "Sess 4-5" Warren from entering the chambers. Only after vocal protestation by Jasper and Warren did the police relent. Then, while over one hundred people were still waiting in line and before attendees had filled all of the two-hundred-plus seats in the chamber or taken up standing positions along the walls—as had been allowed in past large meetings—the police closed the doors for the duration of the meeting. The police followed this by pushing those that remained in line behind a steel gate that blocked off the driveway that led to the chambers. Police chained the gate and had a contingent of several dozen officers, including several on horseback, watch over the crowd.

When the doors were prematurely closed, the public housing activists inside the chambers began agitating against starting the meeting until everyone was allowed inside. Councilwoman Stacy Head, the council's most vocal proponent of demolition, inflamed matters further by blowing a kiss to her detractors as she took her seat. This provocation led even the police to reprimand her, as well as generating a further barrage of booing from the crowd. After Endesha Juakali's failed attempt to engage the council and persuade them to reopen the doors, about twenty other public housing activists and I stood up and began chanting, "Let the people in. Let the people in." After a few minutes of chanting, city council president Arnold Fielkow, flanked by the city's commanding officer, Police Chief Warren Riley, in what was clearly a prearranged plan, told the police to restore order. "At that point," according to the account of *Times-Picayune* reporter Brendan McCarthy, "a police ranking officer began pointing out the most rambunctious protesters and ordering other officers to remove them."[32] The first "rambunctious" activists arrested and hustled out of the chambers following the order were Malcolm Suber, Endesha Juakali, and myself. A few moments later, the relationship between the "economic shock therapy" of demolishing thousands of badly needed public housing apartments and the shock of police tasers directed against those opposing the post-Katrina revanchist agenda was graphically displayed in New Orleans's legislative chamber. Police proceeded to tackle, slam to the floor, and taser Darrel "Sess 4-5" Warren and Robert "Cool Black" Horton while roughing up and arresting several other protestors as officers flooded the council chambers (see Figure 7.7).

While the police were mopping up opposition inside the chambers, they opened another front outside. After those excluded from the meeting—including residents of the homeless encampment in front of city hall—rallied and then forced opened a gate blocking entrance to the council chambers, the police responded with a barrage of pepper spray and tasers.

FIGURE 7.7. Demetrius Warren being arrested by New Orleans police during the December 20, 2007, city council public housing hearing. Photograph by Alex Brandon, used with permission of the Associated Press.

Nine people were treated for injuries by emergency responders, and four were hospitalized, including a woman that went into a seizure after being struck by police tasers. Several were arrested, including the indomitable Jamie "Bork" Loughner. One day after being arrested at Cooper, she was dragged and arrested by police after throwing her body against the gate in an attempt to allow protestors to enter. Public housing activist Mike Howells, after being fingered for arrest by Deputy Police Chief Anthony Canatella, was grabbed, as well.[33]

With their order restored, the city council, under an eerie calmness, began taking what was left of public comment for a vote they had already decided. A few public housing residents and supporters who had not been arrested or blocked from entering the chambers did register their opposition. These voices were drowned out by a train of developers, nonprofits, so-called civic leaders, and official tenant leaders who spoke in favor of demolition. The demolition proponents included Donna Johnigan, the head of the B. W. Cooper tenant council, whose photo testifying before the council was splashed across the front page of the next day's *Times-Picayune* in an obvious attempt to legitimate the highly contested decision. The city's paper of record also celebrated the racial unity reflected in the council's unanimous 7–0 vote, with the three black members joining their four white colleagues to approve bulldozing the homes of thousands of low-income African Americans (see Figure 7.8).

The next day, Kali Akuno chaired a coalition meeting with over fifty people in attendance, including national supporters, to evaluate the city council clash and discuss the group's next move. Instead of having to call a press conference, the press was now coming to the coalition to see what their next move would be, underscoring how the defiance exhibited at the city council had garnered the movement greater attention, support, and momentum. Indeed, the attack on protestors at the city council meeting had been given wide coverage not only by local media but by national and foreign media outlets, as well. Nonetheless, inside the meeting, from which the press was barred, the NGOs continued to thwart resistance. Suber of the PHRF acknowledged, for example, that "we created interest with people that had not been involved" but added that he disagreed that "it showed that the masses had stood up." He therefore continued to oppose any disruptive actions to impede demolition and reiterated his support for a campaign to recall the mayor and the city council, which he had first raised while protestors were in jail. Rev. Marshal Truehill added that there were "too few New Orleanians," and therefore we should work his connections at city hall to "use an inside game," as well as work with the official tenant leaders. The latter recommendation seemed especially problematic considering that the day before these same tenant leaders had spoken at the city council in support of demolition. Carl Dix with the RCP emphasized, in contrast, that "we had exposed their repression" and that we then needed to use our momentum "to carry through this struggle to stop demolition." Mike Howells added that our resistance had "unmasked the propaganda that the people had embraced demolition" and showed that our "heroic resistance would rally people to our cause." But he emphasized that this support would not materialize automatically and that we needed to immediately forge an "emergency action plan to appeal to the much broader audience" we then had. Longtime community activist Eloise Williams endorsed the call to action, declaring, "Just call me, and I will be there," while Jamie "Bork" Loughner, just released from the hospital after being brutalized by the police at city hall, proclaimed, "I want to soldier on. I'm ready." Yet despite Eloise Williams's insistence that "we had to leave the table today" with a plan, Akuno concluded the meeting without one, beyond scheduling another coalition meeting two days later.[34]

he Times-Picayune

FRIDAY, DECEMBER 21, 2007 **NEW ORLEANS EDITION**

YES YES YES YES YES YES YES

UNANIMOUS

COUNCIL VOTES TO RAZE 4,500 UNITS

OLD HOUSING MODEL TO GIVE WAY TO MIXED-INCOME DEVELOPMENTS

STAFF PHOTO BY TED JACKSON

By Coleman Warner and Gwen Filosa
Staff writers

Unbowed by days of caustic protests, the New Orleans City Council on Thursday unanimously approved the demolition of four sprawling public housing developments, launching a new era in the troubled history of a social safety net launched in the World War II era.

The historic vote — embracing sweeping plans to house the poor in mixed-income developments — green-lighted the razing of 4,500 apartments at the B.W. Cooper, C.J. Peete, St. Bernard and Lafitte housing complexes, with teardowns to commence within weeks.

During the next five years, the Department of Housing and Urban Development will

replace the aging complexes with 3,343 public housing units, 900 homes for sale, and 900 homes for rent, with many of them marketed, with financial subsidies, to former public housing residents.

"The past model of public housing in this city has been a failed one," said Council President Arnie Fielkow at the close of a bruising five-hour debate. But he said the

Housing Authority's work in erecting handsome new buildings in the Fischer and Guste complexes in recent years left him convinced that public housing residents "can indeed live in a quality, safe and uplifting environment."

The City Council took up the demolition issue only after plaintiffs in a lawsuit said HUD had failed to com-

See **UNANIMOUS,** A-9

IN FAVOR OF CHANGE: Donna Johnigan, a resident leader at the B.W. Cooper public housing complex, said public housing must change to be part of the recovery of New Orleans. "It's about us walking into a house and saying, 'This is a house, it ain't a project,'" she said, drawing cheers and applause from the chamber.

Both police, protesters came prepared

By Brendan McCarthy
Staff writer

On one side of the wrought-iron fence — closing off a corridor to the City Council chambers, site of a high-temperature housing debate — a small army of police, some on horseback, stood at the ready Thursday.

On the other side, about 100 demonstrators — shut out of the over-full council meeting — chanted "Housing is a human right!" and "Stop demolition now!" along with the odd obscenity and "racist."

New Orleans Police Department officers and Civil Sheriff's deputies stood expressionless as some in the crowd rattled the gate. Eventually, the handcuffs holding the gate in place gave way and the 8-foot-high fence swung open. Two women were Tasered, according to several witnesses. An officer dispersed pepper spray into the throng. The gate swung shut.

See **SECURITY,** A-10

STAFF PHOTO BY MICHAEL DeMOCKER

New Orleans police subdue protesters on the railing inside the City Council chambers before the council's vote Thursday. For weeks, the New Orleans Police Department has been planning for a volatile reaction to the polarized public housing debate. Officials pulled more than 150 officers from their regular roles for the council hearing, according to a copy of the NOPD's incident plan.

---

assified	E	Editorials	B-6	National	A-6	Television	C-5		UNSEASONABLY WARM	
omics	A-21	Living	C	People	A-20	Washington	A-3		HIGH LOW	Weather,
aths	B-4	Money	C-6	Sports	D	World	A-8		74 63	C-8

The interventions made by the NGOs at the subsequent December 23 coalition meeting represented classic examples of their channeling role as they staked out positions that avoided any direct confrontation with bulldozers and the neoliberal agenda while still posturing as defenders of the right of return and affordable housing. Suber's approach was to argue that the set of provisos that Mayor Nagin had attached to the council's demolition order—a set of toothless measures to appear evenhanded and momentarily delay demolition while passions cooled off—was "a victory for us." What we needed to do, he argued, was "exploit the contradictions" between the provisos and the council's approval of demolition. Carl Dix retorted that the provisos were about "how it gets demolished, not if . . . about appearing that they are delivering on housing, when they are not." Sakura Koné backed Dix's position, arguing, "We have to stick to our guns. I am for sticking to our principles of no demolition, no ifs, ands, or buts about it." Several other NGO representatives then chimed in, arguing, basically, that we had to be realistic and accommodate to demolition by working out the best deal possible within the neoliberal framework. For example, Tamara McFarland of the Workers' Center argued that instead of debating whether to stop demolition, we needed to talk about "what we want to happen"—i.e., be realistic and work out a deal with HANO and developers. Shana Griffin of INCITE! and the Rockefeller Philanthropy Advisory board added that demolition of public housing had basically been decided in the 1990s and that now "we had to think about alternative forms of affordable housing . . . the ways that it will happen." Griffin's reasoning—put forward by the representative of a group ostensibly dedicated to exposing and combating violence against women of color—meant abandoning any attempt to defend the homes of thousands of low-income African American families. Nathalie Walker of the AEHR—the major interlocutor with the UN human rights representative who visited the city and studiously avoided any involvement in direct action protests—asserted that we needed "to tell HUD to start building affordable housing" (i.e., accede to demolition and redevelopment while also advocating for passage of Senate Bill 1668, the companion legislation to HR 1227). Even human rights lawyer Bill Quigley accepted Suber's line that we had to get the most out of the mayor's provisos: "The mayor and council handed us some tools. We need to come up with another strategy," as opposed to the direct action aimed at stopping demolition. Suber's position was also backed up by People's Institute trainer, Critical Resistance employee, and former St. Thomas resident Robert "Cool Black" Horton. Denigrating those who were now facing felony charges after courageously occupying the Cooper development, he joked, "It's not about playing hide-and-go-seek in the projects.... It's not about demolition but the right of return." I retorted that, yes, of course, our struggle was about the right of return, and that was precisely why we needed to do everything we could to stop the demolitions. The closing and planned demolition of public housing was one part of the puzzle of why thousands of New Orleanians, dispro-portionally black and poor, remained in the diaspora or homeless in their own city.[35]

The meeting again ended without any plan to stop the ongoing demo-litions at Cooper nor the impending ones at the other developments. The coalition, which was now wholly dominated by the PHRF—with Akuno issuing emails and collecting donations routed to an allied organization—would continue meeting sporadically through January and February but would not play any major role in stopping the demolitions. While plans to protest the NBA All-Star Game never materialized, the coalition did call for and organize national and local actions on January 25 and 26 to push for passage of Senate Bill 1668—a version of which the House had already passed—which would guarantee one-for-one replacement of all public housing units demolished. Locally, the coalition marched on the home of Senator David Vitter, who was the major obstacle to passage of the bill. This was the same type of protest C3 had organized months before and had called for the coalition to organize in December to no avail.[36]

The back-and-forth exchanges and bickering between various activists and factions at coalition meetings should not be considered the minutiae of the public housing movement. Rather, they provide a rich source of data that illuminates the unfolding and inner workings of the public housing movement's crucially important intraclass struggle. As Zeitlin and Ste-pan-Norris emphasize, the process of self-organization of a class—be it at the community, enterprise, or national levels—involves concrete struggles within it and its organizations over aims, strategies, and leadership. The verbal exchanges highlighted show that two main tendencies or factions had emerged and congealed from the intraclass struggle: the NGO and the independent, grassroots tendencies. The NGOs, for their part, varied in the theories and terminology they employed to justify their positions. Some, coming from a Left background, invoked Marxian verbiage, where-as others employed an eclectic mixture of human rights, identity politics, and pragmatic, TINA discourse and ideology. Whatever their rationaliza-tions, the foundation-funded NGO representatives all arrived at the same position on objectives and strategies. Defending public housing through a variety of strategies and tactics, including and especially direct action, was no longer on the table. The retreat was defended by variously arguing that (1) tenant leaders supported demolition and, therefore, the coalition's opposition was illegitimate (identity politics ideology); (2) direct action was futile, since the federal government had long ago decided to demolish and privatize public housing (TINA ideology); (3) the "correlation of forces" was not favorable and, therefore, we still needed to "build our base" (Marxian/Alinskyite ideology). The goal of the movement had now transformed into fighting for an amorphous affordable housing. In contrast, activists operating outside the nonprofit complex, though coming from various ideological and organizational tendencies and framing (Christian pacifist, Maoist, Luxemburgist, Anarchist, human rights), all converged on using direct action to oppose demolition and reaching out to as many supporters as possible. The obstacles presented by the NGOs underscore the weaknesses of analyses that solely focus on exogenous forces, in the form of disaster capitalists, neoliberal state officials, and right-wing think tanks, in understanding how the neoliberal agenda was implanted post-Katrina.[37] Endogenous forces operating within movements ostensibly opposed to privatization must be calculated, as well.

Human Rights: Talking the Talk and Walking the Walk?

In February the movement did get a boost when two UN Human Rights–appointed investigators, or rapporteurs, condemned the demolition of New Orleans's public housing, arguing this policy violated a host of international human rights treaties. In their report they called on federal, state, and local authorities to "protect the human rights of African Americans affected by Hurricane Katrina" by, among various measures, "immediately [halting] the demolition of public housing in New Orleans."[38] A few weeks later, the UN Committee on the Elimination of Racial Discrimination (CERD) raised serious concerns, in their written evaluation, regarding the U.S. adherence to the International Convention on the Elimination of All Forms of Racial Discrimination (ICERD), a treaty the country signed in 1994. Though the UN report did not explicitly refer to public housing, it did criticize the U.S. government for the "disparate impact that this natural disaster continues to have on low income African American residents, many who continue to be displaced more than two years after the hurricane."[39] The NGOs, to their credit, played an important role in garnering the UN's attention. For example, the AEHR, working with the ACLU and the U.S. Human Rights Network, organized and led a New Orleans delegation of Katrina survivors to testify before the UN Human Rights Council in Geneva, Switzerland, in 2006. The AEHR was also instrumental in bringing Walter Kälin, a representative of the UN's secretary general on the human rights of internally displaced people, to visit the city in January 2008. The AEHR organized several hearings where Kälin heard testimony from public housing residents and others negatively impacted by the government's response to Hurricane Katrina during his three-day stay in the city. Kali Akuno (PHRF), Monique Harden (AEHR), and Mayaba Liebenthal (Critical Resistance) traveled to Geneva in February 2008 to testify before the UN Committee on the Elimination of Racism.[40]

The UN's intervention was useful in placing international attention on the human rights violations taking place in New Orleans and legitimating the public housing movement. Nevertheless, the UN rulings and representatives alone would not stop the demolitions; they were simply tools that the public housing movement could draw on to strengthen the coalition's grassroots struggle. Yet, for the NGOs, the junkets to Geneva, the constant invoking of human rights discourse, the organizing of international tribunals—such as the September 2007 event held by the PHRF—to try the United States for human rights violations, and the coordinating of visits by UN representatives became an end in itself, a fetish, a diversion from concretely defending both the right to return and public housing by stopping demolition.[41] Clearly, authorities were not fazed, as Nagin and the city council on February 1 gave final approval to HUD for demolition of St. Bernard, after earlier giving the green light for Cooper and C. J. Peete. Permission was granted even though the mayor's previously issued provisos had not been followed, including the reopening of seventy-five units at St. Bernard as part of a phased-in rebuilding, the expansion of the HANO board to include a public housing and a mayoral designee, and assurances that redevelopment would occur immediately after demolition.[42]

The coalition—that is, the PHRF and Akuno—immediately issued a statement denouncing the mayor and the city council's "callous maneuvers" and promised to "fight" for an "equitable solution to the housing crisis afflicting our beloved city and community."[43] Yet considering the coalition's record of issuing empty rhetoric, Nagin and the city council had nothing to fear by flagrantly violating human rights conventions and allowing demolition at St. Bernard to go forward. Indeed, as with past declarations of war, there was no deployment of troops to the battlefield—in this case, St. Bernard. Endesha Juakali, in the name of Survivors Village, did hold several fruitless meetings in early and mid-February that like earlier coalition gatherings ended without any plans to take action against demolition. But there was now a new twist. At this point, by mid-February 2008, as Juakali was making clear he would not countenance any action and while many of the self-appointed coalition leaders were off to Geneva to testify about human rights violations, St. Bernard public housing residents Sharon Jasper and her daughter, Kawana Jasper, began to chart their own path. They were intent on not allowing a community where they were born, raised their children, developed friendships, and had countless memories to be demolished without taking direct action to oppose this crime.

This new boldness was displayed at the February 14 Survivors Village meeting—a few days before bulldozers began demolition. At the gathering the Jaspers criticized Tessa Jackson, from the AFL-CIO investment arm, for failing to continue backing the residents after the union's investment deal fell through. Jackson then angrily stomped out of the meeting, complaining, "You're always attacking us." On Saturday, February 16, three days before bulldozing began, the Jaspers led the Silence Is Violence protest to denounce and oppose the impending demolition. After demolition began on February 19, Kawana Jasper criticized Juakali at a meeting two days later for not organizing or having any emergency demonstration plans. The younger Jasper at this point made it clear that she was ready "to get in front of the bulldozers," and her mother emphasized that although we may not be able to stop demolition, we could not let it happen without a fight. C3/Hands Off Iberville and other activists, including Jamie "Bork" Loughner and Sam Jackson of B. W. Cooper, worked to support the Jaspers. After a month of going through the torture of seeing the solid brick buildings eaten away by the claws of bulldozers, the Jaspers decided it was time to take bold action. On March 18, they organized a rally in front of the development and proceeded to lead a delegation into the community they had called home for decades. Simultaneously, Jamie Loughner climbed the fence and secured herself on top of one of the bulldozers. Demolition was immediately stopped. After refusing to leave the grounds, following repeated threats, the police arrested Kawana and Sharon Jasper, as well as Loughner and myself. The Jaspers became the first public housing residents subjected to arrest for opposing the internationally condemned demolition of public housing in post-Katrina New Orleans.[44]

Several days later, C3/Hands Off Iberville organized a demonstration to oppose demolition at the Lafitte development, where Jamie Loughner and two Common Ground volunteers—acting independently of the service organization—occupied an apartment and were quickly arrested. Over the next few months, as bulldozers proceeded to level thousands of apartments, C3 members and supporters attended court hearings and organized support for the activists facing felony charges for their nonviolent direct action protests against demolition. At the same time, the group refocused its attention on Iberville, the one public housing development that was saved from demolition but to which developers and their allies in Washington and city hall were increasingly turning their sights.

Nonprofit Radicals and Privatization: Understanding Their Contradictions, Exposing Their Role

"Institutions reveal much about themselves," sociologist Michael Burawoy writes in his treatise on the key precepts of the reflexive social science embedded in his extended case study methodology, "when they are under stress or in crisis."[45] This principle informs my analysis of the protests, from November 2007 to March 2008, against public housing demolition in New Orleans. An in-depth analysis of this period of intense conflict and organizing offered an opportunity to carry out a veritable test of the role of NGOs under neoliberalism, particularly the progressive, activist wing. Clearly, the NGOs were under pressure, an indispensable ingredient, according to Burawoy, for grasping the nature of any social phenomena. The black urban regime and their neoliberal partners in Washington had thrown down the gauntlet. They were going ahead with the destruction of four black public housing communities, human rights treaties or not. How would the NGOs respond? After continually invoking the right of return and denouncing the racist nature of every stage of the human-made disaster, they could not remain silent. At the same time, their incorporation into the nonprofit complex, including receiving funding from foundations directly involved in privatization, placed a restraint on what they could do. Thus, unsurprisingly, what we saw was a schizophrenic response as the contradictions of the progressive NGOs came into full view in their desperate attempt to *appear* opposed to the demolitions. Some, such as Safe Streets, the Soros-funded nonprofit that was the local affiliate of the antigentrification alliance Right to the City, folded under the pressure. Most were nonetheless able to withstand the pressure by continuing to manufacture dissent that created a pretense of doing something.

This study of NGOs under the gun also provided important insights into how they manufacture dissent—that is, how they assert their hegemony within social movements and the intraclass struggle. The process involves, as the public housing case underscores, a double movement. The NGO's manufacturing of dissent involves a simultaneous neutralizing of resistance advocated by their social movement challengers. This neutralization—consistent with Joan Roeofs's observations on how hegemonic institutions elicit consent—takes the form of portraying deviations from NGO-advocated positions as "'extremism,'... 'utopianism,' 'self-defeating,' 'dogmatism' and the like."[46] In New Orleans, neutralization came at times through issuing public statements, as Endesha Juakali did in opposing protests at the Cooper development because of the tenant leadership's support for redevelopment. On other occasions, as documented in the analysis of coalition meetings, neutralization came through labeling the opposition to demolition as ineffectual and quixotic. "It has happened since the 1990s," explained INCITE's Shana Griffin in reference to the federal government privatization and demolition plan for public housing. Being realistic meant "thinking about alternative forms of affordable housing ... ways that it will happen." Nonetheless, the dominant approach employed by the NGOs to neutralize dissent was not accomplished through debates in public forums. Rather, their modus operandi was that of behind-the-scenes whisper campaigns, red-baiting, and character assassination. Akuno's exchange on the Black Left Unity Listserv that "C3, has in the main, been isolated" provides some insight into these behind-the-scenes mechanizations for asserting their hegemony within the coalition.[47] Understanding the roots of their actions and contradictions—which are structural rather than rooted in character flaws or a simplistic selling out—will be crucial for popular, antiracist, working-class movements to both effectively confront the ruling class's soft power in the form of NGOs and mount an effective challenge to the neoliberal capitalist agenda.

Lessons from New Orleans

Business is flourishing upon the ruins. Cities are turned into shambles ... popular rights, treaties ... the holiest words ... have been turned into scraps. ... Shamed, dishonored, wading in blood and dripping with filth, thus capitalist society stands.

Historical experience is his only teacher, his *Via Dolorosa* to freedom is covered not only with unspeakable suffering, but with countless mistakes. ... Self criticism, cruel, unsparing criticism ... is life and breadth for the proletarian movement.

—ROSA LUXEMBURG, *THE JUNIUS PAMPHLET*

In 1965, Bayard Rustin, who had played a leading role (often behind the scenes) in organizing many of the major African American protests of the mid-twentieth century, published his influential essay *From Protest to Politics: The Future of the Civil Rights Movement*. It was a contradictory piece. On one level, Rustin called for broadening and expanding the demands of the civil rights movement, since as he underscores, "Equality cannot be satisfied *objectively* within the framework of the existing political and economic relations." Desegregation of public facilities was important but not sufficient for achieving real freedom. He called for cutting off—just as the Democratic Johnson administration was ramping-up for its budget-busting bloodletting in Vietnam—the trillions spent on the U.S. war machine and redirecting those resources toward prosecuting a serious war on poverty. He demanded as part of that effort a massive direct government employment public works program to address the endemic unemployment that confronted wide swaths of the black working class. The then fifty-four-year-old seasoned peace and civil rights activist also advocated for a massive expansion of federal aid to schools, for national health care, and, yes, for a multibillion-dollar program to create a "future free of slums" through constructing "attractive public housing." All these demands would of course be welcomed by many black and working-class people, even more so today, amid the worst economic crisis since the Great Depression.

The second component of the essay presents Rustin's theory on how this ambitious agenda could actually be achieved—that is, how the civil rights movement and African Americans in particular could forge and assemble the social power necessary to overcome the entrenched political and economic forces who would fight tooth and nail against this radical program. Rustin proposed, paradoxically, a narrowing and conservatizing of the movement's organizing strategies to win his radical agenda. It was time for the civil rights movement to "mature" by moving from "protest" to "politics," defined narrowly as entering into the Democratic Party and electoral politics. Within these confines, the civil rights movement would ally with liberals, religious groups, and organized labor to "take over" the party and push out the urban political machines and big business interest that blocked the social democratic vision laid out by Rustin. "We must see to it," he counsels activists, "that the reorganization of the 'consensus [Democratic] party' proceeds along lines which will make it an effective vehicle for social reconstruction."[1]

This study of New Orleans public housing, post-Katrina redevelopment, and post–civil rights urban politics more generally can be seen as a test of Rustin's thesis. The outcome? Clearly, it was a dismal failure. The insider strategy, far from making headway toward an expansion of the public sector to address pressing social needs and dismantle racial inequality, has instead facilitated a retrenchment of the welfare state concessions that had been gained from the protests of the 1930s and the 1960s. The turn toward a narrowly defined "politics" to confront, for example, racist police brutality by "getting rid of the local sheriff . . . [through] political action within the Democratic Party" have not won relief for the black working class.[2] Instead, indicators, from unemployment to incarceration and civil liberties to health conditions, have deteriorated further for the black working class (and the larger working class) as the black struggle was demobilized through political incorporation.

The emergence of New Orleans's black urban regime and others across the country beginning in the late 1960s typified the type of politics and political path envisioned in Rustin's post-1965 blueprint, which was published in the then liberal Jewish journal *Commentary*. The rise of these regimes, marked by such milestones as the election of Ernest Morial in New Orleans and Kenneth Gibson in Newark, New Jersey, signaled the institutionalization of the civil rights movement and the deeper incorporation into the Democratic Party that Rustin hailed and promoted. These political developments were also ardently supported by many Black Nationalists, who were, ironically, harsh critics of Rustin. The rise of the new black-led local states represented in their eyes, as Cedric Johnson has critiqued in his book *Revolutionaries to Race Leaders*, the realization of Black Power. But as we have seen with New Orleans, whose experience is representative of other "really existing" black urban regimes, the rise of the new black-led political structures did not provide the material benefits and empowerment predicted by Rustin. The regimes did, of course, open doors and nurture an array of black entrepreneurs, professionals, and politically connected ministers. But for the black working class the emergence of black mayors in the 1970s marked the beginning of take backs that would accelerate and deepen in the ensuing decades. Of course, the new black leaders did, at times, lament that they had "not been able to do more for the poor," as Ernest Morial did in a 1985 Keep the Drive Alive campaign speech, a campaign to change the city charter and allow him to run for a third term.[3] Whatever reservations some may have had, this did not stop them from energetically carrying out the neoliberal agenda, despite its negative impacts on their black working-class constituents. They were ready to "meet their responsibilities" placed upon them by Washington and demanded by their local "governing partners," black and white alike.

Yet as this study shows, not everyone embraced the call to move from protest to politics. The public housing movement, for example, showed its ability to do politics, to exercise real power, by operating outside the confines of the Democratic Party and bourgeois electoral politics. They understood that "politics is more than something politicians do." Politics, as the public housing movement's actions underscored, is a

> process of struggle over conflicting interests carried out into the public arena. Politics involves not only the competition among groups within the system but the struggle to change the system itself . . . to pose alternatives to the existing politico-economic structure.[4]

The public housing residents and their activist allies did not hesitate, as seen at St. Thomas in the early 1980s, to do politics by taking their struggles into the public arena. They did not subordinate their demands and actions to protect their mayor but rather forcefully placed their grievances in front of—literally, in some cases—the chief executive and other elements of the new black political class. In the late 1980s, tenants launched a vigorous campaign that derailed the Rochon Plan, pushed by developers and city hall, to massively downsize public housing. Through employing the politics of confrontation, which had been at the heart of the black protest movement, the public housing movement was able to garner real concessions and victories. Likewise, the unruly protests against the 1980 police killings and rampage directed against black residents of the Fischer public housing development and surrounding area were also able to generate concessions. Local struggles forced Mayor Ernest Morial to fire his recently hired police chief, and with federal intervention, at least some New Orleans police were finally prosecuted for brutalizing black people. The post–civil rights struggles were not able, for the most part, to forge and coalesce into a counterhegemonic challenge to the Democrats at the electoral level. Nonetheless, by maintaining adherence to protest rather than being fully incorporated into an ineffectual insider politics, black working-class folks in New Orleans were able to exercise some level of influence and power.

The role of the nonprofit complex was, as demonstrated, to tame these movements, move activists from protest to politics, and facilitate the neoliberal agenda. Rustin's own trajectory provides insight into how this political metamorphosis from protest to politics unfolds and its tragic consequences. By the time of the 1963 March on Washington, as Stephen Steinberg has pointed out, Rustin was already making his transition into being safely ensconced within the Democratic Party and the AFL-CIO bureaucracy.[5] As one of the key organizers of the march, he worked to rein in SNCC activist John Lewis, who had planned, in his speech, to denounce the Kennedy administration for undermining the civil rights movement and for introducing an inadequate civil rights bill. Overall, Rustin used his renowned organizing skills to choreograph an event that would be orderly rather than disruptive, one that would place the Democrats and Kennedy in a favorable light, all of which led Malcolm X to famously denounce the whole affair as the "farce on Washington." Working to tame the movement—strictures enforced upon him due to having entered into the confines of the Democratic Party and its satellite organizations—ensured that the radical program of social transformation he advocated would never be won.

While operating at a local level and a later historical period, New Orleans activists such as Barbara Major went through a similar transformation. She and other PI activists had always maintained some links to the Democratic Party and the local black urban regime. But they still retained enough independence to engage in contentious politics. As Major and her cohorts became incorporated into the nonprofit complex, however, they began a political transformation that required people, as she puts it, to "go outside" of themselves. They were no longer "stuck in the Sixties," in an era of protest, but now had moved into the insider's game of politics. The cementing of Major and a whole layer of activists and tenant leaders allied with her into the nonprofit complex constrained what demands they could raise and actions they might mount. They were free, of course, to hold their Undoing Racism sessions in New Orleans and around the country and denounce the deeply racist nature of American society. But, concretely, on the ground at St. Thomas, in their own backyard, they were not permitted to challenge the transparently racist, corporate-centered development model that the city's governing elite were pursuing. Their political incorporation, as with Rustin, removed the ability of PI and public housing activists to really do politics. That is, they were not able to flex the political power they had at their disposal in the form of disruptive protest to protect besieged public housing communities. Being realistic through inserting themselves into Rustin's narrowly defined politics facilitated the neoliberal revanchist agenda. As with Rustin, the former pacifist who devolved into a fervent backer of the Vietnam War and an unabashed defender of Israeli aggression, Major also underwent a further political transformation. By 2005, in the aftermath of Katrina, she was cochairing the mayor-appointed BNOB commission that backed the mass privatization of public services and the green spacing—demolishing—of several black neighborhoods. Once an unrelenting defender of public housing, she then criticized—in an obvious reference to activists then working to defend public housing and other besieged public services in Katrina's aftermath—"We fight to hold onto things that's no longer working."[6]

Disastrous Politics and Post-Katrina New Orleans

The catastrophic consequences of political realism, of pursuing the insider's game, have been dramatically underscored in post-Katrina New Orleans. The city, more than six years after Hurricane Katrina, is one in which public services have been systematically dismantled and privatized and union contracts have been summarily abrogated and where 100,000 people, disproportionally black and poor, have not been able to return to the city.[7] This landscape is precisely what many elites are celebrating. Illustrating this perspective was the October 2010 conference the Rockefeller Foundation and Tulane University, held at the city's elegant and recently refurbished Roosevelt Hotel in downtown New Orleans, which they shamelessly dubbed "New Orleans as the Model for the 21st Century: New Concepts of Urban Innovation." The gathering, composed of some two hundred attendees drawn from the world of foundations, nonprofits, business, neoliberal think-tanks, universities, and government, made clear what kind of model they admired and wanted replicated. They were celebrating the great strides economic and political elites had made exploiting the clean slate—the metaphor used by Joseph Canizaro to describe the city's post-Katrina redevelopment opportunities—to carry out a thoroughgoing neoliberal makeover of the city. Dramatic neoliberal innovations, from schools to health care to public housing, had either been implanted or were in the process of being rolled out.

Leading the choruses of praise for the New Orleans model was, unsurprisingly, the city's new mayor and chief booster, Mitch Landrieu. In fact, Landrieu, the son of the city's last white mayor and the first in over three decades, represented one significant component of the new New Orleans. His election, along with the five-to-two white majority on the city council and school board, the election of a white district attorney, and the appointment of a white police chief—as a consolation prize, the chief jailer did remain in black hands—highlighted that the old black urban regime model that had managed the city for over a generation had been swept away, as well. The black political class's unwavering commitment to the neoliberal agenda and the racist poor-people displacement it had led to were even undermining the demographic basis of their rule.

Nevertheless, while the pigment of the political leadership did change, their commitment to neoliberal reform was as unwavering as it had been for their black predecessors. Landrieu exemplified this political continuity as he trumpeted New Orleans—delivered in his trademark Kennedyesque oratory and gestures—for becoming the country's "most immediate laboratory for innovation" and a model for other cities. The various neoliberal "innovations" instituted in post-Katrina New Orleans were made possible, Landrieu emphasized in his address to attendees, by "partnerships ... between public and private entities," particularly the nonprofit sector.[8] The conference's keynote speaker, Amy Liu, the cofounder of the Brookings Institution's Metropolitan Policy Program, also expressed "enormous optimism" in public–private partnerships, in "the capacity of the people, the nonprofits, the institutions, the new mayor" to continue moving forward with the emerging "model city." Liu's praise and optimism—which was accompanied with schoolmarmish encouragement to always go further, "to move with more vision, more intentionality and take risks" in the service of the "model"—is not surprising considering her background.[9] Before coming to the Brookings Institution, Liu served as a special assistant to HUD secretary Henry Cisneros from 1993 to 1996, where her duties centered on carrying out the HOPE VI public housing reform program, which had led to the first wave of demolition and privatization in New Orleans and across the country. Therefore, it must have been especially gratifying for Liu and Bruce Katz, her fellow HUD colleague and cofounder of the Brookings Institution's Metropolitan Policy Program, to see their public housing reforms come to full fruition in New Orleans.

A visit the month before the conference by Honduran president Porfirio Lobo underscored that the New Orleans model was also attracting international attention. Lobo's embrace of the model—one imposed by U.S. authorities in flagrant violation of a host of international human rights protections and norms—was unsurprising and fitting, considering his own rise to power through a military coup that was condemned by most other Latin American countries. Therefore, with this background the Honduran head of state had no qualms signing an accord with Mayor Landrieu, Tulane president Cowen, and the city's other universities to help Honduras implement reforms in health care and education, as well as promote student exchanges. The city, which had witnessed the closing of its major public hospital, the firing of over seven thousand public school teachers and support staff, the abrogation of the workers' collective bargaining agreement, and the conversion of most of the system into privately run charter schools, was being touted as an international model. "We have a lot of experience in rebuilding public school systems in New Orleans," President Cowen said at the press conference, without a hint of irony. He added, emphasizing the malleability of the New Orleans model, that "we'll figure out what will work for them." Mayra Pineda, the liaison between the Honduran government and New Orleans, was explicit about the kind of problem solving they were looking for: "We've had a huge problem with teachers' unions. The teachers are striking all the time. . . . Charter schools are certainly one option to try to solve the union situation."[10] The Inter-American Development Bank was also looking to New Orleans for blueprints. Bank officials contracted with Paul Vallas, the former state-imposed head of the so-called Recovery School District who oversaw a variety of charter and nominally public schools, to provide advice on implementing neoliberal educational reforms in earthquake-ravaged Haiti.[11]

Despite this bipartisan record of support for the post-Katrina revanchist agenda, there was hope in some quarters that President Barack Obama, who took power in January of 2009, would follow a different course. But if anyone had followed his political trajectory, they would not have been surprised by his continuation and extension of the neoliberal agenda that his predecessor had promoted in New Orleans. Obama, as Adolph Reed analyzed him in the late 1990s as the young lawyer's political career began its takeoff, was "a foundation-hatched black communitarian . . . a smooth Harvard lawyer with impeccable do-good credentials and vacuous-to-repressive neoliberal politics."[12] Indeed, as a lawyer, as well as a state and U.S. senator, he backed and embraced neoliberal reforms, particularly with regard to public housing. "Public–private partnerships to create affordable housing" were preferable, he argued, to public housing. "Developers," Obama held, "think in market terms and operate under the rules of the marketplace," unlike public service providers, who do not face the same pressure to adequately serve their "consumer."[13] This negative view of public housing has extended to post-Katrina New Orleans, even though thousands remain homeless or stranded in the diaspora due to a dearth of affordable housing. Obama's HUD secretary, in September 2010, awarded a grant to HANO to demolish and privatize the Iberville development, the city's last traditional public housing development and one that even the Bush administration had not been able to do away with. David Gilmore, the Obama administration–appointed HANO director and a former member of the 1989 commission that hatched HOPE VI, awarded the Iberville contract to Pres Kabacoff, who led the St. Thomas redevelopment. The Choice Neighborhood grant HUD bestowed upon New Orleans and several other cities is envisioned as a pilot program to sell off the country's remaining public housing stock of some 1.2 million units under the so-called PETRA plan, introduced in 2010.[14]

The administration has also provided strong support for the mass chartering of public schools in New Orleans begun by their Republican predecessors. As Obama's education secretary, Arnie Duncan, declared in a January 2010 interview with talk show host Roland Martin, "The best thing that ever happened to the education system in New Orleans was Hurricane Katrina."[15] While later apologizing for his "dumb" remark, Duncan's sympathies were clear: the New Orleans model, including the authoritarian measures employed to implant it, was a huge success that should be emulated. Further underscoring this message was the Obama administration's lauding of a Rhode Island school district for firing all the teachers at a "low-performing" school in 2010. This, of course, was an "innovation" first trail blazed in New Orleans.[16]

The People's Silver Lining

The displacement caused by Katrina clearly, as Naomi Klein and many others have argued, provided an opportunity to impose the socially de-structive disaster capitalist agenda initiated under Bush (and Nagin) and extended by Obama (and Landrieu). Yet as Alexander Cockburn has ar-gued in a critique of Klein's thesis, "Capitalists try to use social or eco-nomic dislocation or natural disaster—New Orleans is only the latest instance—to advantage, *but so do those they oppress*" (emphasis added).[17] This is the other side of New Orleans's post-Katrina story, the people's silver lining that top-down analyses like Klein's often miss. "Too often," as radical urban planner Tom Angotti argues, "urban policy narratives fail to include individuals and urban social movements as active agents of social change, thereby contributing to the impression that they are relatively passive subjects of unchangeable globalization trends."[18] This book's bottom–up analysis of pre- and post-Katrina New Orleans has worked to avoid these pitfalls and blind spots by taking seriously the consequential forms of resistance that have been mounted.

The experience of the pre- and post-Katrina Iberville defense cam-paign underscored the ability of a grassroots, non-501(c)(3)-led move-ment to defeat a key component of urban neoliberalism and save people's homes. By operating outside the grasp of the nonprofit complex and not collapsing into narrow Rustian politics, movements from below were able to exercise real power. Despite attempts to pit blacks versus whites and public housing and non–public housing residents against one another, the Iberville movement was able to forge a multiracial alliance to oppose the deeply racist neoliberal capitalist agenda for public housing. In addition, the post-Katrina public housing movement proved it could, just like its neoliberal rivals, put forward a larger vision and not be limited just to defensive demands. Katrina's silver lining, from the perspective of those working to defend public housing and other public services, was that the disaster underscored the bankruptcy of neoliberalism and the need for a massive, direct government employment program to rebuild New Orleans and the entire Gulf Coast. The ability to raise this demand—one that has garnered greater resonance since the 2008 economic crisis and the resulting Depression-era unemployment levels—was also an important gain of the movement.

While saving Iberville, the post-Katrina movement was not successful in preventing the bulldozing of four other larger public housing developments. But at the same time, the movement—unlike at St. Thomas—did prevent the ruling elites from *consensually* introducing neoliberal public housing reform. The resistance—in the developments, in the streets, at public hearings, and through writings—sabotaged the concerted efforts of developers, government officials, academics, and allied nonprofits to frame public housing demolition as a benevolent enterprise to deconcentrate poverty and improve people's lives. Protests against the everyday, normal violence of neoliberal roll back and the subsequent direct state violence inflicted on activists for opposing demolition unmasked the thoroughly coercive, antidemocratic nature of the touted New Orleans model.[19] Thus, the movement contributed to delegitimating neoliberalism or, at least, its public housing agenda by decoupling it from democracy. Democracy and neoliberalism "did not stand as a pair," as held by the ruling ideology, but were shown to be in contradiction to one another.[20] The leading role played by public housing residents—such as Sharon and Kawana Jasper, who faced arrest while defending their homes—was critical to the movement's ability to delegitimate neoliberal public housing reform. The emergence of the Jaspers as leading housing and poor people's activists in New Orleans was also one of the movement's most important gains. Despite continuing attempts to intimidate them—including a heavily armed SWAT team arresting the elder Jasper while at her home in May 2010 for a fabricated assault at a protest the week before—they have become leading activists for jobs and housing and against police brutality in New Orleans.[21]

Despite all these important advances, we cannot avoid the harsh reality that the pre- and post-Katrina public housing and larger antineoliberal movement failed—at least in the short term—to achieve its major goals. Indeed, pre- and particularly post-Katrina New Orleans has been a spectacular success for the neoliberal agenda. But a defeat, even one as thorough as in New Orleans, can still have a silver lining *if* lessons can be drawn from the historical experience to improve the effectiveness of future struggles. As political scientist Cedric Johnson argues in defense of his critical assessment of the Black Power Movement, "The prospects for developing a viable opposition hinge on how well intellectuals and activists understand the historical processes that created our current political conditions."[22] Key to effectively using the historical record is identifying the "sources of failure within the opposition" so as to prevent, as Adolph Reed emphasizes, "a reproduction of failure."[23]

New Orleans's public housing wars, even when the people lost battles and took casualties, did provide invaluable insights into the real role of the nonprofit foundation complex. They operated, as the record shows, as wolves in sheeps' clothing, as the Trojan horse of neoliberalism. The NGOs appeared as an inoffensive humanitarian and even progressive force but, in effect, played a central role in advancing the revanchist agenda. One way the NGOs and their foundation and state funders abetted the neoliberal project was by stepping into replace previously state-delivered services. But their most pernicious role was through co-opting activists and undermining and taming challenges to the neoliberal agenda. The hegemony of New Orleans's neoliberal black urban regime, particularly its public housing privatization agenda, was not unchallengeable but, in fact, "creaked under [its] various contradictions." "But," as Mark Purcell argues in his work on mounting effective challenges to the hegemony of urban neoliberalism, "it takes active, organized, and committed resistance to bring about a collapse."[24] This is precisely what the nonprofit sector undermined, and it helps explain why they are so generously funded by corporate foundations and the state. In the St. Thomas case, the nonprofits channeled residents and activists away from protests and into a negotiating process that conferred legitimacy on the black urban regime's privatization, demolition, and displacement agenda. In the post-Katrina period, some nonprofits did participate in protest, but they simultaneously undermined achieving what coalition activist Carl Dix called the "determined resistance" needed to defeat the drive to demolish badly needed and little-damaged public housing. More broadly, the NGOs and their dissemination of an identity politics ideology and a political practice centered on difference undermined building a broad working class–rooted challenge to neoliberalism. The most promising counterhegemonic alternative to the neoliberal reconstruction plans was the demand for a mass, direct government employment program. Although some groups raised the demand, the network of foundation-funded, single-issue nonprofits operated as an obstacle to generating greater support.

Despite the many obstacles presented by the nonprofit complex, determined resistance *was* mounted against the effort to destroy—"clean up," in

Congressman Richard Baker's words—New Orleans's public housing. For me, one of the most enduring images of this determined resistance was that of seventy-year-old, wheelchair-bound Gloria "Mama Glo" Irving. During the April 4, 2006, action, she led a group of her neighbors and supporters to reclaim their St. Bernard public housing community despite the best efforts of the police to stop them. We lost "Mama Glo" four Aprils later, in 2010. I entitled my commemoration statement "Gloria 'Mama Glo' Irving—Presente!" since her personal warmth and the struggles she threw herself into have indeed left an indelible mark on her beloved city and fellow New Orleanians. The best way to maintain and build on that legacy is to continue the fight for the type of city, country, and world she believed in and fought for, a society whose organizing principle is based on meeting human need.

Notes

Preface

1. William Tabb and Larry Sawers, eds., *Marxism and the Metropolis* (New York: Oxford University Press, 1978), 19.

2. John Saul, *Socialist Ideology and the Struggle for Southern Africa* (Trenton, N.J.: African World Press, 1990), 190.

3. Oliver Cromwell Cox, *Caste, Class, & Race: A Study in Social Dynamics* (1948; repr., New York: Monthly Review, 1959), xvi.

Introduction

1. Michael Burawoy, "The Extended Case Method," *Sociological Theory* 16, no. 1 (1998): 4–33; Alex Vitale, *City of Disorder: How the Quality of Life Campaign Transformed New York Politics* (New York: New York University Press, 2008), 26.

2. Neil Smith, *The New Urban Frontier: Gentrification and the Revanchist City* (New York: Routledge, 1996), 30.

3. Though scholars of the global capitalist system all agree that the 1970s was a key turning point, there is still significant debate regarding the extent to which the system has changed. The strong globalizationist position put forward by sociologist William Robinson and others holds that a new transnational capitalist class is superseding the nationally based capitalists who were dominant during the preceding stage of monopoly capitalism. Consequently, a new global state, which is incipient in such organizations as the World Trade Organization, is developing to serve the emerging global capitalist class and manage the new integrated global economy. In contrast, others, such as James Petras and Henry Veltmeyer, argue that the capitalist class continues to be rooted in the nation-state and that interimperialist rivalries and anti-imperialist challenges continue to define world politics. William Robinson, *A Theory of Global Capitalism: Production, Class, and the State* (Baltimore: Johns Hopkins Press, 2004); James Petras and Henry Veltmeyer, *Globalization Unmasked: Imperialism in the 21st Century* (New York: Zed Books, 2001).

4. Cynthia Anderson, Michael Schulman, Philip Wood, "Globalization and Uncertainty: The Restructuring of Southern Textiles," *Social Problems* 48, no. 4 (2001): 478. The stepped-up attacks on wages and benefits following the 2008 financial crisis have now reached the point where the entire country is seen

as a "capital security zone." As Chad Mountray, the chief economist for the National Association of Manufacturers recently remarked: "A lot of our members tell us that it sometimes is cheaper to produce in the US, because labour costs are lower." The post-2008 restructuring of the auto industry—where CEOs have imposed wage slashing for new hires, cut retiree benefits, and instituted mass layoffs under the guidance of bankruptcy courts and the Obama administration—have led this transformation. During the Fordist-Keynesian era rising wages and benefits for auto-workers set the bar for all wage earners while in the age of neoliberalism the process works in reverse. Floyd Norris, "Making More Things in the U.S.A.," *New York Times*, January 6, 2012; Joseph Kishore, "The Bankruptcy of Kodak," *World Socialist Web Site*, January 20, 2012, http://wsws.org/articles/2012/jan2012/pers-j20.shtml.

5. Even many ostensible manufacturing firms, such as General Motors, and retailers have also developed lucrative financial arms. Therefore, the 40 percent figure actually undercounts the extent to which profits generated through purely financial transactions, rather than by producing goods or services—the "real economy"—has come to dominate the U.S. economy. Fred Magdoff and Michael Yates, *The ABCs of the Economic Crisis* (New York: Monthly Review Press, 2009), 56.

6. Gary Teeple, *Globalization and the Decline of Social Reform* (Toronto: Garamond Press, 1995); William Sites, *Remaking New York: Primitive Globalization and the Politics of Urban Community* (Minneapolis: University of Minnesota Press, 2003).

7. Sites, *Remaking New York*, xi.

8. Jason Hackworth, *The Neoliberal City: Governance, Ideology, and Development in American Urbanism* (Ithaca, N.Y.: Cornell University Press, 2007); Sites, *Remaking New York*, 23.

9. William Robinson, "Latin America in an Age of Inequality: Confronting the New 'Utopia,'" in *Egalitarian Politics in the Age of Globalization*, ed. Craig Murphy (New York: Palgrave, 2002), 53.

10. David Harvey, *A Brief History of Neoliberalism* (Oxford: Oxford University Press, 2005), 19.

11. Alan Sears, "Queer Anti-capitalism: What's Left of Lesbian and Gay Liberation?," *Science & Society* 69, no. 1 (2005): 104.

12. The concept "repertoires of contention" is taken from Charles Tilly, who defines it "as the ways that people act together in pursuit of shared interest." Arthur Stinchombe adds that "the elements of the repertoire are … simultaneously the skills of the population members and cultural form of the population." Destroying public housing eliminates, therefore, not only low-income housing but the communities where "routines … are learned, shared, and acted out." Cited in Sidney Tarrow, *Power in Movement* (Cambridge: Cambridge University Press, 2007), 30–31. Another study also underscores neoliberalism's role in undermining working-class power, describing it as a "new hegemonic political order that [undermines] historically important

institutional bases of political participation." Henry Veltmeyer, James Petras, and Steve Vieux, *Neoliberalism and Class Conflict in Latin America: A Comparative Perspective on the Political Economy of Structural Adjustment* (New York: Macmillan, 1997), 177.

13. Neil Smith, "New Globalism, New Urbanism: Gentrification as Global Urban Strategy," *Antipode* 34, no. 3 (2002): 434–57.

14. Neil Brenner and Nik Theodore, "Cities and the Geographies of 'Actually Existing Neoliberalism,'" *Antipode* 34, no. 3 (2002): 374.

15. Neil Brenner and Nik Theodore, *Spaces of Neoliberalism: Urban Restructuring in North America and Western Europe* (Malden, Mass.: Blackwell, 2002), xi.

16. Brenner and Theodore, "Cities and the Geographies of 'Actually Existing Neoliberalism,'" 349; Loretta Lees, Tom Slater, and Elvin Wyly, *Gentrification* (New York: Routledge, 2008), 166.

17. Peter Dreier, "Does Public Housing Have a Future?," *Shelterforce,* Summer 2010; Edward Goetz, "Gentrification in Black and White: The Racial Impact of Public Housing Demolition in American Cities," *Urban Studies* 48, no. 8 (2011): 1588.

18. Hackworth, *The Neoliberal City,* 12.

19. For coverage of the hoopla in various cities, see Rhonda Williams, *The Politics of Public Housing: Black Women's Struggles against Urban Inequality* (New York: Oxford University Press, 2004), 236–39. New Orleans, with local and national housing officials, Councilwoman Jackie Clarkson, and Mayor Ray Nagin leading the cheers, joined the national revelry by celebrating the destruction of the thirteen-story Fischer high-rise, one of only two in the city's collection of mostly two- and three-story public housing apartments. For the front-page coverage, see Rob Nelson, "38 Years Fall in 30 Seconds," *Times-Picayune,* January 26, 2004.

20. Goetz, "Gentrification in Black and White," 1582.

21. Derek Hyra, *The New Urban Renewal: The Economic Transformation of Harlem and Bronzeville* (Chicago: University of Chicago Press, 2008); Mary Pattillo, *Black on the Block: The Politics of Race and Class in the City* (Chicago: University of Chicago Press, 2007); Michelle Boyd, *Jim Crow Nostalgia: Reconstructing Race in Bronzeville* (Minneapolis: University of Minnesota Press, 2008); John L. Jackson, *Harlemworld: Doing Race and Class in Contemporary Black America* (Chicago: University of Chicago Press, 2001).

22. As Pattillo emphasizes, "Black middlemen are the main characters of . . . [her] book" (*Black On the Block,* 18).

23. Boyd, *Jim Crow Nostalgia,* xiv.

24. Tom Slater, "The Eviction of Critical Perspectives from Gentrification Research," *International Journal of Urban and Regional Research* (2006): 739.

25. Adolph Reed Jr., "The Black Urban Regime: Structural Origins and Constraints," *Comparative and Urban Community Research* 1 (1988): 138–89.

26. Gordon Macleod, "From Urban Entrepreneurialism to a Revanchist

City? On the Spatial Injustices of Glasgow's Renaissance," *Antipode* 34, no. 3 (2002): 604; David Harvey, "From Managerialism to Entrepreneurialism: The Transformation of Governance in Late Capitalism," *Geografiska Annaler* 71, no. B (1989): 3–17.

27. Adolph Reed Jr., *Stirrings in the Jug: Black Politics in the Post-segregation Era* (Minneapolis: University of Minnesota Press, 1999), 102.

28. Robert Whelan, Alma Young, and Mickey Lauria, "Urban Regimes and Racial Politics in New Orleans," *Journal of Urban Affairs* 16, no. 1 (1994): 15.

29. Reed, *Stirrings in the Jug*, 176.

30. Dennis Judd, "Electoral Coalitions, Minority Mayors, and the Contradictions in the Municipal Policy Agenda," in *Cities in Stress: A New Look at the Urban Crisis*, ed. Mark Gottdiener (Los Angeles: Sage, 1986), 164.

31. Antonio Gramsci, *Selections from the Prison Notebooks* (New York: International Publishers, 1971), 12.

32. Unless otherwise indicated, the terms *501(c)(3) organization, nonprofit, and nongovernmental organization (NGO)* will be used interchangeably. The IRS has twenty-eight types of nonprofit organizations that are exempt from federal taxes. For more on nonprofits' legal status and restrictions, see Joan Roelofs, *Foundations and Public Policy: The Mask of Pluralism* (Albany: SUNY Press, 2003), 13–21.

33. Roelofs, *Foundations and Public Policy*, 19.

34. These numbers do not include nonprofits that have not registered with the IRS to receive tax-exempt status. Kennard Wing, Katy Roeger, and Thomas Pollack, *The Nonprofit Sector in Brief* (Washington, D.C.: The Urban Institute, 2010), 2. For more data on the nonprofit sector, consult the website of the Independent Sector, the major trade organization of the foundation and nonprofit third sector (see www.independentsector.org). For more on the IRS, see Roelofs, *Foundations and Public Policy*, 18.

35. Mark Purcell, *Recapturing Democracy* (New York: Routledge, 2008), 12; Hester Eisenstein, *Feminism Seduced: How Global Elites Use Women's Labor and Ideas to Exploit the World* (Boulder, Colo.: Paradigm Publishers, 2009), 160–65; Petras and Veltmeyer, *Globalization Unmasked*, 128.

36. *Ruling class* is defined as the owners of the major means of production, distribution, and finance and the leading state officials, which is what Gramsci means by the "dominant group." For more on understanding Gramsci's use of Aesopian language to obscure Marxist concepts and therefore avoid having his writings censored by his jailers in Fascist Italy, see James Petras, "Venezuela: A Dictionary of Euphemisms of the Liberal Opposition," *The James Petras Website*, January 5, 2008, http://petras.lahaine.org/?p=1725.

37. Gramsci, *Selections from the Prison Notebooks*, 42; Eisenstein, *Feminism Seduced*, 163.

38. Roelofs, *Foundations and Public Policy*, 24.

39. INCITE! Women of Color Against Violence, *The Revolution Will Not Be Funded: Beyond the Non-profit Industrial Complex* (Cambridge, Mass.: South End Press, 2007).

40. James Petras, "US Middle East Wars: Social Opposition and Political Impotence," *The James Petras Website,* July 4, 2007, petras.lahaine.org/articulo.php?p=1704.

41. Underscoring the relationship between revolts and working-class concessions in the form of public housing is the following revealing comment made by Langdon Post, the first chair of the New York City Housing Authority: "All revolutions are generated in slums; every riot is a slum riot. Housing is one of the many ways in which to forestall the bitter lessons history has in store for us if we continue to be blind and stiff necked." Peter Marcuse, "Interpreting 'Public Housing' History," *Journal of Architecture and Planning* 12, no. 3 (1995): 242.

42. D. Bradford Hunt, *Blueprint for Disaster: The Unraveling of Chicago Public Housing* (Chicago: University of Chicago Press, 2009), 32; U.S. Housing Act of 1937, Pub. L. No. 93-383, section 2 (1937).

43. Kevin Gotham, "Urban Space, Restrictive Covenants, and the Origins of Racial Residential Segregation in the U.S. City, 1900–50," *International Journal of Urban and Regional Research* 24, no. 3 (2000): 617, 623.

44. For an interesting discussion of how FHA commissioner Franklin Richards worked to circumvent the 1948 Shelley decision banning racial covenants and therefore ensure that it would "in no way effect the programs of this agency," see John Kimble, "Insuring Inequality: The Role of the Federal Housing Administration in the Ghettoization of African Americans," *Law & Inquiry* 32, no. 2 (2007): 418–21, 423–25; Raymond Mohl, "Making the Second Ghetto in Metropolitan Miami, 1940–1960," in *The New African American Urban History,* eds. Kenneth Goings and Raymond (Los Angeles: Sage, 1996), 284–90.

45. Arnold Hirsch, *Making the Second Ghetto: Race and Housing in Chicago, 1940–1960* (1983; repr., Chicago: University of Chicago Press, 1998). For a similar argument, see Kevin Gotham, "A City without Slums: Urban Renewal, Public Housing, and Downtown Revitalization in Kansas City, Missouri," *American Journal of Economics and Sociology* 60, no. 1 (2001): 285–316.

46. William Julius Wilson, *The Truly Disadvantaged: The Inner City, the Underclass, and Public Policy* (Chicago: University of Chicago Press, 1987); Douglass Massey and Nancy Denton *American Apartheid: Segregation and the Making of the Underclass* (Cambridge, Mass.: Harvard University Press, 1993); Hunt, *Blueprint for Disaster;* Lawrence Vale, *From the Puritans to the Projects: Public Housing and Public Neighbors* (Cambridge, Mass.: Harvard University Press, 2000). For an argument among radical economists that public housing has mainly been used to assist the profit-making ventures of the real estate industry and promote racial segregation, see Midibo Coulibaly, Rodney Green, and David N. James, *Segregation in Federally Subsidized Low-Income Housing in the United States* (London: Praeger, 1998).

47. Massey and Denton, *American Apartheid,* 174.

48. Thomas Sugrue, *The Origins of the Urban Crisis: Race and Inequality in Post-war Detroit* (Princeton, N.J.: Princeton University Press, 1996); Nicholas

Leeman, *The Promised Land: The Great Black Migration and How It Changed America* (Princeton, N.J.: Princeton University Press). For a critique of this literature, see Kevin Mumford, *Newark: A History of Race, Rights, and Riots in America* (New York: New York University Press, 2007), 4–6.

49. Ian Gough, *The Political Economy of the Welfare State* (London: Macmillan, 1979), 11. For further elaboration of this perspective, see Mark Lavalette and Gerry Mooney, eds., *Class Struggle and Social Welfare* (New York: Routledge, 2000).

50. Williams, *The Politics of Public Housing,* 4, 8. For further challenges to the total failure literature and documentation of the political activism of public housing communities, see Roberta Feldman and Susan Stall, *The Dignity of Resistance: Women Residents' Activism in Chicago Public Housing* (Cambridge: Cambridge University Press, 2004); Larry Bennett, Janet L. Smith, and Patricia A. Wright, eds., *Where Are Poor People to Live? Transforming Public Housing Communities* (New York: M. E. Sharpe, 2006).

51. Loïc Waquant, *Punishing the Poor: The Neoliberal Government of Social Insecurity* (Durham, N.C.: Duke University Press, 2009), 42.

52. Williams, *The Politics of Public Housing,* 6.

53. Don Mitchell, *The Right to the City: Social Justice and the Fight for Public Space* (London: Guilford Press, 2003), 25.

54. The study's official title is the *U.S. Report of the National Advisory Commission on Civil Disorders* but is better known as the Kerner Commission Report. The report identifies as a central problem, from the perspective of the police and state, the ability of the poor to assemble very quickly in the streets to protest and challenge authorities: "Ghetto streets come alive with people, especially on summer nights. . . . It takes a little to attract a crowd" (172). Public housing is indicted for facilitating mobilization that overwhelms the ability of police to respond (173–74), with uprisings in New Brunswick (46) and Newark, New Jersey (68), sparked by confrontations at public housing developments. To reduce the likelihood of future riots, a key commission recommendation was to move away from "mammoth size" public housing to "smaller units on *scattered* sites," a policy HUD implemented (262, 263). National Advisory Commission on Civil Disorders, *U.S. Report of the National Advisory Commission on Civil Disorders* (Washington, D.C.: U.S. Government Printing Office, 1968).

55. House Committee on the Budget, *Review of Budget Proposals for Fiscal Year 1988: New Orleans, La.,* February 16, 1987, 100th Cong., 1st sess. (Washington, D.C.: Government Printing Office, 1987), 563; Hunt, *Blueprint for Disaster,* 54.

56. On the changing racial and class dynamics of the land occupied by the Iberville development, see Alecia Long, *The Great Southern Babylon: Sex, Race, and Respectability in New Orleans, 1865–1920* (Baton Rouge: Louisiana State University, 2004). For further background on the political struggles over the creation of public housing and the program's early history in New Orleans,

see Martha Mahoney, "The Changing Nature of Public Housing in New Orleans, 1930–1974" (master's thesis, Tulane University, 1985); J. Arena, "Winds of Change before Katrina: New Orleans' Public Housing Struggles within a Race, Class, and Gender Dialectic" (PhD diss., Tulane University, 2007).

57. Dorothy Coyle, "The New Orleans Housing Projects as Seen by Their Residents" (master's thesis, Tulane University, 1945), 23.

58. October–December 1968, p. 3770, HANO minutes, HANO archives.

59. Kent Germany, "Making a New Louisiana: American Liberalism and the Search for the Great Society in New Orleans" (PhD diss., Tulane University, 1999), 449.

60. November 15, 1968, p. 3422, HANO minutes, HANO archives.

61. Walter Rogers, *To the People of Desire* (New Orleans: privately printed, 1970), political ephemera file, special collections, Tulane University.

62. For more on the Panthers and Desire, see Mahoney, "The Changing Nature of Public Housing in New Orleans"; Orissa Arends, *Showdown in Desire: The Black Panthers Take a Stand in New Orleans* (Fayetteville: University of Arkansas Press, 2009). See also "Black Panthers," Human Relations Committee Papers, box 4, special collections, New Orleans Public Library Archives (NOPLA), as well as the HANO minutes for 1970, for valuable information.

63. Robert Yin, *Case Study Research: Design and Methods* (Los Angeles: Sage, 1994), 92.

1. Confronting the New Boss

1. Allen Johnson, "'Project Residents Human Too'—Morial," *Louisiana Weekly*, August 7, 1982, 1.

2. Leonard Moore, *Black Rage in New Orleans: Police Brutality and African American Activism from World War II to Hurricane Katrina* (Baton Rouge: Louisiana State University Press, 2010), 158–61.

3. Moore, *Black Rage in New Orleans*, 165.

4. For more on the protests against the Algiers murders, see the interview of Mary Howell in Mary Ann Travis, "The Advocate," *The Tulanian*, Summer 2001; "Talkin' Revolution: Malcolm Suber," Vimeo video, 1:49:40, a lecture posted September 20, 2010, by Patois: NOLA Human Rights Fest, http://vimeo.com/15123380. Underscoring the extent of police brutality, a 1992 Justice Department study found that, between 1984 and 1990, New Orleans's citizens registered more complaints of police abuse with federal officials than did the citizens of any other city in the country, even those much larger. See Human Rights Watch, *Shielded from Justice: Police Brutality and Accountability in the United States* (New York: Human Rights Watch, 1998), 250–67.

5. Johnson, "'Project Residents Human Too'—Morial."

6. The voucher program was first created by Congress in 1974. For an informative and thorough overview of the federal government's housing voucher program, see Alex Schwartz, *Housing Policy in the United States*, 3rd

ed. (New York: Routledge, 2010), 177–208. For an analysis of how the LIHTC program furthered privatization of the welfare state, see Doug Guthrie and Michael McQuarrie, "Privatization and Low-Income Housing in the United States since 1986," *Research in Political Sociology* 14 (2005): 15–51.

7. Johnson, "'Project Residents Human Too'—Morial"; Sites, *Remaking New York*, 42.

8. Johnson, "'Project Residents Human Too'—Morial." Morial's call for accommodation to federal government cutbacks to cities, made in an address as head of the U.S. Conference of Mayors, was welcomed by the editorial board of the *Times-Picayune* newspaper, who bemoaned that "cities . . . have become accustomed even addicted, to federal largesse." "Looking into 'New Localism,'" *New Orleans Times-Picayune*, June 15, 1985.

9. Kevin Gotham, "Neoliberal Gentrification: Tourism and the Socio-spatial Transformation of New Orleans' Vieux Carre (French Quarter)" (paper presented at the Annual Meeting of the American Sociological Association, August 18, 2003), 10.

10. Address to Public Housing Authority Directors, May 10, 1979, box B-45, Mayor Ernest Morial Papers, NOPLA.

11. Author's interview with Carol Stewart, November 5, 2003, New Orleans. January–May 1965, p. 861, HANO minutes, HANO Archives.

12. Author's interview with Calean Smith, November 28, 2003, New Orleans.

13. September 30, 1968; April 6, 1972, HANO minutes, HANO archives; Office of Policy Planning, *St. Thomas Neighborhood Profile* (New Orleans: City of New Orleans, 1980).

14. Kevin Gotham, "Separate and Unequal: The Housing Act of 1968 and the Section 235 Program," *Sociological Forum* 15, no. 1 (2000): 13–37; Peggy Lentz, "Public Housing," in *A Place to Live: Housing in New Orleans*, ed. James Bobo (New Orleans: University of New Orleans, 1978), 203.

15. In this study I use census tracts 81.01 and 81.02 to get a general picture of the demographic profile of St. Thomas. These two tracts cover all of St. Thomas and part of the surrounding neighborhood. Nonetheless, these tracts, particularly since the surrounding blocks at this time tended to reflect the demographics of St. Thomas, provide a relatively accurate picture of St. Thomas and the changes over time.

16. Robinson, "Latin America in an Age of Inequality," 70.

17. Christian Parenti, *Lockdown America: Police and Prisons in the Age of Crisis* (New York: Verso Press), 84–86; Human Rights Watch, *Shielded from Justice*, 250–67; editorial, *Louisiana Weekly*, June 27, 1981.

18. Author's interview with Jacqueline Marshall, January, 25, 2004, New Orleans.

19. Interview with Stewart. Antipolice attitudes and an unwillingness to cooperate was widespread not only at St. Thomas but at other developments, as well. In a September 1980 letter to state representative Johnny Jackson, Mayor Ernest Morial decried the unwillingness of residents from the Desire

project to participate in a dialogue with police following a recent confrontation with the community: "Johnny, I am deeply distressed that we have been unable to get any cooperation from the area residents of the Desire/Florida Community to serve on the New Orleans neighborhood police anti-crime advisory council. It appears to me that this is an excellent first step mechanism to allow for citizen input in relation to the New Orleans police department." Letter to Johnny Jackson, HANO file, 1978–81, box B4, Morial Papers, NOPLA. For similar attitudes toward the police among New York City public housing residents, see Liz Robbins, "Relations with Officers in a Crime-Ridden Precinct Are Plagued by Distrust," *New York Times,* January 16, 2012.

20. Eduardo Bonilla-Silva, *White Supremacy and Racism in the Post–Civil Rights Era* (Boulder, Colo.: Lynne Reinner, 2001), 106; Robert C. Smith *Racism in the Post–Civil Rights Era* (Albany: SUNY Press, 1995) 47; Moore, *Black Rage in New Orleans,* 1–3.

21. For examples of the usual focus on drugs and violence, see "2 Children Wounded at St. Thomas By Ex-boyfriend of Mom," *Louisiana Weekly,* April 7, 1984; "High Homicide Rate Leaves New Orleans Fearful," *New York Times,* May 31, 1994; Rick Bragg, "Children Strike Fear into Grown Up Hearts," *New York Times,* December 2, 1994. A more accurate and sympathetic portrait is provided by Sister Helen Prejean, who lived at St. Thomas in the early 1980s, when she began her ministry to death row inmates. See Helen Prejean, *Dead Man Walking: An Eye-Witness Account of the Death Penalty in the United States* (New York: Random House, 1993). Several scenes from the subsequent movie, by the same name, were also filmed at St. Thomas and the Hope House social service center, and a few residents appeared in the production as well.

22. Author's interview with Geraldine Moore, January 5, 2004, New Orleans. A pseudonym has been used at the request of the interviewee.

23. Author's interview with Willie-Mae Blanchard, November 5, 2003, New Orleans.

24. Author's interview with Emilie Parker, December 15, 2003, New Orleans.

25. Al Szymanski, *Class Structure: A Critical Perspective* (New York: Praeger, 1983), 79.

26. See Carol Stack, *All Our Kin: Strategies for Survival in a Black Community* (New York: Harper and Row, 1974); Kathryn Edin and Laura Lein, *Making Ends Meet: How Single Mothers Survive Welfare and Low-Wage Work* (New York: Russell Sage Foundation, 1997), 149–67; Larry Bennett and Adolph Reed Jr., "The New Face of Urban Renewal: The Near North Redevelopment Initiative and Cabrini-Green," in *Without Justice for All: The New Liberalism and Our Retreat from Racial Equality,* ed. Adolph Reed (Boulder, Colo.: Westview Press, 1999), 195–208.

27. William Julius Wilson, *When Work Disappears: The World of the New Urban Poor* (New York: Knopf, 1996), 20.

28. bell hooks, *Yearning: Race, Gender, and Cultural Politics* (Boston: South End Press, 1990), 42; Feldman and Stall, *The Dignity of Resistance,* 342.

29. Interview with Stewart.

30. Interview with Marshall.

31. In 1982, the Reagan administration allowed public housing authorities to increase rent to 30 percent of gross income. Schwartz, *Housing Policy in the United States;* Larry Jones, letter to editor, "HANO Chief on Tenants and the Eviction Process," *New Orleans Times-Picayune,* October 5, 1988.

32. For convenience, I use the initials STRC to refer to the council. Most residents referred to the body as the "resident council."

33. Allen Johnson, "Project Vote, 'A Sleeping Giant,'" *Louisiana Weekly,* November 20, 1982.

34. For an in-depth analysis of how African American men are under-counted by the government in general and their often undetected presence in New Orleans public housing, in particular, see Petrice Sams-Abiodun, "Missing Data, Missing Men: The Role of Adult Men in Inner-City Neighborhoods" (PhD diss., Tulane University, 2003).

35. Johnson, "Project Vote, 'A Sleeping Giant.'"

36. The United States, in turn, leads the world in the number of people incarcerated. J. Arena, "Repression, Racism, and Resistance: The New Orleans Black Urban Regime and a Challenge to Racist Neoliberalism," in *Race and Ethnicity: Across Times, Space, and Discipline,* ed. Rodney Coates (Boston: Brill Press, 2004), 365–96.

37. Author's interview with Fannie McKnight, November 6, 2003, New Orleans.

38. Johnson, "Project Vote, 'A Sleeping Giant'"; House Committee on the Budget, *Review of Budget Proposals for Fiscal Year 1988,* 563; Christine Cook and Mickey Lauria, "Urban Regeneration and Public Housing in New Orleans," *Urban Affairs Review* 30, no. 4 (1995): 538; Sams-Abiodun, "Missing Data, Missing Men."

39. *HANO Annual Report* (New Orleans: HANO, 1972), 20; Vincent Lee, "Role in Use of $6,000,000 Planned," *New Orleans Times-Picayune,* January 23, 1972; "Negro Tenant Elections to Be Held," *Louisiana Weekly,* February 12, 1972, 3; John Bauman, *Public Housing, Race, and Renewal: Urban Planning in Philadelphia, 1920–1974* (Philadelphia: University of Temple Press, 1987), 204; Feldman and Stall, *The Dignity of Resistance,* 49.

40. October 5, 1971, p. 774, HANO minutes, HANO archives.

41. Author's interview with Ron Chisom, January 13, 2004, New Orleans.

42. As mentioned in the introduction, the first HANO board member was longtime civil rights lawyer A. P. Tureaud, appointed in 1966, and the second was Reynard Rochon, who came on board in 1970. The first tenant to sit on the board was Ursula Spencer, appointed in 1973. By the middle of the decade, the board was majority black. The first black executive director of HANO was Floyd McHenry, appointed by Mayor Landrieu in 1972 to replace longtime director J. Gilbert Scheib, who retired that same year after serving in that post since the 1940s. Nonetheless, Scheib and his longtime tenant relations

director, Allen Dowling, who first began with HANO in 1939, continued on as consultants to the agency for several years after their retirements. After the long reign of Scheib, HANO directors, who have all been African American (until the federal takeover of the agency in 2002), have had relatively short tenures, with Elliot Keyes taking the helm in 1977, followed by Sidney Cates in 1980, Jesse Smallwood in 1986, and Larry Jones, two years later, in 1988 (see the HANO annual reports from 1972 to 1988).

43. *HANO Annual Report* (New Orleans: HANO, 1970), 8; see Feldman and Stall, *The Dignity of Resistance*, 119, on role of HUD in promoting tenant councils.

44. *HANO Annual Report* (New Orleans: HANO, 1972), 20; April 6, 1972; August 5, 1976; September–December 1978; January–June 1981, HANO minutes, HANO archives.

45. Author's interview with Jim Hayes, May 23, 2005, New Orleans.

46. James Hodge and Ira Rosenzweig, "Project Residents Make Demands," *Times-Picayune*, July 2, 1982.

47. Allen Johnson, "Cates Knew of Protest," *Louisiana Weekly*, July 10, 1982.

48. Johnson, "Cates Knew of Protest"; Interview with McKnight.

49. July 1, 1982, HANO minutes, HANO archives.

50. Hodge and Rosenzweig, "Project Residents Make Demands."

51. Interview with McKnight; July 1, 1982, HANO minutes, HANO archives; Johnson, "Cates Knew of Protest."

52. *HANO Annual Report* (New Orleans: HANO, 1972), 13.

53. See the commendation HANO and Director Scheib received in 1964 from the State of Louisiana's Department of Civil Service for being a "model of efficiency." The department lauded HANO for its high level of occupancy, negligible rent collection losses, and the budget surpluses—"residual receipts"—it regularly ran. May–August, 1964, p. 869, HANO minutes, HANO archives; see also HANO's special *Twenty-fifth Annual Report* (New Orleans: HANO, 1962).

54. *HANO Annual Report* (New Orleans: HANO, 1978), 15; *HANO Annual Report* (New Orleans: HANO, 1979), 13; Raymond Struyk, *A New System for Public Housing: Salvaging a National Resource* (Washington, D.C.: Urban Institute, 1980), 140–44.

55. The scattered sites, since their creation in the late 1960s, had required tenants to pay utilities used above their monthly utility allowance, whereas the standard public housing complexes, like St. Thomas, from their inception, did not have a separate utility charge. The rent payments covered utilities (October–December 1968, p. 3774, HANO minutes, HANO archives).

56. "Project Residents Sue Housing Authority," *New Orleans Times-Picayune*, September 3, 1982; Author's interview with Bill Quigley, February 4, 2004, New Orleans.

57. Hodge and Rosenzweig, "Project Residents Make Demands."

58. Christina Metcalf, "Race Relations and the New Orleans Police Department, 1900–1972" (senior thesis, Tulane University, 1985), 85. In 1977, Cates was

in the running to replace the outgoing Clarence Giarrusso as police chief. In his application to Mayor Morial, he touted his role in the police–community relations department for keeping a lid on protests in New Orleans in the late 1960s. The program acted as a "conduit between the police department, the city administration and our citizens. What we learned was transmitted from the police department to city hall for action." Sidney Cates III application for New Orleans police chief position, Application for Police Chief file, box 10, Morial Papers, NOPLA.

59. Johnson, "Cates Knew of Protest"; Hodge and Rosenzweig, "Project Residents Make Demands."

60. Interview with McKnight.

61. David Simpson and Mimi Read, "HANO Agrees to Committee; Project Residents Leave Office," *New Orleans Times-Picayune,* July 3, 1982.

62. Interview with Hayes; Crystal Jones, "The Bottom-up Approach to Collaboration for Social Change: A Case Study of the St. Thomas/Irish Channel Consortium," (master's thesis, University of New Orleans, 1993).

63. Interview with McKnight; Interview with Hayes; Bob Ross, "Project Residents Will Relinquish Office," *New Orleans Times-Picayune,* August 5, 1982.

64. Interview with Quigley; Interview with Hayes; Ross, "Project Residents Will Relinquish Office"; August 5, 1982, HANO minutes, HANO archives.

65. Bob Ross, "Project Office Returned to Housing Officials," *New Orleans Times-Picayune,* August 6, 1982.

66. "Project Tenants Sue Housing Authority," *New Orleans Times-Picayune,* September 3, 1982; Ross, "Project Office Returned to Housing Officials."

67. October 31, 1982; September 30, 1983, HANO minutes, HANO archives.

68. Marjorie Roehl, "Project Residents Cry SOS," *New Orleans Times-Picayune,* November 6, 1982. The problems of lead poisoning were particularly severe at St. Thomas. Of 343 confirmed cases of lead poisoning at housing developments between 1980 and 1986, 187 were from St. Thomas. Children were the main victims, poisoned by eating paint flakes and inhaling lead dust. John McQuaid, "Lead Poisoning Causes Kids Pain, Mom Grief," *New Orleans Times-Picayune,* July 7, 1986.

69. Roehl, "Project Residents Cry SOS"; Johnson, "Project Vote, 'A Sleeping Giant.'"

70. T. Jackson, "Project Eviction Ruling Expected Monday," *New Orleans Times-Picayune,* May 8, 1983; Susan Finch, "Most St. Thomas Rent Strikers Get Reprieves," *New Orleans Times-Picayune,* May 11, 1983.

71. Interview with Quigley.

72. Interview with McKnight.

73. Interview with Quigley.

74. Jones, "The Bottom-up Approach to Collaboration for Social Change"; 187; Ira Rosenzweig, "St. Thomas Tenants Agree to End Rent Strike, Pay $250,000." *New Orleans Times-Picayune,* July 21, 1983; Interview with Quigley.

75. October 4, 1984, HANO minutes, HANO archives.

76. Interview with Marshall.

77. Interview with Quigley.

78. Williams, *The Politics of Public Housing,* 8.

79. David Camfield, "Re-orienting Class Analysis: Working Classes as Historical Formations," *Science and Society* 68, no. 4 (2004): 421.

80. Bill Fletcher Jr. and Fernando Gapasin, "Politics of Labor and Race in the USA," *Socialist Register* (2002): 259.

2. Undoing the Black Urban Regime

1. "A Sunbelt City Plays Catch-up," *Business Week,* March 6, 1978; Mickey Lauria, *Waterfront Development, Urban Regeneration, and Local Politics in New Orleans and Liverpool* (New Orleans: Department of Urban and Regional Planning, 1995), 20–23; Greg Thomas, "New Phase to Start in June at Former St. Thomas Site," *New Orleans Times-Picayune,* March 30, 2005.

2. "Moonwalk Won't Rise in Time for Fireworks," *New Orleans Times-Picayune,* December 5, 1999; Lauria, *Waterfront Development,* 25.

3. Author's interview with Press Kabacoff, April 5, 2004, New Orleans.

4. Lewis Pierce, *New Orleans: The Making of an Urban Landscape,* 2nd ed. (Santa Fe, N. Mex.: Center for American Places, 2003), 156.

5. Whelan, Young, and Lauria, "Urban Regimes and Racial Politics in New Orleans," 14.

6. Smith, *The New Urban Frontier,* 211.

7. Author's interview with James Singleton, January 6, 2003, New Orleans.

8. James Wright, Beth Rubin, and Joel Devine, *Behind the Golden Door: Policy, Politics, and Homelessness* (New York: Aldine de Gruyter, 1998).

9. Cited in Smith, "New Globalism, New Urbanism," 438.

10. Wallace Roberts & Todd, *Plan for the Lower Garden District* (New Orleans: Community Resource Partnership, 1995), 2.

11. The extent to which the early "settlers" in the Lower Garden District had embraced the frontier(wo)men identity and metaphors is underscored in a 1973 article about the neighborhood's revival, which profiles Duncan Strachan, one of the first arrivals and a founding member of the neighborhood association: "Duncan Strachan describes his fellow Coliseum Square residents as '*urban pioneers*'" and says that they have shown 'it is possible to carve out and reclaim sections of the *urban wasteland*'" (emphasis added). Carleton Knight, "Urban Pioneers—A Story of Restoration in the Inner City," *Preservation News* 13, no. 7 (1973): 7.

12. Author's interview with former Coliseum Square Park member, September 9, 2011; Knight, "Urban Pioneers."

13. For use of historic landmark designation to further gentrification in Chicago, see John Betancur, "The Politics of Gentrification: The Case of West Town in Chicago," *Urban Affairs* 37 (2002): 790; Phone interview with former Coliseum Square Park member.

14. Wallace Roberts & Todd, *Plan for the Lower Garden District*, 2; Interview with McKnight. The Landrieu planning study used a questionnaire to determine what residents called their neighborhood, since there had been no official designation used in the past. Underscoring the contested nature of neighborhood identity, the class biases of the Landrieu administration, and the influence of the urban pioneers, the Lower Garden District moniker won out over the Irish Channel even though most of the area's working-class residents used the latter term. The Landrieu administration official that led the study explained that "they"—referring to the pioneers—"certainly wouldn't want it to be called the Irish Channel," because of the "demographic stigma" that accompanied the name. Phone interview with former Landrieu official, September 13, 2011.

15. For the crucial role played by Brooklyn Union Gas in the first-wave gentrification in Park Slope, see Lees, Slater, and Wyly, *Gentrification*, 19–30.

16. Author's interview with Larry Schmidt, November 17, 2003, New Orleans; Ann Veigle, "Coliseum Square Wages Rags vs. Riches Battle," *New Orleans Times-Picayune*, December 15, 1986.

17. Interview with Schmidt.

18. Bruce Eggler, "Program Fosters Comeback for Neighborhood," *New Orleans Times-Picayune*, February 22, 1989; "Ministers Host Confab to Promote Local Unity," *Louisiana Weekly*, October 8, 1988.

19. Phone interview with former PRC board member, September 6, 2011.

20. Lees, Slater, and Wyly, *Gentrification*, 23, 174; Betancur, "The Politics of Gentrification," 809; Author's interview with Dave Billings, November 18, 2003, New Orleans; "PRC History," Preservation Resource Center of New Orleans, accessed May 5, 2011, http://www.prcno.org/aboutprc/history.php.

21. Smith, *The New Urban Frontier*, 1–12. For more on stages of gentrification, see Lees, Slater, and Wyly, *Gentrification*, 174; Betancur, "The Politics of Gentrification," 790–91.

22. Interview with Billings.

23. Author's interview with Camille Strachan, December 9, 2003, New Orleans. For further examples of gentrifiers framing their opposition to the presence of the poor and minorities in behavioral or value terms, see Betancur, "The Politics of Gentrification," 802.

24. Interview with Billings.

25. Interview with Billings. For more on the conflict, see Veigle, "Coliseum Square Wages Rags vs. Riches Battle"; Tyler Bridges, "Poor Being Displaced, Minister Says," *New Orleans Times-Picayune*, September 11, 1989.

26. Author's interview with Don Everard, November 10, 2003, New Orleans.

27. Interview with Billings. For further examples of arson as a "mechanism of gentrification . . . to intimidate owners into selling or minorities into leaving, to empty specific properties on the path of gentrification, or to clear land for future development," see Betancur, "The Politics of Gentrification," 788.

28. Pres Kabacoff, interview by Linda Calvert, 1989 (in possession of the author).

29. For similar views by developers and political officials, see Davis Jahnke (architect), interview by Linda Calvert, July 31, 1989 (in possession of the author).

30. Kabacoff, interview by Linda Calvert.

31. Arnold Hirsch, *Dutch Morial: Old Creole in the New South* (New Orleans: College of Urban and Public Affairs, University of New Orleans, 1990), 16–17.

32. Letter from Mayor Morial to Moise Steeg Jr., President of GNO Tourist & Convention Commission, box 18-B, Morial Papers, NOPLA; Charles Chai, "Who Rules New Orleans? A Study of Community Power Structure," *Louisiana Business Survey*, October 1971, 2–11.

33. Reed, *Stirrings in the Jug*, 170; Arnold Hirsch and Joseph Logsdon, ed., *Creole New Orleans: Race and Americanization* (Baton Rouge: Louisiana State University Press, 1992).

34. Interview with Chisom.

35. Interview with McKnight.

36. John McQuaid, "Oust HANO Board, Tenant Leader Urges," *New Orleans Times-Picayune*, July 9, 1986; "Tenant Representatives Sworn In," *New Orleans Times-Picayune*, August 14, 1986.

37. Interview with Hayes. For their attempt at passing a rent control ordinance, see Human Relations Committee Records, Rent Control file, 1975, box 3, NOPLA. For more on Chisom, Dunn, and the origins of the People's Institute, see Orissa Arend, "Undoing Racism & The Kingdom of God," *New Orleans Tribune*, August/September 2003, 10–11.

38. Interview with Chisom.

39. Mitchell, *The Right to the City*.

40. Interview with Chisom; Interview with Hayes; November 6, 1981, p. 248, HANO minutes, HANO archives.

41. "Letter from Ron Chisom and Jim Hayes to Mayor Dutch Morial," September 19, 1978, Contributions file, 1978–1979, box 20, Morial Papers, NOPLA; "Confidential: City of New Orleans inter-office memo, subject: Black Political Organizations, July 16, 1981," Black Political Organizations file, 1981, box 18-B, Morial Papers, NOPLA.

42. Interview with Chisom; see also Ron Chisom to Mayor Morial, re: resignation letter, June 2, 1981, HANO file, 1978–1986, box C5, Morial Papers, NOPLA.

43. Author's interview with anti–police brutality activist, June 10, 2004, New Orleans.

44. One of the PI's most influential graduates is Tim Wise, the well-known antiracist lecturer. Wise, who came into contact with PI while a college student at Tulane University in the late 1980s and later while working for the nonprofit group Agenda for Children, credits PI trainers Chisom, Dunn, Major, and Billings for making "an indelible contribution to my life and my work." Tim Wise, "Appreciation and Accountability," *Tim Wise: Antiracist Essayist, Author and Educator*, www.timwise.org/appreciation-and-accountability.

45. David Billings also argued the Rochon Report was a product of a meeting

Kabacoff called. Like Kabacoff, Billings listed former mayor Moon Landrieu, as well as then–city councilman Lambert Bossier, who was a Barthelemy supporter and member of the same Seventh Ward Creole organization, COUP, as also participating in the meeting. Billings believed the gathering was held on the Mississippi Gulf Coast. Interview with Kabacoff; Interview with Billings.

46. Rochon was the chief accounting officer (CAO)—one of the most important appointed positions—under Mayor Morial. Rochon ran Barthelemy's 1986 run-off campaign against William Jefferson. Jefferson was being backed by Rochon's former employer and now political opponent Morial. Rochon first gained national recognition for his brilliance as a campaign strategist and ability to get out black voters through Morial's 1982 reelection campaign. This success led him to be sought out by aspiring black mayoral candidates in Chicago and Philadelphia, where he led the successful campaigns of Harold Washington and Wilson Goode, respectively. Iris Kelso, "Housing Idea," *New Orleans Times-Picayune,* December 3, 1993; Cook and Lauria, "Urban Regeneration and Public Housing in New Orleans," 583.

47. Rochon & Associates, *A Housing Plan for New Orleans* (New Orleans: Rochon & Associates, 1988), 145–56; John McQuaid, "$14.6 Million Granted to Fix N.O. Projects." *New Orleans Times-Picayune,* November 6, 1987; Frank Donze, "Study: Razing Only Answer for Much Public Housing." *New Orleans Times-Picayune,* February 6, 1988.

48. Author's interview with Sidney Barthelemy, January 20, 2004, New Orleans.

49. Calvert interview with Jahnke.

50. Betancur, "The Politics of Gentrification," 802. On opposition to demolition and dispersal in Minneapolis, see Edward Goetz, *Clearing the Way: Deconcentrating the Poor in Urban America* (Washington D.C.: Urban Institute Press, 2003); For a critique of what Imbroscio calls the "liberal expansionist" model of development advocated by leading urban scholars Peter Dreier, John Mollenkopf, and Todd Swanstrom and a defense of an alternative "community development" strategy that recognizes "the progressive capacities of cities themselves," see David Imbroscio, "Shaming the Inside Game," *Urban Affairs Review* 42, no. 2 (2006): 224–48.

51. Interview with Barthelemy.

52. Frank Donze, "Housing Project Residents Blast Relocation Proposal," *New Orleans Times-Picayune,* February 19, 1988.

53. Clancy DuBos, "The Rochon Report—Facing the City's Thorniest Question," *Gambit,* March 15, 1988; Author's interview with Barbara Major, December 3, 2003, New Orleans.

54. Donze, "Housing Project Residents Blast Relocation Proposal"; Interview with Major; Interview with Hayes.

55. Interview with Major.

56. Author's interview with Jesse Smallwood, January 21, 2004, New Orleans.

57. Ibid.

58. Norbert Davidson, "HANO: Heads Roll after Board Keeps Smallwood," *Louisiana Weekly,* April 2, 1988.

59. Frank Donze and Joan Treadway, "HANO Refuses to Fire Director," *New Orleans Times-Picayune,* March 26, 1988.

60. Interview with Smallwood.

61. Joan Treadway, "HUD Begins Inquiry into HANO's Role in Letter," *New Orleans Times-Picayune,* June 14, 1988; Coleman Warner and Joan Treadway, "HANO Hit on Letter." *New Orleans Times-Picayune,* June 11, 1988.

62. Interview with Hayes.

63. Joan Treadway, "HANO Fires Smallwood Despite Protests," *New Orleans Times-Picayune,* June 15, 1988; Interview with McKnight; Interview with Smallwood.

64. Interview with Barthelemy.

65. Housing Authority of New Orleans, *By-laws of the Housing Authority of New Orleans, as Amended and Restated* (New Orleans: HANO, 1988), 2 (in possession of the author).

66. Interview with Barthelemy.

67. Letter from Sidney Barthelemy to Barbara Jackson, December 8, 1998, file 1, box 56, Mayor Sidney J. Barthelemy Collection, NOPLA.

68. Cook and Lauria, "Urban Regeneration and Public Housing in New Orleans."

69. Housing Authority of New Orleans: Vacancy Comparison Chart, February 1990, file 8, box B 57, Barthelemy Collection, NOPLA.

70. Interview with Marshall.

71. Interview with Quigley.

72. Urban Land Institute, *Canal Street, New Orleans, Louisiana: An Evaluation of Revitalization Strategies for the City of New Orleans and the Downtown Development District* (Washington: Urban Land Institute, 1989), 33; Urban Land Institute, *Downtown New Orleans: An Evaluation of Development Potential and Strategies to Revitalize and Redefine Canal Street* (Washington: Urban Land Institute, 1998), 23.

73. Cook and Lauria, "Urban Regeneration and Public Housing in New Orleans," 553.

74. Tyler Bridges, *The Rise of David Duke* (Jackson: University Press of Mississippi, 1994), 145–46; "MLK March," *Louisiana Weekly* January 7, 1989.

75. Cook and Lauria, "Urban Regeneration and Public Housing in New Orleans," 553.

3. Neoliberalism and Nonprofits

1. Perez, Ernst & Farnet, *A Master Plan: St. Thomas Housing Development, La. 1–1 & La. 1–9* (report prepared for the Housing Authority of New Orleans, 1994), 1.

2. Reed, *Stirrings in the Jug,* 104.

3. For a clear articulation of these politics, see the classic work by Stokely

Carmichal and Charles Hamilton, *Black Power: The Politics of Liberation in America* (New York: Random House, 1967). For a critique of how "demands for black indigenous control" played a conservatizing role by funneling dissent into "conventional political channels," see Cedric Johnson's groundbreaking work on the origins of postsegregation era politics, *From Revolutionaries to Race Leaders: Black Power and the Making of African American Politics* (Minneapolis: University of Minnesota Press, 2007), xxiii.

4. Along with promoting tenant management schemes in public housing, the Ford Foundation, beginning in the 1960s, also became heavily involved in funding community development corporations, which "helped to move groups that started as community organizers and tenant advocates more firmly into the development and ownership of low-income housing." Both interventions were classic examples of liberal foundations channeling radical movements and activists in more moderate directions. Kathyrn Wylde, "The Contribution of Public–Private Partnerships to New York's Assisted Housing Industry," in *Housing and Community Development in New York City,* ed. Michael Schill (New York: SUNY Press, 1999), 81.

5. William Domhoff, *Who Rules America?* (Mountain View, Calif.: Mayfield Publishing, 1998); Ford Foundation, *The Local Initiative Support Corporations: A Private–Public Venture for Communities and Neighborhood Revitalization* (New York: Ford Foundation, 1980), 5; Theodore Koebel and Marilyn Cavell, *Tenant Organization in Public Housing Projects: A Report on Senate Resolution 137* (Blacksburg, Va.: Virginia Center for Housing Research, 1995); Feldman and Stall, *The Dignity of Resistance,* 295–340; *HANO Annual Report* (New Orleans: HANO, 1978), 8–9; *HANO Annual Report* (New Orleans: HANO, 1979), 14.

6. Address to Public Housing Authority Directors, Morial Papers, NOPLA.

7. Preston Smith, "'Self-Help,' Black Conservatives, and the Reemergence of Black Privatism," in *Without Justice for All,* ed. Adolph Reed Jr. (Boulder, Colo.: Westview Press, 1999), 257–58. Similarly, Nikol Alexander-Floyd argues that a "black cultural pathology paradigm," which has gone into ascendency in the post–civil rights era and focuses on family and culture as the source of racial inequality and oppression, has provided an ideological rationale for state retrenchment. Nikol Alexander-Floyd, *Gender, Race, and Nationalism in Contemporary Black Politics* (New York: Palgrave McMillan, 2007).

8. Interview with Major.

9. Smith, "'Self-Help,' Black Conservatives, and the Reemergence of Black Privatism," 408. For more on Gray's former activism with the National Tenants Organization, before her conversion to self-help solutions, see Smith, 279.

10. "Project's Goal Is Home Rule," *New Orleans Times-Picayune,* September 8, 1988; Jonathan Eig, "Housing Project Tenants Want Reins of Management," *New Orleans Times-Picayune,* December 11, 1988; Koebel and Cavell, *Tenant Organization in Public Housing Projects,* 4.

11. For background on Cynthia Wiggins, see "About Cynthia Wiggins:

President/CEO of Guste Homes Resident Management Corporation," http://financialservices.house.gov/media/file/hearings/111/wiggins.pdf. For her eulogy of Jack Kemp for helping "empower" public housing residents through creating RMCs, see "Tributes to Jack Kemp: 'A Man above Men,'" *The Foundary,* May 8, 2009, http://blog.heritage.org. For her corporate portfolio, consult the web page of the Louisiana secretary of state, www.sos.louisiana.gov; Koebel and Cavell, *Tenant Organization in Public Housing Projects,* 18.

12. Jones, "The Bottom-up Approach to Collaboration for Social Change," 120; Coleman Warner, "Tenants of Project Hired to Cut Grass," *New Orleans Times-Picayune,* January 9, 1988; Eig, "Housing Project Tenants Want Reins of Management."

13. Interview with Major.

14. Ibid.

15. Interview with Billings.

16. See Housing Authority of New Orleans, *The New St. Thomas/Lower Garden District HOPE VI/Application* (New Orleans: HANO, 1996), 42; Jones, "The Bottom-up Approach to Collaboration for Social Change," 48.

17. Interview with Major.

18. STICC Articles of Incorporation, STICC History file, St. Thomas Redevelopment box, Hope House archives.

19. Interview with Major.

20. Alma Young and Jyaphia Christos-Rogers, "Resisting Racially Gendered Space: The Women of the St. Thomas Resident Council," in *Marginal Spaces: Comparative and Community Research,* ed. Michael Smith (New Brunswick, N.J.: Transaction Publishers, 1995), 10–11.

21. Alexander-Floyd, *Gender, Race, and Nationalism in Contemporary Black Politics.* The Annie E. Casey Foundation's involvement at St. Thomas was part of the Comprehensive Community Building Initiative (CCI) begun in the late 1980s by a consortium of foundations. The CCI was billed as "a relatively new approach to combating poverty at the neighborhood level." The program, consistent with neoliberal principles, stressed not state intervention but rather a "community-driven process aimed at strengthening the capacity of neighborhood residents, associations, and organizations to work collectively and individually to foster and sustain positive neighborhood change." This wording shares striking similarities with the redevelopment strategy used to forge consensus on redevelopment of St. Thomas. "What Are CCIs," Community Building Resource Exchange, accessed January 21, 2012, www.commbuild.org/html_pages/whatcci.htm (site discontinued). Another major supporter of dismantling public housing, particularly in Chicago, and replacing it with mixed-income communities has been the MacArthur Foundation, which is also a member of CCI. They partnered with Mayor Daley in the city's Plan for Transformation for public housing, contributing $55 million to the $1.6 billion initiative. A major focus of the foundation was ensuring the orderly relocation of residents by "improving the process, by, for example,

engaging residents." Paul Brest and Hal Harvey, *Money Well Spent: A Strategic Plan for Smart Philanthropy* (New York: Bloomberg Press, 2008), 92. The foundation has also been very generous in funding researchers investigating mixed-income communities and public housing demolition and bringing in other foundations, banks, and other businesses to support Chicago's version of the Rochon Plan through the creation of Partnership for New Communities. For more on the MacArthur Foundation and public housing dismantlement, see Pattillo, *Black on the Block*, 16, 145–46, 168, 197; The John D. and Catherine T. MacArthur Foundation, "Program-Related Investments," www. macfound.org/atf/cf/%7BB0386CE3-8B29-4162-8098-E466FB856794%7D/ PRI_8%205X11-A.PDF.

22. Author's interview with Orissa Arend, April 22, 2004, New Orleans.

23. Interview with Billings.

24. Author's interview with Tammi Fleming-White, December 3, 2003, New Orleans.

25. Reed, *Stirrings in the Jug*, 120.

26. Walter Adamson, *Hegemony and Revolution: A Study of Antonio Gramsci's Political and Cultural Theory* (Berkeley: University of California Press, 1980), 243.

27. Adam Przeworski, "Material Basis of Consent: Economics and Politics in a Hegemonic System," *Political Power and Social Theory* 1 (1980): 21–66; Gramsci, *Selections from the Prison Notebooks*, 12, 161.

28. Goran Therborne, "Why Some Classes Are More Successful than Others," *New Left Review* 138 (1983): 44.

29. Stuart Hall, *The Hard Road to Renewal: Thatcherism and the Crisis of the Left* (New York: Verso, 1988), 170.

30. Interview with Everard.

31. On Canizaro's role in forging the DDD and his general influence in New Orleans politics, see Letter from CADD to City, file 26, box 6; Growth Management Program, file 1–2, box 11; Letter from Canizaro to Landrieu, February 23, 1977, file 4, box 133; Committee of 50, file 4, box 133; N.O. Central Area Growth Management Program, February 1974, file 7, box 133—all from Maurice Landrieu Papers, NOPLA. See also Committee of 50, file 78–79, box 20, Morial Papers, NOPLA. A 1978 letter by Morial aid David Marcello points out that Landrieu was going to work for Canizaro after his term ended and he feared that before leaving office the outgoing mayor would appoint members to the Vieux Carre Commission favorable to Canizaro (Vieux Carre Commission file, box 7, Morial Papers, NOPLA). Nonetheless, despite this concern, Canizaro was by no means excluded from the Morial administration. Among various roles, Morial appointed him to the Commission on the Future of New Orleans in 1984, where he served on the economic development committee. Commission on the Future of New Orleans, Commission file, box J31, Morial Papers, NOPLA.

32. Senate Committee on Banking, Housing, and Urban Affairs, *Hearing on Nomination of Moon Landrieu to Be Secretary of Housing and Urban*

Development, September 6, 1979 (Washington, D.C.: U.S. Government Printing Office, 1978), 10–13, 36–39, 54–59.

33. Cited in Bruce Alpert and Bill Walsh, "On the Hill," *New Orleans Times-Picayune,* June 4, 2000.

34. Robert Whelan, "New Orleans: Mayoral Politics and Economic-Development Policies," in *The Politics of Urban Development,* eds. Clarence Stone and Heywood Sanders (Lawrence: University Press of Kansas, 1987), 228; Whelan, Young, and Lauria, "Urban Regimes and Racial Politics in New Orleans," 3.

35. "Bush's 'Rangers,'" *USA Today,* May 20, 2005, www.usatoday.com/news/politicselections/rangers.htm?loc=interstitialskip; Jim Drinkard and Laurence McQuillan, "Bundling Contributions Pays for Bush Campaign," *USA Today,* October 16, 2003. For more on Canizaro's close relations with President Bush, see Sibley Fleming, "Rebuilding Czar," *National Real Estate Investor,* March 1, 2006, http://nreionline.com/mag/real_estate_rebuilding_czar/.

36. Author's interview with Nathan Watson, November 24, 2003, New Orleans; Wallace Roberts & Todd, *Plan for the Lower Garden District,* 14–15; Jeffrey Meitrodt, "Developers Sell Riverfront Acreage to Casino Interests," *New Orleans Times-Picayune,* July 16, 1994. Lettice Stuart, "Focus New Orleans: Builders Betting on Riverboat Gambling," *New York Times,* December 1, 1991.

37. Interview with Strachan.

38. Interview with Watson.

39. Cook and Lauria, "Urban Regeneration and Public Housing in New Orleans," 540.

40. Interview with Watson.

41. Cited in Stuart Alan Clarke, "Black Politics on the Apollo's Stage: The Return of the Handkerchief Heads," in *Spatial Practices,* eds. Helen Liggett and David Perry (Los Angeles: Sage, 1995), 122.

42. Reed, *Stirrings in the Jug;* on this same point, see also James Jennings, *The Politics of BLACK Empowerment* (Detroit: Wayne State University Press, 1992), 22–23.

43. Author's interview with James Singleton, January 6, 2004, New Orleans.

44. Interview with Everard.

45. Mary Jackman, *The Velvet Glove: Paternalism and Conflict in Gender, Class, and Race Relations* (Berkeley: University of California Press, 1994), 16. Cited in Bonilla-Silva, *White Supremacy and Racism,* 72.

46. Interview with Schmidt. Underscoring the extent to which generating consent has become a "best practice" for real estate developers is a recent publication by the Urban Land Institute. The study elaborates on "various forms of engagement processes and the approaches that can be employed *to reach consensus within community groups*" and therefore overcome the "development logjam" (emphasis added). See Doug Porter, *Breaking the Development Logjam: New Strategies for Building Community Support* (Washington, D.C.: Urban Land Institute, 2006), iii. For similar concerns, see *Pulling Together: A*

Planning and Development Consensus-Building Manual (Washington, D.C.: Urban Land Institute, 1994).

47. Interview with Singleton.

48. Todd Swanstrom, *The Crisis of Growth Politics: Cleveland, Kucinich, and the Challenge of Urban Populism* (Philadelphia: Temple University Press, 1985), 4.

49. Interview with Major.

50. Harvey, *A Brief History of Neoliberalism*, 29.

51. Interview with Major; Interview with Billings; Jones, "The Bottom-up Approach to Collaboration for Social Change," 127.

52. Interview with Major; Brian Thevenot, "Canizaro Had Role in Creating River Garden," *New Orleans Times-Picayune*, March 19, 2006.

53. Interview with Billings.

54. Author's interview with Louise Franklin, December 15, 2003, New Orleans.

55. Interview with Moore; Interview with Everard.

56. Interview with McKnight.

57. Interview with Major.

58. House Subcommittee on Housing and Community Opportunity, *The New Orleans Public Housing Authority and the Role of the Department of Housing and Urban Development*, 104th Cong., 2nd sess., July 8, 1996 (Washington, D.C.: Government Printing Office, 1996), 74; Interview with Schmidt; Interview with Billings.

59. Interview with McKnight.

60. ULI Advisory Services, *Lower Garden District, New Orleans, Louisiana* (Washington: Urban Land Institute, 1993), 5.

61. For further background on the members, see House Subcommittee on Housing and Community Opportunity, *The New Orleans Public Housing Authority and the Role of the Department of Housing and Urban Development*, 561–64.

62. ULI Advisory Services, *Lower Garden District*, 9; Wallace Roberts & Todd, *Plan for the Lower Garden District*, 5.

63. Ibid., 11–12, 37–42.

64. Jamie Peck and Adam Tickwell, "Neoliberalizng Space," *Antipode* 34, no. 3 (2002): 380–404; Brenner and Theodore, "Cities and the Geographies of 'Actually Existing Neoliberalism,'" 349–79.

65. Teeple, *Globalization and the Decline of Social Reform*. Harvey explains that a similar populist legitimation tact was used in Britain, where some public housing was sold off to tenants (Harvey, *A Brief History of Neoliberalism*, 61). In the St. Thomas case, developers and government officials included the populist components in the initial plans while residents were being wooed but then later revoked them.

66. Purcell, *Recapturing Democracy*, 12, 27; Harvey, *A Brief History of Neoliberalism*, 66.

67. Interview with Everard; Interview with Billings. When Lane was named to head the Chicago Housing Authority in 1988, HUD waived its rules and allowed him to retain his position with his company, American Community Housing Associates (ACHA). Thus, Lane himself embodied a further extension of privatization—the public–private administrator. In May 1995, Lane resigned from the authority under pressure from HUD. See Scott Farmelent, "Faulty Towers," *Citypaper.net*, October 26, 1995; Jean Amandolia, *The Chicago Housing Authority Time-Line, December 1986–August 1998* (Cambridge, Mass.: Abt & Associates, 1998), 2.

68. Janet Smith, "Mixed-Income Communities: Designing Out Poverty or Pushing Out the Poor?," in *Where Are Poor People to Live?*, eds. Bennett, Smith, and Wright, 97; Susan J. Popkin, Victoria E. Gwiasda, Lynn M. Olson, Dennis P. Rosenbaum, and Larry Buron, *The Hidden War: Crime and the Tragedy of Public Housing in Chicago* (New Brunswick, N.J.: Rutgers University Press, 2000), 31–38.

69. Amandolia, *The Chicago Housing Authority Time-Line*, 2–5; For background on Lane's relationship with President Clinton and support for greater coercive measures as the CHA head, see "Remarks by the President in a Telephone Call to a Town Meeting with Secretary Cisneros," April 11, 1994, http://www.ibiblio.org/pub/archives/whitehouse-papers/1994/Apr/1994-04-11-PRESIDENTs-Remarks-by-Phone-to-Chicago-Town-Meeting; "Remarks by the President to Law Enforcement Officers," April 11, 1994, http://www.ibiblio.org/pub/archives/whitehouse-papers/1994/Apr/1994-04-11-Presidents-Remarks-to-Law-Enforcement-Officers.

70. Pattillo, *Black on the Block*, 232–39, 343–44.

71. Interview with Billings.

72. Stephen Steinberg, "Bayard Rustin and the Rise and Decline of the Black Protest Movement," *New Politics* 6, no. 3 (1997).

73. ULI Advisory Services, *Lower Garden District*, 40

74. Interview with Billings.

75. See Bill Rust, "Walking the Plain Talk: Protecting Sexually Active Teens in Atlanta, New Orleans, and San Diego," *AdvoCasey*, Spring/Summer 2000.

76. Reed, *Stirrings in the Jug*, 5; Cynthia Horan, "Racializing Regime Politics," *Journal of Urban Affairs* 24, no. 1 (2002): 19–33.

77. Reed, *Stirrings in the Jug*, 166, 176.

78. Ibid., 5.

79. Harvey, *A Brief History of Neoliberalism*, 42.

80. David Wilson, "Toward a Contingent Urban Neoliberalism," *Urban Geography* 25, no. 8 (2004): 780.

81. Robinson, "Latin America in an Age of Inequality," 30.

82. On "structuration," see Anthony Giddens, *Profiles and Critiques in Social Theory* (Berkeley: University of California Press, 1982). For the classic statement on the power of poor and working-class people being centered in mass mobilization and disruption, see Francis Fox Piven and Richard

Cloward, *Poor People's Movements: Why They Succeed, How They Fail* (New York: Vintage Books, 1979).

83. Francis Fox Piven, "Whom Does the Advocate Planner Serve?," in *The View from Below: Urban Politics and Social Policy,* eds. Susan Fainstein and Norman Fainstein (Boston: Little, Brown, 1972), 232.

84. Ibid., 232.

85. Roelofs, *Foundations and Public Policy,* 22, 24. For an interesting discussion of the co-optation role foundations and nonprofits played in late- and post-apartheid South Africa, see Patrick Bond, *Elite Transition: From Apartheid to Neoliberalism in South Africa* (London: Pluto Press, 2000), 122–54, esp. 125, 129–30. There, the Urban Foundation, set up by liberal capitalists at the Anglo American Corporation, helped co-opt Left academics and antiapartheid community activists through jobs, consulting contracts, and prestige. The former grassroots activists were put in the service of promoting and legitimizing neoliberal housing reforms and other promarket social policies.

86. Karl Marx and Frederick Engels, *The Communist Manifesto* (1848; repr., New York: International Publishers, 1971). Cited in Roelofs, *Foundations and Public Policy,* 1.

4. No Hope in HOPE VI

1. Michelle Alexander, *The New Jim Crow: Mass Incarceration in the Age of Colorblindness* (New York: New Press, 2010), 56. William Clinton, "State of the Union Address," January 23, 1996, transcript, http://clinton4.nara.gov/textonly/WH/New/other/sotu.html.

2. "Remarks by President at One Strike Crime Symposium," March 28, 1996, William J. Clinton Foundation, accessed May 1, 2011, www.clintonfoundation.org/legacy/032896-speech-by-president-at-one-strike-crimesymposium.htm (site discontinued).

3. Jessica Pardee and Kevin Gotham, "HOPE VI, Section 8, and the Contradictions of Low-Income Housing Policy," *Journal of Poverty* 9, no. 2 (2005): 2.

4. National Commission on Severely Distressed Public Housing, *Final Report,* August 10, 1992 (Washington, D.C., 1992); Center for Community Change, *HOPE Unseen: Voices for the Other Side of HOPE VI* (Washington, D.C.: ENPHRONT, 2003), 3.

5. National Commission on Severely Distressed Public Housing, *Final Report;* Linda Fosburg, Susan Popkin, and Gretchen Locke, *Cross-site Report,* vol. 1 of *An Historical and Baseline Assessment of HOPE VI* (Cambridge, Mass.: Abt & Associates, 1996), i, 8.

6. The official name of the program for revitalizing "distressed" public housing has varied by each funding year. But beginning in 1994, the Clinton administration began to refer to the program, regardless of what was the official title, as HOPE VI. National Housing Law Project, *False Hope: A Critical Assessment of HOPE VI Public Housing Redevelopment Program* (Washington, D.C.: NHLP, 2002), 1. Fosburg., Popkin, and Locke, *Cross-site Report,* 9; Susan

Popkin, Bruce Katz, Mary Cunningham, Karen Brown, Jeremy Gustafson, and Margery Turner, *A Decade of HOPE VI: Research Findings and Policy Challenges* (Washington, D.C.: Urban Institute and Brookings Institution, 2004), 14.

7. U.S. General Accounting Office, *HOPE VI: Progress and Problems in Revitalizing Distressed Public Housing, GAO/RCED-98-187* (Washington, D.C. Government Printing Office, 1998), 18; Fosburg, Popkin, and Locke, *Cross-site Report,* 9–11; National Housing Law Project, *False Hope,* 4.

8. Quality Housing and Work Responsibility Act of 1998, Pub. L. No. 105-276 (1998); Fosburg, Popkin, and Locke, *Cross-site Report,* 23.

9. National Housing Law Project, *False Hope,* 3–4; Jeff Crump, "The End of Public Housing as We Know It," *International Journal of Urban and Regional Research* 27, no. 1 (2003): 184; Fosburg, Popkin, and Locke, *Cross-site Report,* 15, 29.

10. Popkin et al., *A Decade of HOPE VI,* 8.

11. Data on displacement is taken from Edward Goetz's study, which provides the most detailed investigation to date on the racial and class demographic changes produced by public housing demolition. Though less equivocal about the racial impacts of indirect displacement, as compared with the direct variety, the author does emphasize that the "amount of indirect displacement is probably underestimated because very few of the HOPE VI projects that form the basis of this analysis had completed the redevelopment process." To arrive at the figure of 350,000 directly displaced residents, I estimated the number of apartments and residents per unit in eighty-three projects for which HUD did not have data. Even this 350,000 figure is a conservative one, since it does not include residents that left—or were forced out—in the preceding months and years before demolition and whose apartments housing officials then left vacant. This practice, followed at St. Thomas and other developments, further reduced the number of households for which officials had to find replacement housing while having the added benefit of telegraphing to the remaining residents that their days were numbered, as well ("Gentrification in Black and White," 1581–604).

12. P. Brophy and R. Smith, R.N., "Mixed Income Housing: Factors for Success," *Cityscape* 3, no. 2 (1997): 6; Steve Rosenthal, "How Liberal Ideology Assists the Growth of Fascism: A Critique of the Sociology of William Julius Wilson," *Journal of Poverty* 3, no. 2 (1999): 67–87; Bennett and Reed, "The New Face of Urban Renewal," 185–90; Harry Wexler, "HOPE VI: Market Means/Public Ends—The Goals, Strategies, and Mid-term Lesson of HUD's Urban Revitalization Demonstration Program," *Journal of Affordable Housing* 10, no. 3 (2001): 195, 205; Adolph Reed Jr., "America Becoming—What Exactly? Social Policy Research as the Fruit of Bill Clinton's Race Initiative," *New Politics* 8, no. 4 (2002); Sean Zielenbach, "Assessing Economic Change in HOPE VI," *Housing Policy Debate* 14, no. 4 (2003); Yan Zhang and Gretchen Weisman, "Public Housing's Cinderella: Policy Dynamics of HOPE VI in the Mid-1990s," in *Where Are Poor People to Live?,* eds. Bennett, Smith, and Wright, 46–47.

13. Wilson, *The Truly Disadvantaged*, 25–6, 38, 49, 56; Wilson, *When Work Disappears*, 20.

14. Bennett and Reed, "The New Face of Urban Renewal," 186; Rosenthal, "How Liberal Ideology Assists the Growth of Fascism," 74–75.

15. Bennett and Reed, "The New Face of Urban Renewal," 190. Similarly, Nikol Alexander-Floyd argues a "black cultural pathology paradigm," employed by conservatives and Black Nationalists and used in a more nuanced manner by liberals such as Wilson, leads to a focus on family and culture—particularly black women—as the source of black oppression and away from deeply embedded social inequities (*Gender, Race, and Nationalism in Contemporary Black Politics*).

16. "President Clinton's Remarks at the National Medal of Science and Technology Awards Ceremony," April 27, 1999, http://clinton4.nara.gov/WH/New/html/19990427-4646.html.

17. Interview with Kabacoff. This message was further reinforced when Kabacoff, while participating in the Committee for Economic Development's—an influential liberal corporate think tank—subcommittee Tackling the Problems of the Inner City, met Wilson, who was consulted as an expert in the field. The final report, produced by the subcommittee, draws heavily on Wilson's ideas. Committee for Economic Development, Research and Policy Committee, *Rebuilding Inner-City Communities: A New Approach to the Nation's Urban Crisis* (New York: Committee for Economic Development, 1995), 6. For another example of developers invoking Wilson's work to justify demolishing public housing as an antiracist/antipoverty initiative, see comments of Chicago attorney Alexander Polikoff in Patricia Wright, "Community Resistance to CHA Transformation," in *Where Are Poor People to Live?*, eds. Bennett, Smith, and Wright, 159–60.

18. Reed, "America Becoming—What Exactly?"

19. Ibid.

20. Daniel Patrick Moynihan, *The Negro Family: The Case for National Action* (Washington, D.C.: Department of Labor, Office of Planning and Research, 1965); Massey and Denton, *American Apartheid*, 217–23, 229–36.

21. Douglass Massey and Shawn Kanaiaupuni, "Public Housing and the Concentration of Poverty," *Social Science Quarterly* 74, no. 1 (1993): 120.

22. Stephen Steinberg, "The Liberal Retreat from Race," in *Race and Ethnicity in the United States*, ed. Stephen Steinberg (Oxford, UK: Blackwell Publishers, 2000), 47. Cedric Johnson makes a similar critique in his perceptive analysis of the extraordinary import given to the views of minority neoconservatives: "What distinguishes the color-blind conservatism of Ward Connerly, D'Souza and the like from their white counterparts is the social weight afforded to their claims because of their racial identity. Their criticisms are deemed more genuine because of their first-person racial perspective and avoid the stigma of racism that might accompany an attack on redistributive public policy by white pundits" (*Revolutionaries to Race Leaders*, 236).

Johnson's assessment is echoed by white neoconservatives in their recent defense of black anti–affirmative action advocate Ward Connerly following revelations that he was misusing funds from his nonprofit American Civil Rights Institute. Their defense of Connerly emphasized that he had "been particularly effective at what he does . . . because he is black," and therefore they could ill afford to lose his services. For example, Robert Clegg, president of the anti–affirmative action group Center for Equal Opportunity, defended Connerly by emphasizing that there are "few people who can do or would do what he does." He explained that Connerly could handle name calling by "fellow blacks" that would be much harder for a white anti–affirmative action advocate such as himself. Clegg's conclusions on the ability to take flack mirror Steinberg's assessment of why William Julius Wilson was much more effective than Daniel Patrick Moynihan at employing, and getting away with, a victim-blaming diagnosis of black poverty. Charlie Savage, "Affirmative Action Foe Is Facing Allegations of Financial Misdeeds," *New York Times,* January 18, 2012.

23. See footnote no. 22.

24. Waquant, *Punishing the Poor,* 43. For a similar analysis of neoliberalism, see Paul Street, *Racial Oppression in the Global Metropolis* (New York: Rowman & Littlefield, 2007), 36–38, 290. Waquant's conceptualization draws heavily from his mentor, Pierre Bourdieu. The late French sociologist distinguishes between the "left and right hand of the state," with the former defined as the "set of agents of the spending agencies" (i.e., public housing, schools, hospitals, public broadcasting, and other public services). He emphasizes that these services are not bestowed from above but rather "are the trace, within the state, of social struggles of the past." In contrast, the right hand of the state is embodied by the finance ministry and other sections of the state that advocate and impose retrenchment of the left hand, which of course, invariably requires assistance from the coercive arms of the state to contain opposition and deal with the social fallout. Pierre Bourdieu, *Acts of Resistance: Against the Tyranny of the Market* (New York: New Press, 1999), 2.

25. Ed Goetz, "The U.S. War on Drugs as Urban Policy," *Journal of Urban and Regional Research* 20, no. 3 (1996): 540; Corinne A. Carey, "Federal 'One Strike' Legislation," in *No Second Chance: People with Criminal Records Denied Access to Public Housing* (New York: Human Rights Watch, 2004), hrw.org/reports/2004/usa1104/5.htm#_Toc86471128; Charles Lane, "Public Housing Drug Rule Stands," *New Orleans Times-Picayune,* March 27, 2002.

26. Katy Reckdahl, "Thrown Out," *Gambit,* March 9, 2004; Carey, "Federal 'One Strike' Legislation"; "Remarks by the President to Law Enforcement Officers," April 11, 1994, http://www.ibiblio.org/pub/archives/whitehouse-papers/1994/Apr/1994-04-11-Presidents-Remarks-to-Law-Enforcement-Officers; Evelyn Nieves, "Drug Ruling Worries Some in Public Housing," *New York Times,* March 28, 2002; Allen Johnson, "Strike Zone," *Gambit,* October 27, 1998.

27. The financing mechanism for COPS captures the process of refashioning the Keynesian state into its neoliberal version. The $7.6 billion expended

between 1995 and 2000 came from "money saved by the reduction of the Federal work force and [investing] it in crime-fighting programs." *Attorney General's Report to Congress: Office of Community Oriented Policing Services,* September 2000 (Washington, D.C.: U.S. Department of Justice, 2000), 4, www.cops.usdoj.gov/pdf/e12990066_f.pdf.

28. Goetz, "The U.S. War on Drugs as Urban Policy," 547; U.S. Department of Justice, *Weed & Seed* (Washington D.C.: U.S. Department of Justice, 2006); Tulane University, *The Tulane–Xavier Campus Affiliates Program: Building Linkages between Universities and Public Housing Communities in New Orleans* (New Orleans: Tulane University, 1996), 128–32.

29. Chester Hartman and David Robinson, "Evictions: The Hidden Housing Problem," *Housing Policy Debate* 14, no. 4 (2003): 481, 491; Brian Rogal, "CHA Residents Moving to Segregated Areas," *Chicago Reporter,* July–August, 1998; Center for Community Change, *HOPE Unseen.*

30. This theoretical insight is drawn from Louis Althusser's work on the ideological and repressive apparatuses of the state. Even the police, which use primarily repressive measures and strategies to uphold the rule of the dominant class, also have to employ at the same time ideological measures to legitimate the application of force. *Ideology and Ideological State Apparatuses: Notes toward an Investigation, Essays on Ideology* (London: Verso, 1984).

31. Waquant, *Punishing the Poor,* xvii; Kenneth Saltman, *Collateral Damage: Corporatizing Schools—A Threat to Democracy* (New York: Rowman & Litlefield, 2000), 84.

32. For a thorough examination of how the drug war has constructed the system of "mass incarceration," the anchoring institution of contemporary black oppression, see Alexander, *The New Jim Crow.*

33. See Housing Authority of New Orleans, *By-laws of the Housing Authority of New Orleans.*

34. Christopher Cooper, "HANO Kicks Out Newly Hired Manager," *New Orleans Times-Picayune,* September 13, 1991; Fosburg, Popkin, and Locke, *Cross-site Report,* 8–9.

35. House Subcommittee on Housing and Community Opportunity, *The New Orleans Public Housing Authority and the Role of the Department of Housing and Urban Development,* 599–605. For a critique of how C. J. Brown's management at HANO was put together "by some political friends of the mayor," see Jomo Kenyatta Bean, letter to editor, "Management Didn't Deliver," *New Orleans Times-Picayune,* October 3, 1994. The HANO board, with Morial's backing, ended the three-year contract in September 1994. Shelia Danzy, a close aid of Barthemey, was C. J. Brown's last managing director of HANO.

36. Christopher Cooper, "Report Reaps $493,865 for Advisor," *New Orleans Times-Picayune,* October 13, 1996; Alfred Charles, "HANO Awards Contract to Morial Friend," *New Orleans Times-Picayune,* August 4, 1994.

37. Alfred Charles, "Plan to Revamp HANO; Let Private Sector Help," *New Orleans Times-Picayune,* April 19, 1995.

38. Author's interview with Jomo Kenyatta Bean, October 15, 2006, New Orleans; Frank Donze, "HANO Workers: Who Will Be Cut?," *New Orleans Times-Picayune*, March 29, 2005; Alfred Charles, "HANO Approves Management Change," *New Orleans Times-Picayune*, May 9, 1995. Cynthia Wiggins, the most influential public housing resident on the HANO board and a strong supporter of the recommendations, was later named as the cochair of Morial's 1998 reelection campaign ("About Cynthia Wiggins").

39. Susan Finch, "Californian Hired as HANO Director," *New Orleans Times-Picayune*, February 28, 1995; Fosburg, Popkin, and Locke, *Cross-site Report*, 29.

40. Author's interview with Vincent Sylvain, February 17, 2004, New Orleans. For further evidence of Sylvain's support for drastically reducing public housing, see his presentation at a Louisiana Endowment for Humanities panel on New Orleans mayors, where he touted the administration's success at St. Thomas: "When you go out to the old St. Thomas site that was a development conceived of in our administration." "Marc Morial: A Panel Discussion," Humid Beings video, 1:32:00, filmed December 16, 2007, nola.humidbeings. com/features/detail/331/Marc-Morial-A-Panel-Discussion.

41. Interview with Marshall; Leslie Williams, "HANO Might Destroy Units," *New Orleans Times-Picayune*, August 26, 1995; Letter from HUD to Michael Kelly, August 20, 1996, Demolition/Disposition file, St. Thomas box, Greater New Orleans Fair Housing Action Center (GNOFHAC) archives; "New Orleans Zeroes In on Blight, 954 Apartments to Be Torn Down," *New Orleans Times-Picayune*, March 21, 1996; "N.O. Units Will Be Razed," *New Orleans Times-Picayune*, July 30, 1996; "HUD Approval of 954 Plan," Demolition/Disposition file, St. Thomas box, GNOFHAC archives.

42. Leslie Williams, "Florida and Desire Complexes Begin Separation from HANO," *New Orleans Times-Picayune*, November 29, 1995.

43. Housing Authority of New Orleans, *Request for Qualifications for a Development Partner for the St. Thomas Housing Development*, (New Orleans: HANO, 1997), 5.

44. Leslie Williams, "HANO Monitor to Report to HUD; Move Falls Short of Total Takeover," *New Orleans Times-Picayune*, February 9, 1996; House Subcommittee on Housing and Community Opportunity, *The New Orleans Public Housing Authority and the Role of the Department of Housing and Urban Development*, 87–93.

45. HANO Board of Commissioners at Special Meeting, February 10, 1996, Resolution No. 96-01; St. Bernard Resident Council et al. vs. Ronald Mason et al., Docket no. 96-737, Civil District Court, Parish of Orleans, State of Louisiana; Civil Action No. 96-1698 "T" 4, U.S. District Court, Eastern District of Louisiana; "Request for Approval of Non-competitive Award," Memorandum from Henry Cisneros, HUD secretary, to Michael Kelly, HANO executive director, May 16, 1996, Correspondence file, St. Thomas Redevelopment box, Hope House archives; Tulane University, *The Tulane–Xavier Campus*

Affiliates Program, 47; David Maurrasse, *Beyond the Campus: How Colleges and Universities Form Partnerships with their Communities* (New York: Routledge, 2001), 103–44, 202. The last HANO board members were lawyer Ike Spears, the chair; developer Joseph Canizaro; Rev. H. Mayberry; and public housing residents Cynthia Wiggins, Judith Watson, Shirley Bush, and Kim Singleton. House Subcommittee on Housing and Community Opportunity, *The New Orleans Public Housing Authority and the Role of the Department of Housing and Urban Development,* 567–70).

46. Leslie Williams, "HANO to Evict Women, Kids in 40th Drug Case," *New Orleans Times-Picayune,* September 21, 1996.

47. Leslie Williams, "HANO May Evict Drunks; Feds Approve Change in Rules," *New Orleans Times-Picayune,* September 28, 1997; "Agency Praises HANO for Evictions," *New Orleans Times-Picayune,* March 6, 1998; Johnson, "Strike Zone."

48. Moore, *Black Rage in New Orleans,* 230, 234, 240.

49. *New Orleans Police Department Annual Report, 1994* (New Orleans: NOPD, 1994). For more on policing techniques that undermine constitutional protections and have led to a huge expansion of the prison population, especially of African Americans and Hispanics, see Alexander, *The New Jim Crow,* chapters 2 and 3.

50. The first director of the weed and seed program in New Orleans was future city councilman James Carter, while the partnering community, "seed" organization was run by community activist Kojo Livingston. The seed organization affiliated with the initiative also received funding from various foundations, including the Institute for Mental Health, the Greater New Orleans Foundation, the United Way, and national ones, such as the Institute for Community Peace. Valerie Faciane, "2nd District Congressional Race: James Carter Is Working behind the Scenes," *New Orleans Times-Picayune,* August 18, 2008; Interview with the head of the Crescent City Peace Alliance, November 15, 2010; *New Orleans Police Department Annual Report, 1996.*

51. Author's interview with Glynn Alexander, December 16, 2003, New Orleans; *New Orleans Police Department Annual Report, 1994; New Orleans Police Department Annual Report, 1997.*

52. Interview with Alexander. For more on public housing residents and the local war on drugs, see Leslie Williams, "HANO Targets Drugs," *New Orleans Times-Picayune,* January 31, 1998; Johnson, "Strike Zone"; Rhonda Bell, "HANO Gives Cops Drug-Fight Money," *New Orleans Times-Picayune,* March 30, 2001. For further evidence of police harassment being used to drive out public housing residents in other cities, see Associated Press, "Public Housing Tenants Suspect Conspiracy: Police Presence Seen as Pressure to Move Out So Land Can Be Redeveloped," MSNBC, November 15, 2007, www.msnbc.msn.com/id/21821315.

53. Arena, "Repression, Racism and Resistance."

54. On prison expansion, see Arena, "Repression, Racism and Resistance."

On the city's juvenile curfew, see Natalie Pompilio, "Curfew Curbing Crime, Cops Say," *New Orleans Times-Picayune*, January 30, 2001; Christopher Cooper, "Extra Cops Hit Curfew Beat," *New Orleans Times-Picayune*, June 2, 1994. On eviction of HANO residents for juveniles violating the city curfew or fights among teenagers, see Reckdahl, "Thrown Out."

55. Author's interview with Demetria Farve, November 17, 2003, New Orleans.

56. Waquant, *Punishing the Poor*, xviii; Arena, "Repression, Racism and Resistance."

57. Fosburg, Popkin, and Locke, *Cross-site Report*, 10.

58. Interview with Everard.

59. U.S. Department of Housing and Urban Development, *Notice of Funding Availability for Public Housing Demolition, Site Revitalization, and Replacement Housing Grants (HOPE VI), Fiscal Year 1996* (Federal Register, July 22, 1996), 38029. Also, section 24 CFR 970.4 (a) of the federal code required that residents be consulted for HUD to approve any redevelopment plans. Housing Authority of New Orleans, *The New St. Thomas/Lower Garden District HOPE VI/Application*, 156.

60. Center for Community Change, *HOPE Unseen*.

61. By this time, Lane needed a full-time job after being forced out of his position as chair of the board and executive director of the Chicago Housing Authority in June 1995. Bennett, Smith, and Wright, introduction to *Where Are Poor People to Live?*, 8; Author's interview with Robert Mayfield, December 19, 2003; Interview with Billings; *What's Happening*, October 25, 1994, Newspapers file, St. Thomas Redevelopment box, Hope House archives.

62. Interview with Mayfield; Housing Authority of New Orleans, *The New St. Thomas/Lower Garden District HOPE VI/Application*, 26.

63. Piven, "Whom Does the Advocate Planner Serve?," 232; Interview with Mayfield.

64. Housing Authority of New Orleans, *The New St. Thomas/Lower Garden District HOPE VI/Application*, 2, 46.

65. Housing Authority of New Orleans, *The New St. Thomas/Lower Garden District HOPE VI/Application*, 34.

66. Ibid., 34.

67. Ibid., 11, 155.

68. Ibid., 10.

69. Ibid., 33, 157.

70. For these assurances, see *What's Happening*, October 25, 1994, Newspapers file, St. Thomas Redevelopment box, Hope House archives.

71. Interview with Mayfield.

72. Interview with Everard. Nonetheless, Everard, unlike many other non-profit officials involved in St. Thomas, participated in and supported anti-demolition efforts in the aftermath of Hurricane Katrina.

73. Hackworth, *The Neoliberal City*, 11.

74. Brenner and Theodore, *Spaces of Neoliberalism*, ix.

75. Adolph Reed Jr., "New Orleans: Undone by Neoliberalism," *Nation*, September 18, 2006.

76. Reed, *Stirrings in the Jug*, 5.

77. Sociologist Nöel Cazenave's recent book *The Urban Racial State* (New York: Rowman & Littlefield, 2011) provides a theoretically sophisticated analysis of how the local state—of which the black urban regime would be one variant—"manage[s] race relations in ways that foster and sustain both its own immediate political interests, and ultimately, white racial supremacy" (25). This work opens a rich vein for future research, although my analysis of the local black state departs from Cazenave's in that I place greater emphasis on the class origins and class interests of the black officials that head the black-led local state, rather than on state autonomy, to explain the policy agenda they support. Furthermore, my study of neoliberalism and public housing underscores that a class analysis of racial oppression is crucial for identifying its primary beneficiaries and building an effective political challenge.

78. Sharon Collins, *Black Corporate Executives: The Making and Breaking of a Black Middle Class* (New York: Guilford Press, 1997). The role the state played in *forging* this class is similar to Mike Davis's analysis of how the state intervened to *preserve* the old middle strata of peasants, shopkeepers, and artisans in France, Italy and, Japan: "It is well known that the social weight of these groups is artificially preserved by political subvention. Because these strata were indispensable supporters for ruling bourgeois parties (Gaullists, Christian Democrats, and Liberal Democrats), their economic positions have been stabilized by massive state intervention: ranging from agricultural subsidies . . . to special tax relief and 'anti-monopoly' legislation (Like the Royer law of 1973 in France protecting small business from competition from chain stories)." *Prisoners of the American Dream: Politics and Economy in the History of the U.S. Working Class* (London: Verso, 1986), 212. For similar analyses, see Szymanski, *Class Structure: A Critical Perspective*, 83; Morton Wegner, "State Responses to Afro-American Rebellion: Internal Neo-colonialism and the Rise of the New Black Petite Bourgeoisie," *Insurgent Sociologist* 10, no. 2 (1980).

79. Jill Quadagno, *The Color of Welfare: How Racism Undermined the War on Poverty* (New York: Oxford University Press, 1994), 58; Johnson, *From Revolutionaries to Race Leaders*, xxvi; Reed, *Stirrings in the Jug*, 87.

80. Cited in Johnson, *From Revolutionaries to Race Leaders*, xxvii.

81. Collins, *Black Corporate Executives*, 161; Jerry Watts, "What Use Are Black Mayors?," *The Black Commentator*, November 17, 2005; Bruce Dixon, "Failure of the Black Misleadership Class," *The Black Commentator*, November 9, 2006.

82. Whelan, Young, and Lauria, "Urban Regimes and Racial Politics in New Orleans," 10–11; Mickey Lauria, "Reconstructing Urban Regime Theory: Regulation Theory and Institutional Arrangements," in *The Urban Growth Machine*, eds. Andrew Jonas and David Wilson (Albany: SUNY Press), 138;

Louis Miron, "Corporate Ideology and the Politics of Entrepreneurialism in New Orleans," *Antipode* 24, no. 4 (1992).

83. Mary Patillo, *Black on the Block: The Politics of Race and Class in the City* (Chicago: University of Chicago Press, 2007), 17–18, 117–18.

84. Whelan, Young, and Lauria, "Urban Regimes and Racial Politics in New Orleans," 10; Lauria, "Reconstructing Urban Regime Theory," 136.

85. Whelan, Young, and Lauria, "Urban Regimes and Racial Politics in New Orleans," 15.

86. Simon Clarke, "State, Class Struggle and the Reproduction of Capital," *Kapitalistate* 10/11 (1983): 119.

5. When Things Fall Apart

1. Interview with Moore; Minutes of HRI-HANO-STICC-STRC meeting, May 22, 2001, Tri-partite Meetings file; St. Thomas Redevelopment box, Hope House archives.

2. The *Times-Picayune* inaccurately reported that Melancon had lived at St. Thomas longer than any other current resident. In fact, an elderly white resident, Francis Zeiner, who was also relocated (to the Iberville development), had lived there since the late 1940s. Interview with Everard; Rhonda Bell, "Overhaul of St. Thomas: A Complex Undertaking," *New Orleans Times-Picayune,* October 26, 2000.

3. Author's interview with Carlos Crockett, March 2, 2005, New Orleans; Bell, "Overhaul of St. Thomas."

4. Rhonda Bell, "HANO Praises Demolition's Firms Move," *New Orleans Times-Picayune,* January 16, 2001; Interview with Everard.

5. Leslie Williams, "St. Thomas Complex to be Razed, Replaced," *New Orleans Times-Picayune,* October 9, 1996; Leslie Williams, "HANO Notified of Hope 6 Grant for St. Thomas," *New Orleans Times-Picayune,* October 10, 1996; Interview with Everard.

6. U.S. General Accounting Office, *HOPE VI: Progress and Problems in Revitalizing Distressed Public Housing, GAO/RCED-98-187* (Washington, D.C.: Government Printing Office, 1998), 3.

7. Letter from Gregory Byrne, Abt & Associates, to Gayle Epp, Jim Stockard, Ed Marchant, and Marcus Dasher, March 17, 1997, Correspondence file, Brod Bagert Collection (in possession of author).

8. Letter from Alvi Anderson-Mogilles, HANO procurements, to prospective bidders, May 21, 1997, St. Thomas RFQ file, St. Thomas Redevelopment box, Hope House archives; Letter from M. Janis to M. Kelly, March 20, 1997; Demolition/Disposition file, St. Thomas box, GNOFHAC archives.

9. In April 1996, HANO—even before obtaining the HOPE VI grant—awarded the contract to the New York architectural firm Starrett Corporation. The firm later pulled out. Leslie Williams, "New York Firm May Lead HANO Project," *New Orleans Times-Picayune,* April 7, 1996; Housing Authority of

New Orleans, *Request for Qualifications for a Development Partner for the St. Thomas Housing Development;* Creative Choice Homes v. Historic Restorations Inc. and Housing Authority of New Orleans, U.S. District Court, Eastern District of Louisiana, Civil Case No. 99-1569, May 19, 1999, CCH Suit file, Brod Bagert Collection (in possession of author).

10. Leslie Williams, "HANO Signs Pair of Firms; 2 Complexes Will Be Transformed," *New Orleans Times-Picayune,* July 15, 1997; Letter from Michael Kelly, HANO Director, to Elinor Bacon, Deputy Assistant Secretary of HUD, April 1, 1998, CCH Suit file, Brod Bagert Collection (in possession of author); U.S. Department of Housing and Urban Development (HUD), "Developer Selection, St. Thomas HOPE VI Grant, New Orleans Louisiana," memorandum, July 1998, 27, Correspondence file, Brod Bagert Collecton (in possession of author); Creative Choice Homes v. Historic Restorations Inc. and Housing Authority of New Orleans, p. 8.

11. HUD, "Developer Selection," 7; St. Thomas Chronology, Negotiations file, St. Thomas Redevelopment box, Hope House archives.

12. STRC letters file, St. Thomas Redevelopment box, Hope House archives; Creative Choice Homes v. Historic Restorations Inc. and Housing Authority of New Orleans, pp. 8–9.

13. Interview with Everard; Leslie Williams, "Residents Issue Ultimatum on St. Thomas Deal," *New Orleans Times-Picayune,* March 12, 1998; Mary Swerczek, "Report Slams HANO Deal," *New Orleans Times-Picayune,* August 9, 1998; Housing Authority of New Orleans, *Development Agreement among the Housing Authority of New Orleans, the St. Thomas Resident Council and St. Thomas Development Company, LLC for the Housing Authority of New Orleans St. Thomas Development* (New Orleans: HANO, 1998).

14. "Goal . . . ," CRP file, St. Thomas Redevelopment box, Hope House archives; Greg Thomas, "The Plan: Rebirth of the St. Thomas Housing Development Is at the Heart of Hopes for the Lower Garden District," *New Orleans Times-Picayune,* October 22, 1995; HUD, "Developer Selection," 6; Author's interview with Demetria Farve, November 17, 2003, New Orleans; Author's interview with Carolyn Williams, December 1, 2003, New Orleans; Interview with Moore; Interview with Billings.

15. Author's interview with Irma Ricardo, December 15, 2003, New Orleans.

16. Billings moved onto full-time work as a trainer and administrator with the People's Institute; Crystal Jones took an administrative position with the local HUD office; and Major went on to become the executive director of two nonprofits while still continuing as an itinerant PI trainer. Ironically, PI and the Undoing Racism workshops it offered expanded enormously in the late 1990s while, simultaneously, the St. Thomas redevelopment—which they initially touted as an example of empowerment and self-determination—was leading to the expulsion of a low-income black community. By 1997, PI had offices in Berkeley, Seattle, Brooklyn, and Minneapolis, as well as New Orleans, while their revenues increased from $670,000 in 1997, with approximately

$135,000 from foundations, to $1.25 million in 2002, with $600,000 generated from grants. Data on the institute's finances can be obtained from their annual 990 reports filed with the IRS. They can be obtained at the GuideStar website at www2.guidestar.org. For more on the institute, go to www.pisab.org.

17. HUD, "Developer Selection," 5–6; Mary Swerczek, "HANO to Rebid Flawed Rehab Deal for St. Thomas," *New Orleans Times-Picayune,* July 14, 1998.

18. Letter from Gregory Byrne, Abt & Associates, to Gayle Epp, Jim Stockard, Ed Marchant, and Marcus Dasher, March 17, 1997, Correspondence file, Brod Bagert Collection (in possession of author).

19. Interview with Carolyn Williams. Williams, an STRC advisor who attended the meeting, says Barbara Jackson secretly recorded the meeting. Jackson refused to be interviewed for this study, and thus, I could not confirm Williams's claim that a tape exists.

20. Letter to Andrew Cuomo from Barbara Jackson, October 6, 1998, STRC Letters file, St. Thomas Redevelopment box, Hope House archives.

21. Creative Choice Homes v. Historic Restorations Inc. and Housing Authority of New Orleans, 12; Interview with Billings; Don Everard, "Some Notes Concerning the Planned Revitalization of St. Thomas," Numbers file, St. Thomas Redevelopment box, Hope House archives.

22. Brod Bagert, "St. Thomas and HOPE VI: Smoke, Mirrors, and Urban Mercantilism" (master's thesis, London School of Economics, 2002), 14–15.

23. Letter from Mayor Marc Morial in support of HRI, October 3, 1996, CCH Suit file, Brod Bagert Collection (in possession of author).

24. Letter from Barbara Jackson to Andrew Cuomo. Etienne had been on the STICC board. In 1998, he was the STICC treasurer and head of the finance committee (Minutes of the STICC board meeting, February 11, 1998, and March 19, 1998, STICC Board Meetings file, St. Thomas Redevelopment box, Hope House archives). Creative Choice Homes v. Historic Restorations Inc. and Housing Authority of New Orleans, 13; James Varney, "HANO Chooses Local Developer; HRI Chosen over National Rivals," *New Orleans Times-Picayune,* October 29, 1998; Author's interview with Pres Kabacoff, April 5, 2004, New Orleans.

25. Gloria Dauphin, "Black Architects Get a Lift from Airport Work," *Louisiana Weekly,* October 8, 1988; Varney, "HANO Chooses Local Developer"; Interview with Kabacoff. For more on the cooperation among the city's elite black strata and how they narrowly defined African American interests, see "Conference of Black Clergy and Black Professionals," *Louisiana Weekly,* October 8, 1988. For the example of a city bond issue used to provide some benefits for black professionals and entrepreneurs, while the bulk of the proceeds accrued to large, white-controlled corporations, see Gordon Russell, "Bond Deal at City Hall Expected to Cost New Orleans Taxpayers 400 million," *New Orleans Times-Picayune,* October 31, 2008.

26. Varney, "HANO Chooses Local Developer."

27. Interview with Billings; Whelan, Young, and Lauria, "Urban Regimes and

Racial Politics in New Orleans." See the March 16, 1994, issue of St. Thomas's newsletter, *What's Happening*, in which Morial mugs for a photo with St. Thomas residents at the newsletter's office, a visual example of the black mayor's "appearing to be progressive." Newspapers file, St. Thomas Redevelopment box, Hope House archives.

28. Interview with Billings.

29. "St. Thomas Marching to Housing Authority to Protest Development Selection Process," October 29, 1998, STRC file, St. Thomas Redevelopment box, Hope House archives.

30. Interview with Kabacoff; Varney, "HANO Chooses Local Developer."

31. Interview with Quigley.

32. Memo from Bart Stapert to STRC officers and advisors, December 27, 1998, STRC file, St. Thomas Redevelopment box, Hope House archives.

33. Bonilla-Silva, *White Supremacy and Racism in the Post–Civil Rights Era*, 76.

34. Letter from Barbara Jackson to Joseph Canizaro, November 23, 1998, STRC Letters file, St. Thomas Redevelopment box, Hope House archives. Don Everard recalls the funding being $50,000 for six months.

35. Interview with Kabacoff; Letter from Thomas Crumley, Vice-President for Development, to Barbara Jackson, July 6, 2000, HRI file, St. Thomas Redevelopment box, Hope House archives. Attendance at the PI training was one of the few parts of the requirements laid out in the RFQ to which HRI adhered (Housing Authority of New Orleans, *Request for Qualifications for a Development Partner for the St. Thomas Housing Development*, 13).

36. Interview with Billings; CSSP Budget Proposed by HRI, section 3, STICC Notes, STICC Notes file, St. Thomas Redevelopment box, Hope House archives; Interview with Everard; Interview with Kabacoff.

37. STICC board of director meeting minutes, September 16, 1999, STICC Board Meetings file, St. Thomas Redevelopment box, Hope House archives. Under HOPE VI guidelines, 25 percent of infrastructure work was to be performed by residents. See Minutes of HRI-HANO-STICC meeting, May 22, 2001, HRI-HANO-STICC Meetings file, St. Thomas Redevelopment box, Hope House archives; *HOPE VI Community & Supportive Services* (New Orleans: Housing Authority of New Orleans, 2000), 23.

38. Don Everard, "Some Notes Concerning the Planned Revitalization of St. Thomas"; Historic Restorations Incorporated, *St. Thomas Revitalization Plan*, January 15, 2000 (New Orleans: Historic Restorations Incorporated, 2000), cover sheet; Bagert, "St. Thomas and HOPE VI," 22.

39. Letter from Barbara Jackson to Shelia Danzy, May 10, 2000, STRC Letters file, St. Thomas Redevelopment box, Hope House archives.

40. Susan Finch, "Audit Slams Hiring of Consultant; HANO Contract Vague, Work Not Documented," *New Orleans Times-Picayune*, January 31, 2000.

41. Interview with Quigley; Hope House, *Happy 5th Anniversary to the*

St. Thomas Law Center & Farewell to Bart Stapert, August 31, 2001 (in possession of author).

42. Arena, "Winds of Change before Katrina," 353

43. Although HRI originally included Gregory St. Etienne and Liberty Bank as one of their development partners after HUD forced a rebidding of the St. Thomas contract, "it never really materialized," as Kabacoff explains. Interview with Kabacoff.

44. House Subcommittee on Oversight and Investigations, *Inspector General's Report on the Public Housing Authority of New Orleans,* June 4, 2001, 107th Cong., 1st sess. (Washington, D.C.: Government Printing Office, 2001), 3; Housing Authority of New Orleans, *Development Agreement,* 14; Housing Authority of New Orleans, *Request for Qualifications for a Development Partner for the St. Thomas Housing Development,* 11.

45. On collaboration, see the HRI-HANO-STICC-STRC meeting minutes for February 8, March 8, May 22, and June 14, 2001, Tri-partite Meetings file, St. Thomas Redevelopment box, Hope House archives); Historic Restorations Incorporated, *St. Thomas Revitalization Plan,* 55.

46. Form letter from Theresa Richard, acting CSSP coordinator for HANO, to St. Thomas residents, November 1, 1999, Eviction Process file, St. Thomas Redevelopment box, Hope House archives; Historic Restorations Incorporated, *St. Thomas Revitalization Plan,* 20–21. Interviews with Carolyn Williams, Moore, and Everard.

47. *Residents Choosing the Section 8 Options Should Be Aware of the Following,* Eviction Process file, St. Thomas Redevelopment box, Hope House archives; *Resident Housing Decision, September 1997,* Eviction Process file, St. Thomas Redevelopment box, Hope House archives.

48. Housing Authority of New Orleans, *St. Thomas Relocation Report as of 1/29/01,* Eviction Process file, St. Thomas Redevelopment box, Hope House archives; *Relocation Plan for the St. Thomas Development,* p. 9, Relocation file, St. Thomas Redevelopment box, Hope House archives.

49. Interview with Moore.

50. Ibid.

51. James Scott, *Weapons of the Weak: Everyday Forms of Peasant Resistance* (New Haven, Conn.: Yale University Press, 1985); Robin D. G. Kelley, *Hammer and Hoe: Alabama Communist during the Great Depression* (Chapel Hill: University of North Carolina Press, 1990); Adolph Reed Jr., "Mythologies of Cultural Politics and the Discrete Charm of the Black Petite Bourgeoisie," in *African Americans and the New Policy Consensus,* eds. D. Marilyn Lashley and Melanie Njeri Jackson (London: Greenwood Press, 1994).

52. *Gramsci, Selections from the Prison Notebooks, 337.*

53. Interview with Blanchard. Support for Blanchard's insights regarding displacement and health are found in Danya Keene's study of public housing residents in Chicago displaced by HOPE VI. Keene's study found "a marked decline in self-rated health and increased experiences of chronic conditions"

among the displaced. She pointed to the disruption of supportive social networks, which she also measured as a key causal factor. "African American Public Housing Residents in the HOPE VI Era: Relocation, Social Networks and Health" (PhD diss., University of Michigan, 2009), 189. For more on the negative health impacts of gentrification more generally, including HOPE VI–induced displacement, see Mindy Thompson Fullilove, *Root Shock* (New York: Ballantine Books, 2005).

54. Nayita Wilson, "Housing Discrimination Is Significant in New Orleans," *Louisiana Weekly*, March 7, 2005.

55. Author's interview with Emilie Parker, December 15, 2003, New Orleans.

56. Interview with Moore.

57. The 2008 study by the Justice Policy Institute in Chicago found that public housing demolition resulted in "scattered relocation to other segregated, high-crime areas of the city [, which] dislocated people from long-established social networks and increased friction and violence among Chicago gangs." Cited in Alexander Fangmann and Jerry White, "Chicago Youth Violence: An Indictment of the US Democratic Party," *World Socialist Web Site*, June 6, 2008, http://wsws.org/articles/2008/jun2008/chic-jo6.shtml. The tragic death of Derion Albert, a sixteen-year-old public high school student beaten to death while walking home, had its roots in the closing of a school that served youth from the Altgeld public housing development and the placing of these students in another underresourced inner-city school. See Alexander Fangmann and Naomi Spencer, "Chicago Teen Killed in Street Brawl," *World Socialist Web Site*, October 7, 2009, http://wsws.org/articles/2009/oct2009/chic-007.shtml.

58. Rhonda Bell, "Apartments Scarce for Section 8 Renters," *New Orleans Times-Picayune*, June 6, 2000.

59. Ibid.

60. "St. Thomas Residents Have Been Relocated to Segregated Housing," Relocation file, St. Thomas Redevelopment box, GNOFHAC archives. Studies of other relocations as part of HOPE VI have also found those placed in Section 8 program have been resegregated by race and income. A study of 1,044 families relocated in Chicago through the Section 8 program between 1995 and 1998 as part of HOPE VI found that 90 percent ended up in census tracts that were 90 percent black and almost 70 percent ended up in to census tracts with a per capita income below $10,000 (Rogal, "CHA Residents Moving to Segregated Areas"; John Fountain, "Suit Says Chicago Housing Renewal Plan Perpetuates Segregation," *New York Times*, January 24, 2003; National Housing Law Project, *False Hope*).

61. Thomas Kingsley, Jennifer Johnson, and Kathryn Petit, *HOPE VI and Section 8: Spatial Patterns in Relocation: Report Prepared by the Urban Institute for the U.S. Department of Housing and Urban Development* (Washington, D.C.: Urban Institute, 2000); Fountain, "Suit Says Chicago Housing Renewal Plan Perpetuates Segregation."

62. J. Rosenbaum and S. Deluca, *Is Housing Mobility the Key to Welfare Reform?* (Washington, D.C.: Brookings Institution, 2000), 8.

63. Interview with Moore.

64. By public housing units, the plan means Annual Contributions Contract (ACC) units covered by HANO's contract with HUD. The ACC units would involve a subsidy that allows HANO to subsidize low-income renters. Although subsidized by HUD, the public housing, or ACC, units would actually be owned by the developer under the deal.

65. Letter from Shelia Danzy to Bart Stapert, January 18, 2001, HRI file, St. Thomas Redevelopment box, Hope House archives; Historic Restorations Incorporated, *St. Thomas Revitalization Plan*, 14.

66. Greg Thomas and Robert Scott, "Wal-Mart May Build Supercenter Uptown," *New Orleans Times-Picayune*, July 21, 2001.

67. Greg Thomas, "Metro Area Housing Prices," *New Orleans Times-Picayune*, March 11, 2001.

68. Interview with Kabacoff.

69. Bruce Eggler, "Council Approves Financing for St. Thomas," *New Orleans Times-Picayune*, November 23, 2002; Halperin made similar comments at the October 24, 2001, forum held at Tulane University on the Walmart controversy (author's observation notes).

70. Interview with Strachan.

71. "UC St. Thomas Walmart Analysis," *Urban Conservancy*, Augst 29, 2002, http://www.urbanconservancy.org/issues/walmart.

72. Bruce Eggler, "Wal-Mart Conflict Creates Odd Allies," *New Orleans Times-Picayune*, October 24, 2001; "Walmart: The Hits Just Keep on Coming," *Urban Conservancy*, May 1, 2002; http://www.urbanconservancy.org/issues/walmart.

73. Kevin Cox, "Ideology and the Growth Coalition," in *The Urban Growth Machine*, eds. James Andrews and David Wilson (Albany: SUNY Press, 1999).

74. "Recipients of Fees in Soft Costs," Numbers file, St. Thomas Redevelopment box, Hope House archives.

75. Bruce Eggler, "Cries of Racism Enter Debate over Wal-Mart," *New Orleans Times-Picayune*, November 13, 2002; "Walmart: The Hits Just Keep on Coming."

76. Kabacoff made over $2 million simply from selling—flipping—to Walmart 4.5 acres of St. Thomas's property he had acquired from HANO. Another arm of HRI, Riverview Retail LLC, acquired approximately 5.5 acres of the former development, while the remaining 38 acres were awarded to HRI in a long-term lease deal at a nominal fee of one dollar a year. Commercial Land Deal, Letter from Phyllis Eagan to Councilman James Singleton, February 6, 2002, Numbers file, St. Thomas Redevelopment box, Hope House Archives; Bagert, "Smoke and Mirrors," appendix E4; Letter from Ainars Rodins, HUD, Special Applications Center to George Miller, Administrative Receiver, HANO, August 5, 2002; Negotiated Lease and Title Conveyance, St. Thomas

Development, Disposition of Land Correspondence file, St. Thomas Redevelopment box, Hope House Archives; Greg Thomas, "New Phase to Start in June at Former St. Thomas Site," *New Orleans Times-Picayune*, March 30, 2005.
    77. Reed, *Stirrings in the Jug*, 176.
    78. Eggler, "Wal-Mart Conflict Creates Odd Allies"; Author's observation notes, city council hearing, November 21, 2002.
    79. Michael Burawoy, *The Politics of Production* (London: Verso Books, 1985), 150.
    80. Burawoy, *The Politics of Production*, 126.
    81. Cited in Williams, "St. Thomas Complex to be Razed, Replaced."

6. Whose City Is It?

    1. For footage of the march and clash, see "New Orleans St. Bernard Public Housing—April 2006," YouTube video, 20:23, filmed April 4, 2006, uploaded by FluxRostrum, January 23, 2007, http://www.youtube.com/watch?v=4JYMh13viMU&NR=1.
    2. Walter Kälin, *Guiding Principles on Internal Displacement: Annotations* (Washington D.C.: The American Society of International Law, 2008); United Nations Office for the Coordination of Humanitarian Affairs, "Internal Displacement: Overview," http://www.unocha.org/what-we-do/advocacy/thematic-campaigns/internal-displacement/overview. The principles, which outline the rights and guarantees for internally displaced people (IDPs), are not a treaty but have been endorsed by various UN members, and the United States uses them to measure the responsibilities of other countries. IDPs, as distinct from refugees, are defined as persons who have been forced to flee their homes due to or to avoid war, human rights violations, generalized violence, or man-made or human-made disasters but who have not crossed an internationally recognized state border.
    3. See the report by Professor Fernandez of MIT, an expert in building technology, on the limited work needed to repair the four shuttered developments ("Declaration of John E. Fernandez," October 23, 2006, Yolanda Anderson et al. v. Alphonso Jackson et al., Civil Action No. 06-3298, U.S. District Court, Eastern District of Louisiana).
    4. For Reiss's quote, see Christopher Cooper, "Old-Line Families Plot the Future," *Wall Street Journal*, September 8, 2005. For quotes by other prominent officials, see J. Arena, "A Right to the City? Race, Class, and Neoliberalism in Post-Katrina New Orleans," in *Urban Society: The Shame of Governance*, eds. Levon Chorbajian and Robert Grantham (Cornwall-on-Hudson, N.Y.: Sloan Publishing, 2011), 261–84.
    5. Cedric Johnson, ed., *The Neoliberal Deluge: Hurricane Katrina, Late Capitalism, and the Remaking of New Orleans* (Minneapolis: University of Minnesota Press, 2011).
    6. Martha Carr and Jeffrey Meitrodt, "What Will New Orleans Look Like Five Years from Now?," *New Orleans Times-Picayune*, December 25, 2005.

7. Naomi Klein, *The Shock Doctrine: The Rise of Disaster Capitalism* (New York: Metropolitan Books, 2007), 6.

8. Henwood and Alexander Cockburn also critique the work for obscuring the fact that coercion is not something particular to the neoliberal phase of capitalism but has been a defining feature of capitalism from its origins. Doug Henwood, "Awe, Shocks," *Left Business Observer*, March 2008, 117; Alexander Cockburn, "On Naomi Klein's *The Shock Doctrine*," *Counterpunch*, September 23, 2007.

9. Michel Chossudovsky, "'Manufacturing Dissent': The Anti-globalization Movement Is Funded by Corporate Elites," *Global Research*, September 20, 2010, http://www.globalresearch.ca/index.php?context=va&aid=21110.

10. See "Our Work and Progress," Make It Right, http://www.makeitrightnola. org/index.php/work_progress/track_progress.

11. Campbell Robertson, "Smaller New Orleans after Katrina, Census Shows," *New York Times*, February 3, 2011.

12. Michael Barker, "Corporate Social Responsibility or Constraining Social Revolutions," *Corporate Watch* 43 (April/May 2009).

13. Leon Trotsky, *The History of the Russian Revolution*, trans. Max Eastman (New York: Monad Press, 1980), xx.

14. For further comparison of Nagin with previous black mayors, see Arnold Hirsch, "Fade to Black: Hurricane Katrina and the Disappearance of Creole New Orleans," *Journal of American History* 94 (December 2007): 752–61.

15. Development Strategies, *Canal Street Vision and Development Strategy* (New Orleans: Development Strategies, 2005), 12.

16. Bruce Eggler, "Local Developer Floats Plan to Redo Iberville Complex," *New Orleans Times-Picayune*, November 19, 2004.

17. Ibid.

18. Marc Rosenblum, email message to C3 Listserv, December 8, 2004; Jay Arena, email message to C3 Listserv, March 25, 2004; Jay Arena, email message to C3 Listserv, April 2, 2004.

19. By 2009, Wiggins's salary for managing Guste had risen to over $100,000 a year, a figure that does not include income the tenant leader accrues from other for-profit and nonprofit corporations she heads. For financial information on the Guste Homes Resident Management Corporation, including the annual 990 form filed with the IRS, see www2.guidestar.org. For her full corporate portfolio, consult the web page of the Louisiana secretary of state, www.sos.louisiana.gov.

20. Gordon Russell, "HANO to Start Housing Blitz," *New Orleans Times-Picayune*, February 14, 2005; J. Haddad, "Hands Off Iberville," *Data Weekly*, March 12, 2005; *Residents and Community Invited to Open Forum: Stories from Iberville* (New Orleans: C3, 2005).

21. Wendy King, email message to C3 Listserv, April 7, 2005; Jay Arena, email message to C3 Listserv, March 28, 2005; *Speak Out in Defense of Iberville Development and Community City Council Chambers Monday, April 18 10:30 PM,* (New Orleans: C3, 2005); *A Night Out against Gentrification* (New

Orleans: C3, 2005); Jay Arena to City Councilwomen Jacqueline Clarkson, public records request, June 16, 2005.

22. Lili LeGardeur, "A New Activist Group Meets to Propose a Two-Year Plan to Involve Parents in Public Education," *Gambit,* July 6, 2004.

23. Jay Arena, "Hands Off Iberville! Stop the Racist War at Home and Abroad," March 2005 (pamphlet in possession of author); Jay Arena, email message to C3 Listserv, March 10, 2005. Ironically, INCITE! later published a book critical of nonprofits and foundations after the Ford Foundation revoked a grant for its New Orleans conference because of the organization's taking a position in support of the Palestinian liberation struggle (see INCITE!, *The Revolution Will Not Be Funded*, 1–2).

24. Laura Tuggle, email message to Jay Arena, May 23, 2005.

25. On efforts to get on the city council agenda, see Elizabeth Cook, email message to C3 Listserv, May 19, 2005. On analysis of the city council intervention, see Jay Arena, "C3/Hands Off Iberville Coalition Speaks Out against HOPE VI Scam at City Council Hearing and Prepares for June 30th Hearing at HANO," June 21, 2005 (pamphlet in possession of author).

26. Gwen Filosa, "Iberville Stays, HANO Chief Says," *New Orleans Times-Picayune,* July 28, 2005; Gwen Filosa, "HANO Says It Has No Plans to Demolish the Iberville," *New Orleans Times-Picayune,* July 1, 2005.

27. Cited in Street, *Racial Oppression in the Global Metropolis,* 290.

28. Chossudovsky, "'Manufacturing Dissent.'"

29. Purcell, *Recapturing Democracy,* 174.

30. Roelofs, *Foundations and Public Policy,* 24; Ji Giles Ungpakorn, "NGOS: Enemies or Allies?," *International Socialism* 104 (October 2004).

31. Author's interview with Gloria Irving, February 14, 2006, New Orleans.

32. For comments made by Nagin and Compass on the September 6, 2005, *Oprah Winfrey Show* and other venues, see Scott Benjamin, "Some N.O. Chaos Fact or Fiction?," CBS News website, last modified February 11, 2009, www.cbsnews.com/stories/2005/09/28/katrina/main887375.shtml. For a critique of unsubstantiated claims by the media of New Orleans in the storm's immediate aftermath, see Aaron Kinney, "Hurricane Horror Stories: Why Did False Tales of Rape, Shootings, and Murder Flood out of New Orleans in the Wake of Katrina," *Salon.com,* October 24, 2005, http://www.salon.com/2005/10/24/katrina_horror/singleton; Gary Young, "Murder and Rape—Fact or Fiction?," *Guardian,* September 6, 2005. For a critique of photos portraying black survivors as looting and whites as finding necessities, see Aaron Kinney, "'Looting' or 'Finding'?," *Salon.com,* September 1, 2005, http://www.salon.com/2005/09/02/photo_controversy/singleton.

33. "Military Due to Move Into New Orleans," *CNN.com,* September 2, 2005, http://www.cnn.com/2005/WEATHER/09/02/katrina.impact. For further evidence that authorities viewed post-Katrina New Orleans through a military rather than a humanitarian prism, see the comments of Brig. General Gary Jones, head of the Louisiana National Guard operation. As he prepared

to lead hundreds of troops into the city he declared, "This place is going to look like Little Somalia. . . . We're going to go out and take this city back. This will be a combat operation to get this city under control." Joseph Chenelly, "Troops Begin Combat Operations in New Orleans to Fight 'Insurgents,'" *Army Times*, September 4, 2005.

34. There were atrocities taking place beyond people's drowning or being left to die in their homes because of an inadequate rescue operation. These crimes came at the hands of white vigilantes who hunted down and killed black survivors and the New Orleans and other police forces from around the country who descended upon the city and saw their job as securing the city from the lawlessness (i.e., black survivors) that had taken over rather than as a humanitarian rescue operation. On police and vigilante killings, see A. C. Thompson, "Katrina's Hidden Race War," *Nation*, January 5, 2009. On the prosecution of one incident of police killing civilians in the aftermath of Katrina and the subsequent cover-ups, see Laura Maggi and Brendan McCarthy, "Danzinger Bridge Shooting Cover-Up Had a Precedent," *New Orleans Times-Picayune*, March 3, 2011. For coverage of mainly black Katrina survivors being stopped at gunpoint by Jefferson Parish sheriffs while trying to evacuate across the Greater New Orleans Bridge, see Larry Bradshaw and Lorrie Slonsky, "Trapped in New Orleans: First by the Floods, then by Martial Law," *Socialist Worker*, September 6, 2005. On priority given to evacuate white survivors in St. Bernard parish, while blacks languished at the convention center and Superdome, see Lance Hill, email message to undisclosed recipients, June 28, 2008.

35. On the infamous green spacing plan, including a map of the targeted neighborhoods, see Frank Donze and Gordon Russell, " '4 Months to Decide,'" *New Orleans Times-Picayune*, January 11, 2006. For the most comprehensive analysis of the BNOB's formation and the central role played by Canizaro and other business leaders, see Katherine Cecil, "Race, Representation, and Recovery: Documenting the 2006 New Orleans Mayoral Election" (master's thesis, University of New Orleans, 2009).

36. These were the descriptions used by HANO's intergovernment liaison Darren Martin at an October 2005 city council meeting and those of *Times-Picayune* reporter Gwen Filosa in "Faltering Safety Net," October 9, 2005.

37. "New Orleans Resident Discusses Race and Looting at Circle K," *Democracy Now*, September 12, 2005. Author's interview with Mike Howells, May 10, 2008, New Orleans.

38. Gwen Filosa, "Home Depot Gets Turf in Public Housing," *New Orleans Times-Picayune*, January 19, 2006; Kari Lyderson, "New Orleans Public Housing Residents Set to Fight Off Developers," *New Standard*, February 27, 2006, accessed June 10, 2011, http://newstandardnews.net/content/index.cfm/items/2868 (site discontinued). For an article and a video of the march, see M. Black, "Basin Street Blues: Iberville Human Rights March," *Indymedia*, December 5, 2005, www.nyc.indymedia.org/en/2005/12/61297.html.

39. Author's interview with James Perry, July 10, 2009, New Orleans.

40. The most memorable denunciation came from Harvey Bender, a black resident of New Orleans East and a recently laid-off city worker, who shouted into the microphone at a January 11, 2006, hearing on the plan, "Joe Canizaro, I don't know you, but I hate you. I'm going to suit up like I'm going to Iraq and fight this." Gary Rivlin, "Anger Meets New Orleans Renewal Plan" *New York Times*, January 12, 2006. For more on the BNOB's plan and popular opposition, see Arena, "A Right to the City?"

41. Sites, *Remaking New York*, 102, 101–36.

42. The plan, laid out in a report by Eric Lerner and Mike Howells, calls for a mass public works program modeled on the Civil Works Administration to rebuild infrastructure and public services at union wages. This vision differs radically from the Gulf Coast Civic Work Project floated by San Jose State sociologist Scott Myers-Lipton, which calls for a relatively small budget ($3.5 billion), provides for "living" rather than union wages, and allows for the use of private contractors. The differences in political strategies are starker, with Lipton-Myers employing a lobbying campaign to garner the backing of mainstream politicians and nonprofit organizations—many of whom, such as the think tank Policy Link, support demolishing and privatizing public housing. In contrast, Howells and Lerner envision a mass movement, independent of the mainstream capitalist parties, as the only force that could defend currently besieged public services and win a new mass public works program. Mike Howells and Eric Lerner, *Public Works to Rebuild New Orleans* (New Orleans: Workers Democracy Network, 2006); Scott Myers-Lipton, *Rebuild America: Solving the Economic Crisis through Civic Works* (Boulder, Colo.: Paradigm publishers, 2009).

43. Mayaba Liebenthal, email message to NO-HEAT Listserv, March 17, 2006.

44. Adolph Reed Jr., *Class Notes* (New York: New Press, 2000), xxii.

45. Sharon Smith, "The Politics of Identity," *International Socialist Review* 57 (January/February 2008). Film historian Joseph McBride critiques identity politics's epistemological assumptions this way: "When I was a screenwriter in Hollywood and writing a lot of parts for women, some people would ask the same thing: 'Who are you to write about women?' I would say, 'Didn't Tolstoy write a book entitled *Anna Karenina*?'" Cited in David Walsh, "A Discussion with Film Historian Joseph McBride on Steven Spielberg: A Biography—Part 1," *World Socialist Web Site*, May 4, 2011, http://wsws.org/articles/2011/may2011/ssp1-m04.shtml.

46. Reed, *Class Notes*, xxvi

47. The city's official parade route since the establishment of the Martin Luther King Jr. holiday in the mid-1980s had begun in the Lower Ninth Ward. The abandonment of this route by the mayor was interpreted by C3 and other activists as signaling support for the BNOB's green spacing plans for the area and prompted the group to organize a march from the traditional starting point. For more on the politics of the march, see Jay Arena, "The Contradictions of Black Comprador Rule: Understanding New Orleans Mayor Ray

Nagin's 'Chocolate City' Comment," *ZNET*, January 26, 2006, http://www. zmag.org/content/showarticle.cfm?ItemID=9597.

48. For their work in Chicago, see Wright, "Community Resistance to CHA Transformation," 125–67.

49. Graham Burke, "Residents Rally to Re-open St. Bernard Housing Development," *Indymedia*, February 14, 2006, neworleans.indymedia.org/ news/2006/02/7033.php. An April 2007 phone survey of former residents of metropolitan New Orleans displaced by Katrina to other states found that 75 percent of African Americans wanted to return to Louisiana (Louisiana Family Recovery Group, *Recovery Brief, No. 1*, August 7, 2007). For more on the deep desire of residents to return, see the interview with C. J. Peete resident Rosemary Johnson, "Everybody Not Able to Live Like Some People," YouTube video, 9:03, uploaded by WHYNotNews, December 20, 2007, http://www.youtube.com/ watch?v=Nk116RcL92I&feature=related.

50. James Varney, "HANO Only Wants Working Tenants," *New Orleans Times-Picayune*, February 21, 2006. For video coverage of Thomas's statements, support from Cynthia Wiggins, and dissent from Mike Howells, see Martin Savidge, "What's Next for Public Housing in New Orleans," *NBC Nightly News* video, 1:58, February 21, 2006, http://www.msnbc.msn.com/ id/11485681.

51. Gwen Filosa, "Tenants Vow to Retake Housing Complex," *New Orleans Times-Picayune*, June 1, 2006; Susan Saulny, "Residents Clamoring to Come Home," *New York Times*, June 6, 2006. Armand Alfred, a seventy-six-year-old St. Bernard resident, gave these moving words to explain his deep desire to return home: "I want to come home. Simply that. I belong in there. I still have some valuables there. And that's where my bed is. The last bed I owned is in that apartment." Janet McConnaughey, "Demonstrators Demand Return for Housing Project Residents," *Houma Courrier*, June 3, 2006.

52. Lance Hill, email message to undisclosed recipients, June 1, 2006.

53. Interview with Howells. HUD, "HUD Outlines Aggressive Plan to Bring Families Back to New Orleans' Public Housing," June 14, 2006, press statement, no. 06-066, http://archives.hud.gov/news/2006/pro6-066.cfm; Gwen Filosa, "Four N.O. Housing Developments will be demolished," *New Orleans Times-Picayune*, June 15, 2006; Susan Saulny, "5,000 Public Housing Units in New Orleans Are to Be Razed," *New York Times*, June 15, 2006.

54. Katy Reckdahl, "Critics Question Whether New New Orleans Public Housing Will Meet Needs," *New Orleans Times-Picayune*, December 8, 2008. Two other developments, Desire and Florida, were in the process of being redeveloped as mixed-income communities when they were devastated by Katrina. HUD rebuilt Desire, but as of January 2012, nothing had been done to rebuild Florida. The Fischer and Guste low-rises were undergoing redevelopment at the time of the storm. Construction continued, although the residents that were living in the undemolished section of the Fischer development were not officially allowed to return to their apartments after Katrina, even though they were not flooded.

55. See "New Orleans: See How a New Housing Development Is Helping Rebuild a Community," Goldman Sachs, accessed December 21, 2011, http://www2.goldmansachs.com/our-firm/progress/harmonyoaks/index.html?cid=PS_01_02_07_99_01_01.

56. Nicolai Ouroussoff, "High Noon in New Orleans: The Bulldozers Are Ready," *New York Times*, December 19, 2007. Further adding to the tragedy was that it would have been much less costly to rehabilitate rather than demolish the units. Further support for the cost effectiveness of preserving public housing over private sector schemes is found in a recent study that concludes "adequate funding to preserve public housing would cost $6,250 per unit per year, while the annual cost of a replacement voucher, including transition costs, comes to $7,080 per unit per year." *We Call These Projects Home* (New York: Right to the City Alliance, 2010), 13.

57. For more on Enterprise, see Schwartz, *Housing Policy in the United States*, 202.

58. Boyd, *Jim Crow Nostalgia*, xiv.

59. On conflict with the NLIHC and their role in privatization, see Jay Arena, "New Orleans, Public Housing, and the Non-profit Industrial Complex: A Social Movement and Public Works Alternative," *Counterpunch*, July 10, 2007, http://www.counterpunch.org/arena07102007.html; Jay Arena, email message to National Housing Advocates, December 14, 2006.

60. Jackson placed his close aide, Scott Keller, on the panel that decided who would be awarded the contract to redevelop St. Bernard. In addition to Columbia Parc, the nonprofit Bayou District Foundation, comprising powerful local business officials connected to real estate and nationally affiliated with Better Built Communities, was a partner in the effort (Edward Pound, "HUD Probe Heats Up," *National Journal*, December 14, 2007). On the AFL-CIO's plan, see Housing Investment Trust, *Proposal for the St. Bernard Redevelopment Site* (Washington, D.C.: AFL-CIO, 2007).

61. For a critique of ACORN's post-Katrina role and documentation of extensive funding from HUD and the Rockefeller Fellows program, see Mike Howells, "ACORN, Public Housing and Post-Katrina New Orleans," *Indymedia*, October 6, 2008, http://neworleans.indymedia.org/news/2008/10/13166.php. See Tom Angotti, *New York For Sale* (London: MIT Press, 2008), 218–22, for a critique of ACORN's partnership with developers in the Atlantic Yards project in Brooklyn that was vehemently opposed by many community organizations. For more on the Rockefeller Fellows program, see Arena, *New Orleans*.

62. Some of these organizations, such as the PHRF and POC, did not have their own 501(c)(3) designation but were sponsored by other nonprofits, with the Vanguard Foundation for the former and the Interreligious Foundation for Community Organization (IFCO) for the latter. The New Orleans Worker Center for Racial Justice, with which the Ford Foundation has been especially generous, uses the National Immigration Law Center as their fiscal agent. One obstacle to determining the funding of nonprofits is that the 990 annual reports these organizations file with the IRS do not require identification of

the sources and amounts of funding received. For documentation on funding, see the websites of the Ford Foundation, the Rockefeller's Philanthropy Gulf Fund, the Louisiana Disaster Recovery Foundation, and the Greater New Orleans Foundation.

63. On Habitat for Humanity's acquiring scattered site public housing properties from HANO and comments by Jim Pate, director of the local operation, in support of the plan, see Leslie Williams, "Scattered HANO Units in Disrepair," *New Orleans Times-Picayune*, August 12, 2007. The St. Bernard Project received wide media coverage, thousands of volunteers, and financial support from celebrities like Oprah Winfrey, as well as criticism for refusing to publically condemn the racially discriminatory housing policies pursued by the parish government after Katrina (Flaherty, *Floodlines*, 130).

64. Kristin Buras, "'We're Not Going Anywhere': Race, Urban Space and the Struggle for King Elementary School in New Orleans" (unpublished manuscript, 2011).

65. A study by the Corporation for National and Community service found that 1.1 million people had volunteered to help rebuild the gulf in the first two years after Katrina ("More Than 1.1 Million Volunteers Have Responded to Katrina," *Louisiana Weekly*, September 2, 2007). Another example of a radical activist abetting the neoliberal agenda was the work of former New York City teacher Nat Turner, who set up an alternative school rather than oppose the dismantling of the public system.

66. For more on the Community Revitalization Fund, see Valentine Pierce, "Foundations Unite to Revitalize Housing in New Orleans," *Louisiana Weekly*, October 22, 2007. A similar initiative to replace public housing with public–private partnerships is the Louisiana Loan Fund, created by Congress to build affordable housing for buyers and renters that make below 80 percent of the area median income in areas affected by hurricanes Rita and Katrina. The fund is managed by the Enterprise foundation and the Local Initiatives Support Group, originally set up by the Ford Foundation, with funding from a host of banks, foundations, and the state and the federal governments. See David Hammer, "Public, Private Money Brought under One Roof," *New Orleans Times-Picayune*, April 26, 2007, and the fund's website at www.louisianaloanfund.org. Another capture foundation is the Louisiana Disaster Recovery Foundation. For an in-depth analysis of the foundations involved in post-Katrina New Orleans, see Darwin Bon-Graham, "Building the New New Orleans: Foundations and NGO Power," *Review of Black Political Economy*, January 2011, 1–18.

67. Roelofs, *Foundations and Public Policy*, 11; New Orleans–based Activists, "Letter from the People of New Orleans to Our Friends and Allies," *Left Turn*, April 1, 2007, http://www.leftturn.org/letter-people-new-orleans-our-friends-and-allies#. For more on the pleas made by nonprofits to get foundations to direct more funds to the gulf, see Jordan Flaherty, "A Catastrophic Failure: Foundations, Nonprofits and the Second Looting of New Orleans," *Counterpunch*, December 16, 2006, http://www.counterpunch.org/2006/12/16/a-catastrophic-failure. The letter was drafted by Jordan Flaherty, who emerged

post-Katrina as a leading intellectual and chronicler of the radical NGO sector, particularly in New Orleans.

68. Roelofs, *Foundations and Public Policy*, 142.

69. "Mixed-Income Housing Demonstrations Continue," *Louisiana Weekly*, June 26, 2006.

70. Alexander, *The New Jim Crow*, 213.

71. On struggle with lawyers, see Letter from Public Housing Residents and Activists to Judith Browne-Dianes, July 9, 2007 (in possession of author); Email from Tracie Washington to C3 Listserv, July 9, 2007.

72. On the Yes Men action, see Darwin Bond Graham, "Yes Men's Prank Far from 'Cruel' Hoax," *Indymedia*, August 31, 2006, http://neworleans.indymedia.org/news/2006/08/8635.php. On the occupation at Lafitte, see Darwin Bond Graham, "9 Arrested in Action to Reopen New Orleans Public Housing," *Indymedia*, August 28, 2006, http://neworleans.indymedia.org/news/2006/08/8585.php. There was also an attempt in September by C. J. Peete residents to reoccupy their apartments that was thwarted by tenant leader Cynthia Wiggins. On Wiggins's embrace of privatization, see her criticism at the August 2006 HANO board meeting, which was based on the agency's not moving fast enough on redevelopment and the official tenant leadership's needing, as at St. Thomas, to be more closely involved in the redevelopment deals (Minutes of HANO monthly meeting, August 16, 2006, in possession of the author).

73. Sites, *Remaking New York*, 145.

74. See Geoffrey Pax, "Report from HANO meeting," *Indymedia*, November 29, 2006, http://neworleans.indymedia.org/news/2006/11/9195.php.

75. Author's observation notes, December 16, 2006.

76. For coverage, see "Cleaning Out the St. Bernard Housing Complex," *Indymedia* video, downloadable wmv file, uploaded by Logan, January 21, 2007, http://neworleans.indymedia.org/news/2007/01/9521.php; Roy Blumenfeld, "St. Bernard Housing Project Occupation," *Indymedia*, January 15, 2007, http://neworleans.indymedia.org/news/2007/01/9451.php. For coverage of the lawsuit HUD initiated against residents and activists involved in the action, see Darwin Bond Graham, "Has HUD No Heart?," *Indymedia*, January 23, 2007, http://neworleans.indymedia.org/news/2007/01/9534.php.

77. On the day of the protest, Rodrigue did announce in a press release that there would be an occupation but did not disclose what apartment would be taken (Survivors Village, "Solidarity Actions across the City," *Indymedia*, January 15, 2007, http://neworleans.indymedia.org/news/2007/01/9449.php).

78. On the lawsuit, see Bill Quigley, email message to NO-HEAT Listserv, January 22, 2007. For coverage of the raid, see Common Ground Media, "SWAT Team Arrests MayDay Nola Occupiers and Public Housing Resident Council Representative," *Indymedia*, February 3, 2007, http://neworleans.indymedia.org/news/2007/02/9639.php. A report on the occupation did come out on *Indymedia* on January 24, but nothing was done to mobilize support. Another opportune time for a solidarity action would have been during a visit

by Maxine Waters and HANO administrators on January 28 while the occupation was going on. See Infoshop News, "Maxine Waters Visits NOLA Housing Occupation," *Indymedia*, January 29, 2007, http://neworleans.indymedia.org/news/2007/01/9570.php.

79. On agreement that the movement opposed any demolitions, see Darwin Bond Graham, email message to Jay Arena, May 30, 2007.

80. Waters herself openly criticized Landrieu for not pushing the legislation. At a June 2007 conference in Chicago of Jesse Jackson's Rainbow PUSH outfit, she asked rhetorically, "Where is the senator from Louisiana? Why is it that there's a bill that would solve the problems of Louisiana and we don't hear your voice?" Michelle Krupa, "Congressional Leader Faults La. Officials on Recovery; Landrieu Accused of Faltering on Housing," *New Orleans Times-Picayune*, June 4, 2007. Other forms of pressure included speaking at city council hearings. For efforts to get on the agenda of the city council's Housing and Human Needs Committee, see Elizabeth Cook, email message to Councilwoman Stacy Head, May 31, 2007.

81. For criticism by Truehill and Wiggins of C3's protesting of Mary Landrieu, see Marshall Truehill, email message to Elizabeth Cook, June 2, 2007.

82. Harvey, *A Brief History of Neoliberalism*, 177.

83. Ibid., 176.

84. Tine Wallace, "NGO Dilemmas: Trojan Horses of Global Neoliberalism?," *Socialist Register* 40 (2003): 202–19.

85. Mike Howells, email message to C3 Listserv, April 15, 2006; United Front for Affordable Housing, press release, June 14, 2006, in possession of author.

7. Managing Contradictions

1. Harvey, *A Brief History of Neoliberalism*, 161, 159–65, 203; Karl Marx, *Capital: A Critique of Political Economy*, vol. 1 (1867; repr., New York: International Publishers, 1974), 713–74.

2. Judith Stepan-Norris and Maurice Zeitlin, "'Who Gets the Bird' or, How the Communists Won Power and Trust in America's Unions: The Relative Autonomy of Intraclass Political Struggles," *American Sociological Review* 54 (August 1989): 504.

3. Ibid., 504.

4. Author's observation notes, November 13, 2007; Michael Steinberg, "Rally to Save Public Housing," *Indymedia*, November 14, 2007, http://neworleans.indymedia.org/news/2007/11/11404.php; Evan Casper-Futterman, "'What Do We Want? Housing!' Movement Unites in New Orleans to Re-open Public Housing," *Indymedia*, November 14, 2007, http://neworleans.indymedia.org/news/2007/11/11406.php.

5. Then–ACORN head Wade Rathke justified his outfit's absence—issued on his blog while traveling in Lisbon two days after public housing

activists were attacked in the city council chambers on December 20—by repeating HUD's defense that "it was difficult to make a compelling case that there were public housing tenants being denied the right to return to New Orleans." Furthermore, he claimed that ACORN "had not been solicited" to participate, even though Mike Howells had personally invited the group. See Wade Rathke, "New Orleans Public Housing Uproar," Chief Organizer blog, December 22, 2007, http://chieforganizer.org/2007/12/22/new-orleans-public-housing-uproar. No mention was made in Rathke's statement of the group's financial support from HUD. For a further critique of ACORN's role, see Howells, "ACORN, Public Housing and Post-Katrina New Orleans."

6. Author's observation notes, Novemeber 24, 2007.

7. Author's observation notes, Novemeber 24, 2007; "Four N.O. Housing Complexes Expected to Be Razed Dec. 15," *New Orleans City Business,* November 30, 2007.

8. Akuno's previous NGO employer was the advocacy training group SOUL (School of Unity and Liberation). For background on their foundation's funders, see "SOUL Supporters," School of Unity and Liberation, http://www.schoolofunityandliberation.org/soul_sec/about/ab-supporters.html. Jones's career trajectory reads like a textbook case of Joan Roelofs's observation that one key way NGOs and foundations exercise control over social movements and dissent is by providing "jobs and benefits for radicals willing to become pragmatic" (*Foundations and Public Policy,* 24). After leaving the San Francisco–based, Maoist STORM organization, Jones went on to found, in 1995, a police watch program, out of which emerged the nonprofit Ella Baker Center for Human Rights in 1996. Beginning in 1997 with a Rockefeller Foundation Next Generation Leadership fellowship, he was showered with more fellowships and awards. "Van Jones," *Wikipedia,* last modified December 21, 2011, http://en.wikipedia.org/wiki/Van_Jones. For more on how the Oakland-based Urban Peace Movement (led by Nicole Lee, formerly with the Ella Baker Center) worked with the Ella Baker Center, other Bay Area nonprofits, *and* Mayor Ron Dellums to contain protests in the aftermath of the 2009 police killing of Oscar Grant, see Raider Nation Collective, "Lessons Never Learned: Nonprofits and the State, Redux," *Bring the Ruckus,* July 2, 2010, www.bringtheruckus.org/?q=node/112.

9. Cited in Harvey, *A Brief History of Neoliberalism,* 180.

10. Author's observation notes, November 26, 2007. On Willard-Lewis's supporting a ban on multifamily apartment complexes, see Bruce Eggler, "Multi-family Housing Ban Ends," *New Orleans Times-Picayune,* August 2, 2005. At the same time, Willard-Lewis was effective at appearing to be progressive. At the raucous November 2006 hearing held by HANO on their redevelopment plans for the Big Four developments that residents roundly condemned, the city councilwoman screamed, "I am with you in this fight!" She argued the plan was part of the "smaller foot print" agenda devised by the city's wealthy to drive out "true New Orleans." Samhita Mukhopadhyay, "Let the People of New Orleans Know You Haven't Forgotten about Them,"

Colorlines, December 14, 2007, http://colorlines.com/archives/2007/12/let_
the_people_of_new_orleans.html.

11. In fact, in early November PHRF and Survivors Village, even before the coalition was formed, had issued the *Pledge of Resistance,* which urged people to use all "civil and humanitarian means available, including civil disobedience," to resist demolition in New Orleans or "other strategic locales throughout the US." PHRF and Survivors Village, *Pledge of Resistance in Defense of the Right to Housing in New Orleans and the Gulf Coast* (New Orleans: PHRF and Survivors Village, 2007). For the later call, see PHRF, email message to Elizabeth Cook, November 27, 2007.

12. See Kali Akuno, email message to housing activists, December 3, 2007.

13. Edwin Lopez, "Public Housing Supporters Speak Out against Demolition," *Indymedia,* December 7, 2007, http://neworleans.indymedia.org/news/2007/12/11529.php. For video of Quigley's arrest, see "Lawyer Arrested during Housing Protest," YouTube video, 3:03, filmed December 6, 2007, uploaded by wdsutv, December 6, 2007, http://www.youtube.com/watch?v=SZQnSEat50I. At this point, even Akuno had given up on persuading the council. See Kali Akuno, email message (NO Demolition Update) to housing activists, December 6, 2007.

14. On efforts by the city council to ensure the vote was nonbinding, see, Tracie Washington, email message to Councilwoman Midura and housing activists, December 10, 2007.

15. Gwen Filosa, "Panel Balks at Tearing Down Lafitte," *New Orleans Times-Picayune,* December 11, 2007. For a video of the hearing, see Edwin Lopez, "Video Montage of December 10, 2007 Meeting in City Hall," *Indymedia,* QuickTime video, uploaded December 11, 2007, http://neworleans.indymedia.org/news/2007/12/11569.php. For more reporting and photos, see Diane Greene Lent, "Stop the Demolitions," *Indymedia,* December 14, 2007, http://neworleans.indymedia.org/news/2007/12/11603.php.

16. For Juakli's opposition to protests and support for redevelopment, see his flier *Community Organization for Public, Subsidized and Renters Housing Rights* (in possession of the author); Richard Webster, "Resident Challenge HUD on Housing Demolitions," *City Business,* December 17, 2007.

17. See "Caucuses and Auxiliaries," under "National SDS Structure," Students for a Democratic Society, accessed December 21, 2011, www.newsds.org/national-sds-structure.

18. Author's interview with Sakura Koné, April 22, 2011, New Orleans.

19. Edwin Lopez, "Demolition of B.W. Cooper Sets Off Protest," *Indymedia,* December 13, 2007, http://neworleans.indymedia.org/news/2007/12/11577.php.

20. See Safe Streets, "March on Hud," *Homecomingnews,* email newsletter to author, December 12, 2007.

21. Carl Dix, email message to Black Left Unity Listserv, December 15, 2007. The email was posted on the Black Left Unity Listserv and was in response to Kali Akuno's justification for not supporting efforts to stop the bulldozers.

22. Saladin Muhammad, email message to Black Left Unity Listserv,

December 14, 2007; Kali Akuno, email message to Black Left Unity Listserv, December 14, 2007.

23. Suber's political tendency—the official name of his party varied over the years—looked to Albania, under the leadership of Enver Hoxha, as the true heirs of the 1917 Bolshevik revolution. His tendency identified the Comintern's third period, from the late 1920s until the enunciation of the popular front in 1935, particularly the championing of a Black Republic in the U.S. South, as the international Communist movement's high point. The demand for a black republic in the South was consistently raised by his party and mass organization, the Liberation League, as the key solution to ending police repression and other forms of oppression faced by the "Afro-American Nation." For more on the New Communist Movement, see Max Elbaum, *Revolution in the Air* (New York: Verso, 2002).

24. Patricia Hill Collins, *Black Feminist Thought,* 2nd ed. (New York: Routledge, 2009), 5.

25. Juan Gonzalez, "Shocking Act of Class and Racial Cleansing," *New York Daily News,* December 12, 2007; Leslie Eaton, "In New Orleans, Plan to Raze Low-Income Housing Draws Protest," *New York Times,* December 14, 2007. See the December 14, 2007, letter from House Speaker Pelosi and Senate Majority Leader Henry Reid to President Bush requesting a sixty-day moratorium on demolition (in possession of the author). Efforts by Brenda Stokely, a New York community activist, to get Jesse Jackson and Al Sharpton to join the protests proved futile. If the coalition had placed all its resources into carrying out the occupation, Jackson and Sharpton would have been under much greater pressure, in order to maintain their image, to take a public stand (Brenda Stokely, email message to Jay Arena and Sam Jackson, December 6, 2007).

26. See Kali Akuno, email message to Black Left Unity Listserv, December 14, 2007; Jay Arena, "No Demolition Means No Demolition," *Indymedia,* December 15, 2007, http://neworleans.indymedia.org/news/2007/12/11624_comment.php

27. On Safe Streets' defection, see Akuno, email message to Black Left Unity Listserv, December 14, 2007. A further contradictory feature of the RTC is that one of the leading advisors to the foundation-funded outfit is Marxist geographer David Harvey. At the same time, Harvey has detailed and critiqued in his writings the role played by foundations and NGOs in imposing or, at least, undermining resistance to neoliberalism. Safe Streets also was, in addition to being within the orbit of the foundations, closely connected to city council members Midura and Carter, with two former staffers having gone to work for them (Ariane Wiltz, "Citizen Voices," *Gambit,* February 5, 2008).

28. Interview with Koné.

29. Charges included use of a "false explosive device," "criminal; trespass," "terrorizing," and "resisting an officer." See NOPD Report L-23878-07, in possession of author. The reporting officer was Dwayne Scheuermann.

30. Nonetheless, an email bulletin put out by Akuno, in the name of the

coalition, on December 17 indicated that he, Suber, Washington, and other NGO leaders still believed their behind-the-scenes lobbying could lead two black councilpersons—Willard-Lewis and Carter—and possibly two others to vote no on demolition. Susan Finch and Frank Donze, "Judge Puts Demolition in Hands of the Council," *New Orleans Times-Picayune*, December 15, 2007.

31. For more on Scheuermann's role in killings and beatings before and after Katrina, see A. C. Thompson, "Did New Orleans SWAT Cops Shoot an Unarmed Man?," *Propublica*, December 15, 2009, http://www.propublica.org/nola/story/did-new-orleans-swat-cops-shoot-an-unarmed-man-1215. For more on the police department's preparation for December 20, see Chuck Hustmyre, "NOPD SWAT," *Myneworleans.com*, March 2008, accessed June 17, 2011, http://www.myneworleans.com/new-orleansmagazine/march-2008/nopd-swat (site discontinued); Brendan McCarthy, "Both Police, Protesters Came Prepared," *New Orleans Times-Picayune*, December 21, 2007.

32. McCarthy, "Both Police, Protesters Came Prepared."

33. Ibid. A video clip includes coverage of the conflict outside the chambers, including the arrest of Mike Howells, in the green shirt. The unidentified woman on the bullhorn was a resident of the homeless encampment ("New Orleans City Hall Protest—December 20, 2007—Video 1," YouTube video, 1:56, filmed December 20, 2007, uploaded by ehernandeziii, December 20, 2007, www.youtube.com/watch?v=5jvhp4iZFdo& feature=related). For video coverage of the conflict inside and outside the chambers, see "New Orleans City Council Shuts Down Public Housing Debate," YouTube video, 6:19, filmed December 20, 2007, uploaded by bignoisetactical, December 21, 2007, www.youtube.com/watch?v=cMBWAXfGsc4.

34. Author's observation notes, Decemeber 21, 2007.

35. Author's observation notes, Decemeber 23, 2007.

36. For protest against Vitter, see *Stop the Bulldozers of Ethnic Cleansing: Protest Sen. David Vitter on January 25th* (New Orleans: C3/Hands off Iberville, 2007). Even Malcolm Suber—who as recently as December had opposed C3's call for the coalition to confront Vitter, arguing we had no leverage over him—now argued protests were effective in putting pressure on Vitter. See Malcolm Suber, email message to housing activists, January 29, 2008.

37. In addition to Klein, *The Shock Doctrine*, see Jamie Peck, "Neoliberal Hurricane: Who Framed New Orleans?," *Socialist Register 44* (2007): 102–29, for an approach that also fails to address the consensual mechanisms used to introduce neoliberalism from below in post-Katrina New Orleans.

38. United Nations, press release, February 28, 2008, www.unhchr.ch/huricane/huricane.nsf/view01/907604B6DAF5E2F1C12573FD007AD7DC? opendocument.

39. *Concluding Observations of the Committee on the Elimination of All Forms of Racial Discrimination: United States of America* (Geneva: International Convention on the Elimination of All Forms of Discrimination, March 2008), 10.

40. The hearings before the HRC were in regard to U.S. adherence to the International Covenant on Civil and Political Rights, a treaty the United States signed in 1992 ("Victims of U.S. Human Rights Violations Tell Their Stories at UN Meeting in Geneva," ACLU, July 14, 2006, http://www.aclu.org/human-rights/victims-us-human-rights-violations-tell-their-stories-un-meeting-geneva). For testimony of Rev. Lois Dejean before the UN Human Rights Coalition, see "Witness: Reverend Lois Dejean," YouTube video, 6:39, posted to ACLU website, http://www.aclu.org/human-rights-racial-justice/witness-reverend-lois-dejean. Harden and Walker (AEHR) and Akuno (PHRF) also collectively authored a report that was submitted to CERD documenting how U.S. treatment of Katrina survivors violated rights guaranteed in the ICERD. See Monique Harden, Nathalie Walker, and Kali Akuno, *Racial Discrimination and Ethnic Cleansing in the United States in the Aftermath of Hurricane Katrina: A Report to the United Nations' Committee for the Elimination of All Forms of Racial Discrimination* (New Orleans: Advocates for Environmental Human Rights, 2007). The AEHR also coordinated—with the National Law Center on Homelessness and Poverty, the Centre on Housing Rights and Evictions, and national and international NGO advocacy groups—New Orleans's participation in a five-city videoconference on November 5, 2007, that "connected housing and human rights advocates, activists, lawyers, and service providers in each city via videoconference to discuss housing rights violations and the strategies employed by participants to advocate on behalf of homeless and poor Americans." Eric Tars, *National Forum on the Human Right to Housing: Follow up Report* (Washington, D.C.: National Law Center on Homelessness and Poverty, 2007).

41. On the tribunal, see "Rebuilding Gives Way to Reflection on Hurricane Katrina's Anniversary," *New Orleans Times-Picayune*, August 30, 2007; Matt Olson, "International Tribunal: Opening Ceremonies," *Indymedia*, August 29, 2007, http://neworleans.indymedia.org/news/2007/08/10912.php.

42. For an outline of the provisos, see Letter from Ray Nagin to New Orleans City Council, December 20, 2007, in possession of the author.

43. Final approval for Lafitte would be given later the same month. Although HUD promised immediate redevelopment, financing problems related to selling low-income tax credits resulted in developers' not even completing the limited number of apartments promised at Lafitte and Cooper as of 2011. Letter from Ray Nagin to New Orleans City Council, in possession of author. For approving demolition at St. Bernard, see Letter from Ray Nagin, Arnold Fielkow, Cynthia Hedge Morrell to HUD secretary Jackson, February 1, 2008, in possession of author. For the coalition's statement, see Coalition to Stop the Demolitions, "Coalition Condemns Demolition Order for the St. Bernard Projects and the Criminalization of the Homeless," email press release from Kali Akuno, February 2, 2008.

44. For a photo gallery of the event, see "St. Bernard Housing Development Protest," *Nola.com*, http://www.nola.com/katrinaphotos/tp/gallery.ssf?cgi-bin/

view_gallery.cgi/nola/view_gallery.ata?g_id=9871. Juakali did issue a call on March 10 to hold a meeting to plan how we would put "our bodies in front of these bulldozers," warning that if not, "we will forever wonder why we didn't at least try!!!" No action ever materialized. See Endesha Juakali, email message to housing activists, March 10, 2008.

45. Burawoy, "The Extended Case Method," 14.

46. Roelofs, *Foundations and Public Policy*, 2.

47. Kali Akuno, email message to Black Left Unity Listserv, December 14, 2007.

Conclusion

1. Bayard Rustin, "From Protest to Politics: The Future of the Civil Rights Movement," *Commentary*, February 1965. For a critique of how Black Nationalists eventually arrived, a few years later, at the same conclusions as Rustin, their erstwhile ideological nemesis, see Johnson, *From Revolutionaries to Race Leaders*.

2. Ibid.

3. Personal observation, December 1985.

4. Michael Parenti, *Democracy for the Few*, 8th ed. (Boston, Mass.: Thomson-Wadsworth, 2008), 3.

5. Steinberg, "Bayard Rustin and the Rise and Decline of the Black Protest Movement."

6. Daisey Fernandez, "The Future of the Ninth Ward," *Colorlines*, Spring 2006.

7. Campbell Robertson, "Smaller New Orleans after Katrina, Census Shows," *New York Times*, February 3, 2011; David Usborne, "Census Reveals Devastating Effect on New Orleans," *Independent*, February 5, 2011. On increasing residential racial segregation post-Katrina, see Michele Krupa, "Racial Divides among New Orleans Neighborhoods Expands," *New Orleans Times-Picayune*, June 7, 2011.

8. Ryan Rivet, "Model City in Trying Times," *New Wave*, October 4, 2010, tulane.edu/news/newwave/100410_urban_innovation_challenge.cfm.

9. "Moving Forward with Vision," *New Wave*, October 4, 2010, http://tulane.edu/news/newwave/100410_model_city.cfm.

10. Naomi Martin, "President Lobo Meets with Cowen, Mayor: Lobo Looks to New Orleans as Model for Rebuilding," *Hullabaloo*, September 17, 2010.

11. Sarah Carr, "Haiti Rebuilding Effort Draws on the Expertise of RSD Superintendent Paul Vallas," *New Orleans Times-Picayune*, February 20, 2010. For further background on Vallas's work in Haiti, see Jesse Hagopian, "Shock Doctrine Schooling in Haiti," *Socialist Worker*, September 8, 2011.

12. Reed, *Class Notes*, 13.

13. Cited in Binyamin Applebaum, "Grim Proving Ground for Obama's Housing Policy," *Boston Globe*, June 27, 2008. Valerie Jarrett, Obama's influential

mentor and leading advisor, went to work as CEO of Habitat Inc., a real estate firm, after leaving Chicago's Daley administration in the early 1990s. Habitat made millions managing private low-income developments, and Jarrett unsurprisingly was, like her mentee, equally resolute in supporting subsidies. In Applebaum's *Boston Globe* article, Jarrett argues, "Government is just not as good at owning and managing as the private sector because the incentives are not there. I would argue," she adds, "that someone living in a poor neighborhood that isn't 100 percent public housing is by definition better off." Jarrett's and Obama's comments underscore Upton Sinclair's observation that "it is difficult to get a man to understand something when his job depends on not understanding it." For more on the central role played by Jarrett while commissioner of planning and development in facilitating public housing demolition and gentrification in the North Kenwood section, along with Lane, see Pattillo, *Black on the Block*, 240–57. Jarrett hired Michelle Obama in 1991 to work with her as Daley's deputy chief of staff and then brought the future first lady with her when she was appointed commissioner in 1992.

14. Self-styled public intellectual Peter Dreier provides support in his article for PETRA and derides "radical planners" for their opposition (Dreier, "Does Public Housing Have a Future?"). For a critical perspective, see Tom Angotti and Marie Kennedy, "Selling Off Public Housing: PETRA and the Neoliberal Agenda," *Progressive Planning*, no. 185 (Fall 2010). For further critique of the PETRA program and its sister program, Transforming Rental Assistance, see Peter Marcuse, "The Heresies in HUD's Public Housing Policy," *Progressive Planning*, no. 186 (Winter 2011); "The End of Public Housing," *Shelterforce*, Summer 2010. "The End of Public Housing" provides the testimony delivered to the House Committee on Financial Services at its hearing on PETRA and other proposals for public housing, dated May 25, 2010. The statement was signed by twenty leading academics. The summer 2010 edition of Shelterforce provides both pro and con positions with regard to PETRA. It is available at http://www.shelterforce.org/article/2024/the_end_of_public_housing.

15. Cited in Nick Anderson, "Education Secretary Duncan Calls Hurricane Katrina Good for New Orleans Schools," *Washington Post*, January 30, 2010.

16. On the firing, see Katie Zezima, "A Jumble of Strong Feelings after Vote on Troubled School," *New York Times*, February 24, 2010. On support from the Obama administration, see Steven Greenhouse and Sam Dillon, "Schools' Shake-Up Is Embraced by the President," *New York Times*, March 6, 2010. For further Duncan kudos bestowed upon New Orleans's post-Katrina school system—which was led by Paul Vallas, his predecessor in Chicago—especially the authoritarian, top-down way it was imposed, see Sarah Carr, "U.S. Education Secretary Praises School Changes in New Orleans," *New Orleans Times-Picayune*, March 20, 2009.

17. Cockburn, "On Naomi Klein's *The Shock Doctrine*."

18. Angotti, *New York for Sale*, 6.

19. On the relationship between structural violence, represented by the

state's demolition campaign, and the direct state violence used against the public housing movement as simply "different moments of the same relations of domination," see Robinson, "Latin America in an Age of Inequality," 70.

20. Purcell, *Recapturing Democracy,* 170.

21. A grassroots defense campaign was successful in preventing housing authorities from using her arrest as a pretext to revoke her Section 8 certificate. For more on the case, see "Take Action NOW to Defend Sharon Jasper, Free Speech, and Public Housing," C3/Hands Off Iberville, July 16, 2010, http://c3handsoffiberville.blogspot.com/2010/07/campaign-builds-to-defend-sharon-jasper.html.

22. Johnson, *From Revolutionaries to Race Leaders,* xxxviii.

23. Adolph Reed Jr., "Black Particularity Reconsidered," *Telos* 39 (Spring 1979).

24. Purcell, *Recapturing Democracy,* 174.

Index

Abt & Associates, 124
accumulation: by dispossession, 187–88; neoliberal model of, xx–xxi, 187; spatial model of, 31–33
Adamson, Walter, 66–67
Advancement Project, 176
Advocates for Environmental Human Rights (AEHR), 173, 189–91, 211–14, 280n40
AFL-CIO: post–civil rights politics and, 218–19; post-Katrina public housing movement support from, 175, 181–82, 184–85
African Americans: access to professional/management-level jobs, 113–16; census profile for St. Thomas households, 5, 12–13; exclusion from FHA programs, xxx, 92; HANO board representation of, 236n42; identity politics in post-Katrina New Orleans and, 163–70; legitimization of "Negro removal" and, 91–92; New Orleans public housing history and, xxxiii–xxxviii; police brutality against, 1–3; post–civil rights movement politics and, 91–92, 215–16; post-Katrina plans of, 160–61; in public housing, statistics on, 13–14; public housing destruction and displacement of, xxii–xxv, 91–92, 251n11, 264n57; self-help ideology concerning, 57–59; urban migration of, 9. *See also* black urban regime of New Orleans .
Akuno, Kali, 166; Coalition to Stop the Demolitions and, 190–92, 194–95, 197, 199–200, 206, 209, 214, 276n8, 279n30; human rights advocacy and, 211
Albert, Derion, 264n57

Alcohol, Tobacco, and Firearms (ATF), U.S. Bureau of, 104–6
Alexander, Avery C., 24
Alexander, Michelle, 176
Alexander-Floyd, Nikol, 63–64, 244n7, 252n15
Algiers (New Orleans), 2
All Congregations Together (ACT), 191
Allen, Diane, 177
Althusser, Louis, 254n30
American Civil Liberties Union, 79
American Civil Rights Institute, 252n22
American Federation of State, County, and Municipal Employees (AFSCME), xvii
American Federation of Teachers (AFT), 175
American Sociological Association, 94
Amnesty International, 189
Anderson, Una, 171
Anderson et al. v. Jackson, 176, 188–89
Anglo American Corporation, 250n85
Angotti, Tom, 223
Annie E. Casey Foundation, 63–64, 245n21
Anti-Drug Abuse Act, 97
Anti-Racist Working Group, 189, 200
Archdiocese of New Orleans's Providence Community Housing, 148–49
Arena, John (Jay), 152–58, 175–82, 212–14
Arend, Orissa, 64–65
Arendt, Hannah, 66
arson, urban transformation through, 38–39, 240n27
Association of Community Organizations for Reform Now (ACORN), 149, 172–74, 189–90, 275n5
Audubon Institute, 141
Audubon Park Commission, 40
Authentic New Orleans: Tourism,

Culture, and Race in the Big Easy
(Gotham), 31
auto industry, post-2008 restructuring
of, 227n4

Bacon, Elinor, 124–28
Baker, Richard, 145, 226
Baron, Richard, 170–72
Barry, Marion, xxv
Barthelemy, Sidney, 30–31, 36; HANO
and, 40–42, 99; HRI delegitimi-
zation campaign and, 130–36;
Iberville privatization project and,
155; People's Institute support for,
59–60; political strategies of, 53–54;
Rochon Report and, 45–52, 55
Bauer, Catherine, xxx
Bayou District Foundation, 172, 272n60
Bender, Harvey, 270n40
Bennett, Larry, 93
Bickham, Linette, 170
Billes, Gerald, 126–28
Billes/Manning architectural firm,
126–28
Billings, David, 38–39, 44–45, 241n45,
260n16; on CCH contract dispute,
127–29; self-determination ideology and, 60–64; STICC and, 64–67,
73–75, 124; St. Thomas HOPE VI
grant application and, 107–12; St.
Thomas redevelopment plan and,
75–82, 117
Billy, James, 2
black cultural pathological paradigm,
poverty policies and, 63–64, 244n7,
252n15
black gentrification, emergence of,
xxii–xxiii
black mayors, urban gentrification and
role of, xxiv–xxv, 106–12
Black Men United for Change, 111
Black Nationalist movement, 217
Black Panther Party, xxxvii
Black Power movement, 217, 224–25
black urban regime of New Orleans:
bottom-up construction of, 72–79;

class loyalties and, 124–28, 142–44,
261n25; Coalition to Stop the
Demolitions and, 191, 201–14; contradictory alliance within, 40–42;
displacement of poor black communities and, 50–56; gentrification and tourism initiatives and,
33–40; historical background for,
xxxiii–xxxviii; Iberville privatization initiative and, 150–58; nonprofits and, 82–85, 121–24; People's
Institute and, 42–45; political
courage of elected officials and,
45–50; post–civil rights politics and,
113–16, 215–19, 258n78; post-Katrina
politics and, 219–23; public housing
and, xxii–xxv, xxxiii–xxxviii, 106–12;
racial inequality and, 142–44, 261n25;
riverfront redevelopment and,
67–72; spatial containment strategy
of, 52–54; St. Thomas community
targeted by, 30–54; St. Thomas/Irish
Channel Consortium and, 64–67;
Walmart relocation and, 140–42
Blanchard, Willie Mae, 10–11, 134,
263n53
Blanco, Kathleen, 147, 159
Bolan, Lewis, 78
Bond-Graham, Darwin, 174, 273n66,
274n72, 275n79
Bossier, Lambert, 241n45
bottom-up political movements: black
urban regime and, 72–79; post-
Katrina environment and, 223–26
Bourdieu, Pierre, 253n24
Boyd, Michelle, xxiii, 171
Bradberry, Steve, 174
Brenner, Neil, xxi, 112
Bring New Orleans Back Commission
(BNOB), 159–62, 219, 270n47
Broadway Rehab, 141
Brookings Institution Metropolitan
Policy Program, 172, 220–21
Brooks, David, 147
Burawoy, Michael, xix, 143–44, 213
Bush, Barbara, 159

Bush, George H. W., 58, 79, 97
Bush, George W., 67–68, 177–78, 185, 223
Bush–Clinton Katrina Fund, 174
Business Improvement Districts, 67
Business Week magazine, 31
B. W. Cooper public housing development: Coalition to Stop the Demolitions and protests in, 193–209; demolition of, 211; post-Katrina closing of, 146, 160, 162, 176–77, 185. *See also* Calliope public housing development

C3/Hands Off Iberville, 153–61, 212–14. *See also* Community, Concern, Compassion (C3) organization
Cade, Herbert, 201–2
Calliope public housing development, 57–59. *See also* B. W. Cooper public housing development
Camfield, David, 27
Campaign to End the CHA Lockdowns, 79
Canal Place complex, 31
Canal Street development project, 151–58
Canal Street Vision and Development Strategy, 151–52
Canatella, Anthony, 205
Canizaro, Joseph, xviii, 31; black urban elites and, 114; Downtown Development District formation and, 67–72, 246n31; HANO and, 100–101; HTI delegitimization campaign and, 131–36; Lane and, 129–30; nonprofits and, 121–24; post-Katrina vision of, 146, 159–61, 220, 270n40; St. Thomas redevelopment plan and, 76–80; STICC and, 72–75
Capital (Marx), 190
capitalism: neoliberal ideologies and, 83–85; nonprofits' role in, xxvii–xxix, 85–86
capture foundations, post-Katrina activities of, 174–75
Carter, James, 191, 278n30
Carter administration, 3–4, 19

Cates, Sidney (III), 16–17, 21–22, 24, 42, 236n42, 237n58
Cazenave, Nöel, 258n77
Center for Urban Redevelopment Excellence (CURE), 172
Central Atlanta Progress, 67–68
Chai, Charles, 40
Charity Hospital, New Orleans, post-Katrina closing of, 147
Chase, Leah, 171
Chicago, black gentrification in, xxiii
Chicago Housing Authority, 79
Chisom, Ron, 15–16, 22, 24, 41–45, 50
Choice Neighborhood grant, 222
Chossudovsky, Michel, 148–49, 157
Christy, D. J., 176–77
church-affiliated groups, 60–64, 191–92
Cisneros, Henry, 79, 121, 221
Civil Rights Act of 1964, xxxiv, 5
C. J. Brown Management Corporation, 100
C. J. Peete (Magnolia) public housing development, xxxvi, 42, 46, 102–3, 135–36, 146, 162; demolition of, 202, 211; post-Katrina closing of, 171, 176–77, 193, 274n72
Clark, Gordon, 114–16
Clarke, Simon, 116
Clarkson, Jacquelyn, 155, 229n19
class issues: black urban regime of New Orleans and, 124–28; Coalition to Stop the Demolitions and, 209–14; gentrification of New Orleans and, xxii–xxiii, 34–40, 240n14; HRI delegitimization campaign and, 131–36; Iberville privatization project and, 156; nonprofit structure and, xxvii–xxix, 114–16, 230n36; policy formation and, 57–59; post–civil rights black state and, 113–16; privatization initiatives for St. Thomas housing development and, 55–86, 114–16; in public housing, xxix–xxxiii, 1–5, 14–22, 26–27, 187–88; racial inequality and, 142–44; Rochon Report

recommendations and, 46–50; St.
Thomas redevelopment plan and,
76–79; Walmart relocation controversy and, 139–42; working-class
organization and, 11–14
"clean slate" paradigm, post-Katrina
demolition of public housing and,
183–85, 220–23
Clinton, Hillary, 199
Clinton administration, xviii, 79, 87–99;
Hope VI housing program under,
87–99, 106–12; national–local power
sharing under, 101–3, 106; neoliberal
policies of, 118–20; ties to black
urban elite of, 125–28
Coalition to Stop the Demolitions,
187–214
Coates, Geoff, 140
Cockburn, Alexander, 223
coercion, neoliberal mechanisms for,
xxv–xxvi, 96–99, 267n8
Coliseum Square Association (CSA),
35–40, 61, 68, 73, 140–42
collective bargaining, by HANO main-
tenance workers, xxxvii
Collins, Patricia Hill, 113–14, 131, 198
Columbia Residential, 172, 272n60
Columbus Properties, 68–72
Commentary magazine, 216
commodification, privatization and, xxi
Common Ground Relief, 49; Coalition
to Stop the Demolitions and, 189,
198, 213; post-Katrina public hous-
ing movement and, 161, 167–68, 173,
177–78
Communist Manifesto (Marx and
Engels), 85–86
Community, Concern, Compassion
(C3) organization: Coalition to Stop
Demolitions and, 189–214; post-
Katrina public housing initiatives
and, 152–70, 175–82, 270n42. See also
C3/Hands Off Iberville
Community Action Now (CAN), 2
Community Action Program (CAP),
102–3

Community and Housing Development
Act of 1987, 58
community control paradigm, public
housing insurgency and, 57–59
Community Labor United (CLU), 155,
161, 166
Community Oriented Policing (COPS),
98, 103–6, 253n27
Community Resource Partnership
(CRP), 76–79, 109–12, 122–24
Community Revitalization Fund (CRF),
174
Compass, Eddie, 158–59
Comprehensive Community Building
Initiative (CCI), 245n21
Comprehensive Employment and
Training Act (CETA), 43–45
conflict dynamics, nonprofit structur-
ing of, 121–24
Connerly, Ward, 252n22
consensus, manufacturing and genera-
tion of, xxvi, 76–80, 247n46; local
state–nonprofit consensus on priva-
tization and, 114–16
Cook, Christine, 52–53, 69, 144
Cook, Elizabeth, 153, 160–61, 164, 172,
175, 193, 200, 203
Costa, Louis, 35
Cox, Kevin, 141
Creative Choice Homes (CCH), 122–28
Creoles of Color, 30
criminalization of poverty: in
Hurricane Katrina media coverage,
158–61, 269n34; repression in support of privatization and, 96–99
criminal justice system, police partnerships with, 104–6, 254n30
Critical Resistance, 162–63, 173, 189, 194,
208–9
Crocket, Marjorie, 118
Crowley, Sheila, 171–72
culture, poverty and, 92–96
Cuomo, Andrew, 125

Dantas, Luisa, 193
Danzy, Sheila, 48–49, 131–36

Data Weekly newspaper, 154
Davidson, Norbert, 48
Davis, Annette, 161
Davis, Mike, 144, 258n78
Dear, Michael, 114–16
deconcentrating poverty ideology,
    legitimating public housing demoli-
    tion and, 46, 92–96
Democracy Now radio show, 160
Democratic Party, post–civil rights
    politics and, 216–19
Denton, Nancy, xxxi, 95
Desire public housing development,
    101–2; Black Panther Party in,
    xxxvii; Community Center in, 2–3;
    history of, xxxiii; post-Katrina clos-
    ing of, 162, 271n54
Dinkins, David, 69–70
direct action advocacy, importance of,
    199–200
disaster capitalism, post-Katrina pub-
    lic housing demolition and, 148,
    183–85, 223–26
discriminatory real estate practices:
    federal housing programs and
    continuation of, xxx–xxxi, 231n46;
    home ownership patterns and, 5–6
Dix, Carl, 187, 191–92, 194, 197, 206, 208,
    225
Domhoff, William, 57–59
Dowling, Allen, 236n42
Downs, Karen, 169
Downtown Development District
    (DDD), 67–72, 246n31; Nagin's plan
    for, 151–58
Drain-Williams, Brenda, 103
DuBos, Clancy, 47
Duncan, Arnie, 222–23, 282n16
Dunn, Diana, 44–45
Dunn, Jim, 44–45
Dupre, Emilio, 23
Dussett, Mitchell, 145

economic revitalization: global capital-
    ism and, xix–xxi, 227nn3–5; public
    housing redevelopment and, 90–91

Edwards, Edwin, 35
Edwards, John, 199
Eisenstein, Hester, xxviii–xxix
Elbaum, Max, 198
Ellis, Zachary, 49–50
Enterprise Community Partners, 171–72
Ernest N. Morial Convention Center, 33
European Dissent, 189
Everard, Don, 76, 112

Farve, Demetria, 121
Feagin, Joe, 156
federal agencies, 103–6, 113
Federal Housing Administration
    (FHA), xxx, 92, 231n44
federally funded public housing: cut-
    backs to, 3; HOPE VI grant program
    and dismantling of, xviii, 78, 89–91;
    tenant council guidelines and, 15
Fielkow, Arnold, 191, 204
FIRE (finance, insurance, real estate)
    economic sector, xx, 227n4
First Bank and Trust, 132
first-wave gentrification stage, 37
Fischer public housing development,
    xxxvi, 2–3, 218, 229n19, 271n54
Flaherty, Jordan, 273–74n67
Fleming, J. R., 200–201
Fleming-White, Tammy, 65–66
Florida public housing development,
    162, 271n54
Fondal, Arthur, 18
Ford, Kristina, 147
Ford, Selina, 20–21
Ford administration, 19
Ford Foundation, 57–59, 244n4, 268n23;
    post-Katrina initiatives of, 174–75,
    272n62
Fordist-Keynesian capitalist model, xx
Foreman, Ron, 141
foundations: neoliberal capitalism and,
    85–86; post-Katrina initiatives of,
    149, 174–75; structure and charac-
    teristics of, xxvii–xxix
Franklin, Louise, 74–75
Frazier, E. Franklin, 55

Freeport McMoran Corp., 77
French Quarter, 4, 151
Friends and Family of Louisiana's
    Incarcerated (FFLIC), 173
*From Protest to Politics: The Future of
    the Civil Rights Movement* (Rustin),
    215–16

Galatas, Marie, 141
Gambit newspaper, 115
Gates Foundation, 174
gender issues, in public housing, 12–14,
    26–27
gentrification: acceleration of, xviii;
    black urban regime of New Orleans
    and, xxii–xxv, 33–40, 106–12; "Jim
    Crow nostalgia" approach to, 171;
    public housing and, xxxix–xl, 4–5,
    29–54, 56, 154; revanchist agenda
    and, xix–xxi, 33–40
geography, public housing and role of,
    xxxii–xxxiii
Giarrusso, Clarence, 237n58
Gibson, Kenneth, 216–17
Gilmore, David, 222–23
Glass, Ruth, 34
global capitalism, neoliberal revanchist
    agenda and, xix–xxi, 227nn3–7
Glover, Rebecca, 200
Goetz, Edward, 46, 98, 251n11
Goodman, Amy, 160
Gore, Al, xxii
Gotham, Kevin, 31
Gough, Ian, xxxi
governing coalition, nonprofits and, 56,
    82–85
Gramsci, Antonio, xxv–xxvi, 65–66,
    230n36
grant management, community organi-
    zations' control of, 63–65
grassroots organizations, nonprofits
    and, xxviii–xxix
Gray, Jacqueline, 18
Gray, Kimi, 58–59
Greater New Orleans Fair Housing
    Action Center, 134, 136

Greater New Orleans Foundation
    (GNOF), 174
Griffin, Shana, 174, 208, 214
Gulf Coast Bank, 77
Gulf Coast Civic Work Project, 270n42
Gulf Coast Fund for Community
    Renewal and Ecological Health, 174
Guste public housing development,
    58–59, 267n19, 271n54

Habitat for Humanity, 149, 173, 184,
    273n63
Habitat Inc., 281n13
Hackworth, Jason, xxii, 112
Hall, Stuart, 66–67
Halperin, Herbert, 139
Harden, Monique, 174, 190, 211
Harvey, David, xxi, 83–84, 187, 248n65,
    278n27
Have a Heart, St. Bernard Must Restart
    rally, 164–70
Hayes, Jim, 15, 24, 42–45; Rochon
    Report and, 47–50, 59–60
Head, Stacy, 181, 204
hegemony: Burawoy's "hegemonic
    despotism" and, 143–44; Gramsci's
    theory of, xvi
Henwood, Doug, 148
high-rise public housing projects,
    media stereotyping of, xxii–xxv
Hill, Lance, 165, 169–70
Hirsch, Arnold, xxxi, 40
historic districting, public housing
    and, 4
Historic District Landmarks Commis-
    sions, 34
Historic Restorations Incorporated
    (HRI), 119–20, 124–39; Walmart and,
    139–42, 265n76
Historic Row Magazine Association,
    139
Holmes, Lillie, 18
homeless population: activist groups,
    181–82; urban gentrification and
    epidemic of, 34–40
Homeless Pride, 181–82

home ownership: discriminatory real estate practices and, 5–6; St. Thomas redevelopment plan and expansion of, 77–79

Honkala, Sherri, 200–201

Hope House service agency, 82

HOPE VI grant program: Iberville privatization project and, 155–58; privatization of public housing through, xviii, 78, 89–96, 136–39, 170–75, 221–23, 251n11; relocation of poverty as legacy of, 135–36; St. Thomas grant application for, 106–12, 121–24

Horton, Robert ("Cool Black"), 204, 208–9

Housing and Community Development Act of 1992, 90

Housing and Urban Development (HUD), U.S. Department of, 3–4; budget reductions for, 19–22; HANO sit-in and occupation and, 17–18; HOPE VI housing grants and, 90–91; lawsuit against St. Bernard residents, 180–82; one-strike evictions legislation and, 97–99; post-Katrina demolition plans of, 169–70; privatization of public housing and, 50–52, 170–75; public housing downsizing and, 101–3, 222–23; rental income declines and, 18–22; Resident Management Corporation program and, 59–60; section 235 program, 5–6; St. Thomas HOPE VI grant application and, 107–12

Housing Authority of New Orleans (HANO), 1, 5, 10; black urban regime and, 42, 43–45, 73–75, 151–58; board structure of, 236n42; CCH contract irregularities and, 124–30; Coalition to Stop the Demolitions and, 199–202; evictions of St. Thomas residents by, 117–18, 132–36; historical evolution of, xxxiii–xxxviii; HOPE VI

redevelopment grant and, 121–24; Iberville development demolition plans and, 155–58, 222–23; lawsuit against St. Bernard residents, 180–82; national–local power-sharing agreements and, 101–3; organizational restructuring of, 115–16, 211; police partnership with, 103–6; post-Katrina public housing demolition and, 145–46, 160–61, 166–70, 178–82; privatization of public housing and, 50–52, 99–101, 136–39, 259n9; Rochon Report and, 45–50; sit-in and occupation of, xvii, 14–22; St. Thomas Economic Development Corporation and, 59–60; St. Thomas HOPE VI grant application collaboration and, 107–12; St. Thomas redevelopment plan and, 76–79; St. Thomas rent strike and, 22–26; St. Thomas Resident Council and, 13–14; tenant management pilot program and, 57–59

Housing Investment Trust (AFL-CIO), 172

Housing Opportunities Extension Act of 1996, 97

Housing Plan for New Orleans (Rochon Report), 45–50

housing subsidies, federal budget reductions for, 18–22

Howell, Mary, 2

Howells, Mike: Coalition to Stop the Demolitions and, 191, 193, 197–98, 205–6; post-Katrina antidemolition efforts and, 152–58, 160–62, 176, 180, 270n42

Hoxha, Enver, 278n23

HUD v. Rucker, 97–99

Human Relations Committee (New Orleans), 15

human rights advocacy: antidemolition efforts and, 190, 210–14; post-Katrina New Orleans politics and, 221–23

Hunt, Brad, xxxi

Hurricane Betsy, xxxvii
Hurricane Katrina: impact on St.
    Thomas housing project of, 10; New
    Orleans politics in wake of, 219–23;
    privatization of public housing in
    wake of, 145, 158–85
Hyra, Derek, xxii–xxiii

Iberville public housing development,
    defense of, 146, 150–58, 176, 185,
    223–26; Obama demolition plan
    and, 222
identity politics: Coalition to Stop the
    Demolitions and, 194; post-Katrina
    public housing movement and,
    162–70, 270n45
incarceration statistics, New Orleans
    and, 12–14
INCITE! collective, xxviii, 155, 173–74,
    189, 208, 214, 268n23
individual freedom ideology, neoliberal
    paradigm of, 83–85
inequality: class and race and, 142–44;
    concentration of poverty and,
    92–96; nonprofits and reproduction
    of, 82–85; self-determination ideol-
    ogy and, 61–64
Inner-City Building Program (ULI), 77
Institute of Mental Hygiene (IMH), 63
Inter-American Development Bank, 221
interest groups, nonprofit organizations
    and, xxvi–xxix
internally displaced persons, UN guide-
    lines on, 146, 266n2
International Convention on the
    Elimination of All Forms of Racial
    Discrimination (ICERD), 210–14
International Longshore and Ware-
    house Union, 175
International Longshoremen's Associa-
    tion, 175
Interreligious Foundation for Com-
    munity Organization (IFCO),
    272n62
Irving, Gloria ("Mamma Glo"), 145, 158,
    164–66, 176, 180, 226

Jackman, Mary, 71
Jackson, Alphonso, 161, 169–70, 172,
    184–85
Jackson, Barbara, xvii–xviii, 13, 15, 17;
    CCH contract dispute and, 125–30,
    261n19; delegitimization campaign
    against, 130–36; evictions from St.
    Thomas and, 134–35; People's Insti-
    tute ties of, 59–60; Rochon Report
    and, 47, 51; STICC and, 73–75; St.
    Thomas public housing develop-
    ment and activism of, 22–24, 26–27;
    as St. Thomas Residents' Council
    president, 61–64, 122–24, 129;
    Tenants' Fight Back Organization
    and, 42
Jackson, Jesse, 278n25
Jackson, Johnny, 234n19
Jackson, Maynard, xxv, 40–41, 82–83
Jackson, Sam, 160, 176, 190, 193–94, 197,
    199, 212, 272n60
Jackson, Tessa, 212
Jahnke, Davis, 46
Jarmon, Nadine, 155–56
Jarrett, Valerie, 281n13
Jasper, Kawana, 176, 190, 212, 224
Jasper, Sharon: Coalition to Stop the
    Demolitions and, 189–91, 193–94,
    203–4; post-Katrina public housing
    movement and, 170, 176, 178, 183,
    212, 224, 283n21
Jaster, Angela, 195
Jefferson, William, 24, 30, 242n46
Jennings, Bobbie, 177
Jennings, Gloria, 177
Jeremiah Group, 191
Jim Crow Nostalgia, xxiii
Johnigan, Donna, 205, 207
Johnson, Cedric, 113–14, 217, 224–25,
    252n22
Johnson, Palfrey, 15, 17, 21, 24
Johnson, Rosemary, 177, 179
Jones, Crystal, 15–17, 21, 26–27, 47,
    260n16; People's Institute and, 42,
    44–45, 58–59; Rochon Report and,
    47–50; self-determination ideology

and, 60–64; St. Thomas Residents'
Council and, 59–60
Jones, Donald, 50
Jones, Larry, 48–49, 99, 236n42
Joseph, Emma Del, 16–17
Juakali, Endesha: Coalition to Stop the
Demolitions and, 194, 204; human
rights advocacy and, 212; post-
Katrina housing demolitions and,
165, 167–70, 178, 180–82, 184–85;
privatization of public housing and,
172, 214; Rochon Report and, 47,
49–50, 180; tenant organizations
and, 15
Judd, Dennis, xxv
Julian, Elizabeth, 121

Kabacoff, Pres: black urban regime
and, 45–46, 73–75, 241n45; on
CCH contract dispute, 128–30;
gentrification of Lower Garden
District and, 39–40; Iberville re-
development project and, 152–58;
privatization of public housing
supported by, 80, 252n17; river-
front development project and, 31;
STICC delegitimization campaign
and, 130–36; St. Thomas redevel-
opment and, 94, 124–28; Walmart
store location and, 139–42,
265n76; William Julius Wilson
and, 94
KAI Architects, 171
Kälin, Walter, 211
Kanaiaupuni, Shawn, 95–96
Katz, Bruce, 172, 221
Kelley, Robin, 134
Kelly, Michael, 101–3, 121, 126–27
Kemp, Jack, 58, 79, 97
Kenne, Danya, 263n53
Kennedy, Rose, 180, 190
Kerner Commission Report, xxxii–xxxiii,
232n54
Kerry, Augusta, 42, 46, 50
Keyes, Elliot, 236n42
Klein, Naomi, 148, 182, 223

Kohler, Jay, 200, 202–3
Koné, Sakura, 194, 198, 200, 208
Kuji Center, establishment of, 63–65

labor force participation rates: globali-
zation and, xix–xxi, 227nn3–4; of St.
Thomas residents, 6–8, 11–14
Ladas, Harry, 42
Lafitte public housing development:
post-Katrina closing of, 146, 160–62,
171–77, 193, 272n56; redevelopment
of, 202, 213, 280n43
Landrieu, Mary, 181–82
Landrieu, Maurice ("Moon"), xx–viii, 4,
31, 35–36, 240n14, 241n45; Canizaro
and, 67, 246n31
Landrieu, Mitch, 220, 223
Lane, Vincent, 77–82, 89, 96, 249n67;
CCH contract dispute and, 121–24,
128–30; HRI delegitimization cam-
paign and, 130–36, 143–44
Lauria, Mickey, 52–53, 69, 144
lead poisoning problems in public
housing, 24, 238n68
Leeman, Nicholas, xxxi
legal strategies of public housing advo-
cates, 176–82
Lemelle, Ivan, 188–89, 202
Lerner, Eric, 270n42
Lewis, John, 218
"liberal expansionist" development
model, 46, 242n50
Liberation League, 2–3, 198
Liebenthal, Mayaba, 162–63, 194, 211
Lippman, Pauline, 156–57
Liu, Amy, 220–21
Lobo, Porfirio, 221
local institutions: consensus on priva-
tization and, 114–16; national–local
power-sharing agreement and,
101–3
Logsdon, Joseph, 40
Loughner, Jamie "Bork," 178, 200, 203,
205–6, 212–13
Louisiana Justice Institute, 173
Louisiana Loan Fund, 273n66

Louisiana Research Institute for Community Empowerment (LaRICE), 155

Louisiana State Joint Legislative Subcommittee on Public Housing, 24

Louisiana Weekly, 48

Lower Garden District, 4; Canizaro's development initiatives in, 68; gentrification of, 34–40, 56, 239n11, 240n14; home values in, 139–42; tourism development in, 31–32

Lower Ninth Ward, post-Katrina politics in, 149, 162, 164

Low-Income Housing Tax credit (LIHTC) program, 4, 78, 109, 233n6

Loyola University legal clinic, 139, 177, 189

Luxemburg, Rosa, 215

MacArthur Foundation, 245n21

Mahogany, Pam, 176

Major, Barbara, xviii, 44–45, 47–50, 55, 260n16; Canizaro and Singleton and, 72–75; HOPE VI redevelopment grant and, 121; post–civil rights politics and, 218–19; post-Katrina revitalization plans and, 159–61; River Park project and, 71–72; self-determination initiatives of, 60–64; STICC and, 115–16, 122–23; St. Thomas redevelopment plan and, 75–81; St. Thomas Residents' Council and, 60; tenant organizations and, 58, 129

Make It Right Foundation, 149, 184

Making the Second Ghetto (Hirsch), xxxi

Malcolm X, 218–19

Manning, Raymond, 126–28

Marchman, Kevin, 122

Marcuse, Peter, xxx

market rate housing, at River Gardens development, 137–39

Marshall, Cody, 153–56, 160, 177, 190, 194, 197

Marshall, Jacqueline, 8–12, 26, 117

Martin, Paul and Shantrel, 160–61

Martin Luther King Jr. parade, political symbolism of, 53–54

Marx, Karl, 187, 190

Mason, Ron, 122–24, 127, 131

Massey, Douglas, xxxi, 95

May Day New Orleans, 200

Mayfield, Robert, 111

McBride, Joseph, 270n45

McCarthy, Brendan, 204

McCormack, Baron, and Salazar, 170–71

McFarland, Tamara, 192, 208

McGilberry, Charles, 49–50

McHenry, Floyd, 236n42

McKnight, Fannie, xvii–xviii, 13, 15, 17; black urban regime politics and, 41–42, 121, 123–24; HANO board and, 50; political activism of, xxvii–xxviii, 76–82; privatization supported by, 101; STICC and, 66–67, 73–75; St. Thomas HOPE VI grant application and, 108–12; St. Thomas public housing and, 21–23, 25–27, 29, 76–82; St. Thomas redevelopment plan and, 76–82

McLeod, Gordon, xxiv

McNally, David, 197–98

media coverage of post-Katrina New Orleans, 158–61, 268n33, 269n34

Melancon, Evelyn, 117–18, 259n2

Melendez, Edward, 140

middle-class homeowners: exodus from St. Thomas housing development and, 5–6, 76–79; opposition to Walmart from, 139–42

Midura, Shelly, 191

Miles, Reginald, 2

Mingo, Stephanie, 165–66

Miniter, Brendan, 147

Mitchell, Don, xxxii

Mitchell, Randy, 153, 160

mixed-income housing: initiatives for, 89–96, 109–12; post-Katrina plans for, 169–70; at River Gardens development, 137–39

Moonwalk development project (New Orleans), 31

Moore, Geraldine, 9–11, 105–6, 117–18,
123, 132–33, 135
Moore, Theo, 200
Morial, Ernest, xxv; black urban regime
alliance with, 30, 36, 40, 43–44,
124–28, 234n19; Bush administration and, 151; HANO and, 100–101;
national–local power-sharing
agreement and, 101–3; nonprofits
and, 121–24; police–social service
partnerships and, 103–6; post–civil
rights politics and, 216–17; public
housing polices of, 22, 87–89; race
and class issues in regime of, 1–5;
self-determination rhetoric of,
57–59
Morrell, Cynthia, 191
mortgage subsidies, history of,
xxx–xxxiii
Moss, Delena, 153–56, 160
Moten, Emmett, 131
Mountray, Chad, 227n4
Moynihan, Daniel Patrick, 95, 113–14,
252n22
Muhammad, Curtis, 166
Myers-Lipton, Scott, 270n42

Nagin, Ray, 229n19; Downtown Development Project and, 151–58; post-
Katrina public housing demolition
supported by, 148, 159, 162, 169–70,
208, 211; protests against policies of,
178, 181, 193
National Association of Resident Management Corporations, 59
National Commission on Severely Distressed Public Housing, 79, 89–91
National Crime Information Center,
criminalization of poverty and,
97–99
National Housing Law Project, 171–72
National Immigration Law Center,
272n62
national–local power-sharing agreement, New Orleans public housing
policy and, 101–3

National Low Income Housing Coalition (NLIHC), 171–72
National Register of Historic Places, 35
National Tenant Management Program,
57–59
National Tenants Organization (NTO),
43–45
Nation magazine, 160
"Negro removal": demolition of public housing and phenomenon of,
xxii–xxv, 94–96; nonprofits and
politics of, xxv–xxvi, 55–86; postsegregation legitimization of, 91–92
neoliberalism: capitalist ideology and,
85–86; coercive mechanisms of
privatization and, 96–99; defeat of
Iberville privatization project and,
155–58; HOPE VI housing grant
program and, 89–91; institutionalization of reform and, 60–64; post–
civil rights black state and, 114–16;
post-Katrina politics and, 148–85,
219–23; privatization of public housing and, 55–86; public housing and,
xxii–xxv, 29–31; revanchist agenda
and, xix–xxi; undermining of public
housing advocacy by, 197–214
Neupert, Gregory, 2
New Communist Movement, 198
"new federalism," public housing policy
under, 4
New Orleans: history of public housing
in, xxxiii–xxxviii; nonprofit organizations in, xxix
New Orleans Architecture, 34–35
New Orleans Business Council, 141–42,
146; post-Katrina vision of, 159–61
New Orleans Chamber of Commerce,
140–42
New Orleans Convention Center, 33
New Orleans Housing Eviction Action
Team (NO-HEAT), 161–62, 167–68
New Orleans Legal Aid Corporation
(NOLAC), 22
New Orleans Neighborhood Collabo-
rative (NONC), 148–49, 171–72

New Orleans Police Department
(NOPD), 98, 103–6
New Orleans Tenant Organization,
xxxvi–xxxvii
New Orleans 2000 Partnership consortium, 68–72
New Orleans Workers' Center for Racial
Justice, 189, 272n62
New Orleans Works, 100–101
"new urban renewal," emergence of, xxv
New York Times, 171
NGOs. *See* nonprofit organizations
Night Out against Gentrification demonstrations, 154
nonprofit organizations: Coalition to
Stop the Demolitions and, 193–214;
neoliberal agenda of, 82–86, 121–24;
neutralization of dissent by, 128–30;
post–civil rights politics and,
xxv–xxvi, 218–19; post-Katrina
public housing demolition and,
148–85, 225–26, 272n62; privatization of public housing and,
50–52, 55–86, 170–75, 213–14; public
housing movement and, 162–70;
regressive policies supported by,
xviii–xix; STICC formation as,
63–64; structure and characteristics
of, xxvi–xxix, 230n34; St. Thomas
redevelopment plan and, 75–79; St.
Thomas Resident Council alliances
with, 60–64; terminology concerning, 230n32
Notice of Funding Availability (NOFA)
criteria HOPE VI grants, 107–12

Obama, Barack, 199, 222–23, 281n13
occupational distribution, of St.
Thomas residents, 6–8
one-for-one rule in public housing
development, 96–103, 177–78
one-strike evictions policy, 97–99,
104–6, 115–16
Open Society, 174
operating foundations, structure and
characteristics of, xxvii–xxix

Operation Clean Sweep, 79
Operation Comeback, 36–37, 56
Operation Hold-On, 37, 56
Oroussof, Nicolai, 171

Parenti, Christian, 160
Parker, Emilie, 134–35
Park Slope (Brooklyn, New York) gen-
trification, 37, 240n15
paternalism, self-determination ideol-
ogy and, 61–64
Pattillo, Mary, xxiii, 80, 114
Paul, Emelda, 171
Pax Christi, 189
Payment in Lieu of Taxes (PILOT),
139–42
Pendleton, Ollie, 153
Pennington, Richard, 103–4
People's Hurricane Relief Fund (PHRF):
Coalition to Stop the Demolitions
and, 189–92, 194, 197–98, 200, 206,
209; human rights advocacy and,
210–14; *Pledge of Resistance*, 277n11;
post-Katrina public housing movement and, 161, 165, 167, 173, 175,
190–91, 272n62
People's Institute for Survival and
Beyond (PI), 42–45; black urban
regime and, 54, 72–75; C3 criticized by, 163; Coalition to Stop the
Demolitions and, 189, 208–9; expansion of, 260n16; leadership role
of, 64–67; nonprofit alliances with,
61–64; post–civil rights politics and,
219; post-Katrina housing advocacy
and, 173–75; Rochon Report and,
47–54, 241n44; self-help ideology
and, 58–60
People's Organizing Committee (POC),
173, 177, 272n62
Performance Funding System, 19
Perry, James, 161
PETRA housing plan, 222, 281n14
Petras, James, xxix, 227n3, 228–29n12,
230n36
Pineda, Mayra, 221

Pitt, Brad, 149, 184
Piven, Francis Fox, 84–85, 249n82
Planned Parenthood, 63
Pledge of Resistance, 277n11
Police and Public Housing Liaison Section, 103–4
police brutality: Coalition to Stop the Demolitions and experience of, 192–93, 202–6; in public housing, 1–3, 8–11, 218, 233n4
Police Brutality Committee (PBC), 2–3
policing techniques, 103–6, 115–16, 148
political realism: black urban regime and, 45–50; coercive and consensual mechanisms of, xxv–xxvi; in post-Katrina New Orleans, 219–26; public housing residents' role in, 30–54, 52–54
Post, Langdon, 231n41
post-civil rights politics, New Orleans public housing and, 215–19
post-Katrina "exclusionary" agenda, 165–70
poverty: criminalization of, 96–99; deconcentration of, through public housing reform, 91–96; nonprofit attitudes concerning, 63–64; political destabilization and, 52–54; public housing and concentration of, xxxi; relocation of, 134–36; of St. Thomas residents, statistics on, 6
Prejean, Helen, 235n1
Preservation Resource Center (PRC), 36, 56, 73, 139
privatization of public housing: class and racial inequality and, 142–44; coercive mechanisms for, 96–99; criminalization of poverty and, 97–99; final St. Thomas evictions and reconstruction and, 136–39; HOPE VI housing grants and, 90–91, 106–12; local state–nonprofit consensus on, 114–16; national and local cooperation with, 99–101; neoliberal embrace of, xxi; nonprofit organizations and, xxix, 50–52,

55–86, 170–75, 213–14; police–social service partnerships and, 103–6; post-Katrina acceleration of, 145–85, 219–23; St. Thomas redevelopment plan and, 77–79; tenant organization support for, 79–82
procorporate development models, urban gentrification and, xxii–xxv
professional/management-level jobs, African American access to, 113–16
Providence Community Housing, 171–72
Proxmire, William, 67
public charities, structure and characteristics of, xxvii–xxix
public education system of New Orleans, post-Katrina takeover of, 147–48, 171–75, 183, 221–23
public housing: black urban elite retreat from, 50–52; class issues in, xxix–xxxiii, 1–5, 14–22; destruction of, in United States, xxii–xxv, xxxiii, 229n19; discriminatory real estate practices and, xxx–xxxi, 231n46; dismantling of, 87–116; funding reductions for, 19–22; history in New Orleans of, xxxiii–xxxviii; HOPE VI grant program and dismantling of, xviii, 78, 89–91; Hurricane Katrina's impact on, 145, 158–85; legal strategies for protection of, 176–82; negative perceptions of, xxx–xxxiii; neoliberalism and, xxii–xxv, 29–31; political destabilization by residents of, 52–54; political mobilization and advocacy for, 175–82; post-civil rights politics and, 215–19; privatization of, 50–52, 79–82, 96–101; protest terrain in, 22–26; race issues in, xxix–xxxiii, 1–5, 14–22; residents' control of, 57–59; Rochon Report critique of, 45–50; sociological justification for demolition of, 92–96. *See also* privatization of public housing; *and specific public housing developments*

Public Housing Act of 1937: Brooke
Amendment to, 18–19; legacy of,
xxx, 90–91; New Orleans public
housing and, xxxiii–xxxviii
public services, post-Katrina dismantling of, 148, 219–23
public works: demand for, 149, 185, 215;
direct government employment vs.
private contract model, 270n42
public–private partnerships: post-
Katrina political embrace of, 219–23;
public housing and, 4; urban gentrification and, xxiv–xxv
Purcell, Mark, 157–58

Quadagno, Jill, 113
Quality Housing and Work Responsibility Act (QHWR) of 1998, 90–91,
97–99
Quigley, Bill: black urban regime and,
128; Coalition to Stop the Demolitions and, 189–90, 192–93, 208; post-
Katrina antidemolition movement
and, 176–77; privatization of public
housing and, 52; St. Thomas rent
strike and, 22–26, 52

racial cleansing, privatization of public
housing and, 144
racial covenants, establishment of,
xxx–xxxiii, 231n44
racism: class issues and, 142–44; Iberville
privatization proposal and, 156–58;
identity politics in post-Katrina
New Orleans and, 161–70; liberal
retreat from issues of, 92–96, 252n22;
post-Katrina white vigilantism
and, 269n34; privatization of public
housing and, 55–86; public housing
policies and, xxix–xxxiii, 1–4, 26–27,
92–96; racial hierarchy of Louisiana
and, 30; redistribution of public
housing and, 187–88; in St. Thomas
housing project, xxxiii–xxxviii, 5–6,
55–86; urban redevelopment and
legitimacy of, 67–72

"Radical Creole tradition," black urban
regime and, 40–42
Rahim, Malik, 161, 173
Rathke, Wade, 275n5
Reagan administration, xvii, 4, 19, 58,
97, 236n31
real estate development: gentrification
of New Orleans and, 34–40; pressure
on STICC from, 66–67; privatization
of St. Thomas housing development
and, 56, 122–24; Riverfront redevelopment effort and, 67–72
Reed, Adolph, xxiii–xxv; black urban
regime and research of, 40–41, 56,
70, 225–26; on identity politics,
163; on Negro removal, 93–95; on
nonprofits and neoliberal agenda,
82–83; on Obama, 222; reinvention
mechanism of, 141–42, 197; on relocation of poverty, 134
"reinvention mechanism," black urban
regime and, 141–42, 197
Reiss, James, 146
rental income in public housing, history of changes in, 18–22
rent strikes, as protest tool, 22–26
repertoires of contention, commodification of public housing and, xxi,
228n12
repression, privatization of public housing and expansion of, 96–99
Republican Party: Canizaro's ties to,
67–68; New Orleans public housing
politics and, 50
Request for Qualifications (RFQ) for
housing development, 122–24
resident management corporations
(RMCs), 58
revanchist agenda: gentrification and
tourism and, 33–40; neoliberalism
and gentrification and, xix–xxi;
post-Katrina fast-tracking of, 147
Revolutionaries to Race Leaders
(Johnson), 217
Revolutionary Communist Party
(RCP), 164–65, 189–91, 195, 198, 200

Reynolds, Cary, 153–56, 160
Ricardo, Irma, 123–24, 133–34
right of return movement, 271n49, 271n51; post-Katrina coalition for, 145–48, 162–67; St. Thomas public housing privatization and, 119, 130, 142
Right to the City, 189–90, 200, 213–14
Riley, Warren, 204
River Gardens development, 119–20, 150; displaced residents as result of, 136–39; Walmart store and, 139–42
Rivergate Convention Center, 31
River Park Project, 68
Riverwalk Mall, development of, 33
Robinson, Rosalie, 18
Robinson, William, xx, 6–7, 227n3
Rochon, Reynard, xxxvii, 18, 45–50, 101, 165, 236n42, 245n46
Rochon Report on public housing, 45–55, 101, 165, 180–81, 218
Rockefeller Foundation, 148; post-Katrina initiatives of, 174–75, 220–23; Redevelopment Fellowships program, 172
Rockefeller Philanthropy Advisors, 174
Rodrigue, Soleil, 177–78, 180, 274n77
Roelofs, Joan, xxvii–xxix, 85, 129, 164, 174, 276n8
Rohatyn, Felix, 69–70
Rouselle, Bill, 2
Rowland, Marty, 152–58, 160–61
Rummil, Curtis, 178
Rustin, Bayard, 215–19

Safe Streets, 173, 189, 200, 202, 213–14, 278n27
Salaam, Kalamu Ya, 2
Saltman, Kenneth, 99
Samuel, Martha Ann, 35
Sanders, Torin, 122–23
scattered-site housing, history in New Orleans of, xxxiii–xxxviii, 237n55
Scheib, J. Gilbert, xxxvi–xxxvii, 5, 16, 236n42
Scheuermann, Dwayne, 203, 279n31

Schmaltz, Howard, 35
Schmidt, Larry, 36, 71
Scott, James, 134
second-wave gentrification stage, 37
Section 8 voucher program, 1–3, 233n4; post-Katrina relocation using, 176; St. Thomas redevelopment plan and expansion of, 77–79, 135–36
segregation, public housing and promotion of, xxxiii–xxxviii, 95–96, 261n60
self-determination ideology: neoliberal advocacy for, 60–64; privatization linked to, 83–85; St. Thomas Residents Council and, 57–59
self-help ideology: racialized evolution of, 57–59; St. Thomas Economic Development Corporation and, 59–60
Sharpton, Al, 278n25
Shaver, Eileen, 24–25
Shea, Cathy, 175
Sheehan, Cindy, 164–65
shock doctrine theory, public housing movement and, 148, 182–85
Shock Doctrine: The Rise of Disaster Capitalism (Klein), 148
Silence Is Violence protest, 212
single-issue organizations, post-Katrina initiatives of, 149–50
Singleton, James: black urban regime and, 84–85, 113–14; Canizaro and, 70–75; gentrification initiatives and, 33–34, 36; Rochon Report and, 46
Singleton, Sherry, 2
Sites, William, xx–xxi, 162
Slater, Tom, xxiii
Smallwood, Jessie: attempted ouster from HANO of, 42, 48–50; Cates's conflict with, 21, 236n42; as public housing advocate, 14, 17, 53–54; self-help ideology and, 58
Smith, Calean, 5
Smith, Neil, xix, xxi, 27, 33–34, 37
Smith, Preston, 58
Smithburg, Donald, 147

social-cleansing initiatives, gentrification and, 37–40
social justice, neoliberal jettisoning of, 83–85
social networks: black urban regime and, 43–45; in public housing communities, 10–11
sociology: deconcentration of poverty and, 92–94; Hope VI housing program in context of, 92–96; postsegregation legitimization of "Negro removal" and, 91–92
Southall, Charles, 141
Southern Christian Leadership Conference (SCLC), 191
spatial containment, 144; gentrification of New Orleans and, 35–40, 52–54
spatial model of accumulation, New Orleans riverfront tourism and, 31–33
Spencer, Ursula, 236n42
Stapert, Bart, 128–30, 132
St. Bernard Housing Recovery & Development Corporation, 172, 182
St. Bernard Project, 173, 273n63
St. Bernard public housing development, xxxiv–xxxvi, 15, 47, 57; Coalition to Stop the Demolitions and, 200; demolition attempts at, 202, 211–12; post-Katrina public housing movement in, 159, 164–70, 176–78, 180–82; privatization initiatives and, 145–46
Steinberg, Stephen, 80, 95–96, 218–19, 252n22
Stepan-Norris, Judith, 188, 209
St. Etienne, Gregory, 126–28, 263n43
Stets, Paul, 191, 195
Stevens, Evelyn, 135–36
Stewart, Carol, 5, 9–11
Stinchcombe, Arthur, 228n12
Stokely, Brenda, 278n25
Strachan, Camille, 37, 81, 140
Strachan, Duncan, 239n11
structural violence, in St. Thomas housing projects, 6–8

St. Thomas Community Law Center, 129–30
St. Thomas Community Vocations, 130–36
St. Thomas Economic Development Corporation (STEDC), creation of, 59–60
St. Thomas public housing development: African American census profile in, 13–14, 234n15; downsizing of, 101–3; eviction of residents from, 117–18, 132–36; gender, race, and class issues in, 26–27; gentrification efforts targeting, 36–40; HANO sit-in and occupation and, 15–22; historical profile of, xxxiii–xxxviii, 5–6; HOPE VI grant and, 106–12, 122–24; information sources concerning, xxxviii; political destabilization and residents of, 52–54; political transformation in, xviii–xix, xxxix; privatization efforts and, 55–86; protest activities in, 22–26; race and class issues involving, 1–5; razing of, 117–20; redevelopment plan for, xviii, xl, 75–79; River Park Project and, 68–72; Rochon Report critique of, 45–50; state-sponsored control of, 104–6; statistics on displaced residents from, 136–39; structural violence in, 6–11; tourism and gentrification pressures on, 29–54; vacancy rates in, 51–52
St. Thomas Resident Council (STRC), 9–13, 59–60; black urban regime and, 121–28; CCH contract issues with, 124–28; confrontation tactics of, 128–30; evictions from St. Thomas and, 132–36; HOPE VI grant application collaboration and, 107–12; HRI undermining of, 130–36; local state–nonprofit consensus on privatization and, 115–16; rent strike by, 22–26; River Park project and, 71–72; self-determination ideology and, 60–64; STICC alliance with,

72–75; St. Thomas redevelopment plan and role of, 75–82

St. Thomas/Irish Channel Consortium (STICC), xxix, 62; Canizaro and, 72–75; CCH contract dispute and, 125–28; foundation support for, 85–86; grant proposals received by, 64–67; HOPE VI grant application collaboration and, 107–12, 121–24; HRI undermining of, 130–36; local state–nonprofit consensus on privatization and, 115–16; Plain Talk program, 81–82; St. Thomas redevelopment plan and, 75–79, 81–82

Students for a Democratic Society (SDS), 193–94, 198

Suber, Malcolm, 2, 98, 166, 278n23, 278n30, 279n36; Coalition to Stop the Demolitions and, 191–92, 197–98, 204, 206, 208

Sugrue, Thomas, xxxi

Superdome sports stadium, 31

Survivors Village, 168, 172, 176, 189, 194, 212; *Pledge of Resistance* and, 277n11

Sylvain, Vincent, 101–3, 125–26, 127, 255n40

Target Projects Program, elimination of, 19

Tax Increment Financing (TIF), 139–42

Teeple, Gary, 79, 110

tenant management organizations: nonprofit promotion of, 57–59; one-strike evictions expansion and, 97–99; organization of, 15; political alliances among, 56; protest activities and, 22–26; support for privatization from, 79–82

Tenants' Fight Back Organization, 42

Theodore, Nik, xxi, 112

Thomas, Oliver, 141–42, 146, 165, 184

Thomas, Patricia ("Sista Sista"), 176–77

Thompson, Norwood, 191–92

Times-Picayune newspaper, 58–59, 118, 139, 141, 154, 160, 205–7

TINA (There Is No Alternative)

argument: Coalition to Stop the Demolitions and, 209–14; Iberville privatization project and, 156–58; neoliberal accommodationism and, 111–12

Tompkins Square Park (New York City), 37

Total Community Action, 113–14

tourism: accelerated growth of, xviii; impact on public housing of, xxxix–xl, 4–5, 29–54; New Orleans riverfront development and, 31–33; public housing movement's disruption of, 176–82; revanchist agenda and, 33–40

Tremé Community Improvement Association (TCIA), 15, 45–47

Tremé neighborhood, history of, xxxiii

Trinity Episcopal Church, 61–64, 77

Trotsky, Leon, 150

Trouble Funk (hip-hop group), 16

Troyano, Paul, 180

Truehill, Marshall, 161, 206

Truly Disadvantaged (Wilson), 94

Tucker, Robert, 100–101, 114

Tulane University, 114–16, 220–23; national–local power-sharing agreement on public housing and, 101–3

Tulane–Xavier Initiatives agency, 102–3

Tureaud, A. P., xxxvii, 236n42

Turner, Jesse, 2

Turner, Nat, 273n65

Ujamaa Community Development Corporation, 171

unemployment demographics, of St. Thomas residents, 6–7, 11–12

union organizations: post-Katrina dismantling of, 174–75, 219–23; St. Thomas residents' participation in, 11–14

Unitarian Universalist Service Committee (UUSC), 175

United Nations Committee on the Elimination of Racial Discrimination (CERD), 210–11

United Nations Guiding Principles
on Internal Displacement, 146,
266n2
United Nations Human Rights Council,
190, 210–14, 280n40
University of Pennsylvania, 148
Urban Conservancy, 140
urban development, global strategy
for, xxi
Urban Foundation (South Africa),
250n85
Urban Initiatives Program, 19
Urban Investment Group, 171
Urban Land Institute (ULI), 52–53;
post-Katrina revitalization plans
and, 159–61; privatization of public
housing and, 136–39; St. Thomas
HOPE VI grant application collaboration and, 107–12; St. Thomas
redevelopment plan and, 76–80, 123,
129–30, 247n46
urban pioneering paradigm, gentrification and, 34–40, 239n11
Urban Racial State, The (Cazenave),
258n77
urban renewal, public housing and history of, xxii–xxv
Urban Strategies, 172
U.S. Conference of Mayors, 4

Vale, Lawrence, xxxi
Vallas, Paul, 221–22, 282n16
Vanguard Foundation, 166, 272n62
Veltmeyer, Henry, 227n3
Veterans Administration, housing pro-
gram of, xxx
vigilantism in post-Katrina New
Orleans, 269n38
Violent Crime Control and Law En-
forcement Act, 98
Vitale, Alex, xix
Vitter, David, 181, 209
voluntarism, public housing down-
sizing legitimation and, 148–49,
184–85

Wacquant, Loïc, 87, 96–97, 105–6,
253n24
Walker, Nathalie, 208
Wallace, Roberts & Todd consulting
firm, 107–12, 126–27
Wallace, Tina, 183–84
Wall Street Journal, 159
Walmart, 139–42, 197
Warren, Darrel "Sess 4-5," 203–5
Warren, Demetrius, 205
Washington, Andy, 152–58, 160, 180
Washington, Tracie, 176, 191, 201–2,
278n30
Waters, Maxine, 177, 274n78, 275n80
Watson, Nathan, 68–70, 84–85, 152
weed and seed policing program,
98–99, 104–6, 115–16, 256n50
welfare, xvii–xviii, 12–14
Welfare Rights Organization, xxxvi
What's Happening newsletter, 82
White, Felton, 121–24, 130
white corporate elite: ascendancy
in neoliberal politics of, 114–16;
Canizaro's ties to, 68–72; gentrification efforts and, 40–42;
management of HANO by, 100;
post-Katrina politics and, 224–26;
post-Katrina vision of, 159–61;
privatization initiatives for St.
Thomas housing development and,
56; St. Thomas community targeted
by, 29–54; St. Thomas redevelopment plan and, 76–79; Walmart
relocation and, 141–42
Who Rules New Orleans? (Chai), 40
Wiggins, Cynthia, 58–59, 100–101, 153,
169–70, 182, 267n19, 274n72
Willard-Lewis, Cynthia, 191–92, 276n10,
278n30
Williams, Darryl, 12
Williams, Edward, 21
Williams, Eloise, 206
Williams, Michael. *See* Juakali,
Endesha
Williams, Rhonda, xxxi–xxxii, 27

Wilson, David, 84
Wilson, William Julius, xxxi, 46, 252n17, 252n22; deconcentrating poverty and, 92–96
Winfrey, Angela, 174
Winfrey, Oprah, 273n63
Wise, Tim, 241n44
women: dominance in public housing of, 12–14, 26–27; political activism in St. Thomas community of, 56
Workers' Center for Racial Justice, 173, 192, 208
working-class communities in New Orleans: black urban regime and, 55–86; gentrification and displacement of, 34–40, 240n14, 249n82, 264n57; militancy of occupants in, 18–22, 26–27; neoliberalism in relation to, xxi, 228n12; nonprofit cultivation of, 82–85; police targeting of, 104–6; post–civil rights politics and, 217; post-Katrina displacement of, 182–85, 219–23; regressive policies supported by, xviii–xix; revolutionary movements and role of, 231n41; Rochon Report recommendations concerning, 46–50; statistics on, 13–14, 227nn3–4
World's Fair 1984 (New Orleans), 31–33
World Trade Organization, 227n3

Yentel, Diane, 172
Yes Men activist group, 177
Young, Andrew, 41
Young, Coleman, xxv
Young, Mildred, 71

Zeiner, Francis, 259n2
Zeitlin, Maurice, 188, 209
Zinn, Howard, 1

John (Jay) Arena is assistant professor of sociology at the City University of New York, College of Staten Island.